W0007491

Chambéry

The emerald fish-filled waters and beautiful setting of the Làc d'Aiguebelette, France's third largest natural lake, have been attracting tourists since the early 20th century.

Since the early 20th century, binoculars and telescopes have been regarded as essential pieces of equipment for tourists visiting the region. From Le Brévent it was possible to watch the progress of climbers on Mont Blanc.

In the past, many Savoyards lived isolated lives high in the alpine pastures or cut off by the snows, and had restricted access to doctors. For these people, medicinal herbs provided effective cures for many ailments.

THE FRENCH ALPS

SAVOIE
HAUTE-SAVOIE

EVERYMAN GUIDES

All the information contained in this guide has been approved by the many specialists and academics who have contributed to its production.

GEORGES PACQUETET (1)
Assistant managing director of services for the *département* of Haute-Savoie. General reader for the guide.

DOMINIQUE RICHARD (2)
Commissioner-in-chief for heritage 1994–99. General reader for the guide and author of 'Baroque retables'.

JEAN-OLIVIER VIOUT (3)
Member of the Académie de Savoie and president of the Société des Amis du Vieux-Chambéry. General reader for the guide and author of 'Chambéry'.

MICHELE BERLIOZ (4)
Guide-lecturer, member of the Société des Amis du Vieux-Chambéry and vice-president of the Société des Amis de Montmélian et de ses Environs. Author of 'Combe de Savoie'.

GENEVIEVE FRIEH-VURPAS (5)
Director of communications in the Office de Tourisme et de Thermalisme, Aix-les-Bains (1985–96), then project manager for the promotion of the natural heritage of the Lac du Bourget. Author of 'Aix-les-Bains' and the 'Lac du Bourget'.

ANTHIME LEROY (6)
Correspondent for Dauphiné Libéré. Co-author, with Yvette Juge and the park team, of 'Parc Naturel Régional du Massif des Bauges'.

GEORGES GRANDCHAMP (7)
President of the Société des Amis du Vieil Annecy, vice-president of the Académie florimontane. Author of 'Annecy'.

MICHEL VOISIN (8)
Lecturer, local correspondent in Thônes for 30 years, founder-member of Les Amis du Val de Thônes and member of Thônes Patrimoine et Culture. Author of 'Les Aravis'.

GEORGES HYVERNAT (9)
President and founder of the CODERANDO-FFRP Haute-Savoie, photographer and naturalist. Author of 'Genevois'.

PAUL GUICHONNET (10)
Historian and geographer (Savoie), honorary professor and dean of the University of Geneva, corresponding member of the Institut de France and president of the Académie florimontane. Author of 'Lake Geneva'.

BRUNO GILLET (11)
Director of tourist offices in Haute-Savoie for 20 years, tourism consultant, senior lecturer at the University of Lyon II. Author of 'Chablais'.

JEAN-FRANÇOIS TANGHE (12)
Guide-lecturer, president of the Société de Maçons de Samoëns, writer and photographer. Author of 'Vallée du Giffre & Faucigny'.

JEAN-PIERRE DUC (13)
Assistant secretary of the Académie de la Val d'Isère since 1988. Author of 'Tarentaise'.

FRANÇOISE FRANCO-REY (14)
Freelance journalist and researcher who keeps a database on the Vallée de Chamonix. Author of the 'Pays du Mont-Blanc'.

MARTHE AND PIERRE DOMPNIER (15)
Lecturer in history, president of the Société d'Histoire et d'Archéologiede Maurienne, member of the Académie de Savoie. Co-author, with his wife, of 'Maurienne'.

ALAIN BEXON (16)
Jurist and art historian. Author of 'Savoie as seen by painters'.

JACQUES LELEU (17)
Reporter for the Dauphiné Libéré. Contributor to the magazine Alpes Loisirs. Author of 'The Mountains in Summer', 'The Mountains in Winter', 'Skiing areas' and the 'Leisure' pages of the Practical Information section.

JEAN-CLAUDE RIBAUT (18)
Gastronomic editor for Le Monde. Author of the 'restaurants and hotels'.

PARC NATIONAL DE LA VANOISE
ÉLISABETH BERLIOZ, head of communications at the PNV, wrote 'Fauna and flora of the Vanoise' and 'Parc National de la Vanoise', in association with the park team.

EVERYMAN GUIDES
Published by Everyman Publishers Plc

Originally published in France by Nouveaux-Loisirs, a subsidiary of Editions Gallimard, Paris, 1999

French Alps: ISBN 1-84159-031-2

TRANSLATED BY
Wendy Allatson

EDITED AND TYPESET BY
Book Creation Services Ltd, London

OTHER AUTHORS WHO CONTRIBUTED TO THIS GUIDE
Vincent Albouy, Lucien Avocat, Olivier Berclaz, Bruno Berthier, Fernand Berthier, Catherine Blake, René Bozon, Jean-Paul Brusson, Ivan Cadenne, Jacques Chatelain, Laurent Collinet, André Combaz, Pierre Dupraz, Albert Eysseric, Michel Fabre, Chantal Fernex de Mongex, Jean-Pierre Gandebeuf, Michel Germain, Roger Guilhot, Marie-Thérèse Hermann, Yvette Juge, Ronan Kerdreux, Pascale Lapalud, René Lhénaff, Jean Luquet, Patrice Mallet, Maurice Opinel, Jean-Bernard Paillisser, Marc Pépin, Line Perrier, Claude Ponson, Pierre Préau, Abbé Jean Prieur, Raymond Puy, Philippe Raffaelli, Christian Regat, Jean-Paul Rossi, Jeanne-Marie Saisi, Yves Sautier, Karine Schwing, Élisabeth Sirot, Charles Socquet, Jean-Paul Tournier, Bernard Sonnerat, Mireille Védrine, Hélène Viallet, Avant-Pays Savoyard Tourisme, Société d'Économie Alpestre de la Haute-Savoie, Syndicat de Défense du Fromage Beaufort, team of the Parc National de la Vanoise,

WITH SPECIAL THANKS TO:
Georges Pacquetet, Dominique Richard, Jean-Olivier Viout, the Departmental Tourist Agencies of Savoie and Haute-Savoie and Hervé Marcadal, Daniel Debiolles and Geneviève Billet, Rémy Charmetant and Claudie Blanc.
ALSO:
Alain Bexon, Alain Caraco, Nathalie Carret, Laurent Collinet, Mario Colonel, Bernard Coutin, Claire Grangé, Geneviève Frieh, Dominique Pannier, the team of the Parc Naturel Régional du Massif des Bauges, Frédéric Pion and Hélène Viallet.

This guide was produced in association with the departmental tourist agencies and regional councils of Savoie and Haute-Savoie

FRENCH ALPS / SAVOIE, HAUTE-SAVOIE
■ **EDITED BY**
Ædelsa Atelier Tourisme
in collaboration with: Florence Picquot (Practical Information)
■ **LAYOUT**
Karine Benoit, Olivier Brunot, Carole Gaborit
■ **ILLUSTRATIONS**
Bénédicte Bouhours, Odile Domalain, Françoise Arnault

■ **ILLUSTRATIONS**
COVER: Pierre-Marie Valat
NATURE: Lionel Bret, Jacqueline Candiard, Jean Chevallier, Denis Clavreul, Gismonde Curiace, François Desbordes, Claire Felloni, Catherine Lachaud, Alban Larousse, Dominique Mansion, Pascal Robin, John Wilkinson
ARCHITECTURE: Denis Brumaud, Philippe Candé, Jean-Marie Guillou, Bruno Lenormand, Maurice Pommier, Jean-Pierre Poncabare, Claude Quiec, Jean-Sylvain Roveri, Amato Soro
ITINERARIES: Frédéric Bony, Lionel Bret, Philippe Candé, Jean-Philippe Chabot, Jean Chevallier, François Desbordes, Claire Felloni, Jean-Marc Lanusse, Jean-Paul Philippe, Maurice Pommier
PRACTICAL INFORMATION: Maurice Pommier
MAPS: Éric Gillion, Stéphane Girel, Isabelle-Anne Chatellard (colour)
CARTOGRAPHIC COMPUTER GRAPHICS: Paul Coulbois, Édigraphie, Nicolas Grégoire, Patrick Mérienne

Printed in Italy by Editoriale Lloyd

EVERYMAN GUIDES
Gloucester Mansions, 140a Shaftesbury Avenue,
London WC2H 8HD

Encyclopedia section

Alpine itineraries

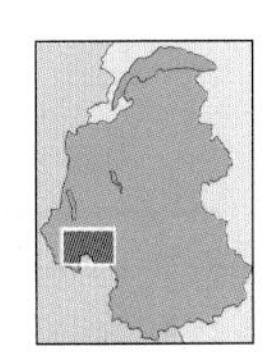

Chambéry

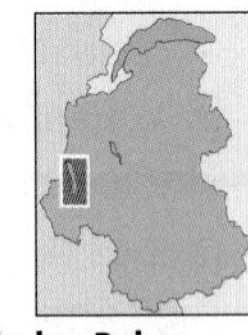

Aix-les-Bains

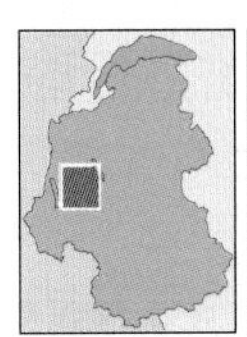
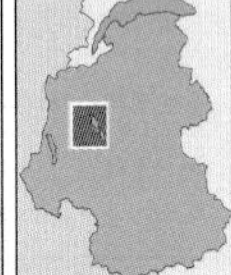

Bauges-Albanais, Annecy

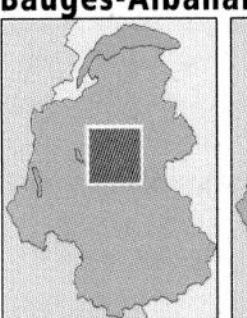
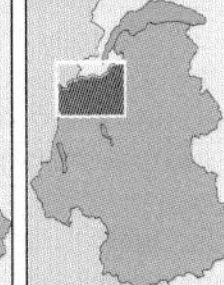

Aravis, Genevois

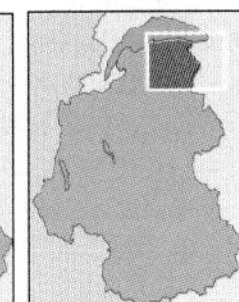

Lake Geneva, Chablais

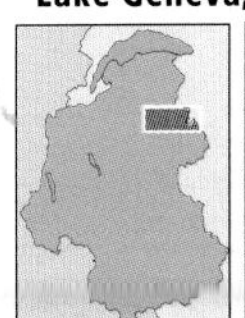
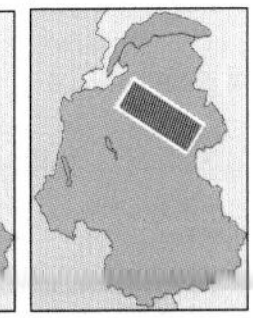

Giffre, the Faucigny

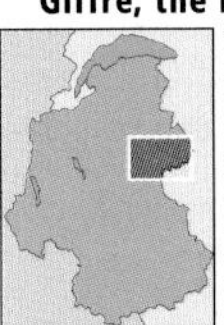
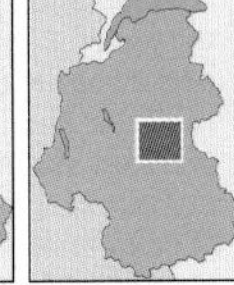

Pays du Mont-Blanc, Val d'Arly and Beufortain

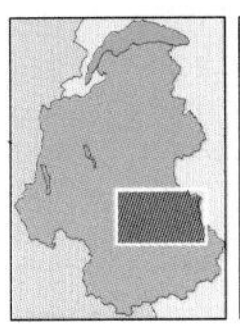

Tarentaise, Maurienne

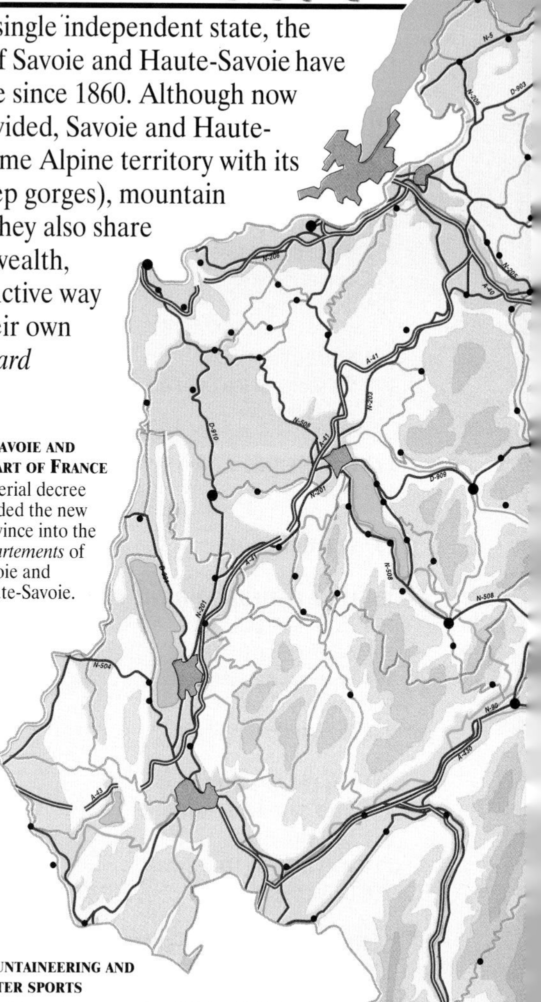

Profile of Savoie

Once existing as a single independent state, the two *départements* of Savoie and Haute-Savoie have been part of France since 1860. Although now administratively divided, Savoie and Haute-Savoie share the same Alpine territory with its glaciers, *cluses* (deep gorges), mountain passes and lakes. They also share the same touristic wealth, and the same distinctive way of life rooted in their own particular *montagnard* heritage.

April–June 1860: Savoie and Haute-Savoie Become Part of France

On April 22–23, 1860 the people of Savoie voted overwhelmingly to become part of France. Napoleon III had promised that Savoie would be a free zone. The official act signed by Victor-Emmanuel II in the Château de Chambéry marked the end of 1000 years of political autonomy for the state of Savoy. On June 15 an imperial decree divided the new province into the *départements* of Savoie and Haute-Savoie.

The Alps of Savoie and Haute-Savoie

The distinctive personality of Savoie and Haute-Savoie reflects the natural contrasts of the Alps: the magnificence and majesty of the Mont Blanc Massif; the solitude and unspoiled natural beauty of the nature reserves; and the pleasant green plains of Lake Geneva (Lac Léman), Lac d'Annecy, Lac du Bourget and Lac d'Aiguebelette. From 650 to 15,771 feet, from the heat of summer to the deep snowfalls of winter, Savoie and Haute-Savoie are first and foremost an Alpine region.

Mountaineering and Winter Sports

Mont Blanc has been familiar territory for climbers since the ascent made by Frenchmen Jacques Balmat and Michel-Gabriel Paccard in 1786. Its towering beauty also impressed a number of Britons, explorers rather than tourists, who went to Chamonix to 'breathe the invigorating air and lark about in the snow'. The fashion for winter sports, which took off at the start of the 20th century, became firmly established when the first ever Winter Olympics were held in Chamonix in 1924. The Winter Olympics held in nearby Albertville in 1992 celebrated a leisure industry which now attracts tourists from all over the world. With 120 resorts and more than seventy percent share of the national market, this industry accounts for fifty percent of the local economy. Tourist attractions range from sports and culture to gastronomy and health spas.

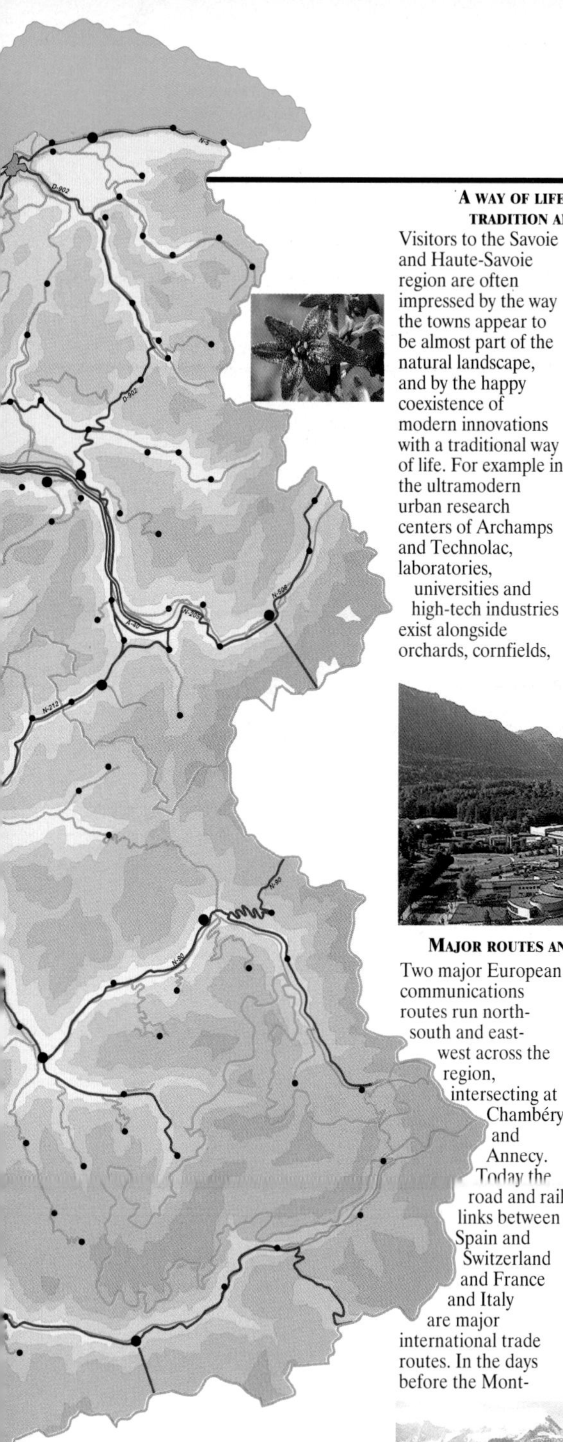

A WAY OF LIFE THAT COMBINES TRADITION AND MODERNISM

Visitors to the Savoie and Haute-Savoie region are often impressed by the way the towns appear to be almost part of the natural landscape, and by the happy coexistence of modern innovations with a traditional way of life. For example in the ultramodern urban research centers of Archamps and Technolac, laboratories, universities and high-tech industries exist alongside orchards, cornfields, snowfields, beaches and vineyards. Traditional agricultural practices continue to produce quality products, especially cheeses (Beaufort, Reblochon) and wines (Apremont, Chignin, Gamay de Savoie, Mondeuse), while the future looks rosy with new wealth created by the leisure and industrial sectors. But there is a price to pay for this success, and the population of the two *départements* continues to increase.

MAJOR ROUTES AND FUTURE PROJECTS

Two major European communications routes run north-south and east-west across the region, intersecting at Chambéry and Annecy. Today the road and rail links between Spain and Switzerland and France and Italy are major international trade routes. In the days before the Mont-Blanc and Fréjus tunnels were built, goods were carried by donkey over the high Alpine passes (Petit-Saint-Bernard, Mont-Cenis) and the counts of Savoie were regarded as the 'gatekeepers' of the Alps. The mountains of Savoie and Haute-Savoie have never been a barrier to trade and the European market would certainly not have allowed them to create one.

FACTS AND FIGURES

Surface area: 40,020 square miles
Population: 1 million
Tourist accommodation: 113,000 beds
Principal town (Savoie): Chambéry
Principal town (Haute-Savoie): Annecy

HOW TO USE THIS GUIDE

The symbols at the top of each page refer to the different parts of the guide:

■ NATURE

● ENCYCLOPEDIA

▲ SECTION

◆ ITINERARIES

The itinerary map shows the main points of interest along the way and is intended to help you find your bearings.

The mini-map locates the particular itinerary within the wider area covered by the guide.

● ▲ ■ ◆
The symbols alongside a title or within the text itself provide cross-references to a theme or place dealt with elsewhere in the guide.

Nature

THE MONT BLANC MASSIF
The Mont Blanc Massif originated from the rock strata of the Eurasian plate, part of which fragmented and was pushed upward to high altitudes by tectonic pressures.

The regions of Savoie and Haute-Savoie rise from 690 feet above sea level at the confluence of the Rivers Guiers and Rhône to 15,771 feet at the summit of Mont Blanc. In the west is the 'Alpine fringe', a sandstone and shale foreland dominated by the secondary chains of the Jura: the Salève range and the massifs bordering the Lac du Bourget. Further east are the ranges of the Préalpes (the Chartreuse and Bauges massifs), which in turn give way to the snow-covered peaks of the central (Mont Blanc and Vanoise) massifs. Deep valleys penetrate this relief: the Alpine trench, between the Préalpes and the central massifs, is crossed by the valleys of the Rivers Isère and Arc, while the gorges of Annecy, Chambéry and the River Arve score deep into the mountains.

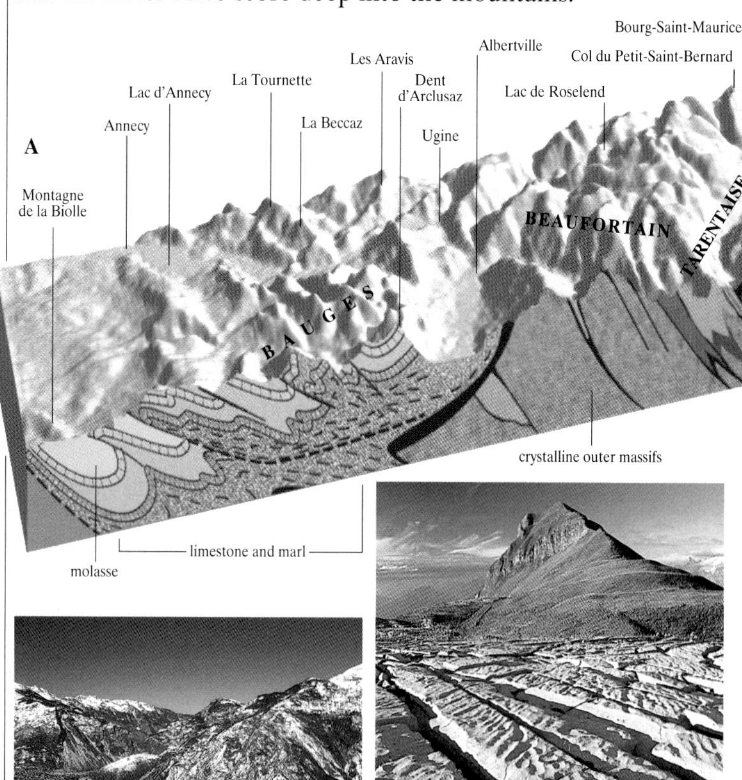

LA MAURIENNE
The major Alpine valleys were formed by a succession of tectonic upheavals. The valleys were later hollowed out and formed into a series of depressions and thresholds by glacial activity.

DÉSERT DE PLATÉ. Thick limestone deposits have created a spectacular Alpine karst landscape in the upper valley of the River Giffre. Rainwater and melting snows have dissolved the limestone, carving out networks of fissures, sink-holes and underground galleries.

The Bauges Massif. This pre-Alpine massif is a moderately sized range. Walls of limestone rock rise on its outer edges and the folding of secondary sediment has created an arrangement of parallel ridges and trenches. Its position in the Alpine foreland means that it has high levels of precipitation, giving rise to forest-clad slopes (beech and fir give way to spruce and mountain pine higher up).

The Combe de Savoie. The Alpine trench (*sillon alpin*) is a deep depression that lies between the Préalpes and the central massifs. Originally cut through deep layers of slaty marl, during the Quaternary Era it was further eroded by glaciers and occupied by a lake. The Isère and its tributaries filled the lake with sediment, turning it into a marshy plain that has been reclaimed by embanking the river and draining off the water.

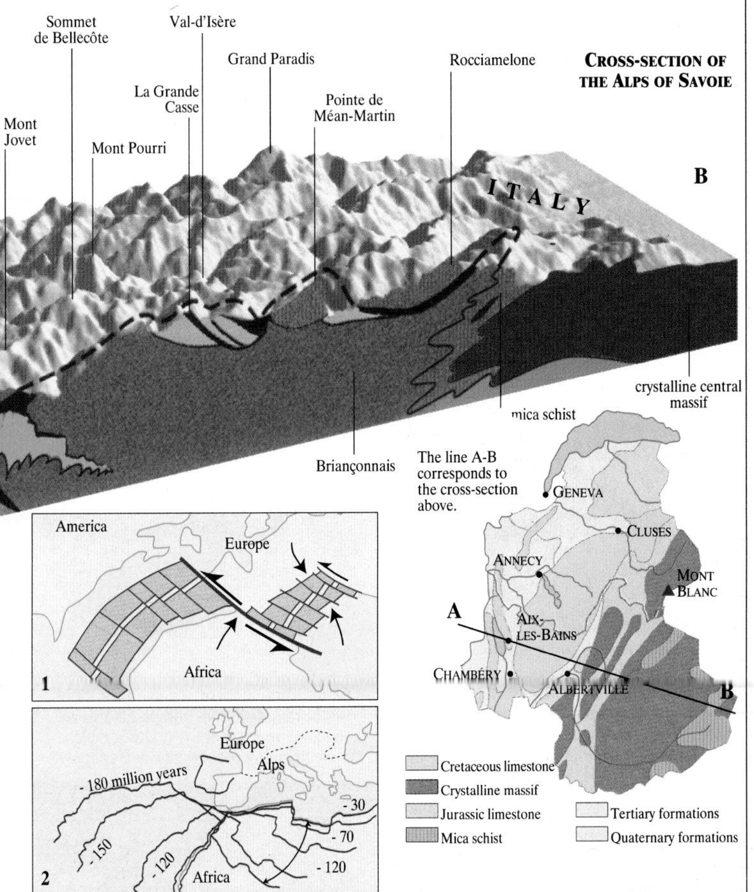

Cross-section of the Alps of Savoie

The line A-B corresponds to the cross-section above.

Formation of the Alps

The separation of the Eurasian and African tectonic plates during the Triassic and Jurassic periods (230 to 158 million years ago) gave rise to a great sea that covered the region of what is now Savoie and Haute-Savoie. Sedimentary deposits of vast thicknesses were laid down by the sea on the crystalline rock strata. Tectonic upheavals, which began 110 million years ago and culminated 40 million years ago, thrust the seabed upward and northward, forcing it to gradually fold so that it formed great ridges and valleys. In some areas large masses of rocks were pushed on top of others. The layer folded about 10 million years ago when it overthrust the Miocene molasse (sandstone and shale) of the foreland, forming the Préalpes and the folds of the Jura.

Climate

Summer storms
These are usually violent and can be accompanied by localized hailstorms.

The climate of the Savoie region is temperate, tending toward continental. It is characterized by wide variations between summer and winter temperatures, which become even more marked in the high mountains, and by a regular, sometimes abundant, rainfall that is heaviest in the summer. Much of the rain falls during storms, which in the mountains can be quite violent. Altitude has major ecological consequences for the region's flora and fauna, which have to adapt to long periods of snow, wide variations in temperature and irregular rainfall.

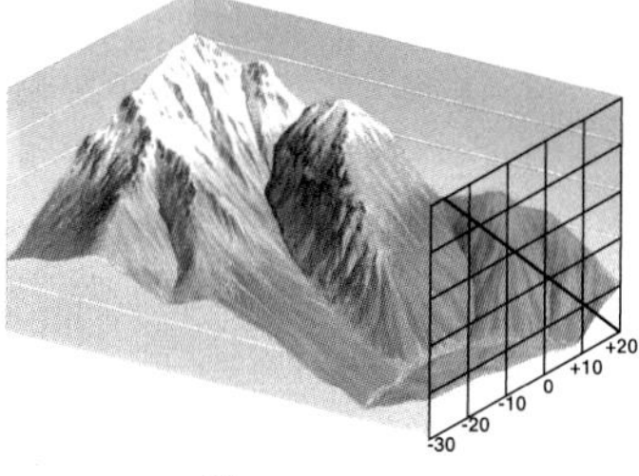

Temperature
The temperature drops as altitude increases: 1°F for every 330 feet. The characteristically wet mountain climate makes temperatures feel even cooler.

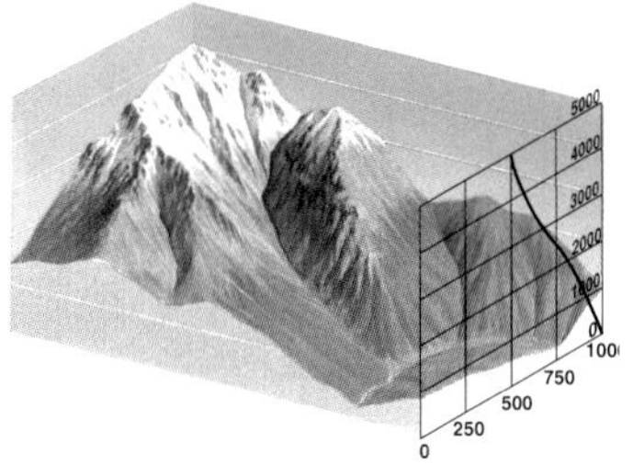

Atmospheric pressure
Pressure decreases with altitude; at 8000 feet the pressure is about half that at sea level. Above 8000 feet, the drop in pressure can cause physiological disorders.

Ultraviolet rays
The sun's ultraviolet rays are much more intense in the mountains as they are less effectively filtered by the atmosphere. Effective protection against sunlight reflected by the snow is also extremely important.

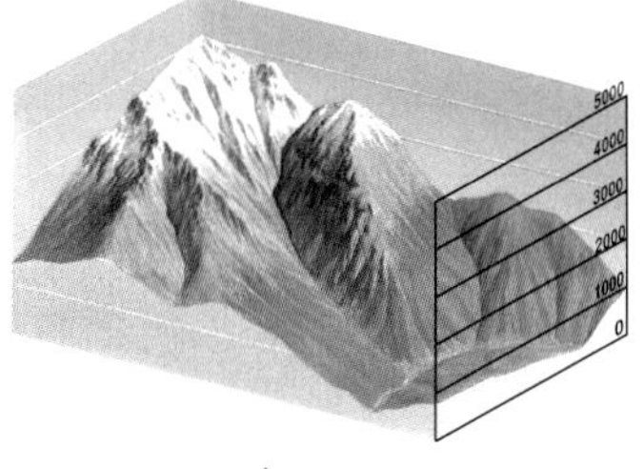

Altitude
As the altitude increases, the conditions under which animals and plants survive become much more restrictive, which significantly reduces their diversity.

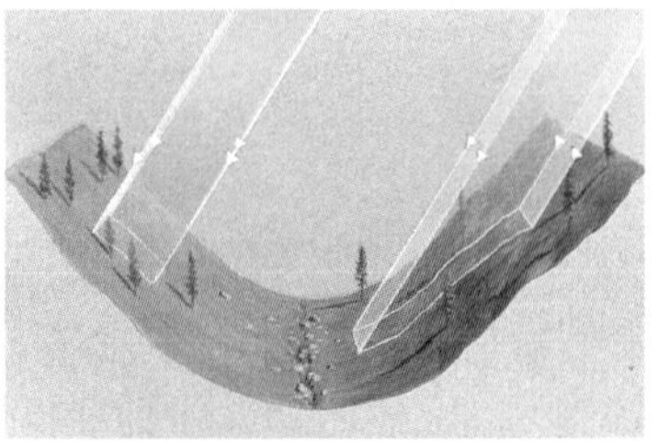

Situation and exposure
Differences in exposure between the south-facing and north-facing slopes determines the distribution of plant and human colonization.

Temperature regulation
The vast size and depth of Lake Geneva prevents it from freezing over. It acts as a huge regulator to the region's temperate climate.

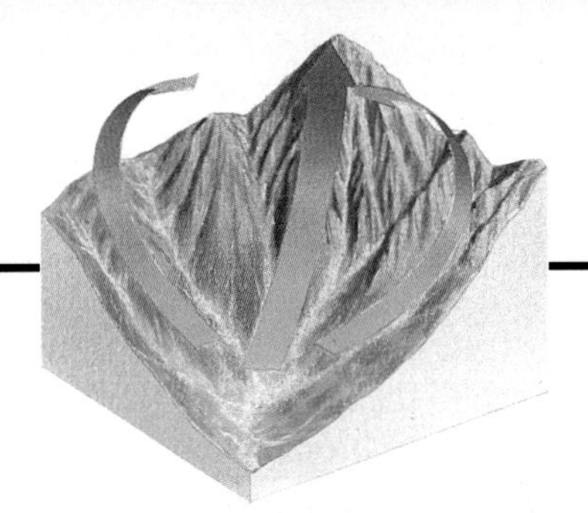

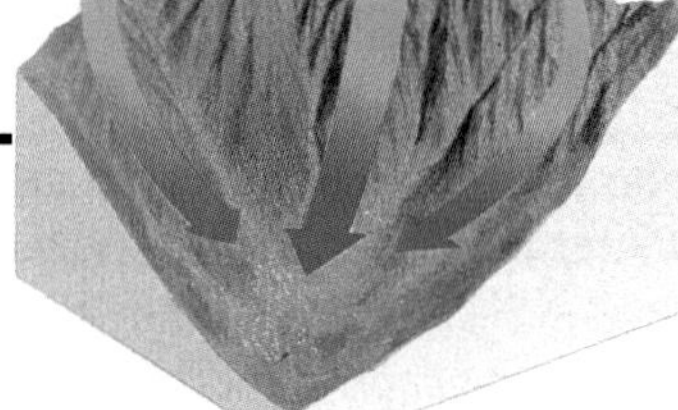

Diurnal aerology
The mountains have a complex system of air currents that affects the valleys and slopes during the summer months. During the day, the sun heats the mountains and upper slopes of the valleys, warming the surrounding air, which rises. It is replaced by cooler air from the valley bottoms, so creating a current of air from the valleys to the mountain peaks.

Nocturnal aerology
At night, the mountains cool down much more quickly than the valleys (because of the higher altitude) and the circulation of air is reversed.

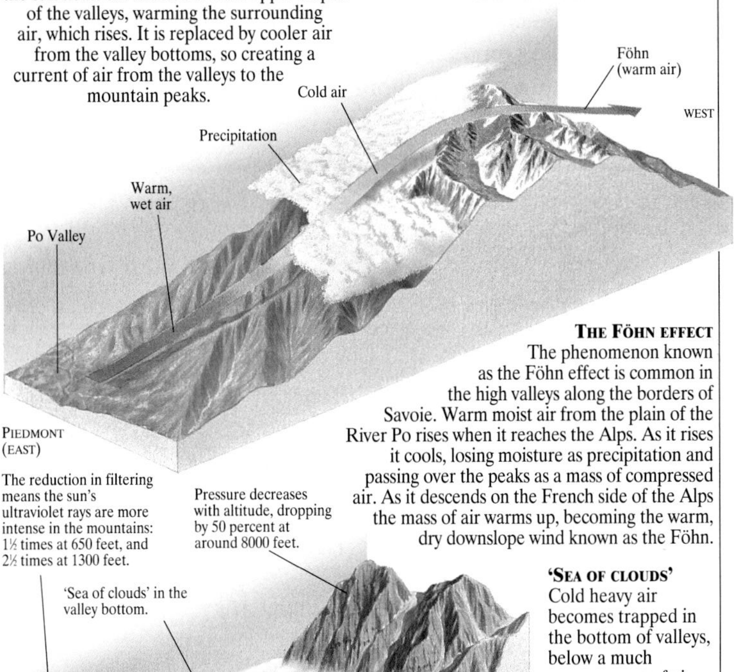

Föhn
(warm air)
WEST
Cold air
Precipitation
Warm,
wet air
Po Valley
Piedmont
(East)

The Föhn effect
The phenomenon known as the Föhn effect is common in the high valleys along the borders of Savoie. Warm moist air from the plain of the River Po rises when it reaches the Alps. As it rises it cools, losing moisture as precipitation and passing over the peaks as a mass of compressed air. As it descends on the French side of the Alps the mass of air warms up, becoming the warm, dry downslope wind known as the Föhn.

The reduction in filtering means the sun's ultraviolet rays are more intense in the mountains: 1½ times at 650 feet, and 2½ times at 1300 feet.

Pressure decreases with altitude, dropping by 50 percent at around 8000 feet.

'Sea of clouds' in the valley bottom.

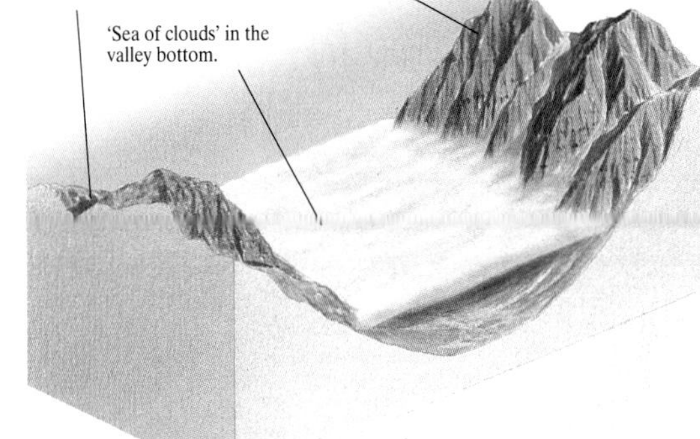

'Sea of clouds'
Cold heavy air becomes trapped in the bottom of valleys, below a much warmer mass of air. The boundary between these two air masses takes the form of a 'sea of clouds' which is in fact a layer of condensation caused by the contact between the warm and cold air.

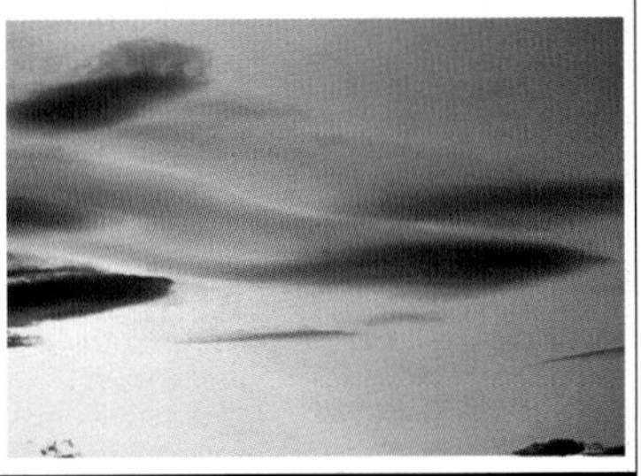

Orographic clouds
As it approaches a mountain, a mass of air is diverted upward by air currents. As it rises, it cools at a rate of about 33°F for every 320 feet. The colder the mass of air, the less able it is to hold water vapor. This vapor condenses rapidly and gives rise to an orographic cloud.

WIND CRUST. Snow crystals blown by the wind into sheltered areas form a rigid crust. Its poor cohesion with the snow pack means that the crust fractures and slips easily.

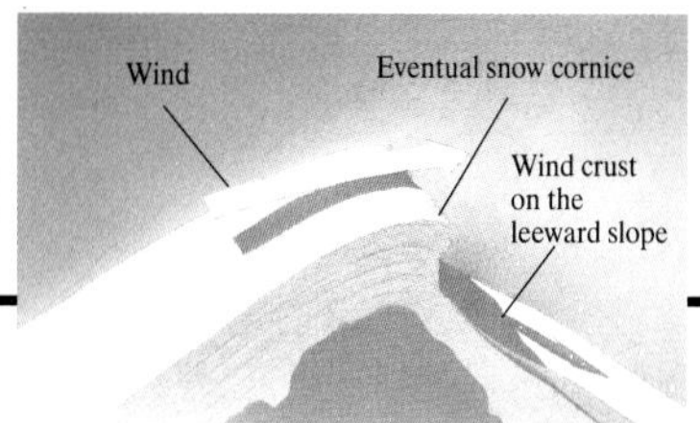

Snow is an integral part of the winter landscape in the Savoie region. From the first snows of the fall to the last flurries of spring, the snow undergoes transformations brought about by the changing weather conditions. These changes in size, form and structure of the settled snow are caused by the wind, temperature and localized falls. They result in a snow pack made up of different layers that, depending on their structure, can cause avalanches. The number of days of snowfall ranges from several days on the plains and shores of the lakes to over 100 days on the summit of Mont Blanc.

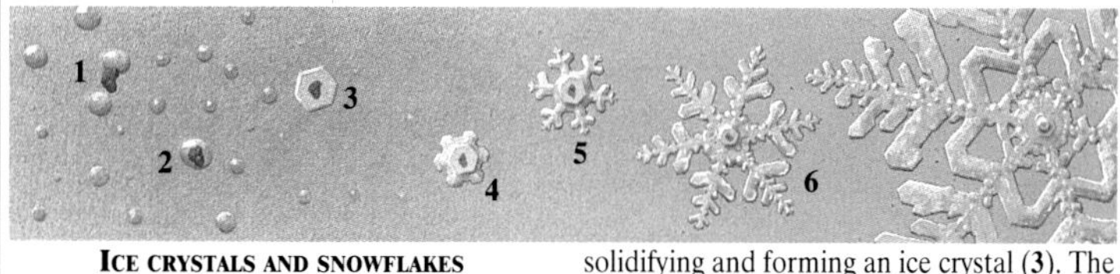

ICE CRYSTALS AND SNOWFLAKES
Ice crystals are formed in a mass of air saturated with water vapor, at temperatures between –4° and –40° F. The water vapor condenses (**2**) around dust nuclei (**1**), solidifying and forming an ice crystal (**3**). The crystals increase in size and weight, and form composite snowflakes (**4**) as they fall to earth. The complexity of their hexagonal structure (**5** and **6**) depends on temperature.

PLATELIKE CRYSTALS
Small, smooth-surfaced hexagonal plates are formed between 14°F and –4°F.

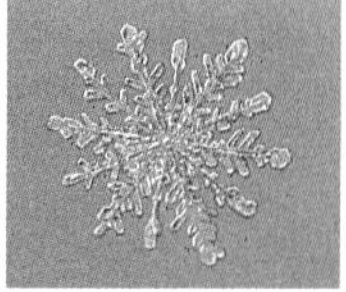

STAR CRYSTALS
Six-armed, geometric flakes are formed between 5°F and –0.5°F.

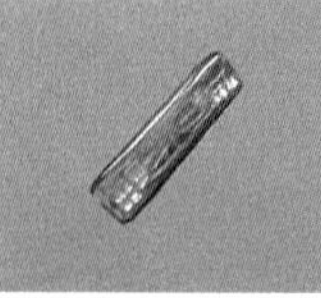

COLUMNAR CRYSTALS
Prisms (solid or with cavities) are formed between 14°F and –8.5°F.

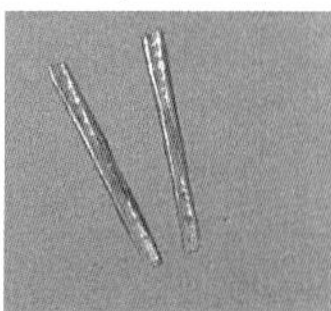

NEEDLE CRYSTALS
Fine crystals (solid or with cavities) are formed between 24°F and –17° F.

'CUFF-LINK' CRYSTALS
Prisms with a plate at either end are formed at temperatures below –0.5° F.

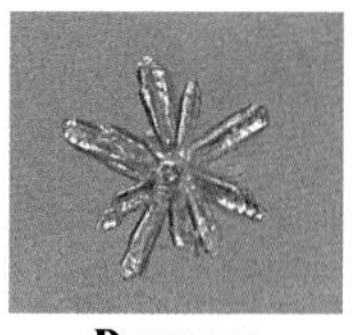

DENDRITIC, SPHERICAL CRYSTALS
Needles, plates or prisms around a central nucleus.

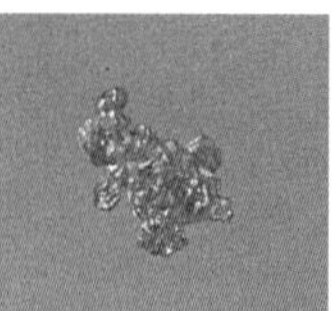

IRREGULAR PARTICLES
A formation without any particular geometrical form.

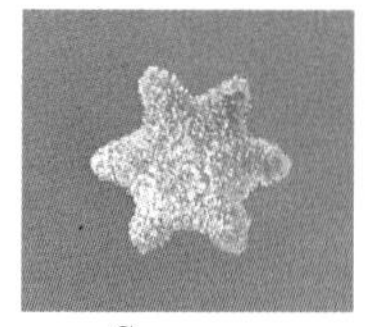

SOFT HAIL
Soft hail or 'snow pellets' are formed from a collision of ice crystals.

SNOW PACK
This is a permanent feature of much of the mountain landscape. Overloading or structural changes within the snow pack can cause it to fracture and lead to an avalanche.

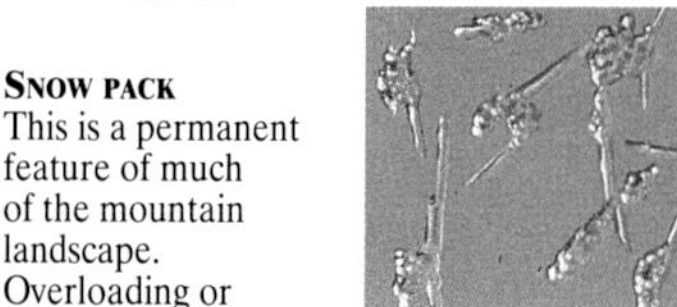

DESTRUCTIVE METAMORPHOSIS
Fractured and reduced crystals break up into particles.

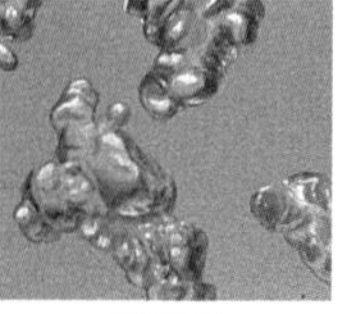

'MELT' METAMORPHOSIS
Rising temperatures create large, smooth crystals.

CONSTRUCTIVE METAMORPHOSIS
'Goblet' crystals are formed by low stable temperatures.

Avalanches

Avalanches are most likely occur on steep slopes (greater than 22°), where the delicate balance of the snow pack may suddenly be disturbed by the effects of additional weight and slip down the mountainside. There are three types of avalanche.

Wet snow avalanche

Generally occuring in spring, this type of avalanche is a mass of wet, dense snow. They can cause heavy erosion of the mountain slopes.

Slab avalanche

Slab avalanches are caused by the fracturing of one of the upper layers of the snow pack that is only partially bound to the lower layers.

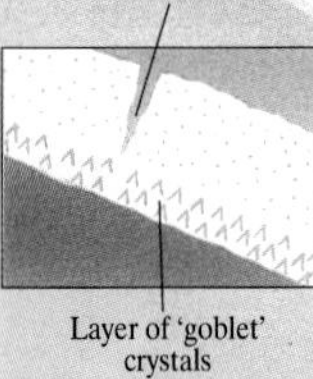

Dry snow avalanche

Dry snow avalanches consist of powdery snow and air and can move at more 100 miles per hour. They occur in very cold weather after a heavy snowfall.

Alpine pastures on Mont Bochor, at the foot of La Grande Casse.

The variation of the rock structure of the Parc National de la Vanoise and its location at a climatic 'crossroads' result in a remarkably rich variety of landscapes, flora and fauna. In addition to the native Alpine flora, the 1000 plant species recorded on this massif also include Asian and Mediterranean species, and the Arctic-Alpine species that survived from the Quaternary glaciations.

The River Arc winds it way through the Bessans valley.

Alpine hay meadow below the massif of La Grande Casse.

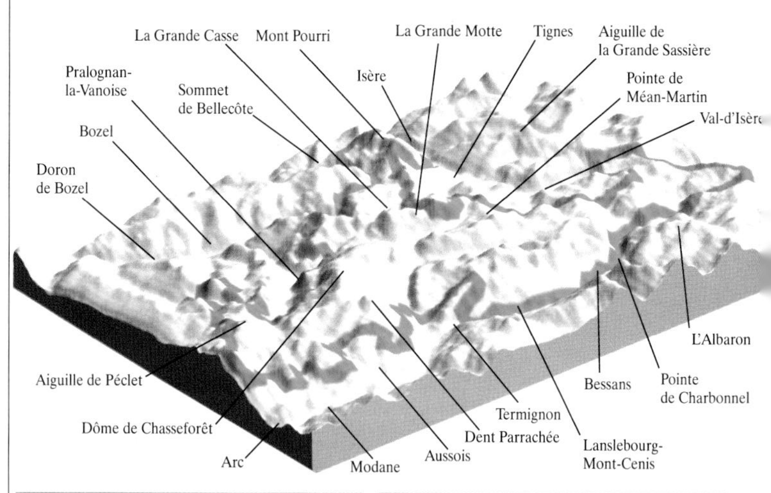

Alpine pastures on the Col de l'Iseran, from the Signal du Mont Iseran.

The leading edge of the Glacier de Gébroulaz, a tongue of flowing ice.

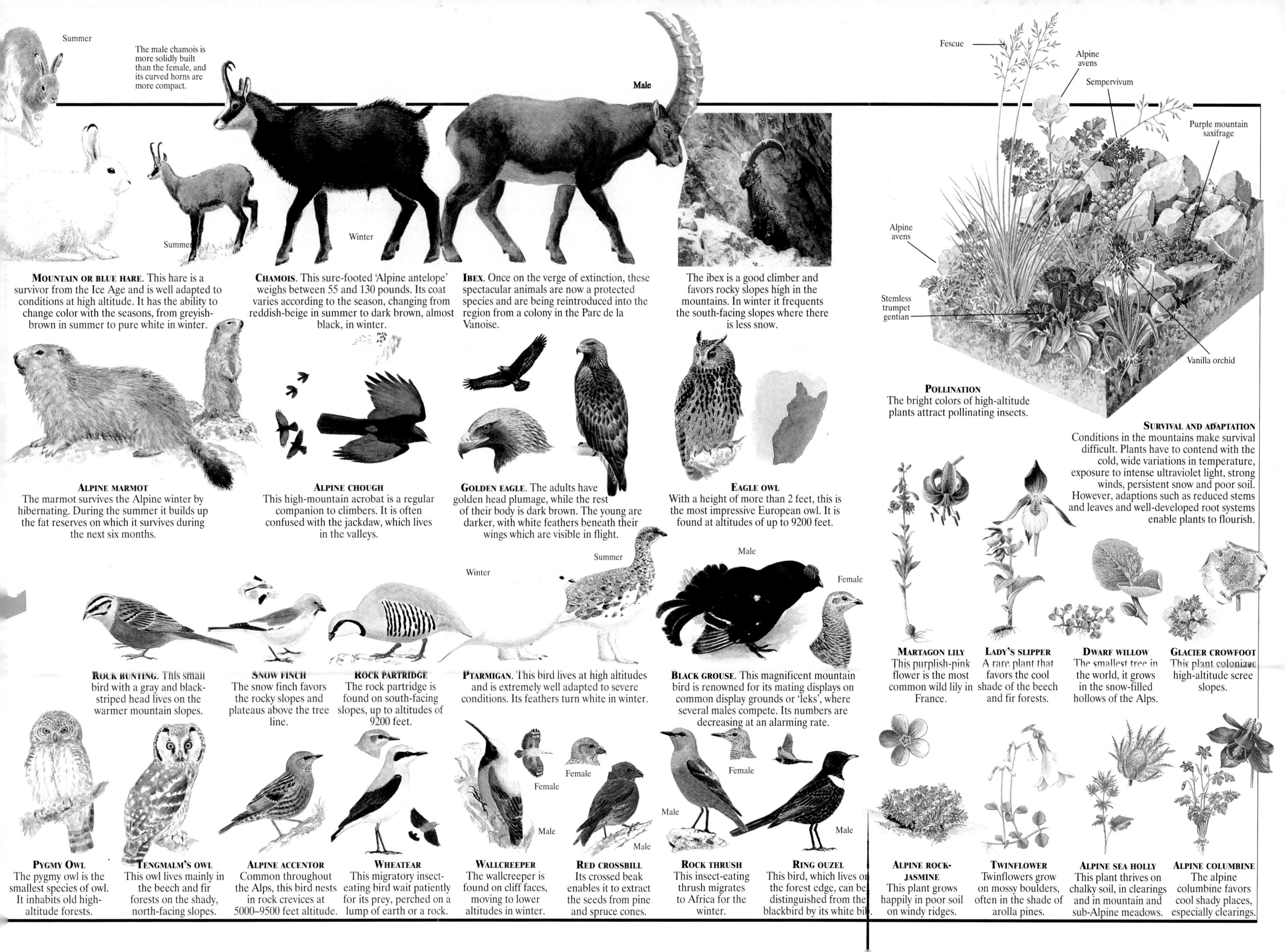

Mountain or blue hare. This hare is a survivor from the Ice Age and is well adapted to conditions at high altitude. It has the ability to change color with the seasons, from greyish-brown in summer to pure white in winter.

Chamois. This sure-footed 'Alpine antelope' weighs between 55 and 130 pounds. Its coat varies according to the season, changing from reddish-beige in summer to dark brown, almost black, in winter.

Ibex. Once on the verge of extinction, these spectacular animals are now a protected species and are being reintroduced into the region from a colony in the Parc de la Vanoise.

The ibex is a good climber and favors rocky slopes high in the mountains. In winter it frequents the south-facing slopes where there is less snow.

Pollination
The bright colors of high-altitude plants attract pollinating insects.

Survival and adaptation
Conditions in the mountains make survival difficult. Plants have to contend with the cold, wide variations in temperature, exposure to intense ultraviolet light, strong winds, persistent snow and poor soil. However, adaptions such as reduced stems and leaves and well-developed root systems enable plants to flourish.

Alpine marmot
The marmot survives the Alpine winter by hibernating. During the summer it builds up the fat reserves on which it survives during the next six months.

Alpine chough
This high-mountain acrobat is a regular companion to climbers. It is often confused with the jackdaw, which lives in the valleys.

Golden eagle. The adults have golden head plumage, while the rest of their body is dark brown. The young are darker, with white feathers beneath their wings which are visible in flight.

Eagle owl
With a height of more than 2 feet, this is the most impressive European owl. It is found at altitudes of up to 9200 feet.

Rock bunting. This small bird with a gray and black-striped head lives on the warmer mountain slopes.

Snow finch
The snow finch favors the rocky slopes and plateaus above the tree line.

Rock partridge
The rock partridge is found on south-facing slopes, up to altitudes of 9200 feet.

Ptarmigan. This bird lives at high altitudes and is extremely well adapted to severe conditions. Its feathers turn white in winter.

Black grouse. This magnificent mountain bird is renowned for its mating displays on common display grounds or 'leks', where several males compete. Its numbers are decreasing at an alarming rate.

Martagon lily
This purplish-pink flower is the most common wild lily in France.

Lady's slipper
A rare plant that favors the cool shade of the beech and fir forests.

Dwarf willow
The smallest tree in the world, it grows in the snow-filled hollows of the Alps.

Glacier crowfoot
This plant colonizes high-altitude scree slopes.

Pygmy Owl
The pygmy owl is the smallest species of owl. It inhabits old high-altitude forests.

Tengmalm's owl
This owl lives mainly in the beech and fir forests on the shady, north-facing slopes.

Alpine accentor
Common throughout the Alps, this bird nests in rock crevices at 5000–9500 feet altitude.

Wheatear
This migratory insect-eating bird wait patiently for its prey, perched on a lump of earth or a rock.

Wallcreeper
The wallcreeper is found on cliff faces, moving to lower altitudes in winter.

Red crossbill
Its crossed beak enables it to extract the seeds from pine and spruce cones.

Rock thrush
This insect-eating thrush migrates to Africa for the winter.

Ring ouzel
This bird, which lives on the forest edge, can be distinguished from the blackbird by its white bib.

Alpine rock-jasmine
This plant grows happily in poor soil on windy ridges.

Twinflower
Twinflowers grow on mossy boulders, often in the shade of arolla pines.

Alpine sea holly
This plant thrives on chalky soil, in clearings and in mountain and sub-Alpine meadows.

Alpine columbine
The alpine columbine favors cool shady places, especially clearings.

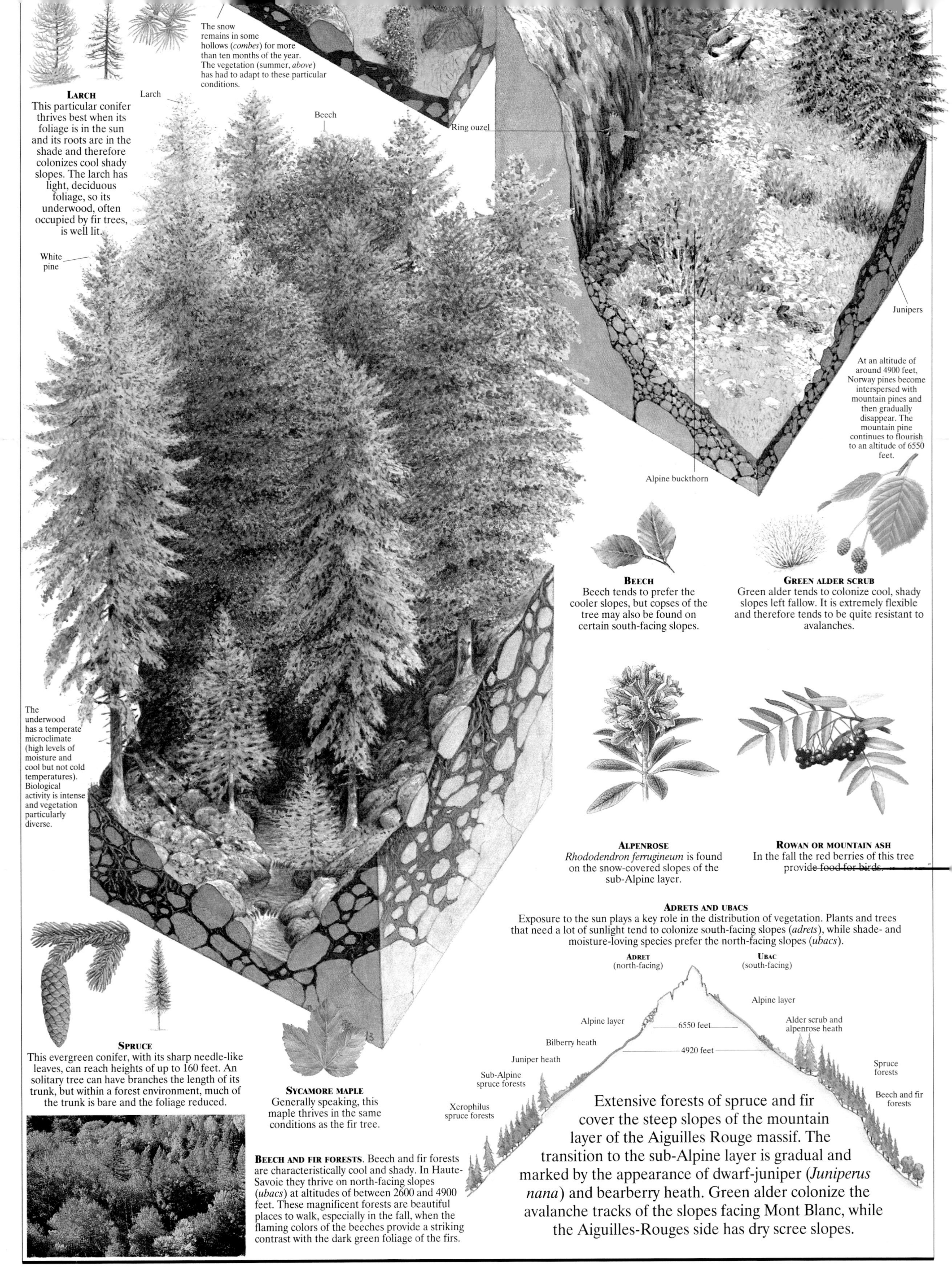

LARCH
This particular conifer thrives best when its foliage is in the sun and its roots are in the shade and therefore colonizes cool shady slopes. The larch has light, deciduous foliage, so its underwood, often occupied by fir trees, is well lit.

BEECH
Beech tends to prefer the cooler slopes, but copses of the tree may also be found on certain south-facing slopes.

GREEN ALDER SCRUB
Green alder tends to colonize cool, shady slopes left fallow. It is extremely flexible and therefore tends to be quite resistant to avalanches.

ALPENROSE
Rhododendron ferrugineum is found on the snow-covered slopes of the sub-Alpine layer.

ROWAN OR MOUNTAIN ASH
In the fall the red berries of this tree provide food for birds.

ADRETS AND UBACS
Exposure to the sun plays a key role in the distribution of vegetation. Plants and trees that need a lot of sunlight tend to colonize south-facing slopes (*adrets*), while shade- and moisture-loving species prefer the north-facing slopes (*ubacs*).

SPRUCE
This evergreen conifer, with its sharp needle-like leaves, can reach heights of up to 160 feet. An solitary tree can have branches the length of its trunk, but within a forest environment, much of the trunk is bare and the foliage reduced.

SYCAMORE MAPLE
Generally speaking, this maple thrives in the same conditions as the fir tree.

BEECH AND FIR FORESTS. Beech and fir forests are characteristically cool and shady. In Haute-Savoie they thrive on north-facing slopes (*ubacs*) at altitudes of between 2600 and 4900 feet. These magnificent forests are beautiful places to walk, especially in the fall, when the flaming colors of the beeches provide a striking contrast with the dark green foliage of the firs.

Extensive forests of spruce and fir cover the steep slopes of the mountain layer of the Aiguilles Rouge massif. The transition to the sub-Alpine layer is gradual and marked by the appearance of dwarf-juniper (*Juniperus nana*) and bearberry heath. Green alder colonize the avalanche tracks of the slopes facing Mont Blanc, while the Aiguilles-Rouges side has dry scree slopes.

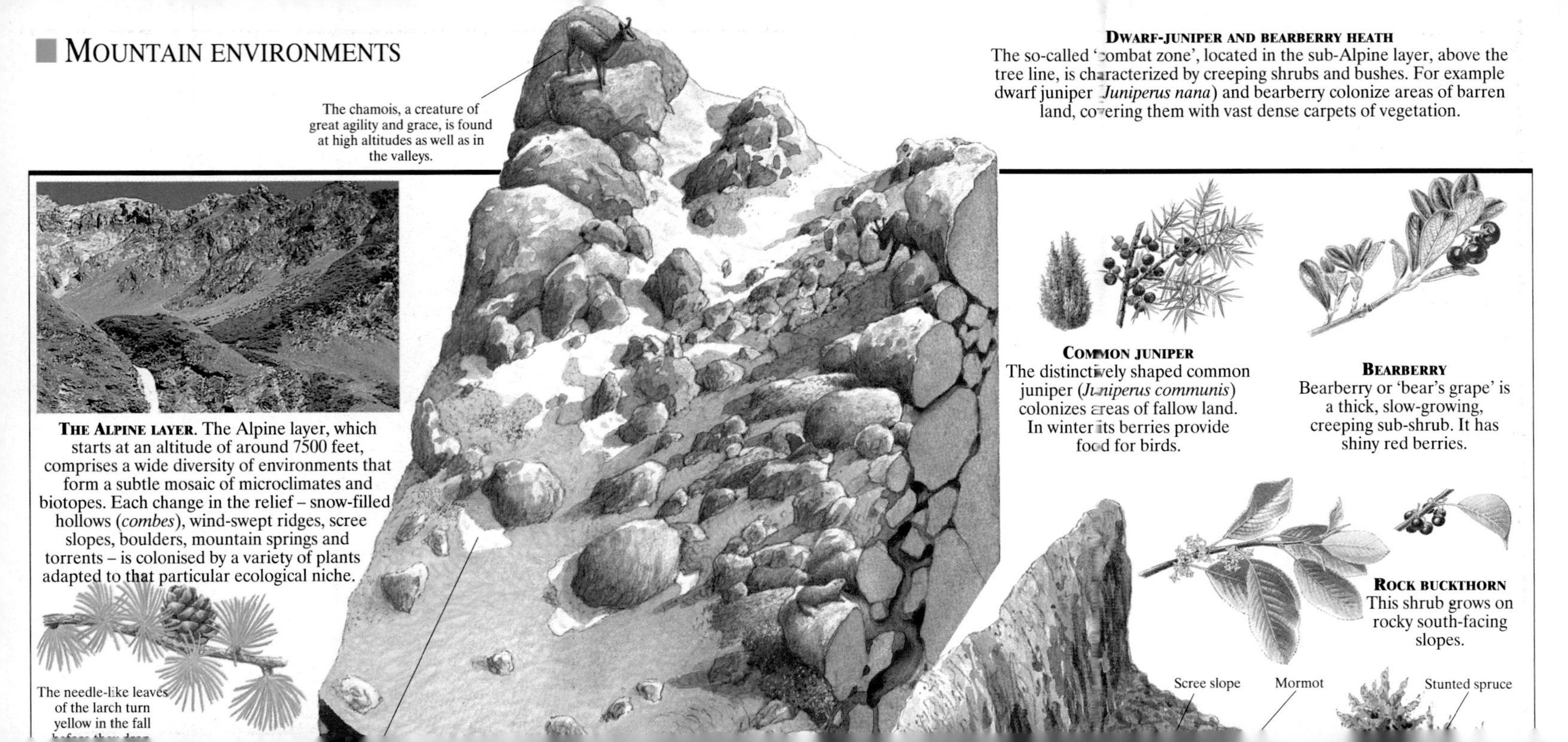

The chamois, a creature of great agility and grace, is found at high altitudes as well as in the valleys.

DWARF-JUNIPER AND BEARBERRY HEATH
The so-called 'combat zone', located in the sub-Alpine layer, above the tree line, is characterized by creeping shrubs and bushes. For example dwarf juniper (*Juniperus nana*) and bearberry colonize areas of barren land, covering them with vast dense carpets of vegetation.

THE ALPINE LAYER. The Alpine layer, which starts at an altitude of around 7500 feet, comprises a wide diversity of environments that form a subtle mosaic of microclimates and biotopes. Each change in the relief – snow-filled hollows (*combes*), wind-swept ridges, scree slopes, boulders, mountain springs and torrents – is colonised by a variety of plants adapted to that particular ecological niche.

COMMON JUNIPER
The distinctively shaped common juniper (*Juniperus communis*) colonizes areas of fallow land. In winter its berries provide food for birds.

BEARBERRY
Bearberry or 'bear's grape' is a thick, slow-growing, creeping sub-shrub. It has shiny red berries.

ROCK BUCKTHORN
This shrub grows on rocky south-facing slopes.

The needle-like leaves of the larch turn yellow in the fall

Lake Geneva (Lac Léman) lies at an altitude of 1220 feet and occupies an area of 225 square miles. Its shoreline is 103 miles long, 32 miles of which lie in Haute-Savoie. Situated in the heart of a temperate zone, at the edge of the Alps, the lake lies on a major migratory route. Certain species of bird visit the lake in summer and migrate south in winter, to be replaced in turn by other species escaping the harsher Scandinavian and Siberian winters. Lake Geneva is one of Europe's richest microclimates and offers a rich and varied supply of food to the 100,000 species of birds (including ducks, swans and gulls) that spend the winter here.

GREAT CORMORANT
In the past 15 years the cormorant, a big fish-eating relative of the pelican, has become a regular winter visitor to Lake Geneva.

YELLOW-LEGGED HERRING GULL
The gull population is at its highest in summer when thousands of these birds fly to the lake from the Mediterranean.

GOOSANDER
The goosander nests in holes in trees and other such cavities. More than 90 percent of France's goosander population is found in Haute-Savoie.

TUFTED DUCK
These diving birds are the most numerous of the ducks spending winter on the lake. Their increasing numbers are due to the expansion of the zebra mussel which forms their staple diet.

Fennel pondweed
These aquatic plants form huge colonies or 'beds' wherever the lake floor slopes gently,

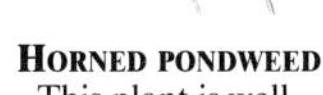

Horned pondweed
This plant is well-adapted to deep water and occupies the lower section of the 'beds' (over 16 feet).

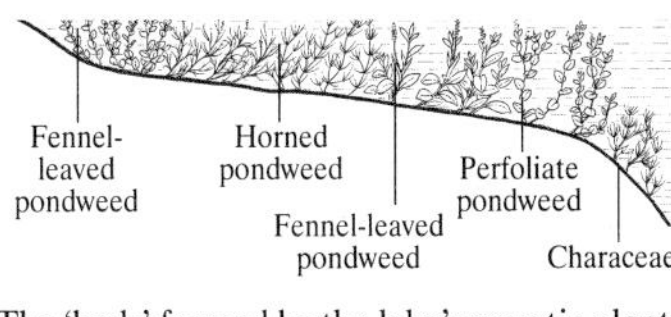

The 'beds' formed by the lake's aquatic plant communities constitute a valuable food resource for waterfowl. Surface-feeding ducks and swans feed on the pondweed along the shoreline, while certain diving birds feed on the characeae found in deeper water.

Zebra mussel
This tiny mussel forms the staple diet of many diving ducks.

Bleak
This small fish lives in large compact shoals and is an easy prey for certain waterfowl, especially the black-necked grebe.

Perch
Hundreds of tonnes of this popular freshwater fish are caught each year. The population varies hugely from year to year, depending on the breeding season.

Goldeneye
A native of northern Europe, the goldeneye migrates to Lake Geneva during the winter. Large concentrations are found near Excenevex and Sciez.

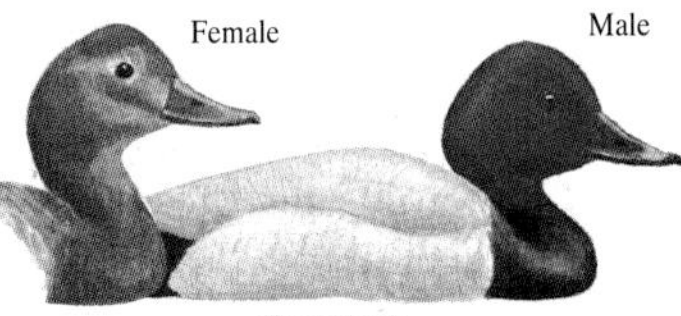

Pochard
Together with the tufted duck, the pochard is the dominant species of duck on the lake during the winter. However, its numbers appear to have declined in recent years.

The people of Savoie have always exploited the natural resources of the region. Local plants formed the basis of many recipes for remedies, liqueurs, sauces and dishes at a time when the distinction between culinary and medicinal use was less clearly defined. Today, except for wormwood, which has become the victim of its own success, most of these plants are no longer used in these traditional methods. However, they are often extremely common and can be found by the wayside, in a meadow, forest or on mountain pasture.

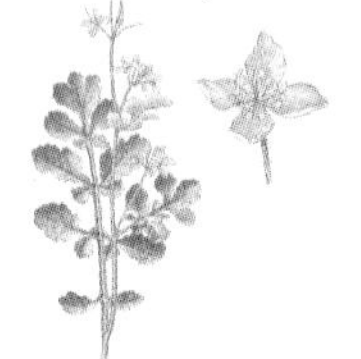

GREATER CELANDINE
The corrosive yellow sap of this plant was used as an eye ointment and as a popular and effective cure for warts.

WORMWOOD
This aromatic plant is used to flavor liqueurs, including absinthe. The harvesting of its fruit is now strictly controlled.

COMMON JUNIPER
The scented berries are used as a condiment and are also a traditional remedy for stimulating the kidneys.

COMMON OR BLACK-BERRIED ELDER
Elder flowers and fruit are used to make drinks and desserts. Elder wood is used to make whistles, toys and other objects.

WHITE MUGWORT
White mugwort is used to flavour liqueurs and as a traditional cure for chills. The harvesting of its fruit is now strictly controlled.

DANDELION
Dandelion leaves can be eaten in salads. Its roots are used in the preparation of diuretics, which is why it is popularly known as 'pissabed'.

BILBERRY
The bilberry's delicately flavored, purple fruits have medicinal properties. They are picked for home consumption or for sale.

NETTLES
Young nettle shoots can be eaten like spinach, while their leaves are good for the circulation. In the past its fibers were woven.

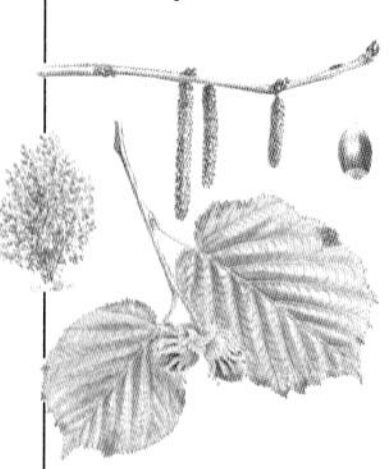

HAZEL (NUT TREE)
Hazelnuts are extremely popular in desserts. According to legend, magic wands were made of hazel wood.

SPRUCE
Spruce resin had a number of medicinal uses. Cooked with honey it makes delicious cough sweets.

ST JOHN'S WORT
The cornerstone of traditional medicine, this plant was used to heal wounds, as a remedy for anxiety and ulcers and to treat animals.

HYSSOP
This aromatic Mediterranean plant was cultivated in the gardens of the valleys for culinary purposes and as a remedy for digestive complaints.

History

HISTORY

- **– 5000** Neolithic settlements
- **– 3000**
- **– 2000** Bronze Age
- **– 1000**
- **– 900** Hallstatt culture
- **– 800** The Iron Age
- **– 500**
- **– 450** Celtic occupation
- **– 218** Hannibal crosses the Alps
- **– 121** Roman conquest
- **– 100**
- **– 52** Siege of Alesia. Roman occupation.
- **– 15** Conquest of the Alps
- **0**
- **c. 300** Martyrdom of Saint Maurice and the Theban legion at Agaune
- **300**

THE EARLIEST INHABITANTS

The earliest traces of human habitation in Savoie were left by the hunters who moved into the subalpine valleys and massifs as the glaciers began to retreat (c. 12,000 BC). During the Neolithic Period the first farmers settled in the region and, c. 3000 BC, colonized the high valleys. Toward the end of the Bronze Age (1000–800 BC) the inhabitants of the lakeside villages (Lake Geneva, Lac du Bourget, Lac d'Annecy) became skilled craftsmen in bronze and ceramics.

By 900 BC all the best land in the region was occupied: the Préalpes by the Hallstatt and then the Gallic cultures, and the Alpine valleys by another civilization. The Allobrogi settled in the area between Geneva and Vienne, except for the Maurienne (inhabited by the Medulles) and the Tarentaise and Arly valleys and the upper valley of the Arve (inhabited by the Ceutrons). In 218 BC Hannibal crossed the Alps with thirty-seven elephants, possibly via the Maurienne Valley.

ROMAN OCCUPATION

Between 121 and 61 BC the Romans conquered the region, which became part of the colony of Narbonna. The Allobrogi resisted for a long time, but finally submitted when Caesar conquered Gaul. The Alpine tribes were not conquered until c. 15 BC, when present-day Savoie was divided between the city of Geneva, founded during the Late Empire, and two provinces: the Graian Alps and the Cottian Alps. The Romans improved the Gaulish tracks and developed a road network, complemented by the Lake Geneva–Rhône river route. Towns grew up: Geneva, Boutae (Annecy), Aquae (Aix-les-Bains) and Lemuncum (Chambéry). By the end of the 4th century the region was known as Sabaudia, which later became Savoie. In 443 Burgundians from the Rhine swore allegiance to Rome and settled in Sabaudia, whose principal city was Geneva. Their king, Gondebaud, created the united kingdom of Burgundy between 474 and 516. In the 6th century Savoie was divided between five dioceses: the Maurienne, Tarentaise, Geneva, Belley and Grenoble.

FROM THE KINGDOM OF BURGUNDY TO THE HOLY ROMAN EMPIRE

The kingdom of Burgundy was short lived and was finally defeated by the sons of Clovis in 534. Under the Merovingians the early kingdom of Burgundy was in conflict with the Alemanni, in the northeast, and the Lombards, in Italy. The dioceses of the Maurienne and Tarentaise and a region known as Saboia each corresponded to a *pagus*, the seat of a count. The abbeys of St-Maurice-d'Agaune (in the Valais), founded c. 515, and Novalaise (in the Susa Valley), founded in 726, emerged as major religious and political centers until the 10th century.

The accession of Charlemagne made his victory over the Lombards complete, and in 843 the Treaty of Verdun gave Savoie to Lothair. Lotharingia (Lorraine), which stretched from the North Sea to Italy, was soon divided under pressure from its Frankish and Germanic rivals, but also as a result of internal divisions. The regions that later formed Savoie under the Ancien Régime were also divided. In 855 the southern regions came under the jurisdiction of the kingdom of Provence. In 888 Rudolf I, Duke of Burgundy, took advantage of the fall of the Frankish Emperor Charles II to declare himself King of Transjuran (Upper) Burgundy. His territory stretched from the Jura to the Great Saint Bernard Pass. In 947 Rudolf II acquired the lands of Savoie dependent on the Duke of Provence. Rudolf III (d. 1032) was succeeded by Humbert I, a native of Burgundy and was possibly already Count of Savoie. His services to Emperor Conrad II, who inherited Rudolf's domains in 1033, were rewarded with gifts of land from the Bugey, Chablais, Valais and Val d'Aoste to the Maurienne. His successors did their utmost to strengthen the state that he had founded.

500 | **534** End of the kingdom of Burgundy | **700** | **800** Charlemagne becomes Emperor of the West | **900** | **1100** | **1401** Purchase of the countship of Geneva | **1430** Amadeus VIII's *Statuta Sabaudiae* | **1450**

443 Burgundian federation | **773** Charlemagne, king of Lombardy | **888** Rodolph I, king of Transjuran Burgundy | **1032** Death of Rodolph III; Savoie annexed by the Holy Roman Empire | **1416** Savoie becomes a dukedom

THE HOUSE OF SAVOIE ● 40

Through clever alliances and skillful diplomacy, the House of Savoie occupied a key position within the balance of power in Europe, while its counts became the 'gatekeepers' of the Alps. From the reign of Thomas I (1189–1233) to Amadeus VIII (1383–1451), the dynasty produced such exceptional figures as Peter II (1203–68), known as 'Little Charlemagne'. The antagonism between the houses of Geneva and Savoie began in the 11th century, when the Genevan Count Gerold opposed the Emperor, who was supported by Humbert I of Savoie. The territory of Gerold's successors stretched from the Albanais to the countship of Vaud. The lords of Faucigny, members of the same family and vassals of the counts of Geneva, owned almost the entire valley of the Arve, except the Chamonix Valley, which had been ceded to the abbey of Saint-Michel-de-la-Cluse, in Piedmont, c. 1091. But these two dynasties did not present armed resistance to the counts of Savoie. From the 12th century, the counts of Geneva were forced to accept the power of the Church and recognize the authority of the Bishop of Geneva, transferring their capital to Annecy. Their dynasty came to an end in 1394 with the death of Robert, the last of the five sons of Amadeus III, Count of Geneva, who was also elected Pope Clement VII.

CASTELLANIES: A FEUDAL ADMINISTRATION

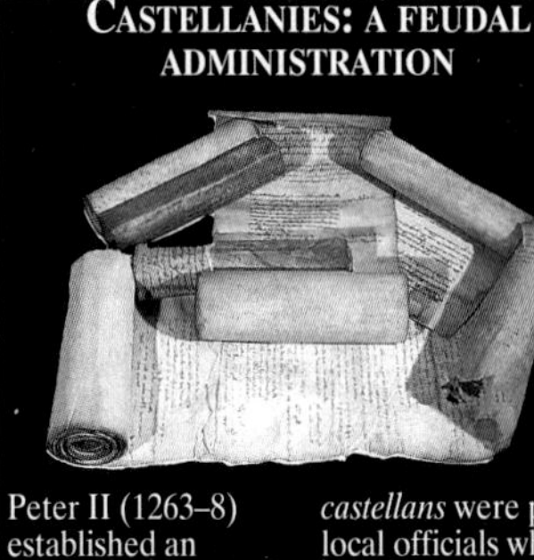

Peter II (1263–8) established an administrative system based on that of England, a country with which he had family connections. The *castellans* were paid local officials who submitted regular accounts. These were copied onto sheets of parchment and sewn end to end to form scrolls.

AN ORGANIZED STATE

Between the 13th and 15th centuries the countship of Savoie acquired extensive new territories, mainly through the activities of three counts. The first was Amadeus VI (r. 1343–83), who acquired Faucigny and the homage of the count of Geneva in 1355. His son, Amadeus VII (r. 1383–91) acquired Nice in 1388. But the reign of Amadeus VIII (r. 1391–1440) marked the height of the power of the House of Savoie. As soon as he came to power, he added the lands of the counts of Geneva to his domain. That dynasty had come to an end, and so he bought the inheritance rights of Odon de Villars. He thus acquired the last missing piece of his territory (August 5, 1401) and Piedmont finally became part of Savoie. He established a permanent council and exchequer, and in 1430 established the administrative and legislative code known as the *Statuta Sabaudiae*. In 1416 the Emperor Sigismund made Savoie a dukedom. At the height of his power Amadeus VIII withdrew to the monastery he had founded at Ripaille on Lake Geneva, where he led a pious life but without relinquishing the reins of power. In 1439 the rebellious Council of Basel elected Amadeus pope – under the name of Felix V (*below*) – in opposition to Pope Eugenius IV. Amadeus-Felix found it difficult to impose his authority and resigned ten years later, thus helping to resolve the Great Schism. He died Cardinal and Bishop of Geneva.

1536 Edict of Reformation. Calvin in Geneva.

1559 Treaty of Cateau-Cambrésis

1500 **1550** **1600**

1514 The Genevois-Nemours appanage

1536 First French occupation

1559 Creation of the Senate of Savoie

1600–1 Second French occupation. Treaty of Lyon.

TURIN AND ITALY

The marriage of Louis, son of Amadeus VIII, to Anne of Cyprus conferred the first royal title on the House of Savoie. Yolande of France, the wife of Amadeus IX and sister of king Louis XI, proved a competent regent acting in place of her sick husband, and then her son. She drew artists and men of letters to Chambéry and successfully confronted the rebellion of the great feudal lords. A number of her successors supported France and gave 'safe passage' to the troops fighting in the Italian wars. However this alliance with her more powerful neighbor cost Savoie the Genevois, Faucigny and Beaufortain regions. When the alliance with Charles V resulted in the French occupation of Savoie in 1536, Duke Charles III fled to Verceil. In 1559 the Treaty of Cateau-Cambrésis restored Savoie and Piedmont to Duke Emmanuel-Philibert. However, considering Savoie too vulnerable to invasion the duke transferred his capital to Turin (1563) and Savoie became the province 'beyond the mountains'. In 1559 he founded the Senate of Savoie, based on the French *parlements*, at Chambéry, and now established permanent troops and regular taxation. These included a tax on salt, wine and tobacco, a tax on individuals and income, and a tax levied in the form of food and forage for the army. In 1561 a census was carried out for the salt and income taxes.

A DISPUTED BORDER FOR TWO HUNDRED YEARS

Charles-Emmanuel I (1580–1630) had a confrontation with France which ended in the invasion of Savoie (1600) and the exchange of the Bresse, Bugey and Gex regions for the marquisate of Saluces. When Richelieu's troops invaded Savoie under Victor-Amadeus I, the latter formed an alliance by marrying Christine of France, sister of Louis XIII. On his death, she acted as regent until Charles-Emmanuel II came of age, pursuing Savoie's ambitions toward Italy. Her son recovered Faucigny and the Genevois through marriage to Jeanne-Baptiste de Savoie-Nemours.

THE GENEVOIS-NEMOURS APPANAGE (GRANT OF LAND)

Geneva was Savoie's most recent acquisition. In 1434 Amadeus VIII gave it to his son Philip, together with Faucigny. Philip died without an heir and the appanage reverted to the dukedom. The second appanage, given to Janus (1460–91), had administrative autonomy, with the prince and his court, a private council, permanent council and a revenue court in Annecy. On Janus's death, the lands again reverted to Savoie. In 1514, Charles III formed a third appanage for his brother Philip. Having received the duchy of Nemours from the king of France (1528), the counts of Geneva led independent policies from Savoie, making Geneva an 'island' state. During the French occupation 1536–59 the appanage preserved its independence and its law courts. The descendants of Philip spent most of their time at the French court and often opposed their Savoyard cousins. The appanage finally reverted to the Savoie in 1659, when Marie-Jean-Baptiste de Savoie-Nemours married Charles-Emmanuel II.

THE CATHOLIC RECONQUEST

During the 17th century Savoie experienced a period of Catholic organization and reconquest dominated by such figures as St François de Sales (1567–1622), Antoine Favre, president of the Senate, and the *intendants*, the loyal officials of an authoritarian government. François de Sales converted the Chablais and became Bishop of Geneva and Annecy ▲ *169*. Under him the diocese became a major religious center. After founding the literary Académie Florimontane in 1606 ▲ *170*, he founded the Visitation of Holy Mary with St Jeanne de Chantal, in 1610. The work of this great theologian and writer was continued by his 17th-century successors, who firmly established Catholicism in the region. During this period the construction of Notre Dame de Chambéry and other baroque churches not only fueled public fervor, but also provided employment and increased the wealth of the mountain communities.

1630 Third French occupation
1639 End of the Genevois-Nemours appanage

1650

1661 Beginning of the personal reign of Louis XIV

1690 Fourth French occupation

1700

1706 Turin besieged by the French, victory of Prince Eugene

1706 Montmélian destroyed. Fifth French occupation.

1713 Royal title for the House of Savoie. Treaty of Utrecht.

1740–8 Savoie occupied by the Spanish. War of the Austrian Succession.

1750

1790

1792 Creation of the 'Mont Blanc *département*'

Wars and occupations

During the 17th century the House of Savoie was subjected to French domination and suffered another invasion by the troops of Richelieu (the Defense of Rumilly, 1630). The dukedom was devastated by occupations, food shortages and epidemics. Between 1690 and 1696, and again between 1703 and 1713, Savoie was occupied by French troops. In 1713 the Treaty of Utrecht made Victor-Amadeus II (above) king of Sicily. In 1718 he exchanged Sicily for Sardinia, which gave rise to the term 'Sardinian States'. During the reign of Charles-Emmanuel III Savoie suffered a ruinous occupation by the Spanish army during the War of the Austrian Succession (1740–8). But in spite of these setbacks the rulers of Savoie succeeded in establishing centralized government and carrying out extensive administrative reforms, including the creation of *intendants* (stewards) and a land register (*cadaster*). Within an absolutist context, the monarchy became an enlightened dictatorship, with the purchase of feudal rights made possible in 1771.

Savoie, a French 'département'

The caution of Victor-Amadeus III was not enough to protect Savoie from the French Revolution. On September 24, 1792 revolutionary troops occupied Chambéry. The Assemblée des Allobroges proclaimed the Republic and the civil constitution of the clergy and demanded annexation with France. Their demands were ratified by the Convention on November 27, 1792 and Savoie became the Mont-Blanc *département* (*below*), which lay more or less within the borders of present-day Savoie and Haute-Savoie. However, support for the ideals of the Revolution was soon diminished by the intransigence of the regional representatives. The sale of national wealth contributed to the destruction of such historic sites as Aillon and Hautecombe. In 1798 Geneva was annexed by the Directoire and became the principal town of the Léman *département*, which included the Gex region, Carouge, Thonon and Bonneville.

The Sardinian land register

In 1728 Victor-Emmanuel II (1673–1730) decided to draw up a land register of each *commune* for taxation purposes. It was innovative in the extremely detailed cartography of the maps drawn up for each area. This register is the only one of its kind in Europe.

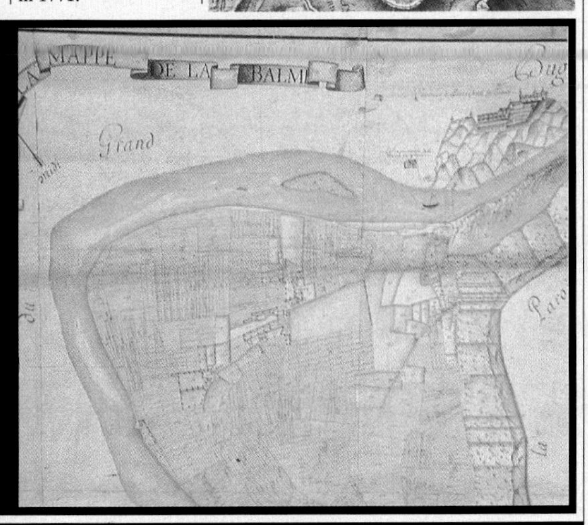

1790 — 1850 — 1900

1815 Sardinian restoration. Congress of Vienna.

1849 Austrian victory over the kingdom of Piedmont-Sardinia (Battle of Novara)

1851 Coup d'état by Louis-Napoléon Bonaparte

1859 Franco-Sardinian victory at Solferino

1860 Savoie becomes part of France. Creation of the 'Grande Zone'.

1870–71 Franco-Prussian War

Victor-Amadeus and his son Charles-Emmanuel IV tried to take advantage of counter-revolutionary rebellions to attempt a reconquest. The failure of these movements forced Charles-Emmanuel IV to surrender Savoie and Nice (1796) and seek refuge in Sardinia. In 1798 part of the Mont-Blanc *département* was attached to the newly formed *département* of Léman around Geneva. Napoleon carried out a major reorganization of Savoie's administrative and legal systems, constructed such strategic routes as the road over Mont-Cenis (the present N6) and introduced massive conscription to supply the manpower for his European wars. In 1814 Napoleon's defeat was compounded by the Austrian invasion of Savoie, with heavy fighting involving irregular troops. Initially only the eastern states were restored to the dynasty, but after Waterloo, the Congress of Vienna restored all the states of Savoie to Victor-Emmanuel I (*left*).

THE SARDINIAN MONARCHY

The restoration of the Savoyard dynasty was represented by a conservative government that was sometimes described ironically as *il buon governo*. The Royal Constitutions of the 18th century were once again the order of the day. New political factions gradually emerged which were opposed to absolutism and, in 1848, Charles-Albert granted his subjects a Constitution. Savoie became increasingly detached from Piedmont since the House of Savoie was involved in the unification of Italy under the Piedmontese banner. Victor-Emmanuel II gave a free hand to his minister Cavour (1852–9), who conducted an anti-clerical policy and advocated free trade. He was opposed by the conservatives, but supported by the clergy and industrialists, who favored the previous protectionism. The people of Savoie, who had learned about France through emigration (*Savoyard passport, left*), were attracted by this prosperous country.

UNION WITH FRANCE

Savoie was the price paid for an alliance with Napoleon III, who was persuaded by Cavour to help the Piedmontese create a united Italy against Austria. After the Battle of Solferino, the Treaty of Turin (March 24, 1860) provided for Savoie and Nice to be annexed to France. The plebiscite – like the one in the Italian principalities, which had united under the House of Savoie – was thus held when the anticlerical government of Piedmont was too unpopular and France too prosperous. On April 22–23, 1860 Savoie voted overwhelmingly in favor of union with France (*plebiscite at Annecy, below*) and the former dukedom was transformed into the *départements* of Savoie and Haute-Savoie. The government built schools, administrative buildings and road and rail networks. Union with France occurred when the Second Empire was becoming more liberal and embarking upon industrial and commercial expansion. The economic revolution was symbolized by the advent of hydro-electricity and the construction of the Mont-Cenis (Fréjus) Tunnel. Ugine and the Maurienne became major industrial sites. But Savoie's integration into the economy and a competitive market was not without its problems, and its essentially *montagnard* heritage has played a decisive role in the region's history.

1900 | 1950 | 2000

1924 Winter Olympics held at Chamonix

1940 The Alpine *chasseurs* land at Narvik. The Alpine army resists the Italians and Germans.

1944 Resistance in the Glières, Bauges and Tarentaise

1963 Creation of the Parc National de la Vanoise

1965 Opening of the Mont-Blanc Tunnel

1992 Winter Olympics held at Albertville

In tune with the Republic

The Franco-Prussian War (1870–1) and World War One (1914–8) showed the extent to which Savoie had been integrated into France, education being the most powerful means of assimilation. This predominately rural, Catholic and conservative region had become firmly attached to the Republic. Toward the end of the 19th century Savoie entered the age of hydroelectric power. This revitalized traditional activities such as metalworking in the Arve basin, and enabled electrometallurgy to thrive at Ugine and the Maurienne. Agriculture was gradually modernized and dairy and fruit cooperatives became widespread. The region lived in close partnership with Geneva, due to the 'Grande Zone' which was abolished in 1919. After a long struggle, smaller zones were reestablished in 1934. Tourism, centered around such spa towns as Aix-les-Bains, Saint-Gervais and Évian, was developed by the construction of vast hotels and an improved transport system, and the region welcomed its first skiers. Population movement had previously been outward emigration. This was reversed in the 1930s and Savoie became a host region.

Alpine hunters in the early 20th century.

World War Two

In Savoie the war began with the Alpine army's successful opposition to Italian and German attacks. Then came the tragedies of the Occupation. After the Italian occupation (November 1942 –September 1943) repression of the Resistance intensified. In response the Secret Army was formed in January 1944. An increasingly large proportion of the population was disillusioned with the Vichy regime, which was moving toward collaboration. In the summer of 1943 the first *maquis* groups were formed, their ranks swelled by the large numbers evading the Nazis' enforced labor program (STO). The Glières plateau ▲ *186* incident in 1944 became the symbol of the Resistance ● *46*. Between August 15 and 20 the Resistance freed the region (*liberation of Annecy, left*), which had nevertheless been badly damaged by these tragic years.

The rise of Savoie

Economic activity was helped by a rapid increase in population, the completion of hydroelectric works and the improvement of communications. The development of the electrochemical and metalworking industries and winter sports all contributed to this growth, which was marked by a sometimes aggressive urban development and the end of a rural way of life. But Savoie was regarded as a privileged region, in which work was combined with a pleasant living environment. Agriculture began to specialize in quality cheeses and dairy products, market garden produce, fruit and vineyards. The region's double tourist season (summer and winter) has made it France's most popular resort. During the 19th century Aix-les-Bains and Chamonix (the site of the first Winter Olympics in 1924) were favorites with wealthy Europeans. However the creation of Courcheval (1946) and the development of the major ski resorts marked the beginning of the mountain leisure industry. The Parc National de la Vanoise, created in 1963, attests to an awareness that the natural heritage of Savoie is an extremely fragile resource. The Winter Olympics at Albertville, 1992, was seen as the symbol of this new age of economic growth.

Like so many families of its kind, the House of Savoie – descended from the Carolingian counts – could well have stagnated in its little mountain kingdom before disappearing at the end of the Middle Ages. History decreed otherwise. Originally a modest Alpine countdom, the dynasty frequently crossed swords in the late 19th century as the political ideal of an independent Savoie was abandoned in favor of the creation of the kingdom of Italy. The rise of the Risorgimento (liberal movement for Italian unity) illustrated the age-old facility for adaptation of an ambitious family that did not hesitate to sacrifice the land of its forbears on the altar of political advancement.

HUMBERT I
(c. 980–1048)
Humbert, the founder of the dynasty, inherited the countdoms of Bugey and Savoie which lay within the kingdom of Burgundy. His acceptance of the sovereignty of the Holy Roman Emperor was rewarded with gifts of land which, from the early 11th century, formed the nucleus of the state of Savoie.

PETER II
(c. 1203–68)
Although he considerably extended the territory under the control of the House of Savoie, Peter II made his mark by the development of a rational government, and by promulgating the Statutes of Savoie, which formed the foundations of the modern state of Savoie.

AMADEUS VIII
(1383–1451)
Pursuing the work begun by Peter II, especially with the promulgation of his own *Statuta Sabaudiae*, Amadeus VIII was rewarded with the title of Duke of the Holy

Roman Empire. His reign evokes the golden age of a state still deeply rooted in the western Alps.

EMMANUEL-PHILIBERT (1528–80)
As well as hastening the modernization of the monarchy, Emmanuel-Philibert also initiated the dynasty's future role in Italian unity. After thirty years of French occupation he transferred his capital to Turin. This gave Savoie the status of a simple western march, and was intended to preempt any further invasion attempts on the part of France.

CHRISTINE OF FRANCE (1606–63) and **MARIE-JEANNE-BAPTISTE DE SAVOIE-NEMOURS** (1644–1724)
During their regencies the states of Savoie stagnated under the influence of French politics. But public institutions were strengthened, paving the way, with the accession of Victor-Amadeus II, for the establishment of absolute monarchy.

VICTOR-AMADEUS II (1666–1732)
Obsessed by the example of Louis XIV, he embarked on a bold diplomatic policy, together with a reorganization of the administrative system. The Treaty of Utrecht rewarded his efforts by making him king of Sicily, a title which he soon exchanged for the less prestigious king of Sardinia.

VICTOR-EMMANUEL II (1820–78)
A pragmatist, in 1860 he exchanged the countdom of Nice and the dukedom of Savoie in return for French military aid, the only way he could defeat Austria in northern Italy. But by exchanging the land of its forbears for the crown of Italy, the House of Savoie sacrificed a thousand years of autonomous history on the altar of the Risorgimento.

GODS OF THE ALPINE PASSES
According to Greek and Roman legend, Hercules, returning on foot from Spain, tried to rejoin the Etruscans of the Po Valley via an Alpine route. Hercules became the protector of the Alpine roads, while Mercury protected the low-lying valleys and Jupiter watched over the mountain passes. A figurine of Hercules and a silver bust of Jupiter were found on the Little-Saint-Bernard Pass.

The Alps lie across the major routes between the Atlantic and the East. The low Alpine passes, above steep valleys, have always been a crossing point for soldiers, merchants, pilgrims and travelers. The roads built by the Romans disappeared due to neglect, and for over 1200 years goods were carried over the mountains by pack animals. Roads suitable for vehicles, such as the Napoleonic road over Mont-Cenis (1803–5) and the road over the Little-Saint-Bernard Pass (1858–73) appeared late in the day. Now technology has removed all obstacles, and crossing the Alps is no longer an exploit.

MULE TRAINS AND SLEDS
A great many mule trains once used the road between Chambéry and Susa, transporting cloth and cereals on the outward journey, and rice and salt on their return. Carts and carriages had to be dismantled at the foot of Mont Cenis and the various sections loaded onto mules. Passengers were carried over the pass by 'bearers', an operation that took an average of five hours and required between two and eight bearers per person, depending on their weight. Only pilgrims and the poorest travelers crossed the pass on foot. On the Savoyard side of the pass, the descent was made by sled in winter.

EARLY TRANSALPINE TRADE AND ROMAN ROADS
Identical objects found on either side of the Mont-Cenis and Little-Saint-Bernard passes attest to the fact that regular trade took place over these mountains during Neolithic times. During the Bronze Age (1800 BC) these passes lay on a major trading route. In the 1st century AD the Greek geographer Strabo recorded that one of the major routes across the Alps was via the Little-Saint-Bernard Pass. An Iron-Age cromlech (menhirs arranged in a circle) and Roman remains – traces of a road, the foundations of a temple dedicated to Jupiter, a staging post (*mansio*) with an inn and stables, a small Gallo-Roman temple (*fanum*) – can still be seen on the pass today.

HANNIBAL'S EXPLOIT
Like Hercules and the great Gallic chieftain Bellovèse before him, the Carthaginian general Hannibal crossed the Alps in 218 BC. The exploit has been remembered because it was only after a long detour, and with thirty seven elephants, that Hannibal crossed the Alps to attack the Romans on their own territory. Although it is not known with any certainty which pass Hannibal crossed, the general consensus is that it was Mont-Cenis. Two 20th-century expeditions tried to reenact the event that has fired so many imaginations by taking elephants over the Mont-Cenis (1959) and Clapier (1979) passes.

HOSPICES
Crossing mountain passes in winter was a dangerous business and hospices were built early on in the history of Savoie. On the Little-Saint-Bernard Pass, the major part of the construction, attributed to Saint Bernard ▲ *261*, dates from 1050 and the most recent from the 19th century. The hospice founded (825) by Lothair I on Mont Cenis was engulfed by an avalanche in 1968.

RAILROADS
The first great Alpine tunnel – the Fréjus rail tunnel (7¾ miles long) – was built between 1857 and 1870 by the Piedmontese authorities. The line linking Saint-Michel-de-Maurienne and Susa via Mont Cenis (*inauguration of the tunnel, left*) was built between June 1868 and November 1871.

Savoie had always been the envy of its powerful French neighbor. Between late 1792 and 1814 it was occupied five times by France, and then annexed. In 1815 the ancestral monarchy of Savoie was restored. Some thirty years later, influenced by the 1848 rebellions, the monarchy tried to form a united Italy against the Austrian threat and asked the people of Savoie to make a major contribution to the war effort. However its request was accompanied by anticlerical measures. The people, abandoned by their prince and accusing Piedmont of 'living off Savoie', finally turned to France.

HABITANTS DE LA SAVOIE

Vos vœux sont accomplis! Muni des pleins pouvoirs de Sa Majesté l'Empereur, je viens de signer avec le Commissaire extraordinaire de Sa Majesté le Roi de Sardaigne l'acte qui constate la remise du territoire savoisien et sa réunion à la France.

A dater de ce jour vous êtes Francais

SAVOIE: BETWEEN ITALY AND FRANCE
Savoie was little more than an appendage of the nascent kingdom of Italy. Savoyard parliamentary representatives in Turin demanded complete autonomy for Savoie, because the former conqueror of Piedmont was tired of being its vassal state. At a secret conference held at Plombières (July 21, 1858), Napoleon III pledged military support to Victor-Emmanuel II from the Alps to the Adriatic, in exchange for Savoie and Nice.

THE PEACE OF VILLAFRANCA
Following the bloody Franco-Sardinian victories at the Battles of Magenta and Solferino, a peace treaty was signed with the Emperor of Austria in June 1859, to the great disappointment of Cavour. In November 1859 the Treaty of Zurich gave Lombardy to the French, who gave it to Piedmont, while Venetia remained Austrian: Savoie did not become an issue again until March 1860.

March 24, 1860: the Treaty of Turin

Under the Treaty of Turin (1860), signed by Victor-Emmanuel II and Napoleon III, Savoie and Nice were ceded to France, subject to a popular referendum. Thus 'the people' were party to the agreement between the two states. Through Swiss agency the neutral status of northern Savoie, acquired by the kingdom of Sardinia at the Congress of Vienna (1815) in exchange for the *communes* surrounding Geneva, was confirmed.

The 'Grande Zone' of 1860

Since northern Savoie, of which Geneva had always been the natural capital, was in favor of becoming part of Switzerland, France promised to grant it the status of a 'free zone' – a great improvement on the little Sardinian zone of 1816 – if it voted in favor of 'annexation and the zone'.

The plebiscite of April 1860

On April 22 and 23, 1860, the people of Savoie, urged by their clergy, voted overwhelmingly in favor of union with Catholic and imperial France. Although 99.8 percent of voters voted in favor of annexation, 25 percent of these – i.e. the majority of voters in northern Savoie (Chablais, Faucigny and northern Genevois) – had voted for 'annexation and the zone' (see right). On June 14 the official act of union was signed at the Château de Chambéry.

Union with France

On June 15, 1860, an imperial decree created the *départements* of Savoie and Haute-Savoie. The borders, which followed the watershed, took little account of the cultural reality and left French-speaking valleys in Piedmont. In 1945 General de Gaulle's government tried unsuccessfully to restore the Val d'Aoste to France. In 1973 a small majority of representatives put an end to the project to create a region of Savoie that would be part of the administrative division of Rhône-Alpes.

Lieutenant Tom Morel, who embodied the spirit of the Resistance, devised the famous motto: *Vivre libre ou mourir* ('freedom or death').

The 'lads' of the Dents de Lanfon Resistance, and a member of the militia during a search carried out in a village, February 1944 (*below*).

Because of its shared border with Switzerland Savoie was a transit place for refugees during World War Two. During the Italian occupation (November 1942– September 1943) many Savoyards sought refuge in the mountains to evade the STO (forced labor program). They soon became *maquisards* (resistance fighters) and the increasing number of mountain camps received forty parachute drops between March 1943 and August 1944. During the German occupation Nazi barbarity, supported by the militia, was rife. The conflict came to a head when, after intense fighting, the *maquisards* of Glières were forced off the plateau, losing one-third of their men. Fighting intensified and the liberation of Savoie began on August 11. The Germans surrendered at Annecy on August 19, and a few days later at Chambéry. Savoie was the first *département* to be liberated by its own efforts.

FRENCH-SWISS RESISTANCE

Savoie's shared border with Switzerland led to the formation of organized pockets of resistance. People living on both sides of the border played an active part in establishing routes to ensure the safe passage of refugees fleeing from the Nazi regime and the Vichy government. At Annemasse, where the Gestapo hindered the activities of the Resistance, the mayor, Jean Deffaugt, often acted as a mediator between his fellow-citizens and the occupying army. Fathers Marius Jolivet and Claudius Fournier were decorated by the Israeli government for their bravery at Collonges-sous-Salève and Vers. In August 1944 fifteen houses were burned in the villages of Chenex, Vulbens and Chevrier by way of reprisal against the Resistance during the German retreat. The village of Éloise was awarded the Military Cross and a monument was erected to its mayor, Robert Gassilloud, one of the pioneers of the Resistance.

La RESISTANCE SAVOISIENNE

THE MARSHAL'S TREE

On September 23, 1941 some 80,000 Haut-Savoyards went to hear a speech given by Marshal Pétain in Annecy. They believed he was the only person able to keep Savoie within France in the face of Italian demands. On April 25, 1942 the Foreign Legion and the SOL (Services d'Ordre Légionnaires) planted a tree to commemorate the marshal's visit, but by May 2 it had been chopped down. The SOL retaliated by manhandling Count François de Menthon, the founder of *Liberté*, the first underground newspaper in southern France. The incident aroused strong emotions and resulted in a section of the local population joining the Resistance.

EVER GREATER NUMBERS OF 'MAQUISARDS'

Those evading the STO (*service du travail obligatoire*), the program of enforced labor introduced by the Nazis, sought refuge in isolated farms high in the mountains. They were soon transformed into *maquisards* by the Secret Army, Franc-Tireurs and Partisans. The Secret Army, founded in January 1941, originally consisted of some of the members of the 27th Battalion of Alpine *chasseurs* (mountain light infantry), members of other Alpine units and volunteers. In February 1941 they were joined by the FTP (Franc-Tireurs and Partisans) *maquisards* from the Communist Party. In March 1943 the first parachute drops of equipment took place on the Dents de Lanfon. The German occupation, in September 1943, marked the beginning of an intensive repression which affected many civilians. At the same time Savoie became a key point in Allied strategy and, in early 1944, the Plateau des Glières and the Col des Saisies were selected as targets for massive parachute operations ▲ *186*.

THE CRADLE OF THE RESISTANCE

The Resistance movement was founded in the Beaufortain region in 1941 at the instigation of Captain Bulle, who trained the *maquisards* of the Secret Army. On August 1, 1944 one of the largest parachute drops of weaponry of World War Two was made by 78 Flying Fortresses on the Col des Saisies. It equipped Bulle's unit with pistols, hand grenades and anti-tank weapons. But the euphoria of the liberation was overshadowed by the captain's death. He was assassinated by the Germans, who had guaranteed him safe passage when he went to negotiate conditions for the surrender of Albertville on August 21, 1944.

THE SPIRIT OF GLIÈRES

According to André Vignon, a veteran of Glières: 'We were proud to be the first inhabitants of the first corner of free French soil. One day when we were going for supplies we met Lieutenant Morel who told us: "We're going to have to fight, you know [...] It won't be easy, but we'll prove there are still some Frenchmen left in France."' Tom Morel, a former instructor at Saint-Cyr, was head of the Haute-Savoie *maquis*. Under his command were soldiers of the Secret Army, units of Francs-Tireurs and a detachment of Spanish Republicans. On the night of March 9–10, 1944 Lieutenant Tom Morel was shot in Entremont during negotiations with Vichy forces ▲ *186*.

The language of Savoie

The Savoyard language belongs to the Franco-Provençal languages of France, Switzerland and Italy. It is spoken in an area bounded to the northeast by Neuchâtel, in French-speaking Switzerland; to the north by Pontarlier, in the Jura; to the west by Montbrison, in the Loire; to the south by La Mure, in Isère; and to the southeast by Pont-Saint-Martin in the Val d'Aoste and the Piedmontese valleys above Susa. Although the same root language is spoken, each town and village has its own particular dialect, especially in the high mountains. The people of Savoie are proud of the richness of their language which they regard as part of their cultural heritage. From Lake Geneva to the Préalpes, Savoyards have no difficulty in understanding each other. The dialects of eastern Savoie, from Aime and Saint-Jean-de-Maurienne, are very different, but not incomprehensible.

Sayings and expressions

◆ *L ivir, le la l a jamé mdja*: wolves have never eaten winter.
◆ *La montanye rè po to s k le prè*: the mountain does not always give back what it has taken.
◆ *La nèy èl tïn po, ta kè l èharnyua èy-i po bo*: the snow doesn't settle until the larch has lost its needles.
◆ *Kan janvi bemôte, fevri shevrôte*: as January begins, February's kids are on the way (goats drop their young in the coldest part of winter).
◆ *La bize ninre a tan koru ke le polâlye on sarâ lo ku*: The north wind has been blowing so hard that the chickens have been sitting tight (i.e. not laid).
◆ On fine days people sit outside to *akouto le soleuy* (listen to the sun), *le soleuy i le boui dè lè pouè dzïn* (the sun is the firewood of the poor).
◆ (Said of a young bride who is the victim of an arranged marriage) *Kan l ara po d égue djè son sizelin, l n ara p lou zu beu*: when she doesn't have any water in her pail, she will always have the water from her eyes.
◆ (Said to a young girl who is still a virgin) *Te n o po onkô vyu pétâ l leû su la pira d boué*: you haven't seen Peter the wolf yet.
◆ *On gran dékapa-djô*: a big sausage hook (used to describe a very tall man i.e. tall enough to unhook the sausages hanging from the ceiling).
◆ *On tota-ku dè polalye*: a pernickety person (the sort who checks chickens' behinds to ensure they are good layers).
◆ *Koujïn du lo du pyeuy de l one*: a very distant cousin (literally: a cousin on the donkey's side).

Place names and family names ending in 'z' and 'x'

During the Middle Ages Savoie developed its own written form for place names and family names. Unlike the corruptions that exist in modern French, z and x are not pronounced at the end of place and family names. The z indicates a non-accentuated final vowel: *La Clusaz* is pronounced *La Clus(a)* and *Cohennoz*, *(Le)Cohenn(o)*. Certain accentuated final vowels can take a z by analogy, for example Pra(z)-sur-Arly. An x indicates an accentuated final vowel: *Chamonix* is pronounced *Chamoni* and *Conjux*, *Conju*, but *ez* is pronounced *é*: *Albiez*, *Sciez*. The same rules apply to family names.

Regional French

Savoyard dialects have survived in and enriched many regional French words and phrases: *être à l'abade*: to set out in complete freedom or without knowing where you are going; *des agassins*: corns on the feet; *des carottes rouges*: beetroot; *la châlée*: a path or track made through fresh snow; *un crochon*: a crust (of bread); *une éclape*: a splinter of wood; *une filoche*: a string shopping bag; *une gouille*: a pool; *gremailler*: to shell nuts; *un fayard*: a beech tree; *une pate*: a rag; *une pôche*: a ladle; *un tara*: an earthenware pot; *être à borgnon*: to grope your way along; *faire des gôgnes*: to put on airs and graces; *faire la pôte*: to sulk; *la patioque*: mud or slush; *rebioller*: to gather one's strength; *redresser*: to put away; *ça terraine*: the ground is appearing (as the snow melts); *tu viendras puis*: so, you'll come then (*puis* used as a reinforcement); *prends-y*: take it; *une pernette*: a ladybird; *un rhabilleur*: a bone-setter.

Le Cmaclie
Cahiers périodiques savoyards
Littérature, Poèmes en Patois et du Terroir
Chansons et Dessins

Arts and traditions

TYPES OF WOOD
Carpenters and cabinet makers in the low valleys tended to use walnut and the wood from other fruit trees. The craftsmen of the high valleys used the wood from mountain species ● *26*: all types of conifers and especially the Arolla pine (*Pinus cembra*), the 'noble wood' of the Alps.

Traditional furniture from the high mountain valleys of Savoie was remarkably skillfully made and unique to the region. While craftsmen in the towns and villages of the lower valleys formed corporations and reproduced the styles of Burgundy, Lyonnais, Dauphiné and Piedmont in walnut for the bourgeoisie and clergy, their high-mountain counterparts made furniture and domestic objects for their own or village use. The infinite variety of designs and decorations was the result of each craftsman's individual skill and inspiration.

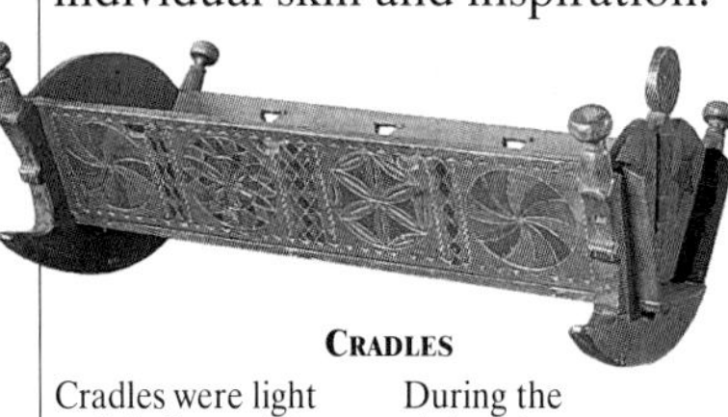

CRADLES
Cradles were light and shallow, with curved feet that enabled them to be rocked. The baby was tightly wrapped with its arms at the side of its body, and held in with a cord laced through the holes along either edge. During the christening ceremony tradition required the godmother to carry the child on her head, which is why the sloping sides were so carefully decorated.

INGENIOUS DESIGNS
The production of dairy produce in traditional mountain homes greatly affected the design of rural furniture, which was often quite ingenious. For example the table-chair (*above, left*) was a chair whose back could be lowered onto the arms and used as a table; the table-dresser (*above, right*) was a storage unit whose door could be lowered onto a folding leg and used as a kitchen table; beds had an array of drawers and were concealed during the day. As well as this dual-purpose furniture there were also more traditional pieces.

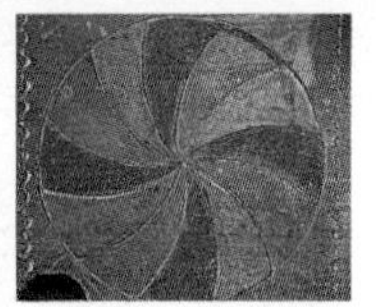

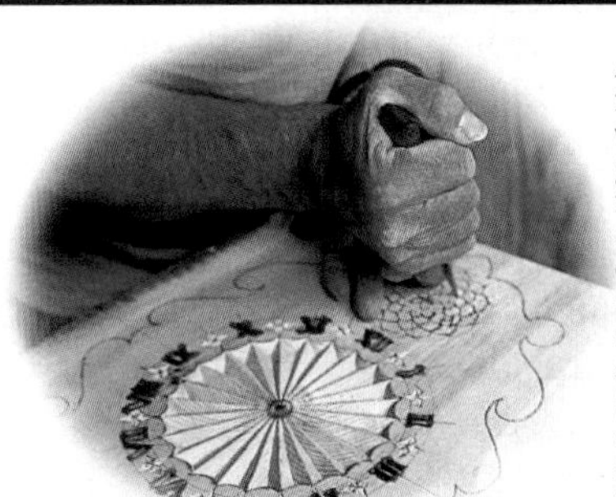

Decorations

Although essentially functional, furniture was carved with geometric and figurative motifs, according to the craftsman's imagination. The rosette (six-branched star) and the roundel (a spinning sun) were combined with flowers, hearts, Savoie crosses and knots. All these designs were hand carved with a knife and used to decorate trunks, chests and bedposts. They were sometimes highlighted with color: red (iron oxide), black (soot), green and greenish-blue (plant- and fruit-based dyes).

Traditional furniture

The chest was the most typical piece of Alpine furniture. It was widely used between the 15th and 20th centuries and was usually a 'wedding chest' given to a young couple by their parents. From the 16th century, cupboards, dressers and furniture with doors began to appear. The craftsmen of the high valleys sometimes incorporated elements inspired by the Baroque decor of mountain churches and chapels, or by the more sophisticated styles (Renaissance, Louis XIII, Louis XIV) introduced by traveling craftsmen. Techniques and decorative themes were handed down until the early 19th century.

Travelers have always been amazed by the strange and colorful costumes of the valleys of the Maurienne, or the headdresses worn by the women of the Tarentaise region. The richness and detail of the various elements and the wide diversity of women's costumes reflects an individuality and cultural identity, a desire to be different from the next village. Savoie's costumes, way of life, ceremonies and rites of passage still varied from one valley to the next at a time when a certain conformity was developing in other regions.

THE 'FRONTIÈRE' (*above and top left*)
The *frontière*, a headdress worn in the Tarentaise region, is rather like the cap worn by the women of the courts of Europe during the second half of the 16th century. Two braids (*couaches*) bound with black velvet are wound round the head.

HEADDRESSES
These developed during the 16th century onward: the last headdress worn in Sixt was a hat for outdoor wear (*right*). The *béguine* or *bedzonas* from Megève (*left*) consists of a crown made of rows of fluted lace: white lace for Sundays and festivals, black lace for funerals and mourning.

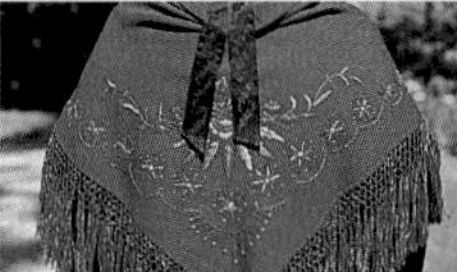

The Tarentaise costume
Folklorists and the development of tourism have helped to establish the costume worn by the women in the greater part of the Tarentaise valley as the typical Savoyard costume and the emblem of Savoie.

Bridal couple from the Arves
The pleats of the bride's dress are formed by a series of bands (*apponsures*) sewn one onto the other to create the garment's 'tucked up' effect. The broad belt is made of black or blue fabric and decorated with colored fabric or silk ribbons and sometimes beads, sequins or braid. This element is not found on any other costume in Savoie.

Marriage
The tradition of buying jewelry for the bride-to-be and piercing her ears so that she could wear earrings was known as 'ringing' the bride in the Chablais region and 'fettering' her in Talloires. In Thônes the term 'slave collar' was used to refer to the chain that bore the heart and the cross.

Hearts and crosses
There are up to fourteen types of cross in Savoie. The most widely found are the openwork cross, 'Jeannette' cross and flat cross. Each is associated with a particular place of origin: the baton-cross with Peisey-Nancroix, the six-cabochon cross with Bessans, the flat silver cross (up to six inches long) with Saint-Colomban or Les Villards.

Although the Counter-Reformation provided the Catholic Church with an opportunity to strengthen the basis of its credo and establish its religious doctrines, it was forced to compromise by allowing traditional beliefs and rituals to exist. The vast majority of the population, who lived with the constant threat of natural disasters, was firmly attached to certain devotional practices and beliefs, especially in the ability of saints to protect and heal human beings and animals. The parish church was the ultimate place of worship where the principal dogmas of Catholicism were expressed according to ritual, but the Church had to accept the existence of other places where popular piety could be freely expressed.

CHAPELS
The many chapels built between 1650 and 1725 attest to the extent of popular piety. Rural chapels existed alongside parish churches as alternative places of worship, which were more accessible to the ordinary people. Here they could worship the saints who healed (saints Sebastian and Roch for epidemics) and protected (Saint Antony for domestic animals and Saint Grat for crops). They prayed to Our Lady of the Snows to protect them against avalanches and Our Lady of the Puy for protection against fire.

CROSSES AND CRUCIFIXES
In 1608 the British traveler Thomas Coryate wrote: 'In Savoie there are a great many wooden crosses'. There are crosses everywhere: crosses on costumes, crosses on houses, huge crosses that stand in the extension of chapels and on mountain tops. In the upper Maurienne, they often bear the symbols of the Passion. The function of the crosses that stand in chapels, at intersections and on mountain tops is to consecrate the ground. The crosses in chapels were mostly erected by the clergy to commemorate a key point in the spiritual life of the parish, while the others were erected to commemorate tragic events.

S^T GRAS

S ROCH

Processions

Processions used to be widely held for Corpus Christi and during religious festivals. They were also held in times of great misfortune and to pray for good weather for the harvest. These ceremonies involved the use of religious objects which usually hung on the interior walls of the church or on the balustrade of the gallery.

Pilgrimages

Until the 19th century, with the exception of the official pilgrimage to the tombs of saints François de Sales and Jeanne de Chantal, most pilgrimages were made on the initiative of the people under the watchful eye of the clergy. Even so Saint François de Sales ● *36* ▲ *169*, Bishop of Geneva (1602–22), established such pilgrimages as the pilgrimage of the Bénite-Fontaine (holy fountain) near La Roche-sur-Foron, which still exists today. From 1830 the clergy took over the organization of pilgrimages.

The Virgin Mary

There is not a church or chapel in Savoie that doesn't have a statue, image or inscription dedicated to the Virgin Mary. Many chapels are dedicated to her under a wide range of names, and every church has an altar 'of the Rosary' or 'of the Carmelites'. Iconography varies depending on the period and ranges from 15th-century pietà and 16th-century Trinities to Our Lady of Lourdes or the Sacré-Coeur (19th century).

HIGH MOUNTAIN PASTURES

The mountain pastures or 'high mountains' comprise the Alpine meadows situated at between 5000 and 8000 feet. During the 'hundred days', from June to September, cattle from small farms in the valleys are combined into large herds of up to 200 heads which help to maintain the mountain pastures. There are two types of farming in the 'high mountains': individual, where a *montagnard* rents cows from small peasant farmers in the valley, and communal, where the cows from a village or *commune* are put together in one herd and the profits from the sale of cheese are shared out at the end of the season.

'COMMON LAND'
On the 'common land' of the Tarentaise region (areas of mountain pasture), the milk produced by each farmer is measured on the Sunday nearest to July 24. The quantity is then used as a basis to calculate the amount payable to the farmers in the autumn. This is a day of celebration in these mountain areas.

THE 'HUNDRED DAYS'
Farming on the mountain pastures is far from easy. When farmers leave the valleys and take their cattle up into the Alpine pastures for several months (*l'emmontagnée*), they know that for the next 'hundred days' they will be cut off from the rest of the world in the silence of the high mountains.

ALPINE PASTURES
Alpine pastures have to be constantly maintained, a process begun in the 12th century by monks and continued by farmers.

MILKING
The management of the Alpine pastures has kept pace with technological progress.

The Tarine has a tawny-colored coat and dark patches around its eyes and on its back and tail.

Mobile milking machines are one of the key developments in mountain farming.

AN ACTIVE LIFE
Life in the high mountains revolves around twice-daily milking, maintaining the Alpine pasture and cheese-making. The milk is transformed twice a day into soft, creamy uncooked cheese (Reblochon ▲ *180*) or once a day into pressed, uncooked cheese (Tomme de Savoie, Abondance). The milk is poured into a copper vat and rennet is added. Then the curds are removed and the milk is gently heated. The cheeses are shaped, dried, washed and left to mature.

ABONDANCE
This breed has a distinctive dark red and white coat and dark red patches around its eyes. Like the Tarine, the Abondance is a traditional Alpine breed. Introduced into the Alps by the Burgundians in the 5th century, it was bred by the monks of the abbey of Abondance ▲ *202* and officially recognized in 1892. It is well adapted to the harsh conditions of the high mountains and is renowned for its endurance and stamina and the quality of its milk.

DAIRY PRODUCE
The high mountain pastures produce huge quantities of milk used in the manufacture of such cheeses as Beaufort and Reblochon.

NURSERIES
Vast quantities of young vines from various AOC vintages are grown at Fréterive, in the Combe de Savoie. The vines are sent all over the world and the village is known in certain quarters as the 'nursery capital' of Savoie.

Vines seem to have been grown in Savoie since early Roman times. In the 1st century AD the Roman writers Columella and Pliny (23–79 AD) refer to the vineyards of Allobrogia and their *picatum*, a resinous wine which was extremely popular in Rome. This traditional production has not only marked the landscapes of Savoie but has also influenced its place names, such as La Plantaz. The quality of Savoie's wines has greatly improved over the last two hundred years. However, it is still mainly produced for regional consumption (88 percent), by Savoyards and tourists alike.

CHÂTEAU DE RIPAILLE
The wine press is the only surviving piece of infrastructure from the vineyard's former wine-growing activities. Today it grows the Chasselas grape variety which produces a good-quality, slightly sparkling white wine.

BOTTLED IN SAVOIE
In 1991 the Comité Interprofessional des Vins de Savoie approved a new type of bottle for AOC wines produced in Savoie. It is taller than Burgundy bottles, but shorter than those used for Alsace wines, and has the Savoie cross stamped on the shoulder.

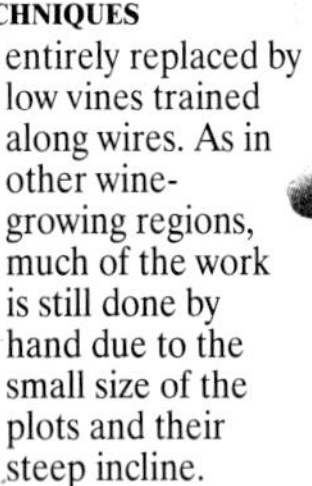

THE VINEYARDS OF SAVOIE
In the Middle Ages vines were grown anywhere in Savoie, often for the aristocracy and clergy. In the 19th century most of the estates were taken over by the middle classes and peasant farmers. Between 1876 and 1894 Savoie's vineyards were devastated by phylloxera. They were recreated by grafting vines onto new root stock, and the quality was greatly improved. The 'Seyssel' AOC was established in 1942, and the 'Vin de Savoie' and 'Roussette de Savoie' in 1973. In 1975 quality table wines produced outside the AOC zone were awarded the 'Vin de pays d'Allobrogie' appellation.

SIZE AND TECHNIQUES
Until the 19th century espalier-trained vines were grown on a series of posts or chestnut trees whose bark was stripped off to a height of 25–40 feet, or on vine props (wooden stakes). This method of cultivation has been almost entirely replaced by low vines trained along wires. As in other wine-growing regions, much of the work is still done by hand due to the small size of the plots and their steep incline.

'SARTOS' AND 'LIBOTS'
Because vines need attention throughout the year, many vineyards have *sartos*, small two-story buildings where tools are kept, wine is stored and which once provided temporary shelter for wine-growers from the Bauges. During the end-of-winter celebrations, known as *libots,* the winter prunings were burned and *diots* (sausages) cooked slowly in white wine were eaten. After the grape harvest the still did the rounds of the villages so that the villagers could make *gnôle* (spirit). When they had used it for the last time they ate *diots* cooked with potatoes.

WHITE GRAPE VARIETIES
The chalky soils of Savoie are ideal for white varieties, which produce three times the volume of red. The most popular, Jacquère, flourishes on the slopes of Les Abymes and the Combe de Savoie (Apremont and Abymes growths and the 'Perlant' *appellation*). The Altesse variety favors the vineyards of Frangy and Seyssel (AOC 'Roussette de Savoie'). Chasselas grapes are used in some villages near the Swiss region of Le Valais. Roussanne is grown further south, in the Chignin vineyards, and produces Chignin-Bergeron.

RED GRAPE VARIETIES
The plain of Chautagne produces Gamay de Chautagne. The best known red variety, Mondeuse, thrives on the Bauges mountains, between Fréterive and Arbin. Arbin, Montmélian and Saint-Jean-de-la-Porte are among the best-known vineyards.

FACTS AND FIGURES
- ◆ 22 AOC vineyards, 14 in Savoie and 8 in Haute-Savoie
- ◆ Total vineyard area: 6175 acres; AOC wines: 4695 acres of which 629 acres are in Haute-Savoie
- ◆ Annual production: 5,283,400 US gallons, representing 0.2 percent of French production
- ◆ Authorized yield of 'Vin de Savoie': 586–696 US gallons per acre
- ◆ Wine production represents 16 percent of Savoie's annual agricultural income.

It was inevitable that this mountainous region should develop a cuisine that was rich, generous and satisfying. Forcemeat, for which the recipe varies from valley to valley, is typical of the rural home-cooking of Savoie. This traditional dish, which combines potatoes, bacon and dried fruit to produce a subtle blend of sweet and savory flavors, requires a special mold and takes several hours to cook. It was prepared on Sundays and during periods of intensive agricultural work.

Recipe from Haut-Faucigny
Ingredients (serves 6)
25 thin slices of smoked bacon
2½ pounds potatoes
1 handful of raisins
10 prunes
10 dried pears
Salt and pepper

1. Peel and finely grate the raw potatoes.

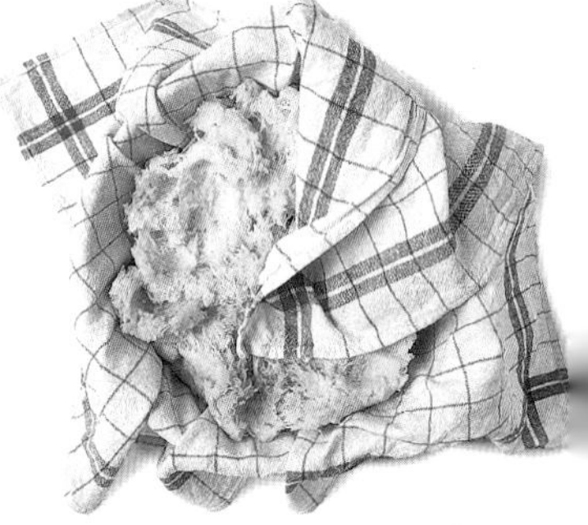

2. Drain and carefully dry the grated potatoes in a teatowel.

3. Chop the prunes and dried pears and add, with the raisins, to the potato.

4. Mix well to obtain a smooth, doughy consistency. Season to taste.

5. Line the mold with the slices of bacon.

6. Fill the lined mold with the mixture.

7. Put the lid on the mold and place in a large pan of boiling water. Leave to cook gently for 3–4 hours.

8. Turn the forcemeat out of the mold onto a dish: it should be firm and not collapse.

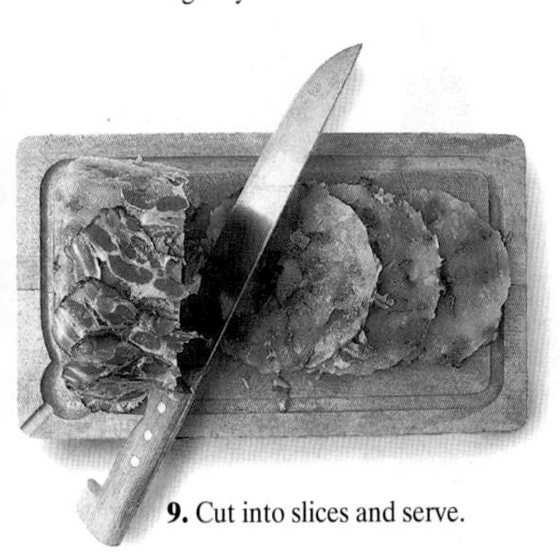

9. Cut into slices and serve.

10. If there are any slices left, they can be served with the next meal by browning in a lightly greased pan.

Regional specialties

Mineral water
Mineral water from Evian ◆ *198* and Thonon ◆ *194* are renowned for their lightness and diuretic properties. Water from Aix-les-Bains ◆ *138* has also been bottled in recent years.

Alpine cheeses
Milk from the Tarine and Abondance cows is used to make delicious cheeses such as Beaufort ◆ *247* (a pressed, cooked cheese), Tomme de Savoie and Tome des Bauges ◆ *157* (pressed, uncooked cheeses). Reblochon ◆ *180* is a semi-pressed, uncooked cheese. Abondance, made from cow's milk, and Chevrotin des Aravis, made from goat's milk, are delicious farmhouse cheeses.

'Crozets' and 'polenta'
'Crozets' are small, square pieces of pasta made from soft wheat flour, sometimes mixed with buckwheat flour. 'Polenta' is a corn meal which is made into a thick porridge.

Cooked meats
Regional specialties include *pormoniers* (fresh sausages made from pig's offal and herbs), sausages made from donkey and goat's meat, *diots* (small, fresh pork sausages simmered in white wine with onions and herbs), *grelots* (pork sausages with herbs and nuts) and Savoie ham.

Regional wines
'Perlant' wines make a good aperitif, the whites go well with fondues (especially *raclette*), seafood, fish, cheese and cakes, while the reds and rosés make an ideal accompaniment for game, white meat, salt-cured fish and meat, and Savoie cheeses.

The mountains

In the early 20th century Mont Blanc was already well known to climbers, but only a few Britons were mad enough to go to Chamonix to 'breathe the invigorating air and lark about in the snow'. Strange, long wooden planks began to appear and were used by the military to transport reinforcements and supplies, strengthen their lines of defense and organize the first ski competitions… Hotels and transport companies in the region realized the potential for a second tourist season. Megève and Val d'Isère, with their high mountain peaks, modeled themselves on the Swiss resorts of Davos and St-Moritz. The high mountains ceased to be considered dangerous and became the setting for the new fashion in winter sports.

WINTER OLYMPICS, 1924
Following the introduction of ski competitions in 1907, Chamonix ▲ *236* hosted the first Winter Olympics in 1924. The municipal authorities built the world's largest ice-rink and an equally impressive ski jump and bobsled run. In doing so Chamonix joined the ranks of the leading Alpine ski resorts.

AN INVITATION TO TRAVEL
Paris to Chamonix in 12 hours, Geneva to Chamonix in 4 hours: this was the promise given by the PLM (Paris-Lyon-Méditerranée) company to promote its new railroad lines and luxury hotels. Its posters fired the imaginations of millions of people throughout France. The 1920s and 30s marked the golden age of the travel poster which reflected an idealized image of the fashion for winter sports, the aspirations of the general public and the means of transport that gave them access to the resorts.

MEGÈVE: A FASHIONABLE RESORT

Baroness Noémie de Rothschild had been impressed by the fairy-tale settings, luxury hotels, sophisticated atmosphere and clientele of the Swiss and Austrian ski resorts. In France she chose Megève and launched the town's career as a winter sports resort when she opened the Mont-d'Arbois hotel in 1919. The more daring guests ventured onto the slopes – well before Émile Allais, a native of Megève, started the general fashion for skiing.

COURCHEVEL: AN INNOVATIVE RESORT

Courchevel was the first ski resort to be built 'from scratch' at the foot of the ski slopes. This innovative project (involving urban planning and the layout of the skiing area) became a leading resort and led to the renaissance of winter sports.

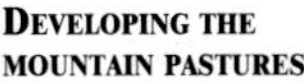

DEVELOPING THE MOUNTAIN PASTURES

Courchevel was built in 1945. It had been known since 1930 that the best snow was to be found at high altitudes. Surveys were therefore carried out in the vast snowfields of the Trois Vallées and ski lifts were developed. The process became widespread and gave rise to clusters of resorts such as La Plagne (1960).

WINTER OLYMPICS, 1992

When the International Olympic Committee chose Albertville as the venue for the 16th Winter Olympics, it had not only selected the town but the entire region of Savoie to host the event. Between February 8 and 23, 1992, after a colorful and spectacular opening ceremony which went down in the annals of Olympic and sporting history, the various events reflected a region that combined modernism with its traditional *montagnard* heritage.

FASHION ON THE SKI SLOPES

Was it better to ski with one or two sticks? In the early days of skiing there were two opposing theories on the subject. On the other hand nobody thought to question fashion. Women wore long skirts to their ankles and waisted, woolen jackets. There was an uproar when the aviator and skier Marie Marwingt had the audacity to take to the slopes in trousers!

Until the 1880s and 1890s access to high mountains was the prerogative of a privileged élite, and excursions were made on foot or by mule. At the end of the 19th century the advent of the railroad made the ski resorts more accessible to a cosmopolitan clientele and marked the transition from 'pioneering' to 'middle-class tourism'. Between 1890 and 1914 the rail network was developed in the valleys and then extended into the mountains. However the various rail systems had certain weaknesses and the cable, which had been used for a long time to transport merchandise, revolutionized methods of transport and promoted the development of winter sports.

Construction of a cableway pylon.

THE MONT-BLANC TRAMWAY

Originally the Mont-Blanc tramway was intended to run to the summit of the 'roof of Europe'. After two years the line to the Col de Voza was completed and opened in 1909. It had been extended to Mont Lachat by 1912 and to the Bionnassay glacier – 7780 feet – by 1914, when the project was interrupted by World War One. Steam locomotives operated on the 7½ mile line until 1956 when electric rail cars were introduced.

MONT REVARD ▲ *143*

A cog railroad opened in 1892 gave summer visitors to the spa town of Aix-les-Bains access to the plateau of Mont Revard at an altitude of 4900 feet. Luxury hotels were built and, in 1908, Mont Revard became one of the first ski resorts. In 1935 the cog railroad was replaced by a cableway which has since disappeared.

THE MONTENVERS RAILROAD ▲ *238*

This railway was built between 1905 and 1908 and fully opened in 1909. Since then it has given tourists easy access to the Mer de Glace (6275 feet), the region's largest glacier.

THE AIGUILLE DU MIDI CABLEWAY ▲ *238*

In 1905 two engineers, Feldmann and Strub, had the idea of linking Chamonix to the Aiguille du Midi. The line was designed to shorten the ascent of Mont Blanc and give the public easier access to the high mountains and the ski slopes of the Vallée Blanche. The project, taken over by the French geographer Joseph Vallot (1854–1925), never reached the Aiguille du Midi and the line ceased to operate in 1951. In 1949 a different route was developed and the work carried out in 1951–5. It resulted in the present cableway whose upper station is at an altitude of 12, 450 feet. From there, a second cableway runs to the Italian border.

ENVIRONMENTAL CONCERNS

Since the 1990s environmental concerns have been high on the agenda. Cableways have become more discreet and underground funiculars have even been built at Val d'Isère and Tignes. Val-Thorens, whose cableway to the Cime de Caron is one of the largest in the world, has protected its environment by building underground stations. At Courchevel the cars of the world's other largest cableway each carry 161 people to the Sommet de la Saulireat at a speed of 36 feet per second.

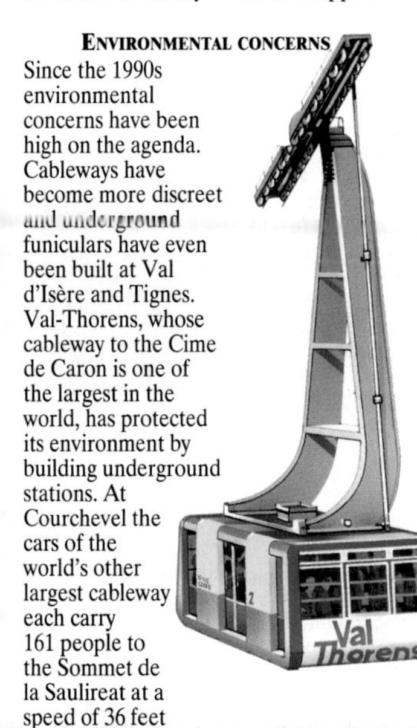

Thousands of miles of marked footpaths, three nature reserves, paths that wind their way above lakes and across mountain passes at heights of almost 10,000 feet.... The best way to discover Savoie is undoubtedly on foot. Walking in the mountains gives an insight into the geological upheavals that formed the Alps, and the people who settled and lived in the region's unique landscape and climate.

'READING' THE MOUNTAINS

Although the Alps were formed 300 million years ago they are continually changing and regenerating. They are a living geology lesson that can be read like an open book: from the legendary tracks of the Drus ▲ 226, carved into the granite of the Mont-Blanc Massif, to the exploits of the pioneers of the west face of the mountain at 12,250 ft, which were erased in September 1997 by a huge rock fall.
The region's diverse vegetation adapts and changes with altitude. As the valleys give way to the mountain layer (2600–5250 ft on the north-facing slopes and 5900 ft on the south-facing slopes) beeches are gradually replaced by firs, Scotch pines and spruces. The sub-Alpine layer, which begins at 5900–6560 ft, is characterized by spruce and mountain pines in the Préalpes, and larch and Arolla pines in the more southerly zones. Above 7550 ft are the meadows and pastures of the Alpine layer. The different climates, reliefs and soil types of the various layers have affected the way of life of the people who live there. Even so this exceptional environment was inhabited early on in history: the Préalpes de Savoie were a hunting ground in the Paleolithic Period, while the first traces of a human presence date from the Neolithic Period.
Walking in Savoie also gives an insight into the legends carved in the rocks along the mountain paths. Every mountain pass is associated with an historical event or legend, for example Hannibal's famous crossing of the Alps in 218 BC ● *43*. But for every famous figure there were many more peddlers and traders of all kinds who, without maps or compasses, crossed these mountains to sell salt and matches. Farmers and herdsman on the high mountain paths will explain to interested hikers how the Beaufortain has successfully kept its identity and herds intact, the guarantee of a low-key agri-tourism and the best defense against the advance of fallow land that threatens certain abandoned areas.

SAFETY PRECAUTIONS

As in all extreme environments certain precautions should be taken before setting off into the mountains. Mist, storms and sudden snowfalls in July can have dramatic consequences. Always consult the weather forecast (Tel: 04 36 68 02 73/74), which is updated several times a day, before setting off. The mountains are there to be enjoyed, but they should be treated with respect. Contrary to popular belief, more accidents occur at middle-range altitudes than in the high mountains that are the preserve of experienced climbers. The rescue services are having to respond to an increasing number of accidents resulting from people slipping down grassy slopes, falling off mountain bikes or while canyoning (a sport where rescue operations are always problematic).

‘Going climbing means setting out, reaching the summit and returning safely. Relying on the rescue services to intervene in the event of difficulty is a betrayal of the concept of mountaineering.’

President of the Compagnie des Guides de Chamonix

Tomorrow is another day

Mountain guides are constantly reminding impatient or inexperienced climbers that the Alps will still be there tomorrow. Even a relatively minor injury can become serious due to high altitude, cold and exhaustion.

It is well worth taking a few simple precautions:

- choose a route suited to your ability and physical condition;
- seek advice from the professionals regarding the difficulties and distance of your chosen route;
- consult the weather forecast and ensure your equipment is suitable for extreme temperatures;
- tell people where you are going (route, estimated time of return);
- don't set off alone and don't be reluctant to take a guide.

Above all you should always remember that the high mountains are not a place in which to improvise or be careless.

Putting your best foot forward

You can't spend too long choosing a good pair of walking boots. Don't buy a cheap pair if you don't want to risk being reminded of the fact at every step. There is a wide range of boots of different types, but the ideal boots should be light and support your ankles. In summer they should allow your feet to breathe and dry out easily. Choose your rucksack with the same care and ideally fill it before trying it on so that you get an idea of how it feels. As when choosing boots there isn't a ‘standard’ model: a rucksack that is ideal for a day's walking in the mountains will not hold the equipment required for several days. However, too large a rucksack hinders your movements, so look for one large enough to hold what you need without hurting your shoulders or back.

Essential equipment

A map (1/25,000 or 1/50,000), compass and altimeter. Alternatively you can use GPS, a system that uses satellites to calculate position and altitude and which is becoming increasingly affordable. However you should still make sure you can read a map! Other essential equipment include a water bottle, a rain cape, a survival blanket, a high-protection sun cream, sunglasses that filter UV rays, a small first aid kit and signaling equipment (pocket flares and a whistle).

For centuries the snow had condemned many of the region's wage earners to leave home and find work as peddlers, chimney sweeps and coach drivers during the winter months. Today it supports tens of thousands of people and represents a major part of the wealth produced in Savoie, including winter-sports equipment with an international reputation.

'WHITE GOLD'

The middle classes of the 19th century would be surprised to learn that the pleasures of a privileged élite have today become an industry that provides thousands of Savoyards with a job. With a turnover of several billion francs, ski resorts are one of the leading sectors in the production of the region's wealth. Although the overall number of people skiing in France is decreasing, the pioneering role of Chamonix and the impact of the Winter Olympics held at Albertville in 1992 ▲ *248* are still having a positive effect. This is particularly true with regard to foreign visitors who are increasingly attracted by the largest area of ski slopes in the world.

However the professionals view the future with a certain degree of caution. The emphasis is on rehabilitating the existing infrastructure, with an eye to the external appearance of the buildings as well as the renovation of aging installations. The trend is toward wooden boarding and stone facings to make modern buildings blend with traditional architecture, to the point that metal structures are being painted to look like wood. This great 'face lift' divides architects and environmentalists. Its opponents consider this neo-rustic renaissance creates a uniform appearance which is a caricature of the traditional architectural style. Others are disappointed by the architects' lack of innovation and their unimaginatively traditional reproductions. The debate also fuels the arguments of the proponents of a low-key development that respects the vast Alpine spaces. This recent environmentalism is accompanied by an unprecedented development of such activities as snow-walking, excursions on snow shoes, husky sledding and horse-drawn skiing (*ski-joëring*).

NATURAL HAZARDS

For more than 130 years the mountain restoration service has protected people and buildings against such natural hazards as avalanches, landslides, falling rocks and flooding. Members of the service responsible for maintaining ski runs have been given special training, along with the region's *gendarmes*, CRS (state security police) and mountain rescue service. Météo-France (the French weather service) has two mountain forecasting stations – at Chamonix and Bourg-Saint-Maurice – linked to observation posts. This network makes it possible to issue daily bulletins which predict the risk of avalanches on a scale of 1 (low-risk) to 5 (high-risk) outside the marked ski runs that are open. It can be accessed daily from 3.30 pm, by telephone (08 36 68 10 20) or on the French Minitel system (3615 MÉTÉO or 3615 MFNEIGE).

Architecture

The remarkable homogeneity of Savoie's traditional architecture is due to the use of local materials from the actual construction site (wood, stone, pebbles) or one of the many nearby quarries (slate, stone, tufa). In spite of the rustic appearance of these materials, the wood and masonry elements in this 'land of chalets' produce an interesting combination of shades and textures, especially after a few years when the raw materials – which are often treated and painted for decorative effect – have acquired their final colors.

STONE
Savoyard stone masons have a generous supply of differently colored and textured stone at their disposal. Limestone, schist and granite are used in their simplest form in whitewashed rough-cast masonry. Tufa and *molasse* – crumbly, bluish- or greenish-gray marly sandstones – are mainly used for window and door frames. The light gray slate from the quarries of Morzine, the Val d'Arly and the Maurienne and Tarentaise regions is widely used for roofing. Roofing stones are only found in the high valleys.

TILES AND COBWORK
Tiles are used in the region's vineyards (rounded tiles) and on the lake shores (scalloped tiles at Duingt). Cobwork is only found in the Préalpes de Savoie.

METAL
Galvanized corrugated iron is widely used to replace traditional roofing such as thatch. When it is not painted black, its color changes from matt gray to rust. Many balcony railings are made of wrought iron or cast iron.

Rendering
Although the stonework is still visible through some renderings, most cover it completely and consist of a – more or less granular – monochrome blend of local sand and earth and crushed brick. In the pink-tinged and raw sienna façades of Chambéry ▲ *120*, window and door frames are emphasized with a band of lighter color. Many façades are also whitewashed and highlighted with border lines, friezes, corner stones, diamond-point and *trompe l'oeil* effects. By contrast the architects of Turin used a typically Sardinian range of colors to highlight the public buildings of Annecy ▲ *160*, Cluses ▲ *222* and Sallanches ▲ *222*.

Wood
In the wetter regions of Savoie spruce from the nearby forests has a wide range of constructional uses: frameworks, boarding, roofing in the form of shingles ▲ *182* or wooden tiles, and balcony friezes. Further south spruce is replaced by larch, which is traditionally left untreated and acquires a range of colors when exposed to the elements. It turns gray in a north-facing position, is burnt by the sun when exposed to the south and remains brown under eaves and balconies, sometimes acquiring a soft orange hue. These different colors can be seen in piles of firewood and timber stored for construction.

As well as the famous 'wooden chalet' there are many other different types of rural architecture in Savoie and Haute-Savoie. Some of the principle characteristics are similar to those found in other regions: the houses of the low-lying valleys and deep gorges are similar to those of the Lyonnais and Dauphiné regions; predominantly wooden houses are also found in Switzerland and the Val d'Aoste; while predominantly stone houses are also found further south in the Dauphiné and Piedmont. However, each region of Savoie has its own unique architectural characteristics in respect to dimensions, materials, design and use.

HOUSE AND BARN FROM THE PRÉALPES DE SAVOIE
The division of use is represented by two separate buildings: one made of shuttered cobwork for agricultural use, while the living accommodation is in rendered stonework. Dauphiné-type houses are characterized by a two- or four-paneled roof with a pitch of around 50°, usually covered with scalloped tiles. Some buildings in the Chautagne and Petit Bugey regions have overhanging, stepped gables.

FARM FROM THE LOW-LYING VALLEYS AND THE ALBANAIS ▲ *158*
The cellar door is located at the foot of the flight of stone steps leading to the house. The flatter terrain in these regions allows easy access to the barn, which has a wide, double door. As everywhere else in Savoie the eaves provide protection when moving between the house and the outbuildings.

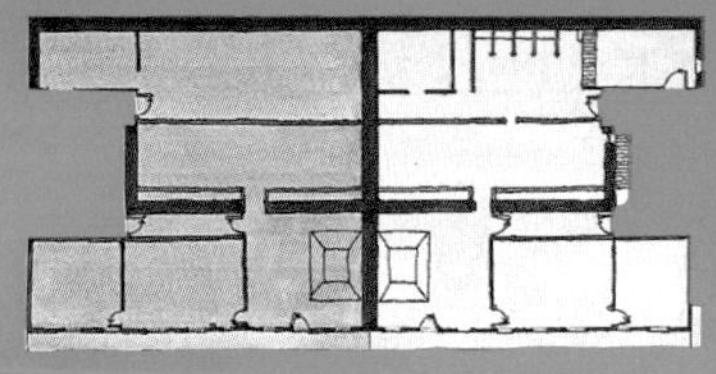

Double chalet from the Abondance ▲ *203*
The chalet comprises two symmetrical structures, with the living accommodation at the front separated from the stables by a long corridor. The façade has two galleries. The upper gallery, on the same level as the barn, is used for drying crops. The roof and huge wooden chimney (*bourne*) are covered with shingles.

Storehouse from the Beaufortain
Storehouses are built of wooden planking and stand some distance from the house in case of fire. These one- or two-story structures are used to store such precious possessions as seeds and festival costumes.

Ventilation
The wooden walls of barns and storehouses have openwork motifs (dates, initials, crosses, playing card symbols) to allow the air to circulate and the crops to dry.

Traditional farmhouse
This traditional farmhouse from the Massif des Bornes ▲ *178* in the Préalpes has a cape-like, double-pitched, or 'German', roof. Here, as in the mountains, a layer of hay on the floor of the huge barn provides effective insulation against the cold.

The proportions of stone and wood used in rural buildings changes in relation to altitude, with a predominance of stone and *lauzes* (roofing stones) at higher altitudes. The region's many Alpine chalets are built according to the same techniques used for permanent buildings. People and animals live under the same roof, sometimes sharing the ground floor, whose vaulted masonry provides better ventilation.

WOVEN GABLE FROM THE MOYENNE MAURIENNE
The wall section beneath the gable must ensure that the interior of the barn is adequately ventilated. Here, in the Arves, it is made of woven branches (green alder) with boarding on the lower section.

FARMHOUSE FROM THE HAUTE MAURIENNE
These fairly low houses have solid stone walls. They are mainly given over to agricultural use and until the 1900s, people and animals lived under the same roof. The lower rooms are vaulted and the upper floors are often reached from the inside. The wooden balconies are protected by a slightly overhanging roof and are used for drying.

COLUMNED HOUSE FROM THE MOYENNE TARENTAISE
These houses, built with stone from the Bourg-Saint-Maurice (Sainte-Foy-Tarentaise, Montvalezan) region, are widely found in neighboring Piedmont. On the south-facing façade, columns support the eaves which protect the entrance, a small farmyard and a drying balcony.

WOOD AND DRY-STONE PIERS FROM THE HIGH VALLEYS
In some regions, especially Polset, the walls are supported by piers with double interlocking beams, one in the wall, one on the outside. Overhanging roofing stones protect the ends of the beams from the elements.

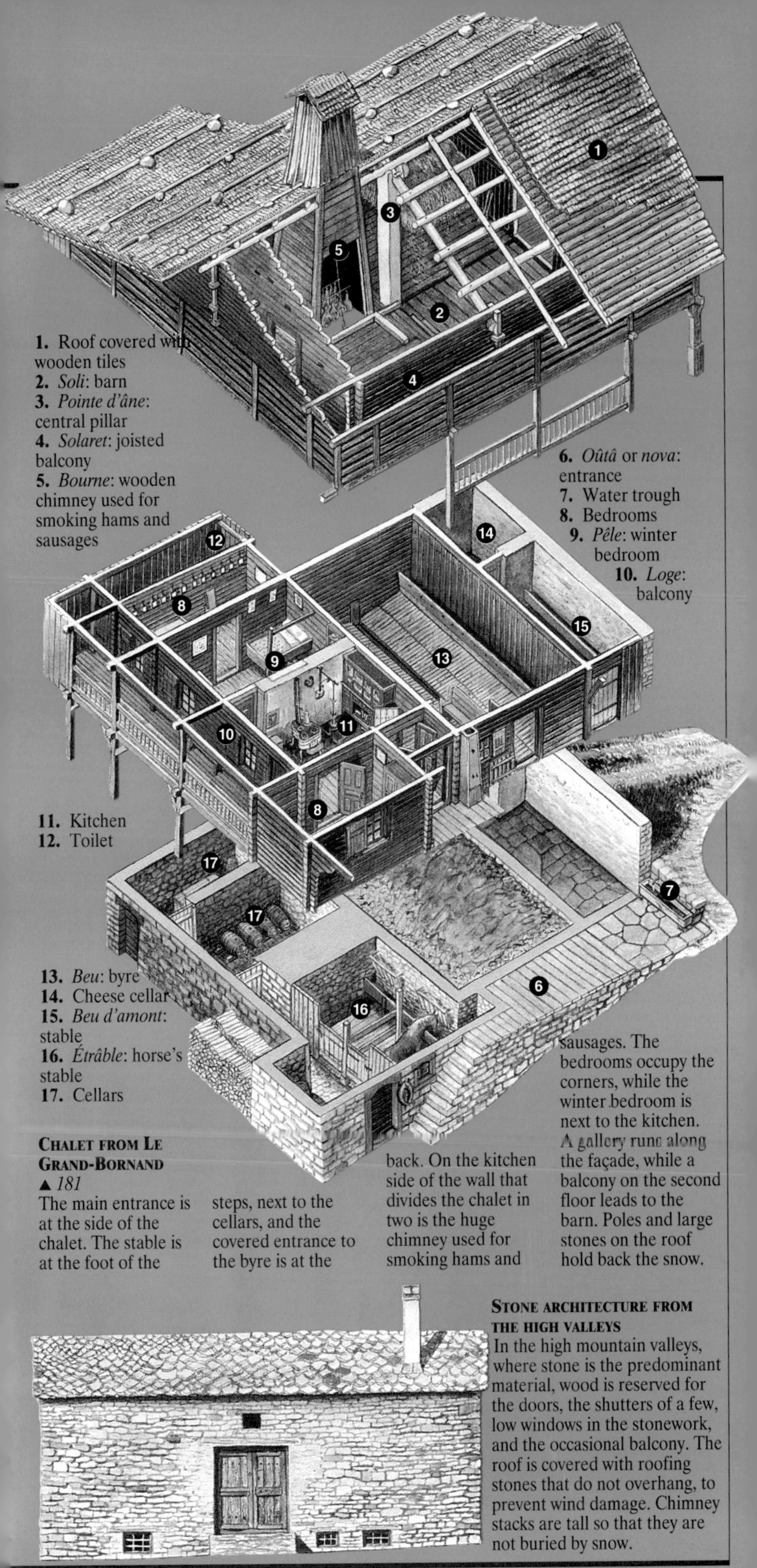

1. Roof covered with wooden tiles
2. *Soli*: barn
3. *Pointe d'âne*: central pillar
4. *Solaret*: joisted balcony
5. *Bourne*: wooden chimney used for smoking hams and sausages
6. *Oûtâ* or *nova*: entrance
7. Water trough
8. Bedrooms
9. *Pêle*: winter bedroom
10. *Loge*: balcony
11. Kitchen
12. Toilet
13. *Beu*: byre
14. Cheese cellar
15. *Beu d'amont*: stable
16. *Étrâble*: horse's stable
17. Cellars

CHALET FROM LE GRAND-BORNAND
▲ *181*
The main entrance is at the side of the chalet. The stable is at the foot of the steps, next to the cellars, and the covered entrance to the byre is at the back. On the kitchen side of the wall that divides the chalet in two is the huge chimney used for smoking hams and sausages. The bedrooms occupy the corners, while the winter bedroom is next to the kitchen. A gallery runs along the façade, while a balcony on the second floor leads to the barn. Poles and large stones on the roof hold back the snow.

STONE ARCHITECTURE FROM THE HIGH VALLEYS
In the high mountain valleys, where stone is the predominant material, wood is reserved for the doors, the shutters of a few, low windows in the stonework, and the occasional balcony. The roof is covered with roofing stones that do not overhang, to prevent wind damage. Chimney stacks are tall so that they are not buried by snow.

From 1150 onward most of the region's castles belonged to three families who had divided Savoie between them: the counts of Savoie, the counts of Geneva and the lords of Faucigny. These castles were built on high ground and made use of the natural relief. The large amount of space devoted to residential and domestic buildings suggests a comfortable and sophisticated lifestyle. During the 13th century the minor aristocracy built country houses that consisted of residential buildings flanked by towers. Much of the medieval structure of these houses has survived.

FEUDAL CASTLE (CHANTEMERLE ▲ *252*)
In the 12th century the feudal keep formed an 'upper court', the 'upper residence' and annexes being dominated by a 'great tower', both watchtower and storehouse. During the 13th century the feudal practice of co-seigneury brought about changes: palisaded enclosures surrounded several baronial keeps and the towers and fortified residences of their vassals.

RESIDENTIAL CASTLE (ANNECY ▲ *164*)
The residence of the counts of Geneva from the mid-13th century had four residential wings (logis) flanked by square towers. Only the Tour de la Reine ('queen's tower'), built in the late 12th century, appears to have been a defensive structure with two lower levels equipped with loopholes. The Vieux Logis and Logis Perrière have retained some of their interior structure (15th century).

CHÂTEAU DES ALLINGES ▲ *193*
This site was originally occupied by two castles, *Châteauneuf* and *Châteauvieux*, one on each side of a pass. They belonged to the rival lords of Allinges and the counts of Savoie. All that remains today is a chapel.

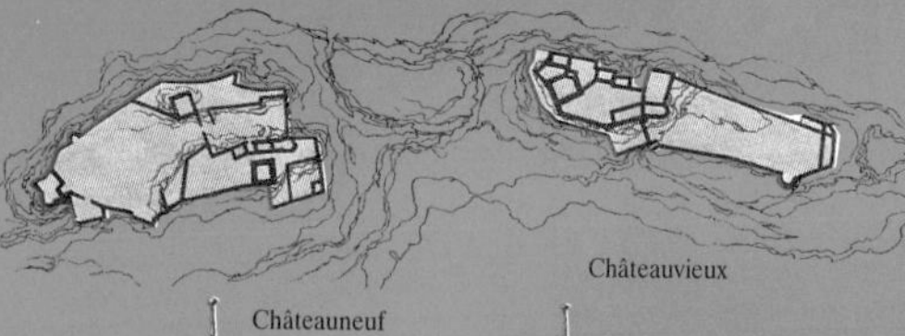

FORTIFIED RESIDENCE, MAGLAND
This fortified baronial residence is in the center of the village. The massive structure has an upper defensive story which is more symbolic than functional. It has retained its original layout with two stories separated by remarkable ceilings dating from 1439. The rooms were lit by broad windows and heated by monumental chimneys.

ARISTOCRATIC RESIDENCE
This 15th-century residence (Maison de Marclaz, Thonon) is surrounded by an outer wall. Its many outbuildings attest to the importance of domestic activities and the cultivation of food crops. The rectangular residential wing is flanked by a staircase turret.

A SOPHISTICATED DECOR
The decorative elements of the Maison de Marclaz – doors surmounted by an ogee arch and mullioned windows surrounded by grooved moldings and crowned by a drip stone – are typical of the Flamboyant style ● *81*.

CHÂTEAU DE RIPAILLE (THONON ▲ *195*)
The 14th-century Château de Ripaille belonged to the counts of Savoie and was extended by Amadeus VIII ● *40*. It had seven wings, seven towers and the tower of the Chevaliers de l'Ordre de Saint Maurice, founded in 1434. It was reminiscent of the Palais des Papes in Avignon, which were built at about the same time. (Reconstruction, *below, left;* the château today, *right*.)

The churches and chapels of Savoie were usually built in the form of an elongated rectangle, based on a basilical plan. Occasionally they had a more central layout in the form of a Greek cross or a circle. Several Romanesque churches, two Gothic cathedrals and the Sainte-Chapelle have survived from the Middle Ages. Romanesque architecture was essentially monastic and was influenced by the styles of northern Italy, southern Germany, the Rhône Valley and Burgundy. Gothic architecture, introduced by the Cistercians in 1160, gave rise to the local Flamboyant style in the 15th century.

A FAITH THAT IS VERY MUCH ALIVE (Chapelle Saint-Roch, Jarrier ▲ *274*)
The Alpine valleys of Savoie have a great many rural chapels. The chapel in the village of Jarrier was built in 1565, following a plague epidemic, and is dedicated to saints Roch and Sebastian. Its pink façade (colored whitewash rendering) stands out on the Aiguilles d'Arves.

ROMANESQUE (Basilica of Saint-Martin d'Aime ▲ *258*)
This 11th-century priory church, which stands on the foundations of a Roman building, is a masterpiece of Romanesque Lombard architecture. The nave with its timber framework opens onto a *chancel* with a groined vault and an oven-vaulted apse flanked by two chapels. The blind arcades that heighten the chevet enabled roofing stones to be placed on sloping masonry without a timber framework. The basilica has an elegant crypt and wall paintings dating from the 13th century.

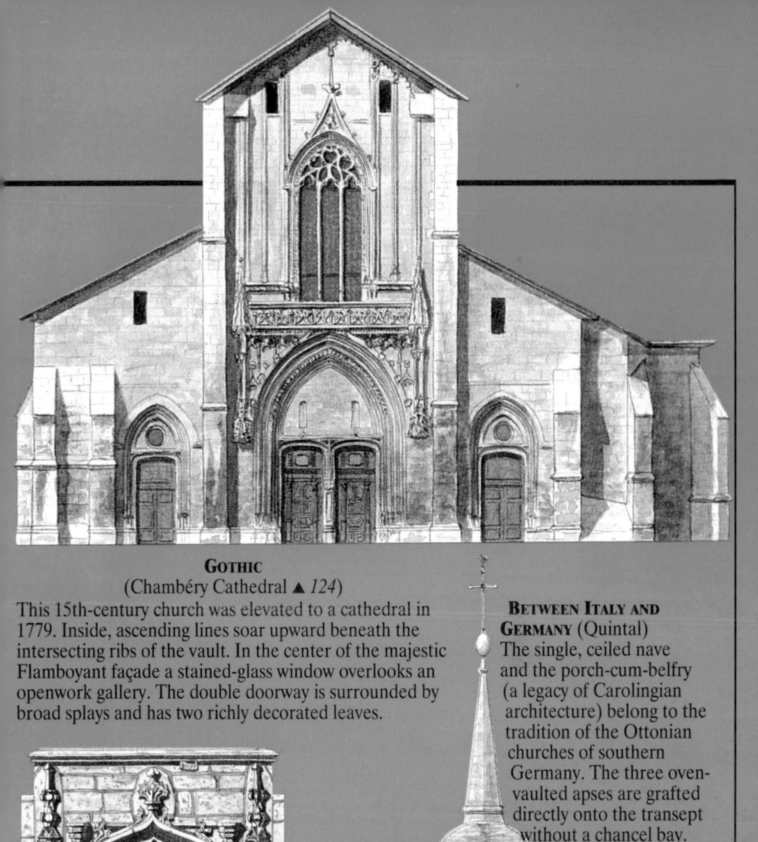

Gothic
(Chambéry Cathedral ▲ *124*)
This 15th-century church was elevated to a cathedral in 1779. Inside, ascending lines soar upward beneath the intersecting ribs of the vault. In the center of the majestic Flamboyant façade a stained-glass window overlooks an openwork gallery. The double doorway is surrounded by broad splays and has two richly decorated leaves.

Flamboyant
(Mieussy ▲ *212*)
The Flamboyant (French Late Gothic) architectural style was characterized by the replacement of capitals with unbroken wave moldings, prismatic bases and Mannerist sculpted elements.

Between Italy and Germany (Quintal)
The single, ceiled nave and the porch-cum-belfry (a legacy of Carolingian architecture) belong to the tradition of the Ottonian churches of southern Germany. The three oven-vaulted apses are grafted directly onto the transept without a chancel bay. Their decorative bands, still known as Lombard bands, and the frieze of small blind arcades reflect the influence of northern Italy.

The archaic style of Faucigny
(Chartreuse de Mélan ▲ *214*)
Although the vault has intersecting ribs, the rustic tufa masonry, narrow windows and solid buttresses of this late-13th-century Carthusian church give it an extremely Romanesque appearance.

Baroque architecture developed in Italy in the wake of the Catholic Reformation and spread rapidly through Savoie as a reaction to Calvinism. From 1650 an increase in population was accompanied by renewed religious fervor. Many churches were transformed or rebuilt. The choice of decorative and religious themes (the importance of protective saints) and the systematic use of wood (Arolla pine) were distinctive features of Savoyard Baroque, while polychrome and gilding made the concept of paradise more accessible to the rural imagination.

1. La Riche-sur-Foron ▲ *218*
2. Ballaison
3. Combloux ▲ *241*

THE ORIENTAL TOUCH
Baroque churches often had characteristic onion-shaped bell towers. The simplest form consisted of a lantern, 'bulb' and spire, sometimes complemented by heavy moldings and a balustrade. The most elegant had two superposed modules.

BAROQUE DECOR
The religious sentiments of the faithful were reflected in the exuberance of this elaborate style, dominated by curves and counter-curves. Sculpted or painted, triumphant images combated Protestantism and illustrated the catechism of the Council of Trent (1566): the source of faith (the Bible and traditions), the primacy of Rome, the Eucharistic presence, the cult of the Holy Virgin, the saints and angels (117 cherubs in the church of Valloire and 160 in the church of Champagny). There were no empty spaces: Baroque abhorred a vacuum!

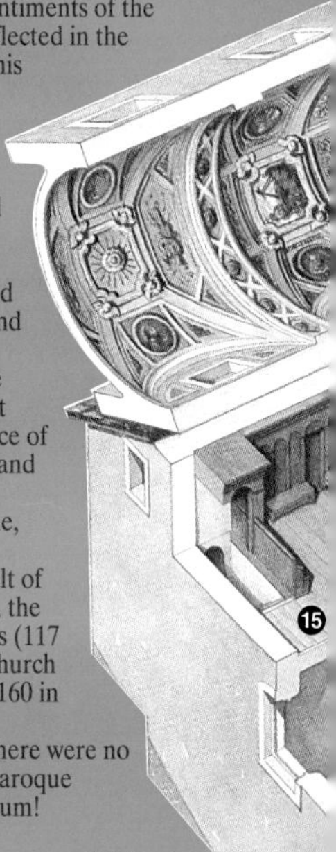

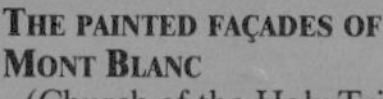

THE PAINTED FAÇADES OF MONT BLANC
(Church of the Holy Trinity, Les Contamines-Montjoie)
The painted façades of these 'hall-churches' – so called because there are no side aisles – contrast with the absence of exterior decoration on the rest of the building. The paintings are usually dedicated to the patron saint of the town or village, in this case the Holy Trinity.

1. Steps 'taken by the dead'
2. Steps leading to the crypt
3. Outer crypt-chamber
4. Temporary altar
5. Crypt
6. Steps to the chancel
7. Chancel
8. High altar
9. Dome
10. Nave
11. Secondary altars
12. Side aisles
13. Ceiling of the nave
14. Gallery
15. Steps to the gallery

Church of Avrieux
(1678) ▲ *278*
The beautiful wooden door of the vaulted vestibule opens onto the central nave with its groined vault, flanked by smaller side aisles. The choir is surmounted by an octagonal dome decorated with stucco medallions.

The crypt
In 1685 the priest installed a crypt in the extension of the priests' vault in order to house the dead when it was too cold to bury them. A flight of steps leads down from the vestibule to a nave (outer crypt-chamber), a small chapel (temporary altar) and the priests' vault (crypt). Sculptures and paintings evoke the Passion and Resurrection of Christ.

'CLUSURAE AUGUSTANAE'
These 'imperial gates' controlled the passes through the Alps in the Roman era (beginning of the 5th century).

Since antiquity the art of fortification has adapted to the diversity of Savoie's Alpine relief. Deep gorges (*cluses*), glacial thresholds and the foot of mountain passes formed strategic natural defenses and became key points from which to control roads and tolls. From the 11th century the counts of Savoie were the 'gatekeepers' of the Alps and developed a network of fortifications which they continued to modify and strengthen until the mid-19th century. After 1860 French and Italian defense systems on either side of the Alps were used to protect the border between the two countries. In 1940 the Alpine section of the Maginot line held off the Italian offensive.

THE ADVENT OF ARTILLERY (Miolans ▲ *133*)
The Château de Miolans is one of the finest examples of medieval military architecture adapted for artillery. The fort had loopholes, battery galleries, 14th- to 15th-century ramparts and an early 16th-century artillery tower.

THE ITALIAN SCHOOL OF FORTIFICATION
(Fort of Montmélian ▲ *133, below*)
In the 16th century the medieval castle was surrounded by a bastioned fortification. Sheer, high ramparts and bastions were characteristic of these polygonal or rectangular structures which practiced enfilading fire.

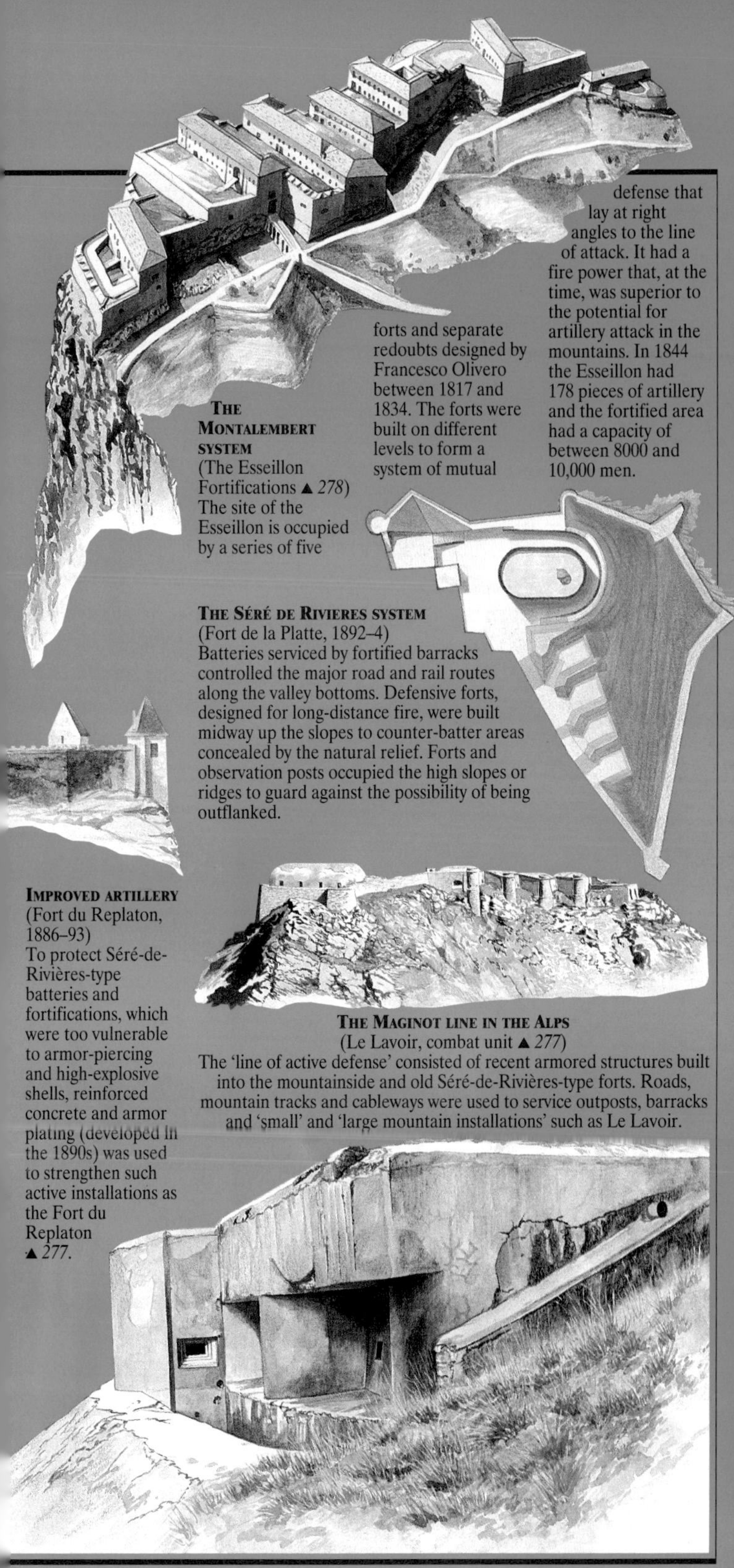

The Montalembert system
(The Esseillon Fortifications ▲ *278*)
The site of the Esseillon is occupied by a series of five forts and separate redoubts designed by Francesco Olivero between 1817 and 1834. The forts were built on different levels to form a system of mutual defense that lay at right angles to the line of attack. It had a fire power that, at the time, was superior to the potential for artillery attack in the mountains. In 1844 the Esseillon had 178 pieces of artillery and the fortified area had a capacity of between 8000 and 10,000 men.

The Séré de Rivieres system
(Fort de la Platte, 1892–4)
Batteries serviced by fortified barracks controlled the major road and rail routes along the valley bottoms. Defensive forts, designed for long-distance fire, were built midway up the slopes to counter-batter areas concealed by the natural relief. Forts and observation posts occupied the high slopes or ridges to guard against the possibility of being outflanked.

Improved artillery
(Fort du Replaton, 1886–93)
To protect Séré-de-Rivières-type batteries and fortifications, which were too vulnerable to armor-piercing and high-explosive shells, reinforced concrete and armor plating (developed in the 1890s) was used to strengthen such active installations as the Fort du Replaton ▲ *277*.

The Maginot line in the Alps
(Le Lavoir, combat unit ▲ *277*)
The 'line of active defense' consisted of recent armored structures built into the mountainside and old Séré-de-Rivières-type forts. Roads, mountain tracks and cableways were used to service outposts, barracks and 'small' and 'large mountain installations' such as Le Lavoir.

ANTIQUITY REVISITED
(*right*, Thonon)
This beautiful public washhouse reflects the architectural canons of antiquity. The frieze of the entablature has alternate triglyphs and metopes.

In 1815 the Sardinian monarchy, traumatized by the French Revolution, embarked upon a reactionary policy which was supported by the Church. Neoclassical architecture provided the perfect medium for the expression of this new ideology. Its often overwhelming monumentalism, austere majesty, and a grandeur that stood in stark contrast to its surroundings, were designed to glorify divine and royal power. The style originated in Turin, which produced the region's architects and civil engineers. In the space of 35 years the diocese of Annecy acquired 85 Neoclassical churches. Town halls, covered markets, fountains and public washhouses were also built in this grandiose style. When the towns of Cluses and Sallanches were destroyed by fire, their reconstruction reflected the austerity and rigor of Neoclassical urban planning.

CHURCH OF LA BATHIE (SAVOIE)
The curves and counter-curves of the Baroque style have been replaced by an orthogonal composition reminiscent of the façades of classical temples. Here the single-story façade is surmounted by an entablature and a triangular pediment. The three vertical sections, separated by pilasters, correspond to the three naves of equal height (hall-church). The semicircular bay window, high above the door, is characteristic of this architectural style.

'GRENETTE' (Sallanches ▲ *222*)
The *grenette*, a covered corn market, was an integral part of the urban landscape in such towns as Boëge, Rumilly ▲ *158*, La Roche-sur-Foron ▲ *218* and Sallanches. The simplicity of the colonnades is reminiscent of the temples of antiquity.

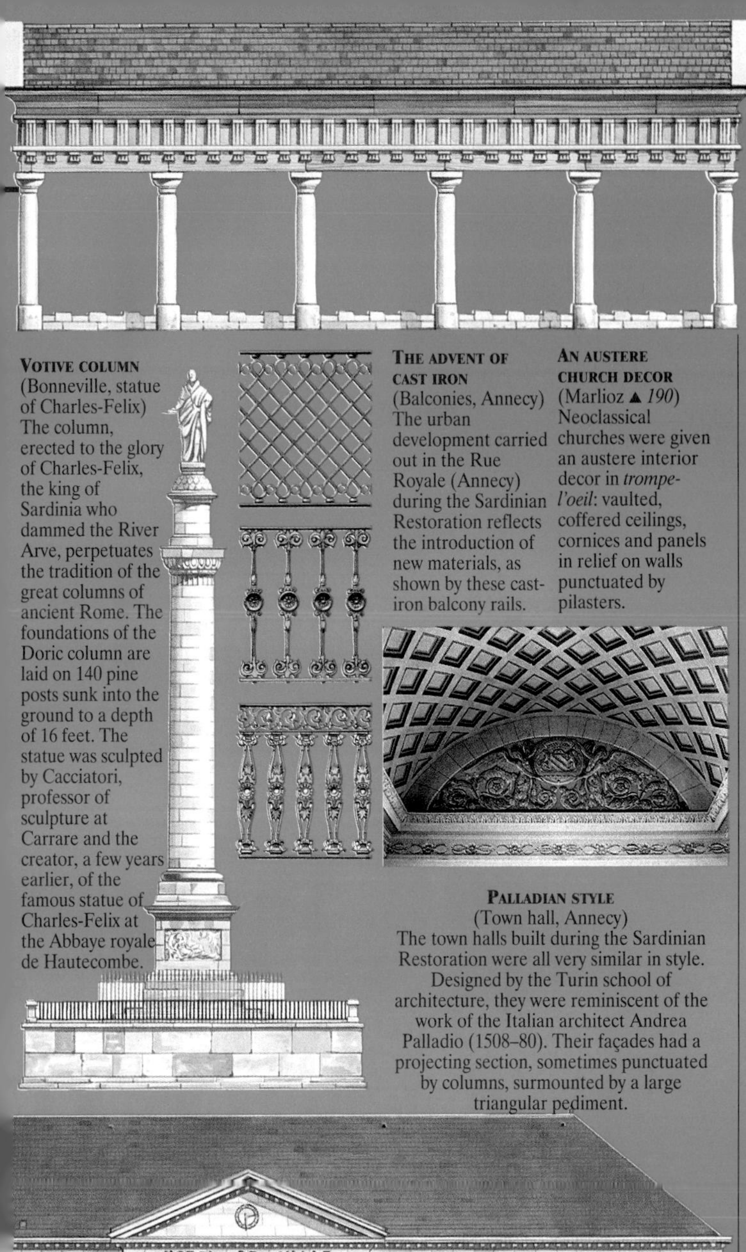

VOTIVE COLUMN
(Bonneville, statue of Charles-Felix)
The column, erected to the glory of Charles-Felix, the king of Sardinia who dammed the River Arve, perpetuates the tradition of the great columns of ancient Rome. The foundations of the Doric column are laid on 140 pine posts sunk into the ground to a depth of 16 feet. The statue was sculpted by Cacciatori, professor of sculpture at Carrare and the creator, a few years earlier, of the famous statue of Charles-Felix at the Abbaye royale de Hautecombe.

THE ADVENT OF CAST IRON
(Balconies, Annecy)
The urban development carried out in the Rue Royale (Annecy) during the Sardinian Restoration reflects the introduction of new materials, as shown by these cast-iron balcony rails.

AN AUSTERE CHURCH DECOR
(Marlioz ▲ *190*)
Neoclassical churches were given an austere interior decor in *trompe-l'oeil*: vaulted, coffered ceilings, cornices and panels in relief on walls punctuated by pilasters.

PALLADIAN STYLE
(Town hall, Annecy)
The town halls built during the Sardinian Restoration were all very similar in style. Designed by the Turin school of architecture, they were reminiscent of the work of the Italian architect Andrea Palladio (1508–80). Their façades had a projecting section, sometimes punctuated by columns, surmounted by a large triangular pediment.

In 1869 the French engineer Aristide Bergès (1833–1904) built a paper mill in the Isère region with the idea of harnessing the power of a 650-foot waterfall by means of a pressure pipeline. This exclusively hydraulic installation was the first stage in the development of hydroelectric power, produced some twenty years later using the power of Savoie's many rivers and waterfalls. Once the problem of transporting this energy over long distances had been resolved, the interwar period witnessed the development of major reservoirs designed to regulate the high-water level.

The first large-scale hydroelectric power stations built in the Alpine valleys in the late 19th century were designed to meet the needs of the region's developing electrochemical and electrometallurgical industries. At the time, the problem of transporting electric energy over long distances had not been resolved, so it tended to be produced and used *in situ* in the valleys. The interwar years saw the construction of vast reservoirs capable of supplying the entire national grid. It had become necessary to develop the means of producing, transporting and distributing a form of energy that would make up for the shortfall in coal and thermal energy. A multiple-vault dam **(2)** was built on the Lac de la Girotte (Beaufortain) and completed just before the end of World War Two. In the Tarentaise region there were plans to harness the upper reaches of the Isère since the EDF (Électricité de France), nationalized in 1946, wanted to offset the industrial and energy-related underplanting of the

valley. The Tignes-Le Chevril dam **(3, 4, 5, 6)** was brought into service in 1952 after seven years' work and strong resistance from the local population. It was followed in 1961 by the vast and elegant reservoir dam – 2625 feet long – built on the Lac de Roselend **(1, 7, 8)** in the Beaufortain region. Between 1963 and 1968, the Mont-Cenis dam (**11**) was built in the Maurienne: almost one mile long and 400 feet high, with a capacity of more than 70,000 million US gallons. The Plan d'Amont dam **(12)** complemented the Plan d'Aval system. To meet the increasing demands of the nuclear energy sector in the 1980s the EDF adopted a power-station design with two reservoirs. Each night the waters of the lower reservoir are pumped and stored in the upper reservoir to meet the heavy energy demands of the next day. This mountain hydraulic-power system compensates for the lack of flexibility in the traditional power stations which are limited to a regular production, for example Grand-Maison (**9,10**) on L'Eau d'Olle.

THE MAURIENNE FREEWAY
In the valley of the River Arc the river, road, railroad and freeway (40 miles) form a major traffic corridor.

The broad, fast-flowing rivers Rhône, Arve, Isère and Arc, the steep-sided Gorges des Usses and Gorges du Chéran, the inaccessible Chamonix valley and the Haute-Tarentaise, and the need to link Europe north and south via the Alps of Savoie are all challenges that have led the *départements* of Savoie and Haute-Savoie to develop exceptional infrastructures. These are often works of art: stone bridges built by Piedmontese engineers in the 18th century, vertiginous suspension bridges, rail viaducts of the PLM transport company, 20th-century road viaducts using the latest techniques in reinforced concrete and, last but not least, cable-stayed bridges. The damming of the Arve and the Griaz are other examples of the spectacular engineering feats that have overcome the challenges presented by this mountain environment.

CONQUERING THE MOUNTAINS
(Viaduc Sainte-Marie, Les Houches ▲ *224, below*)
In 1900 the railroad was extended to Chamonix via a number of freestone tunnels and viaducts. The elegant viaduct across the Arve at Les Houches has become an integral part of the landscape.

THE ENLIGHTENMENT
(Pont de Saint-Martin-sur-Arve)
The remarkable works of architecture constructed by engineers from the Turin school during the 18th century include the single-arched stone bridge (1783) which spans the Arve at Saint-Martin-sur-Arve.

GROUNDBREAKING NEW TECHNOLOGY
(Ponts de la Caille ▲ *190*, above and below)
In 1838 the French engineers Belin and Lehaître began to construct a 636-foot suspension bridge across the Gorges des Usses, almost 500 feet above the river. The Charles-Albert bridge took 16 months to complete. Between 1924 and 1928 a second bridge, designed by the engineer Caquot, was built across the gorge. The 750-foot bridge was supported by two piers and had a single arch, whose span of 460 feet was then the largest in the world.

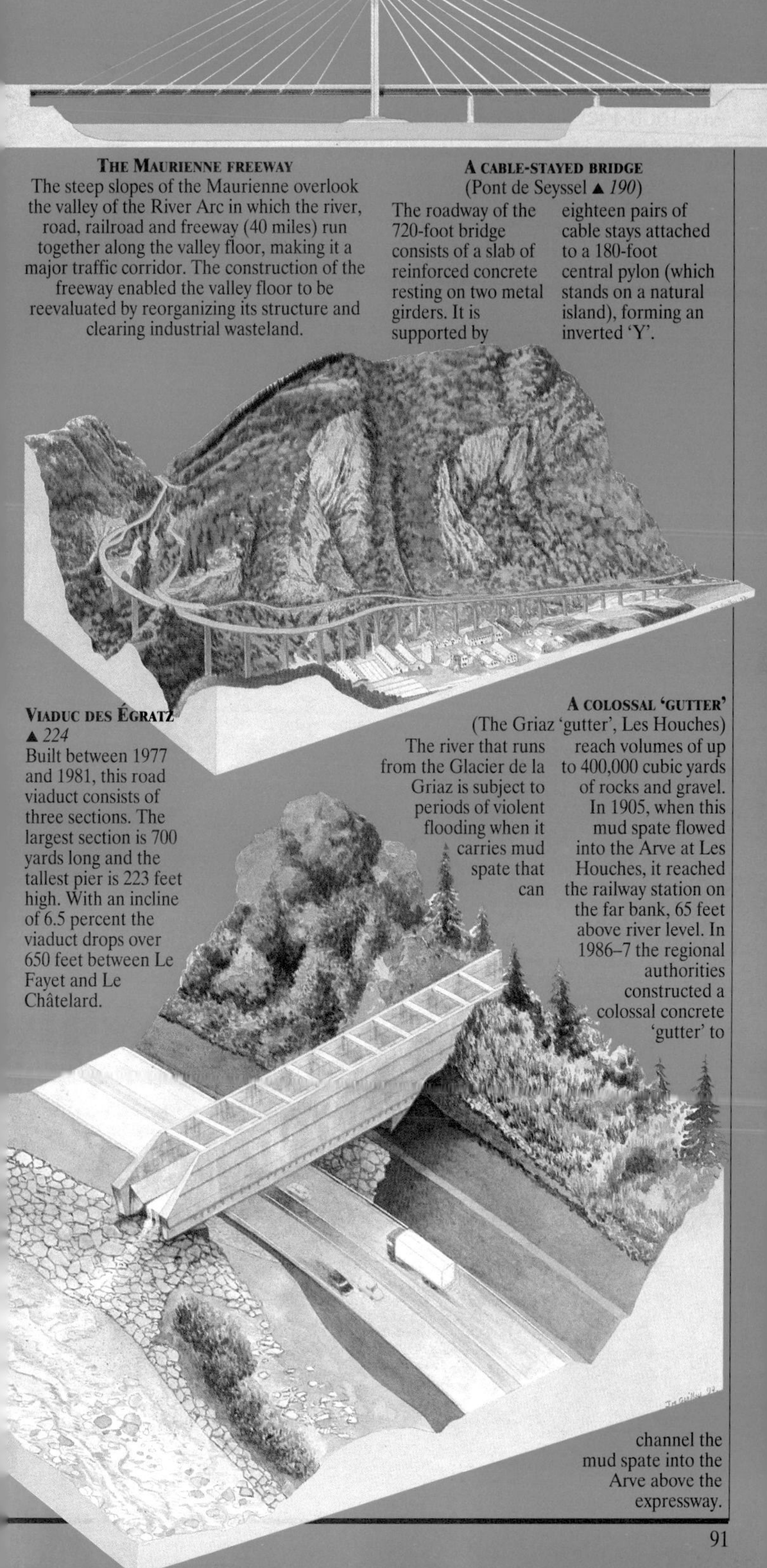

THE MAURIENNE FREEWAY
The steep slopes of the Maurienne overlook the valley of the River Arc in which the river, road, railroad and freeway (40 miles) run together along the valley floor, making it a major traffic corridor. The construction of the freeway enabled the valley floor to be reevaluated by reorganizing its structure and clearing industrial wasteland.

A CABLE-STAYED BRIDGE
(Pont de Seyssel ▲ *190*)
The roadway of the 720-foot bridge consists of a slab of reinforced concrete resting on two metal girders. It is supported by eighteen pairs of cable stays attached to a 180-foot central pylon (which stands on a natural island), forming an inverted 'Y'.

VIADUC DES ÉGRATZ
▲ *224*
Built between 1977 and 1981, this road viaduct consists of three sections. The largest section is 700 yards long and the tallest pier is 223 feet high. With an incline of 6.5 percent the viaduct drops over 650 feet between Le Fayet and Le Châtelard.

A COLOSSAL 'GUTTER'
(The Griaz 'gutter', Les Houches)
The river that runs from the Glacier de la Griaz is subject to periods of violent flooding when it carries mud spate that can reach volumes of up to 400,000 cubic yards of rocks and gravel. In 1905, when this mud spate flowed into the Arve at Les Houches, it reached the railway station on the far bank, 65 feet above river level. In 1986–7 the regional authorities constructed a colossal concrete 'gutter' to channel the mud spate into the Arve above the expressway.

Arc 1600-Pierre Blanche is one of the so-called 'integrated' resorts built between 1960 and 1980. It was built from scratch on a site overlooking the Isère valley, at the foot of a vast skiing area. The resort is a well-coordinated entity whose distinctive architecture and urban design are the product of the nature and position of the site. The intention was to create a rational and untraditional style of architecture which meets the needs of a modern leisure-based society.

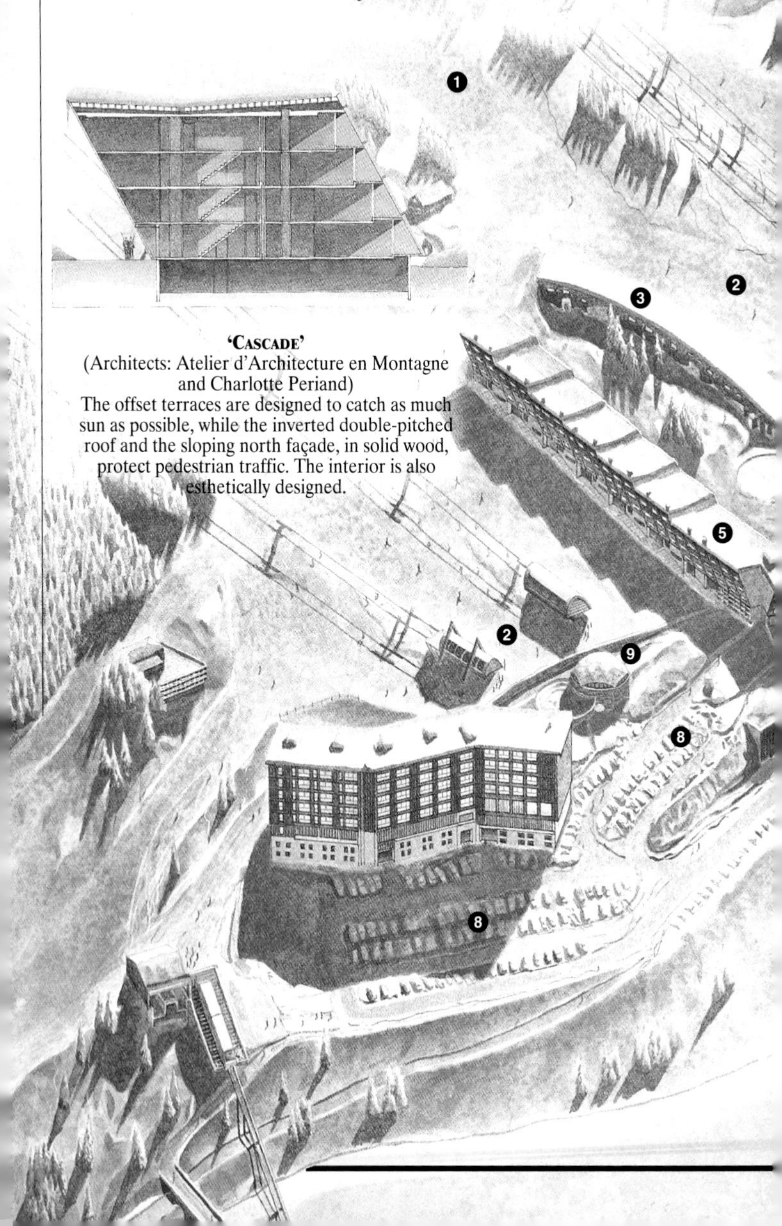

'CASCADE'
(Architects: Atelier d'Architecture en Montagne and Charlotte Periand)
The offset terraces are designed to catch as much sun as possible, while the inverted double-pitched roof and the sloping north façade, in solid wood, protect pedestrian traffic. The interior is also esthetically designed.

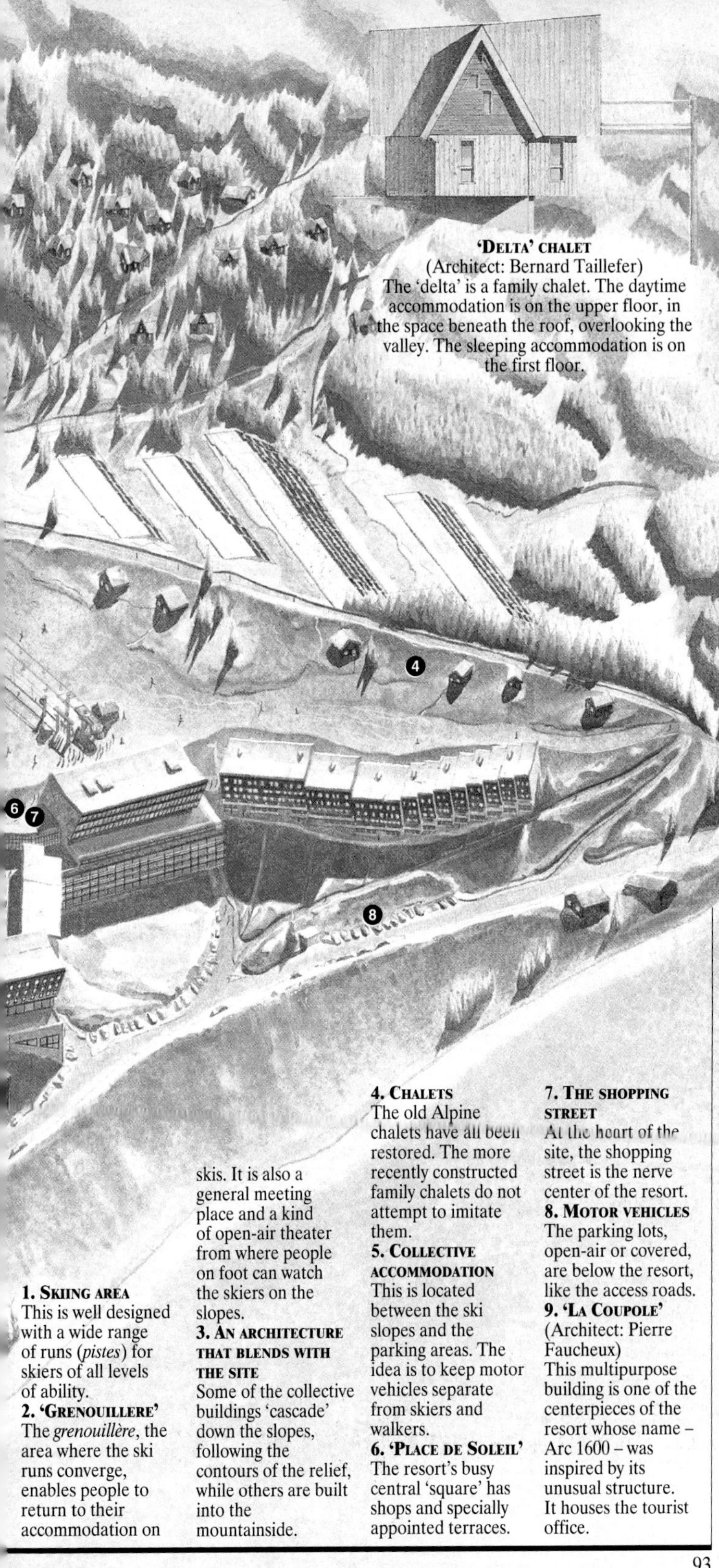

'Delta' chalet
(Architect: Bernard Taillefer)
The 'delta' is a family chalet. The daytime accommodation is on the upper floor, in the space beneath the roof, overlooking the valley. The sleeping accommodation is on the first floor.

1. Skiing area
This is well designed with a wide range of runs (*pistes*) for skiers of all levels of ability.

2. 'Grenouillere'
The *grenouillère*, the area where the ski runs converge, enables people to return to their accommodation on skis. It is also a general meeting place and a kind of open-air theater from where people on foot can watch the skiers on the slopes.

3. An architecture that blends with the site
Some of the collective buildings 'cascade' down the slopes, following the contours of the relief, while others are built into the mountainside.

4. Chalets
The old Alpine chalets have all been restored. The more recently constructed family chalets do not attempt to imitate them.

5. Collective accommodation
This is located between the ski slopes and the parking areas. The idea is to keep motor vehicles separate from skiers and walkers.

6. 'Place de Soleil'
The resort's busy central 'square' has shops and specially appointed terraces.

7. The shopping street
At the heart of the site, the shopping street is the nerve center of the resort.

8. Motor vehicles
The parking lots, open-air or covered, are below the resort, like the access roads.

9. 'La Coupole'
(Architect: Pierre Faucheux)
This multipurpose building is one of the centerpieces of the resort whose name – Arc 1600 – was inspired by its unusual structure. It houses the tourist office.

THE CREATION OF WINTER SPORTS RESORTS

The Le Même chalet, with its steeply sloping roof, is an essential element in the contemporary mountain scene. It offers a comfortable, elegant interior, with magnificent views of the countryside.

Ski chalets were invented at Megève, in the 1920s, by Henry-Jacques Le Même whose colorful architectural style broke with tradition. After World War Two purpose-built resorts were constructed in the Alps within the context of a national 'snow program'. Some resorts, such as Avoriaz, designed by the architects Roques, Labro and Orzoni, used organic forms and natural wood, while others (Flaine by Breuer and Gatje) favored the stark simplicity of concrete which echoed the rock faces of the surrounding mountains. Today this architecture has been replaced by the more reassuring neo-traditional style.

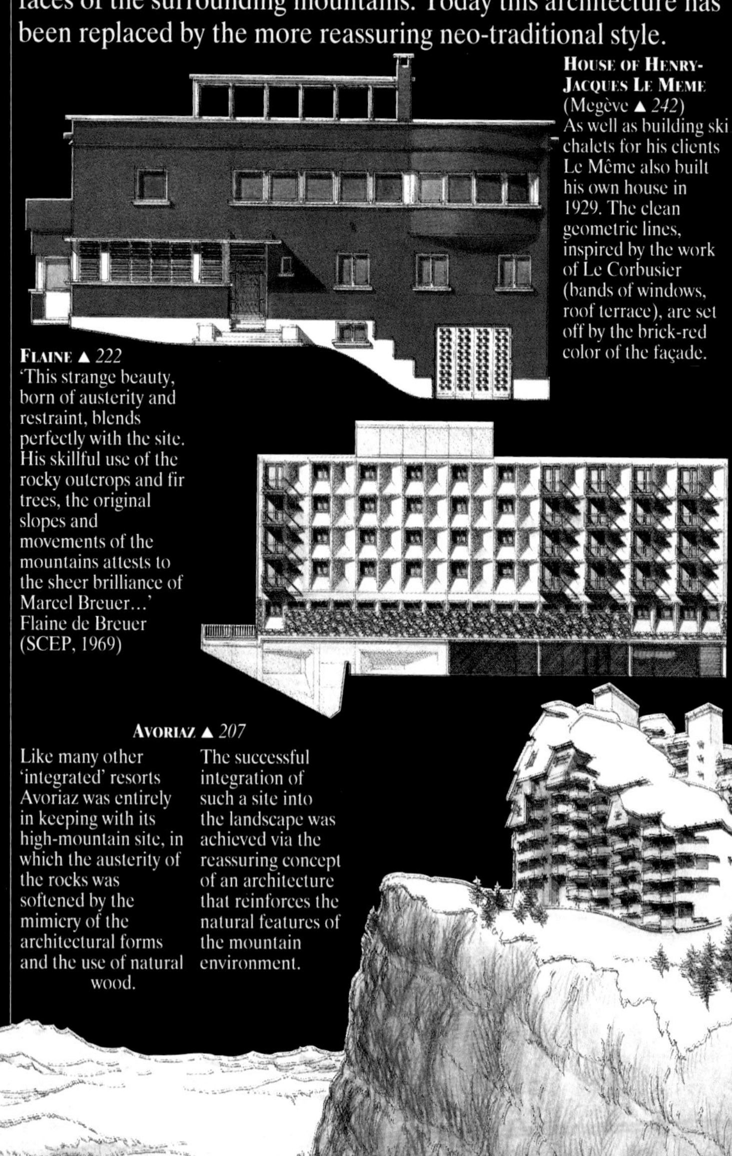

HOUSE OF HENRY-JACQUES LE MEME (Megève ▲ *242*)
As well as building ski chalets for his clients Le Même also built his own house in 1929. The clean geometric lines, inspired by the work of Le Corbusier (bands of windows, roof terrace), are set off by the brick-red color of the façade.

FLAINE ▲ *222*
'This strange beauty, born of austerity and restraint, blends perfectly with the site. His skillful use of the rocky outcrops and fir trees, the original slopes and movements of the mountains attests to the sheer brilliance of Marcel Breuer...'
Flaine de Breuer (SCEP, 1969)

AVORIAZ ▲ *207*
Like many other 'integrated' resorts Avoriaz was entirely in keeping with its high-mountain site, in which the austerity of the rocks was softened by the mimicry of the architectural forms and the use of natural wood.

The successful integration of such a site into the landscape was achieved via the reassuring concept of an architecture that reinforces the natural features of the mountain environment.

Savoie as seen by painters

Alain Bexon

1 | 3
2

In 1444 **Konrad Witz** (1400–46) painted *La Pêche Miraculeuse* (the Miraculous Draught of Fishes) (**1**) for the retable of Saint Peter's Cathedral in Geneva. In this first pictorial representation of Lake Geneva and the Mont-Blanc Massif, the artist contrasts the imagery of the miracle with his realistic depiction of the landscape. In the 16th century, although Calvin permitted the representation of tangible subjects, the control of Geneva by the Protestants effectively cut off the principal source of public financing for art by banning commissions for religious works. The Genevan landscape school did not emerge until the 18th century (the School of Art was founded in 1751 and the Society of Fine Arts in 1776) but from the 18th to the 20th centuries, Genevan artists visited Savoie on a regular basis. For a number of years the Château de Duingt, on the shores of the Lac d'Annecy, was their rallying point. Prosper Dunant (1790–1878), a native of Annecy, was one of the first to convey the poetry of sunlight on the lake. Firmin Salabert (1811–95), Dunant's son-in-law and a pupil of Ingres, portrayed it with great subtlety, while Pierre Alexandre Janniot (1826–92) captured its majesty by the skillful use of contrasting planes. In July 1896 **Paul Cézanne** (1839–1906) was staying at Talloires ▲ *176*. He 'did some painting to amuse himself' and produced several watercolors. In *Le Lac d'Annecy: le château de Duingt vu de Talloires* (**2**), he tried to capture the light and color that played around the 'little lake' by using alternate warm and cold colors for light and shade. Acutely aware of the curves, ridges and mountains, he developed a new language – the language of geometrically simplified shapes – to reflect their basic structure. In so doing he developed the precursor of Cubism. From the Swiss shores of Lake Geneva artists such as the Bernese painter **Ferdinand Hodler** (1853–1918) often painted the Alps of Savoie. Hodler, who portrayed the history of Switzerland in a realistic, energetic style that placed emphasis on symbolism, learned to apply the principles of geometry to art (parallelism, symmetry, rhythm) from his Genevan master Barthélemy Menn. A few months before his death Hodler, confined to his room overlooking Lake Geneva, painted fifteen or so versions of the view from his window (**3**). Through the simplicity of his composition and his strongly evocative use of color he 'takes his landscapes to the brink of abstraction' (Guido Magnaguagno) and foreshadows some of the characteristics of the German expressionists: broad planes, an intensity of flat color and a Pantheistic view of nature.

'Annecy is such a beautiful place, this verdant, remote region with its own lake, surrounded by cool orchards, high valleys and summits within easy reach!'

Rodolphe Töpffer

'Lake! Silent rocks! Caves! Dark forests!
Unscathed or regenerated by time,
Beauteous Nature, remember, and keep at least the
memory of this night alive!'

Lamartine

In 1818 Charles Humbert Despine, founder and director of the baths at Aix-les-Bains, decided to publish an annotated book of the principal views of the Lac du Bourget, drawn and engraved by **Prosper Dunant** (1790–1878) from watercolors painted between 1812 and 1817 (**1**): 'Since several foreign visitors have expressed their regret at only being able to take away a vague memory of this agreeable, enchanting and unspoiled region, a young artist had the idea of producing a collection of various series of etchings and lithographs.' Influenced by the Swiss *vedutisti*, who received a classical training and produced a great many color prints, Savoyard and foreign artists searched constantly for ideal combinations of composition, color and light in order to produce sensitively and realistically painted landscapes. Union with France ● *44* promoted tourism in the new *département* of Savoie and the more remarkable sites were illustrated in the lithographs of a work entitled: *Nice et Savoie.* The artist **Jacques Morion** (1863–1904) chose the Lac du Bourget and its surroundings as his principle subject: *Fin d'été en Savoie. Après-midi au lac du Bourget* (**2**). Although Corot did not paint in southern Savoie, **François Cachoud** (1863–1904) was a sort of nocturnal Corot, a past master in the art of painting the effects of moonlight, without however neglecting daylight (**3**). When **Louis-Eugène Ginain** (1818–86) – an artist more usually associated with violent cavalry charges – stayed in Aix, he was captivated by the peace and serenity of the lake (**4**).

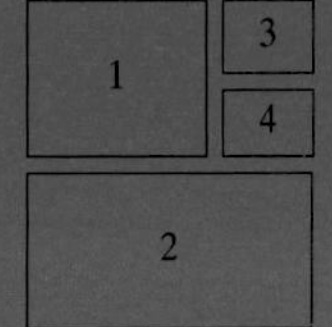

Mountains were generally considered to be magnificent and overpowering, and initially tended to provide the backdrop for landscape paintings. However, over the years, they gradually began to play a leading role. As the school of modern landscape painting founded at Barbizon became closely associated with Romanticism, the resonance of the atmosphere merged with successive planes of mountains and valleys. In the 18th century artists from northern Europe, especially England, were fascinated by the Alps. The great British artist **Joseph Mallord William Turner** (1775–1851), whose perception and representation of landscapes embodied the movement from Romanticism toward pre-Impressionism, returned continually to Savoie to paint the grandiose presence of the Alps. Caught in a storm on his way to Italy, *Snowstorm on Mont Cenis* (**1**) conveys the extraordinary intensity of light in a masterly depiction of the violence and fury of the elements. Long after the artists of the Swiss school, alpinist-painters took to the mountain paths of the Maurienne and Tarentaise regions. A new trend in the history of local art was founded by artists such as Gabriel Loppé; Eugène Viollet-le-Duc; Paul Cabaud; Firmin Salabert (the pupil of Ingres); and, in the 20th century, Joseph Communal, Francis Carrifa, Lucien Poignant, **Jean Bugnard** (1880–1947) – a native of Chambéry who was strongly attached to Le Bourget, the Tarentaise and the Maurienne (*Chapelle sous la neige*, **2**) – and **Frédéric Sauvignier** (1864–1950) (*Paysage de montagne*, **3**). The mountains became a subject in their own right. Artists abandoned the smoothness produced by the brush in favor of the more striking representations of the harshness of rocks and the crevasses of glaciers that could be achieved by using a knife. In the solitude of the high mountains they tried to capture moments of great emotion on the paper, canvas and plywood transported by mule.

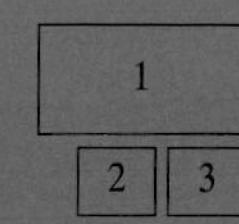

'It is always a piece of good fortune for those traveling on foot when they have to cross these mountains, where walking is so easy and free, and the spectacles so varied and beautiful.'

R. Töpffer

In the 18th century Bernese artists produced admirable *vedute* of glaciers and waterfalls, and the English discovered Chamonix. Then Mont Blanc began to attract a great many artists, including the Genevan painter **PIERRE LOUIS DE LA RIVE** (1753–1817). When he painted the 'roof of Europe' in all its splendor (1802, **1**) it was the first time Mont Blanc had been the principle subject of a major work. Minor artists from all over Europe published a great many 'commercial' prints of the valley of Mont Blanc. At the other end of the scale, in his *Mer de Glace* (1860, **2**), the painter and art historian **JOHN RUSKIN** (1819–1900) presents the idea that the artist must believe in what his eye really sees. Gabriel Loppé (1825–1913) was a real alpinist-painter who devoted himself to painting the high mountains. In his *Sunset* (1906, **3**) **WENZEL HABLIK** (1881–1934), a pupil of the Prague academy, portrayed Mont Blanc in brilliant colors rendered fragile by the ephemeral rays of the setting sun. The watercolors of Samivel (1907–92) are dominated by every shade of blue and white in an interplay of simple lines that combine the lyricism and delicacy of the brush strokes.

1

2

3

1

2

The paintings of Lake Geneva by **FRANÇOIS BOCION** (1828–90), a native of Lausanne, were imbued with a sublime serenity. He also painted views of interiors in the surrounding villages: *Yvoire, scène villageoise* (**2**). Eugène Burgat-Charvillon (1844–1911) was born in Manigod and portrayed scenes from the rural life he had known before his Parisian exile. His *Sortie de la mariée* ● *53* attests to the skill and realism of his work. The pencils, brushes and etcher's needles of Annecy-born **ANDRÉ-CHARLES COPPIER** (1866–1948) (*Femmes de Savoie*, **1**) and the Parisian artist André Jacques (1880–1962) often depicted the proud expressions of women from the Tarentaise and Maurienne regions. The English artist **ESTELLA CANZIANI** (1887–1967) captured the customs of the people from the valleys of Savoie with great accuracy.

Savoie
as seen by writers

THE SAVOYARD IDENTITY

In the 18th and 19th centuries, the magnificence of the Savoy attracted many travelers from the educated classes and literary society – who often made rather individual comments and observations about its towns and their people. Among them were Lady Mary Wortley Montagu (1689–1762), whose erudite and amusing letters home have assured her a place in literary history, the surgeon John Moore (1729–1803), who published an account of his travels in Europe, Edward Gibbon (1737–94), who finished his Decline and Fall of the Roman Empire *in Lausanne, the eccentric novelist and travel writer William Beckford (1759–1844), and the journalist, critic and essayist William Hazlitt (1778–1830), who left for Europe in 1824 with his fortunes at a low ebb.*

“Why suicide is more frequent in Great Britain and Geneva than elsewhere, would be a matter of curious investigation. For it appears very extraordinary, that men should be most inclined to kill themselves in countries where the blessings of life are best secured. These must be some strong and peculiar cause for an effect so preposterous. Before coming here, I was of the opinion that the frequency of suicide in England was occasioned in great measure by the stormy and unequal climate, which, while it clouds the sky, throws also a gloom over the minds of the natives. – To this cause, foreigners generally add, that of the use of coal, instead of wood, for fuel… But neither can account for the same effect at Geneva.”

JOHN MOORE, *A VIEW OF SOCIETY AND MANNERS IN ITALY, SWITZERLAND, GERMANY, ETC.*, 1779

GENEVA

“This Place is exactly like an English Country Town, the Prospects very pretty to any Eye that had not seen Naples or Genoa. This little Republic has an air of the Simplicity of Old Rome in its earliest Age. The Magistrates toil with their own Hands, and their Wives litterally dress their Dinners against their return from their little Senate. Yet without dress or Equipage, 'tis as dear living here for a stranger as in Places where one is oblig'ed to both, from the price of all sort of provision, which they are forc'd to buy from their Neighbours, having almost no Land of their own.”

LADY MARY WORTLEY MONTAGU, *LETTERS TO HER HUSBAND, OCTOBER/NOVEMBER 1741*

CHAMBERY

“You know this town is very old and ill built, but is wholly inhabited by the poor Savoyard Nobility, who are very well bred and extremely carressing to strangers.

Here is the most profound peace and unbounded plenty, that is to be found in any corner of the universe; but not one rag of money.”

(*TO LADY POMFRET, DECEMBER 3*)

AIX-LES-BAINS

“...Arrived in Aix in Savoy, famous for its baths; which, as disagreeable things are generally the most salutary, ought, doubtless, to be of the greatest efficacy; for more uninviting objects one seldom meets with.

Advancing beneath a little eminence, partly rock, partly wall, we discovered the principal bath, filled with a blue reeking water, whose very stream is sufficient to seethe one, without further assistance.”

WILLIAM BECKFORD, *AN EXCURSION TO THE GRANDE CHARTREUSE IN 1778*

LAUSANNES

“My passion for my wife or mistress (Fanny Lausanne) is not palled by satiety and possession of two years. I have seen her in all seasons and in all humours, and though she is not without faults, they are infinitely overbalanced by her good qualities. Her face is not handsome, but her person and everything about her has admirable grace and beauty; she is of a very cheerful and sociable temper, without much learning she is endowed with taste and good-sense, and though not rich the simplicity of her education makes her a very good economist; she is forbid by her parents to wear any expensive finery, and though her limbs are not much calculated for walking, she has not yet asked me to keep her a Coach.

The only disagreeable circumstance is the increase of a race of animals with which this country has been long infested, and who are said to come from an island in the Nothern Ocean.”

EDWARD GIBBON, *LETTER TO LORD SHEFFIELD,* OCTOBER 1 1765

THE MAGNIFICENCE OF THE MOUNTAINS

THE EDGE OF FEAR

Jean-Jacques Rousseau (1712–78), one of the dominant writers and thinkers of the age and a forerunner of Romanticism, was born in Geneva. The mountain scenery of the Savoy had a huge effect on him, as he spent his some of his most formative years (1728–41) first at Annecy and then at Chambéry. His autobiographical work Confessions, *an exercise in self-justification and self-analysis, was published after his death.*

"In telling the story of my travels, as in travelling itself, I never know how to stop. My heart throbbed with joy as I drew near to my dear Mamma, but I did not go any the quicker for that. I like to walk at my leisure, and halt when I please. The wandering life is what I like. To journey on foot, unhurried, in fine weather and in fine country, and to have something pleasant to look forward to at my goal, that is of all ways of life the one that suits me best … I need torrents, rocks, firs, dark woods, mountains, steep roads to climb or descend, abysses beside me to make me afraid. I had these pleasures, and I relished them to the full, as I came near to Chambéry. At a place called Chailles, not far from a precipitous mountain wall called the Pas de l'Échelle, there runs boiling through hideous gulfs below the high road – which is cut into the rock – a little river which would appear to have spent thousands of centuries excavating its bed. The road has been edged with a parapet to prevent accidents, and so I was able to gaze into the depths and make myself as giddy as I pleased. For the amusing thing about my taste for precipitous places is that they make my head spin; and I am very fond of this giddy feeling so long as I am in safety. Supporting myself firmly on the parapet, I craned forward and stayed there for hours on end, glancing every now and then at the foam and the blue water, whose roaring came to me amidst the screams of the ravens and birds of prey which flew from rock to rock and from bush to bush, a hundred fathoms below me. At those spots where the slope was fairly smooth, and the bushes thin enough to allow of stones bouncing through, I collected some of the biggest I could carry from a little way off and piled them up on the parapet. Then I threw them down, one after another, and enjoyed watching them roll, rebound, and shiver into a thousand pieces before they reached the bottom of the abyss.

Nearer to Chambéry, I saw a similar sight, though from an opposite angle. The road passes the foot of the finest waterfall I have seen in all my life. The mountain is so sheer that the water springs away and falls in an arc wide enough for a man to walk between the falls and the rock-face, sometimes without getting damp. But unless one is careful one can easily make a mistake, as I did. For, because of its immense height, the water breaks and falls in a spray; and if one goes a little too near without at first noticing that one is getting wet, one is soaked in a moment."

JEAN-JACQUES ROUSSEAU, *CONFESSIONS, BOOK FOUR* (1732), PENGUIN 1953

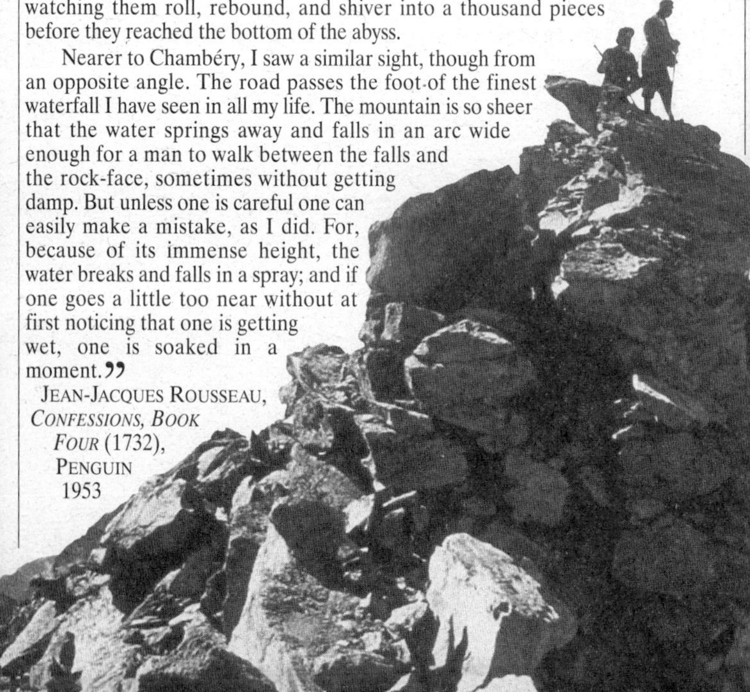

Scaling the heights

On the return journey from his long visit to Italy in 1845, Charles Dickens (1812–70) crossed the Alps, and was struck by the seductive beauty of the mountain scenery. One year later, he returned to Chamonix, and he described his experience of the mountains in a letter to his friend James Forster.

“Going by that Col de Balme pass, you climb up and up and up for five hours and more, and look – from a mere unguarded ledge of path on the side of the precipice – into such awful valleys, that at last you are firm in the belief that you have got above everything in the world, and that there can be nothing earthly overhead. Just as you arrive at this conclusion, a different (and oh Heaven! what a free and wonderful) air comes blowing on your face; you cross a ridge of snow; and lying before you (wholly unseen till then), towering up into the distant sky, is the vast range of Mont Blanc, with attendant mountains diminished by its majestic side into mere dwarfs tapering up into innumerable rude Gothic pinnacles; deserts of ice and snow; forests of firs on mountain sides, of no account at all in the enormous scene; villages down in the hollow, that you can shut out with a finger; waterfalls, avalanches, pyramids and towers of ice, torrents, bridges; mountain upon mountain until the very sky is blocked away, and you must look up, overhead, to see it. Good God, what a country Switzerland is, and what a concentration of it is to be beheld from that one spot!”

Charles Dickens, *Letter, August 2 1846, in Forster, Life of Dickens, 1872–3*

Savoyard flora and fauna

Nature sublime, nature grotesque

In 1608 Thomas Coryat (1577–1617) traveled through France, Italy and Northern Europe, mostly on foot. He was known for his eccentric and amusing character, and became an almost legendary figure in his own lifetime. In 1611 he published the stories of his travels as Coryat’s Crudities.

“The worst wayes that ever I travelled in all my life in the Sommer were those betwixt Chamberie and Aiguebelle, which were as bad as the worst I ever rode in England in the midst of Winter: insomuch that the wayes of Savoy may be proverbially spoken of as the Owles of Athens, the peares of Calabria, and the Quailes of Delos... On every Alpe I saw wonderfull abundance of pine trees, especially about the toppe, and many of them of a very great height; and betwixt the toppe and the foote there are in many of those mountains wilde Olive-trees, Chestnut-trees, Walnut-trees, Beeches, Hasel-trees, &c. The whole side of many a hill being replenished with all these sorts of trees... The countrey of Savoy is very cold, and much subject to raine, by reason of those clouds, that are continually hovering about the Alpes, which being the receptacles of raine do there more distill their moisture, then in other countries.

I observed an admirable abundance of Butter-files in many places of Savoy, by the hundred part more then ever I saw in any countrey before, whereof many great swarmes, which were, (according to my estimation and coniecture) at the least two thousand, lay dead upon the high waies as we travelled. When I came to Aiguebelle I saw the effect of the common drinking of snow water in Savoy. For there I saw many men and women have exceeding great bunches or swellings in their throates, such as we call in latin strumas, as bigge as the fistes of a man, through the drinking of snow water, yea some of their bunches are almost as great as an ordinary foot-ball with us in England. These swellings are much to be seen amongst these Savoyards, neither are all the Pedemontanes free from them.”

Thomas Coryat, *Crudities*, 1611

SUBLIME INSPIRATION

The Romantic movement developed out of the 18th-century fashion for the Picturesque, with its scenic descriptions and new esthetic values that embraced roughness and irregularity. Romanticism was rooted in contemporary ideas of the Sublime – with its associations of enormity, the magnificence of nature, awe, solitude, and terror – as the ultimate source of strong emotion and imaginative stimulus. For the poet seeking inspiration, the Savoy was an obvious destination.

'STILL AND SOLEMN POWER'

Percy Bysshe Shelley (1792–1822) led a dramatic and often traumatic life. Leaving his history of controversy, outrage and personal strife behind him in Britain, Shelley spent the summer of 1816 on Lake Geneva with Lord Byron. Here he wrote two philosophical poems, 'Hymn to Intellectual Beauty' and 'Mont Blanc', a meditation of the nature of power in a godless universe.

“Mont Blanc yet gleams on high: the power is there
The still and solemn power of many sights
And many sounds, and much of life and death.
In the calm darkness of the moonless nights,
In the long glare of day, the snows descend
Upon that Mountain; none beholds them there,
Nor when the flakes burn in the sinking sun,
Or the starbeams dart through them: – Winds contend
Silently there, and heap the snow with breath
Rapid and strong, but silently! Its home
The voiceless lightning in these solitudes
Keeps innocently, and like vapour broods
Over the snow. The secret strength of things
Which governs thought, and to the infinite dome
Of heaven is as a law, inhabits thee!
And what were thou, and earth, and stars, and sea,
If to the human mind's imaginings
Silence and solitude were vacancy.”

PERCY BYSSHE SHELLEY, *'MONT BLANC, LINES WRITTEN IN THE VALE OF CHAMOUNI'* (JUNE 23, 1816), WORDSWORTH EDITIONS 1994

CHAMONIX

William Wordsworth (1770–1850), whose friendship with Coleridge was partly based on their mutual love of hillwalking, went on a walking tour of the Alps in 1790, returning to France for another year in 1791. Two years later, he published 'Descriptive Sketches', containing predictably picturesque descriptions of the alpine landscapes.

“Last, let us turn to Chamouny that shields
With rocks and gloomy woods her fertile fields:
Five streams of ice amid her cots descend,
And with wild flowers, and blooming orchards blend; –
A scene more fair than what the Grecian feigns
Of purple lights and ever-vernal plains;
Here all the seasons revel hand in hand:
'Mid lawns and shades by breezy rivulets fanned,
They sport beneath that mountain's matchless height
From age to age, throughout his lonely bounds
The crash of ruin fitfully resounds;
Appalling havoc! but serene his brow,
Where daylight lingers on perpetual snow;
Glitter the stars above, and all is black below.”

WILLIAM WORDSWORTH, *DESCRIPTIVE SKETCHES* (1791–2), WORDSWORTH EDITIONS, 1994

'O DREAD AND SILENT MOUNT!'

It has been said of Samuel Taylor Coleridge (1772–1834) that his best works possessed 'the inescapable glow of the authentic visionary'. Despite this, however, his personal life was never easy, and he was constantly beset by difficult relationships and bouts of depression, while his addiction to opium grew ever stronger. In the early years of the new century he made many trips abroad in an attempt to restore his health and remake his career.

"Hast thou a charm to stay the morning-star
In his steep course? So long he seems to pause
On thy bald awful head, O sovran BLANC.
The Arve and Arveiron at thy base
Rave ceaselessly; but thou, most awful Form!
Risest from forth thy silent sea of pines,
How silently! Around thee and above
Deep is the air and dark, substantial, black,
An ebon mass: methinks thou piercest it,
As with a wedge! But when I look again,
It is thine own calm home, thy crystal shrine,
Thy habitation from eternity!

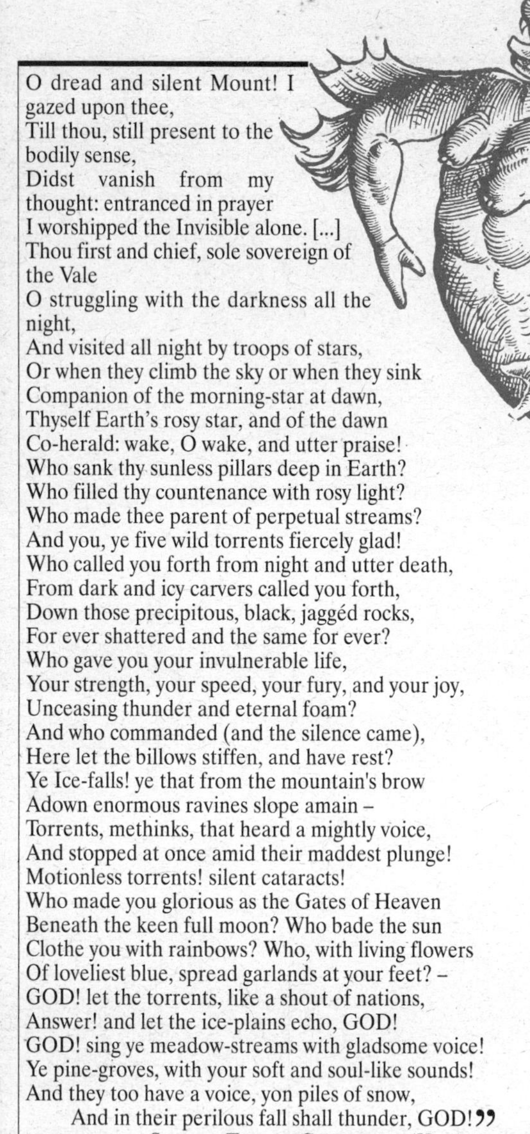

O dread and silent Mount! I gazed upon thee,
Till thou, still present to the bodily sense,
Didst vanish from my thought: entranced in prayer
I worshipped the Invisible alone. [...]
Thou first and chief, sole sovereign of the Vale
O struggling with the darkness all the night,
And visited all night by troops of stars,
Or when they climb the sky or when they sink
Companion of the morning-star at dawn,
Thyself Earth's rosy star, and of the dawn
Co-herald: wake, O wake, and utter praise!
Who sank thy sunless pillars deep in Earth?
Who filled thy countenance with rosy light?
Who made thee parent of perpetual streams?
And you, ye five wild torrents fiercely glad!
Who called you forth from night and utter death,
From dark and icy carvers called you forth,
Down those precipitous, black, jaggéd rocks,
For ever shattered and the same for ever?
Who gave you your invulnerable life,
Your strength, your speed, your fury, and your joy,
Unceasing thunder and eternal foam?
And who commanded (and the silence came),
Here let the billows stiffen, and have rest?
Ye Ice-falls! ye that from the mountain's brow
Adown enormous ravines slope amain –
Torrents, methinks, that heard a mightly voice,
And stopped at once amid their maddest plunge!
Motionless torrents! silent cataracts!
Who made you glorious as the Gates of Heaven
Beneath the keen full moon? Who bade the sun
Clothe you with rainbows? Who, with living flowers
Of loveliest blue, spread garlands at your feet? –
GOD! let the torrents, like a shout of nations,
Answer! and let the ice-plains echo, GOD!
GOD! sing ye meadow-streams with gladsome voice!
Ye pine-groves, with your soft and soul-like sounds!
And they too have a voice, yon piles of snow,
And in their perilous fall shall thunder, GOD!”

SAMUEL TAYLOR COLERIDGE, *'HYMN BEFORE SUNRISE IN THE VALE OF CHAMOUNI' (1802)*, OXFORD, 1925

▲ Châtillon on the Lac du Bourget.
Abbaye Royale de Hautecombe.▼
▼ Boats on the Lac d'Annecy.

▲ Lac Saint-André with Mont Granier in the distance. Lac de Roy on the Roc d'Enfer.▼

▼ Lac Guichard and the Aiguilles d'Arves.

▲ Summit of Mont Blanc. Aiguille du Plan. ▼

Arête Kufner on Mont Maudit.▼

▲ The Grand Chatelard and the Dent Parrachée.

Dent du Géant. ▼

▼ Mountain pastures near Valloire.

Arête du Midi; the Grandes Jorasses in the distance.▶

Chambéry, gateway to the Alps

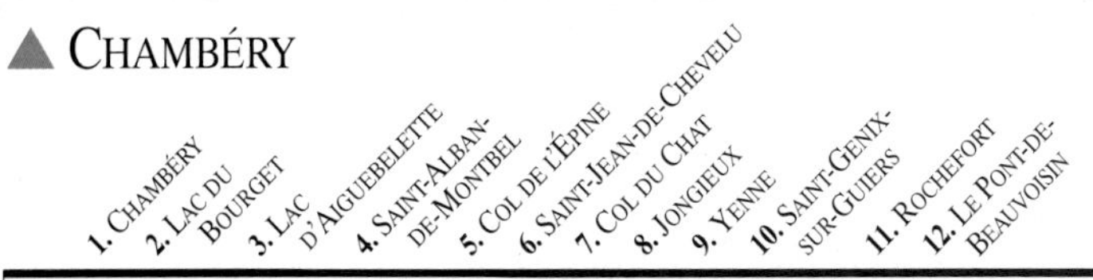

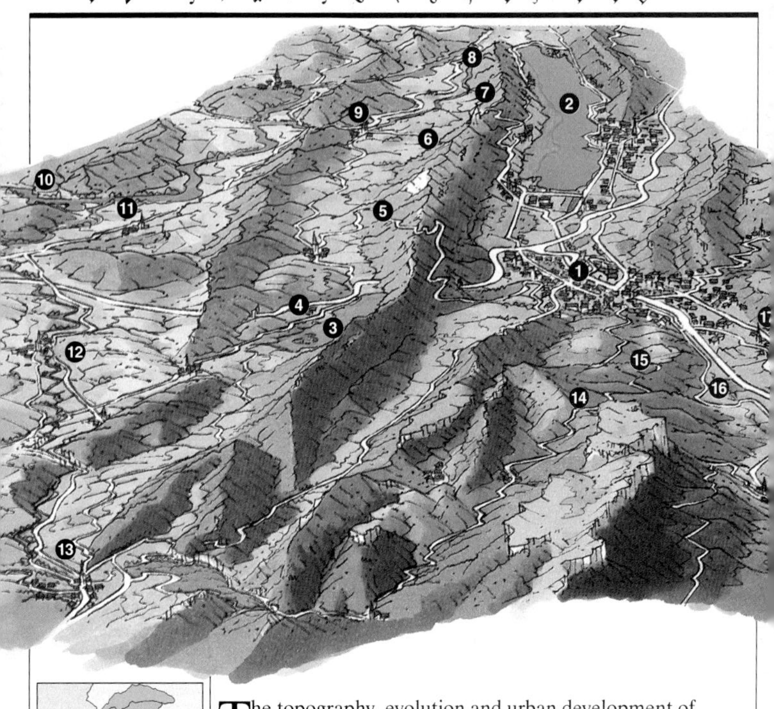

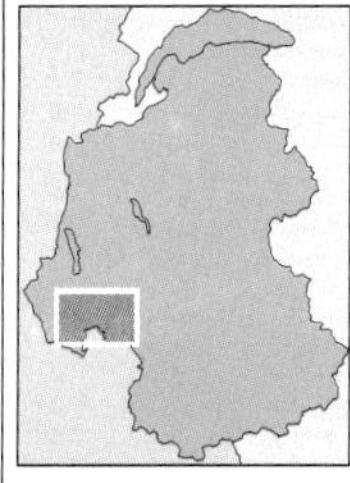

TRADITION AND MODERNITY
Modern Chambéry has caught the attention of the wider world. It is the venue of many conferences and major national and international events, including trade fairs and conferences, literary and film festivals, as well as an international festival of mountain life. However Chambéry also carefully preserves its unique historic and cultural heritage. The town has an aristocratic elegance and a rare sense of the art of good living.

The topography, evolution and urban development of Chambéry has largely been determined by the presence of water. For eons water lay in the bottom of the *cluse* (deep gorge) that was formed by glaciers during the Quaternary period and where the modern town now lies. In the 1st century the stagnant water and marshland in the bottom of the gorge forced the Romans to choose a hill (*Lemincum*) as the site of the town on the road linking Milan and Vienne. In the 11th century the first lords of Chambéry also built their castles on high ground. When the buildings of the agglomeration began to encroach on the marshland the architects resorted to constructing them on larch piles. The remains of these piles were later discovered immersed in the underground water that lies just below the subsoil of the old part of the town. Over the centuries life in Chambéry was punctuated by floods and the underground water would often rise above the surface. For a long time flooding was caused by the Leysse and Albanne rivers, which flowed through the town and burst their banks at fairly regular intervals. After the great flood of 1551 the municipal authorities, weary of seeing their town under constant threat from flooding, levied a tax on the population to finance the damming of the two rivers. This vast undertaking continued until the end of the 16th century and weighed heavily on the municipal treasury. Even so the townspeople still lived in fear of the floods. The great flood of 1875 (commemorated by plaques that are still to be seen at various points in the city center) was followed by the flood of 1910, which the town's oldest inhabitants can still remember. Since then major civil engineering works have brought the flooding under control, though it nevertheless remains the major natural threat to

13. Les Échelles
14. Col du Granier
15. Apremont
16. Myans
17. Challes-les-Eaux
18. Chignin
19. Montmélian
20. Arbin
21. Saint-Pierre-d'Albigny
22. Miolans
23. Col de Tamié

Chambéry, the historic capital of Savoie. However Chambéry's relationship with water has not been entirely negative. Throughout its history the town has always been attracted by

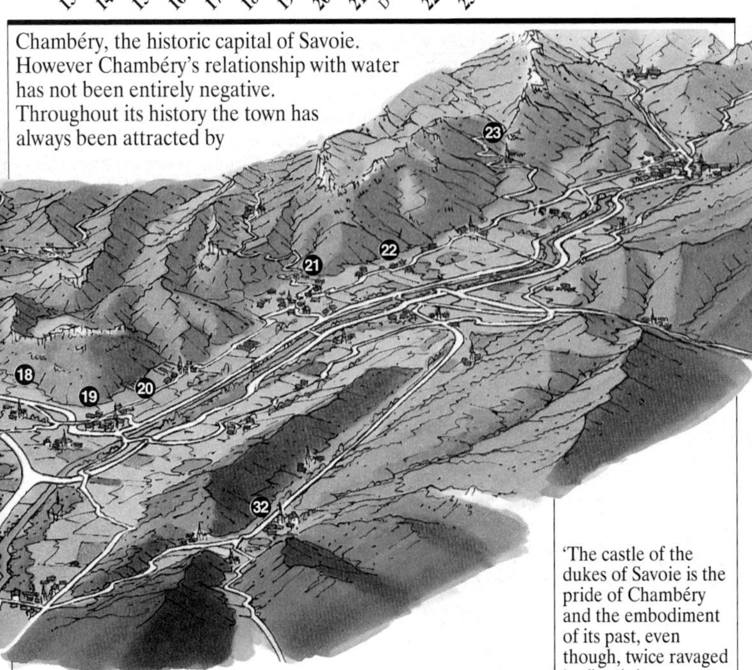

the Lac du Bourget. It is on the shores of this lake that the faculties and research laboratories of this university town are laid out. Chambéry proudly retains the memory of its former status as capital of the states of Savoie, and its long-term prosperity lies in its cultural heritage and tourist potential. The Lac du Bourget is not the only natural attraction that Chambéry has to offer; the town's geographical location means that it is within easy reach of three important and extensive nature reserves – the Parc National de la Vanoise ▲ *264*, Parc Naturel Régional de Chartreuse ▲ *134* and the Parc Naturel Régional du Massif des Bauges ▲ *152*, the latter forming a natural promontory between the Combe de Savoie and the basin of the Lac d'Annecy ▲ *160*.

Castle of the dukes of Savoie

The castle was the former residence of the counts and dukes of Savoie. It was they who decided to make the modest town of the lords of Chambéry the capital of the states of Savoie. Their possessions extended to what is today Suisse Romande (French Switzerland), Bresse, Piedmont (with the exception of an open corridor) and Nice, on the Mediterranean. All traffic across of the Alps had to pass inexorably through their territory, and this was how they became the much-envied 'gatekeepers' of the Alps. Up until 1562 their castle in Chambéry was the center of an economic, diplomatic and military power that was well respected in medieval and Renaissance Europe. The ghosts of these noble members of the House of Savoie can almost be sensed in the buildings that surround the Place du Château, rather like the scenery of a timeless stage.

'The castle of the dukes of Savoie is the pride of Chambéry and the embodiment of its past, even though, twice ravaged by fire, it is no more than a shadow of the old monument, part palace, part fortress, that once dominated the town. However, the Tour des Archives, the Sainte-Chapelle and the long building of the Chambre des Comptes are still impressive enough to fire the imagination.' (Henry Bordeaux)

PLACE DU CHATEAU. The buildings on the square are framed by two towers. On the right stands the massive TOUR TRÉSORERIE, its lower section pierced by loopholes. These are a legacy of the reign of Amadeus VI, the legendary Green Count, so named after the colors that adorned his cuirass during tournaments. The Tour des Archives and watchtower, on the left, were built by Count Amadeus V in the 15th century. The tower's grilled windows attest to the fact that it served as a prison during the count's reign. In the center is the façade of the residential wing of the Chambre des Comptes (Audit Office), once surmounted by four monumental gable windows, of which only two remain. When Duke Emmanuel-Philbert transferred his capital to Turin in 1563, he insisted on keeping this major government institution in Chambéry. Separated from this building by a small courtyard is the SAINTE-CHAPELLE (*left*), whose apse is a fine example of early-15th-century Gothic architecture. The apse, in the Flamboyant Gothic style, was commissioned by Amadeus VII, the last count and first duke of Savoie, shortly before he became Pope Felix V. Its high wall, pierced by elegant stained-glass windows set above the level of the surrounding rooftops, stands as a reminder of the duke's wish that this religious building should not compromise the security of the square's fortifications.

INTERIOR COURTYARD. The courtyard is reached via a ramp bounded by tall buildings that have been renovated over the centuries. Since the 17th century access to the Bâtiment de la Porterie, on the left, has been via a broad, straight flight of steps preceded by four arcades supported by wooden pillars. The gateway opposite – surmounted by a stone framework containing the vestiges of a salamander painted at the time of the town's occupation under François I (r. 1515–47) – leads to the rooms of the former Chambre

des Comptes. A surprise lies in store beyond the ancient portcullis gateway: the architecture of the ducal age has been replaced by a building whose style and layout very obviously date it to the 19th century. When Savoie became part of France in 1860 ● 44 the French government chose this building as the seat of the *préfecture* (town council) and *conseil général* (departmental council) of Savoie. Two devastating fires, one in 1743 and another in 1798, destroyed the former ducal residence. All that remains of the building's prestigious past are the TOUR DEMI-RONDE (occupied since the 19th century by a monumental staircase that is open to the public), the upper section of the Tour Trésorerie, on the edge of the wooded grounds, and the Sainte-Chapelle, whose elaborate Baroque façade (*below*), designed by the Italian architect Castellamonte, provides a striking contrast with the apse.

The fire of 1798 (*top*), as depicted by Joseph Masotti, a draftsman in the office of the chief civil engineer in Chambéry, and the monumental staircase inside the Tour Demi-Ronde (*above*).

SAINTE-CHAPELLE. Access to the building is via a small courtyard that lies to the right of the parvis. The *trompe-l'oeil* ceiling frescos, painted in 1836 by the Piedmontese artist Casimir Vicario, are remarkable for their technical skill (*opposite page, left*). In the course of restoration work carried out between 1958 and 1960, the walls and fittings were stripped to expose the fire damage of 1532, which had subsequently been concealed by the application of colored renderings. The stained-glass windows, most of which were installed after the fire, combine influences from the Italian Renaissance and from German and Flemish art. The many representations of scenes from the Passion of Christ are a reminder that the Holy Shroud, acquired by the House of Savoie in 1453, was deposited here in 1502. The presence of the holy relic transformed the royal chapel into a major centre of European pilgrimage and brought the town unexpected economic prosperity. To the great disappointment of the people of Chambéry this came to an end in 1578, when the shroud was transferred to Turin. The departure of the court to Turin also marked the end of the royal ceremonies that had punctuated the life of the chapel. Among some of the most memorable were the marriages of Duke Charles-Emmanuel of Savoie to Clotilde of France, sister of Louis XVI, in 1775, and of the French romantic poet Alphonse de Lamartine to his English wife Maria Ann Birch, in June 1820.

CARILLON OF THE SAINTE-CHAPELLE
The carillon of the 1937 World Fair was among Chambéry's proudest acquisition. In keeping with the town's position in the field of campanology, the carillon was replaced by a modern peal of seventy bells, complete with the latest technical refinements. The new peal, installed in the Tour Yolande in 1993, is the second largest in Europe.

The alleyways of the old town.

A CHURCH ON 30,000 FOUNDATION PILES
When the Franciscans built their church in the early 15th century, they had to take into account the instability of the terrain, which consisted of mud overlain with a thin layer of permeable soil. Traditional foundations would have been inadequate; instead they used 30,000 larch piles, which they sank into the mud, to support and stabilize the building's foundations. Two of these rustic piles can be seen in the cathedral treasure.

IN THE FOOTSTEPS OF JEAN-JACQUES ROUSSEAU

'If there is one place in the world where one can enjoy the sweetness of life in agreeable and friendly society, it is the little town of Chambéry.' This description, in Book V of the *Confessions* by the French philosopher and writer Jean-Jacques Rousseau (1712–78), illustrates the importance of his stay in the capital of Savoie. He came to Chambéry in 1731, to join Mme de Warens, the first love of his life ▲ *130*. The woman he called 'Mamma' gave him food, shelter and more besides. She also used her influence to obtain for him a position in the local surveyor's office. However, the young man hated the administrative work and decided instead to teach music to the young ladies of Chambéry's polite society.
OLD CHAMBÉRY. On the right of the steps leading down from the foot of the castle to the Place Maché is the Rue Trésorerie. At no. 10 is the 15th-century vaulted store with stone moldings, the former *Épicerie Lard*, where Rousseau found a café-crème waiting for him each morning when he came to teach Péronne, the grocer's daughter, whom he described as 'the true model of a Greek statue'. A little further on, on the left, the Rue Juiverie leads to two former private mansions. The Hôtel des Allinges (no. 104), badly damaged by two successive fires, still has the flight of steps on the right of the courtyard that were climbed in turn by General de Montesquiou, the prefect of the Mont-Blanc *département* and the magistrates of the Senate of Savoie who occupied the premises for a time. The arrangement of the interior façade of the Hôtel Chabod de Saint-Maurice, at no. 60, is a fine example of the type of architecture found in the town's old aristocratic residences. The alleyway leading to

The Hôtel Chabod de Saint-Maurice in the Rue Juiverie, and the Place Saint-Léger, the commercial center of the town.

no. 39, surmounted by a decorative metalwork tympanum, evokes the old Savoyard Morand family. In 1786 one of the daughters married the French writer and philosopher Joseph de Maistre, who was born in the nearby Place de Lans. As you leave the alleyway you come to the RUE BASSE-DU-CHATEAU which has barely changed since the days it constituted the most direct route to the royal palace. At that time it was virtually a covered way since it was crossed by a great many overhead passageways. The one remaining example illustrates how easily these passageways enabled fires to spread, the reason why they were demolished in the 18th century. The broad PLACE SAINT-LÉGER, on the left, is also haunted by memories of Rousseau. In 1735 the de Mellarède family lived at no. 120, behind the elegant façade of the 15th-century Maison Dieulefils. Their daughter, 'a most lively brunette, but tender in her liveliness which was graceful and never hoydenish', was one of his most devoted pupils. So too was Mlle de Challes, who lived at the far end of the passageway of no. 110, in the Hôtel Cordon, reached via a broad, exterior flight of steps at the back of the house. Jean-Jacques and Mme de Warens lived close by, in rooms on the top floor of the house of the Count of Saint-Laurent, which occupied the right-hand side of the courtyard. Back in the passageway a vaulted archway on the left leads, via another courtyard, to the Rue Métropole and the PLACE MÉTROPOLE, dominated by the sober façade of the cathedral. The austerity of the Franciscan architecture is reflected in the high nave whose starkness has not been tempered by its 19th-century *trompe-l'oeil* paintings. The cloister, which opens off the left-hand aisle of the church, offers a view of the old convent building which today houses the MUSÉE SAVOISIEN ▲ *126*. Here the memory of Rousseau is associated with that of Father Caton, who took every opportunity to leave the monastery for the comfort of Mme de Warens' drawing room. As you walk past the façade of the cathedral, you come to a narrow alleyway on the right; it leads to the central courtyard of a mansion occupied by another of Rousseau's confidants, François Joseph de Conzié, a highly cultured man, as evidenced by his library of some 2500 volumes. The alleyway leads to the RUE CROIX-D'OR, where there are several former aristocratic residences: the Hôtel de La Pérouse (no. 70), the Hôtel Castagnery de Châteauneuf, with its elegant 17th-century metalwork entrance (no. 18); the Hôtel de Bellegarde (no. 13), where such prestigious visitors as Pope Pius VII and Napoleon once stayed.

'The house that she lived in was dark and melancholy, and my room was the darkest and most melancholy in the whole house. A wall for a view, a blind alley instead of a street, little air, little light, little space, crickets, rats, rotten boards… But I was in Mamma's house, close beside her.'
Jean-Jacques Rousseau

SAVOYARD PRIMITIVES IN THE MUSÉE SAVOISIEN

Artistic activity flourished in Savoie in the 15th century. It was characterized by a style of painting resulting from various influences emanating from the flourishing European schools of painting, particularly the Flemish and German schools. Among the works from this period on display in the Musée Savoisien is a delicate *Annunciation*, a *Martyrdom of Saint Catherine* and a *Last Supper* attributed to Godefroy (1482).

The Musée Savoisien, housed in a former Franciscan convent, presents Savoie and its history through its collections of archeology, ethnology and works of art. The Musée des Beaux-Arts, which occupies a former corn exchange, acquired most of its collections during the 19th century in the form of donations from enlightened art lovers. It contains one of the richest collections of Italian paintings in France, including some exceptional 15th-, 16th- and 17th-century works. Other schools – for example, French Neoclassicist and Realist painting, and the German, Dutch and Flemish painting – are represented by works spanning the 16th to 18th centuries.

WALL PAINTINGS FROM CRUET
These polychrome murals, covering a panel 125 feet long, are one of the few examples of secular wall paintings dating from the early 14th century. The anonymous work, consisting of a series of scenes enclosed within a banded border, depicts chivalric deeds: combats, cavalcades, sieges and ceremonial events. The cycle, undoubtedly inspired by legends, historical chronicles and epics, decorated the great hall of the Château de la Rive, at Cruet.

DEPARTMENT OF ARCHEOLOGY, MUSÉE SAVOISIEN
The department's collections were formed largely as a result of excavations carried out around the Lac du Bourget in the 19th century. The excavations proved that the lakeside was inhabited some 3000 years ago, during the Bronze Age.

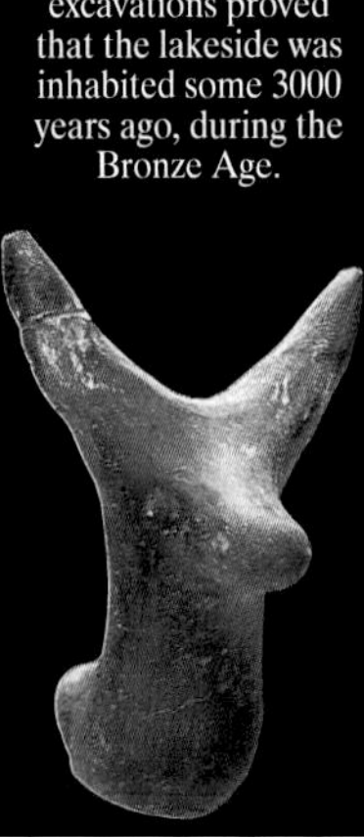

VENUS DE DÉTRIER
This beautiful bronze figure of Venus emerging from the waves dates from the Hellenistic period. It was found in a tomb at Détrier, near Pontcharra, and proves a Roman presence in the region, as does a coin with the head of Marcus Aurelius, struck in AD 163 and discovered nearby.

‘PORTRAIT OF A YOUNG MAN’
This exceptional portrait is traditionally attributed to Paolo Uccello (1397–1475). It can be regarded as one of the first examples of the ‘Florentine profile’ portrait, a genre that was clearly inspired by images on ancient coins. Although the identity of the subject is unknown, the strong depiction of the face, the use of light and the linear treatment of forms anticipate the techniques and style developed by Renaissance art.

‘ADORATION OF THE MAGI’, Jan van Dornicke (c. 1520)
As indicated by the inscriptions on the frame this panel originally formed part of triptych. The richness of detail, the treatment of the garments and the architecture of the idealized background reflect the sophistication of early Antwerp Mannerism.

‘THE ASTRONOMER’, Luca Giordano (c. 1655)
This Baroque work is one of a series of ‘philosophers’ (another can be seen in the Musée des Beaux-Arts). The low-angle perspective, the use of light and shade, the spiral of the composition and the use of large areas of flat color give the subject great dignity and a remarkable sense of presence.

‘TRIBUNAL DE BESSANS’ (19TH CENTURY)
The figures, costumes and attitudes of this local court scene are extremely realistic. The model, which turns a legal judgment into a work of art, conveys a sense of popular respect for justice combined with a fear of the law and its immediacy.

CHAMBÉRY IN THE MOVIES
The town's streets and buildings have attracted movie-makers. Movies shot in the town include *Les Roquevillard* (1943), *Mort où est ta victoire?* (Death, Where is Thy Victory?, 1964), *Allons z'enfants* (Children, Come On!, 1980) and *L'Effrontée* (An Impudent Girl, 1985).

'ON A VALLEY SLOPE' ▲ *130*
About 1½ miles along the road leading from Chambéry to the Col du Granier and Col de la Chartreuse lies the valley of Les Charmettes. It was here that Mme de Warens and Jean-Jacques Rousseau rented a country house in the late summer of 1735 and stayed until winter. At the time there were a great many of these solidly built country houses, surrounded by a piece of land with a kitchen garden, vines and fruit trees, on the outskirts of the town. The richer members of Chambéry society would rent them during the hot summer months.

COMTE DE BOIGNE, THE PATRON-GENERAL

THE PHILANTHROPIST. The rebuilding and renovation work carried out in Chambéry in the 1820s was financed by the son of a local hide merchant who had made his fortune in India. Benoît Leborgne (*above*), whose father's business was on the Place Saint-Léger, not only had a distinguished career in the Indian army but also amassed a comfortable fortune. He returned to Chambéry in 1802 and devoted a large part of his wealth to improving the lot of his fellow-citizens and foreign travelers. He built a hospital, an old people's home for the poor and for destitute '[persons] of standing who had fallen on hard times', a poor house and a school. Nothing escaped the attention of the munificent general, who took up residence on the Buisson-Rond estate, a 'little folly' on the edge of the suburbs of Montmélian (now a public park).

RUE DE BOIGNE. De Boigne's major work was the ambitious urban development project that he financed in 1824. It involved the construction of a broad, straight road through the built-up area, giving direct access to the castle ▲ *121* from the eastern end of the town. He graced the central section with Italianate porticos and, in so doing, gave the town's historic center new life. It is well worth taking a walk beneath these vaulted porticos, which won the acclaim of the French writer Stendhal and were once occupied by the the town's famous *chocolateries* whose specialties included the much sought-after *truffes de Savoie* (chocolate truffles). All that remains of these nostalgic times is the *pâtisserie* at no. 15 whose sign – *Au fidèle berger* – records the fact that it was established in 1832. At the far end of the Rue de Boigne stands a column flanked by four elephants (*left*). It is surmounted by a bronze statue of the heroic general, by the Grenoble sculptor Victor Sappey, erected by the people of Chambéry as a token of their gratitude.

FONTAINE DES ÉLÉPHANTS
The fountain's four elephants commemorate the Indian campaigns of General de Boigne (1751–1830). It is the town's best-known monument and is known locally as the 'Quatre sans cul' as the elephants have no rear end.

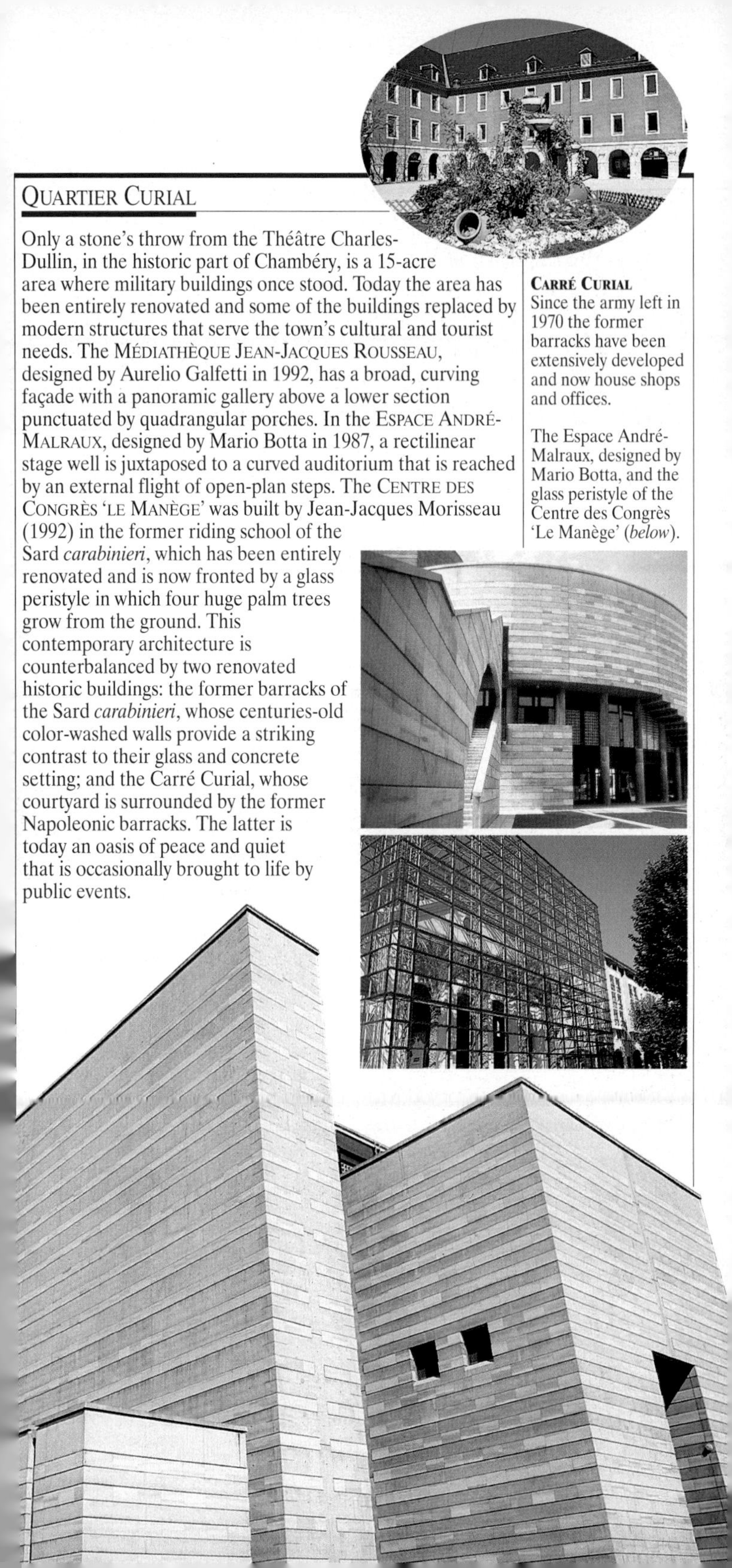

QUARTIER CURIAL

Only a stone's throw from the Théâtre Charles-Dullin, in the historic part of Chambéry, is a 15-acre area where military buildings once stood. Today the area has been entirely renovated and some of the buildings replaced by modern structures that serve the town's cultural and tourist needs. The MÉDIATHÈQUE JEAN-JACQUES ROUSSEAU, designed by Aurelio Galfetti in 1992, has a broad, curving façade with a panoramic gallery above a lower section punctuated by quadrangular porches. In the ESPACE ANDRÉ-MALRAUX, designed by Mario Botta in 1987, a rectilinear stage well is juxtaposed to a curved auditorium that is reached by an external flight of open-plan steps. The CENTRE DES CONGRÈS 'LE MANÈGE' was built by Jean-Jacques Morisseau (1992) in the former riding school of the Sard *carabinieri*, which has been entirely renovated and is now fronted by a glass peristyle in which four huge palm trees grow from the ground. This contemporary architecture is counterbalanced by two renovated historic buildings: the former barracks of the Sard *carabinieri*, whose centuries-old color-washed walls provide a striking contrast to their glass and concrete setting; and the Carré Curial, whose courtyard is surrounded by the former Napoleonic barracks. The latter is today an oasis of peace and quiet that is occasionally brought to life by public events.

CARRÉ CURIAL
Since the army left in 1970 the former barracks have been extensively developed and now house shops and offices.

The Espace André-Malraux, designed by Mario Botta, and the glass peristyle of the Centre des Congrès 'Le Manège' (*below*).

Jean-Jacques Rousseau (1712–78) ran away from his home town of Geneva in 1728. When he was sixteen he met Mme de Warens, the first love of his life, in Annecy. He went to live with her in Chambéry in 1731 and in 1736 found 'a place of refuge' in 'a lonely house on a valley slope' on the outskirts of the town. Rousseau described this time of 'pure and complete happiness' at Les Charmettes in Books V and VI of his *Confessions* and the 10th *promenade* of his *Reveries of the Solitary Walker*. This was the awakening of love and the discovery of nature, reading and music, and it had a profound effect on his personality: 'in the space of four or five years I enjoyed a century of life.'

'ON A VALLEY SLOPE'
The house at Les Charmettes was the sort of 'sanctuary somewhat wild and aloof' that Rousseau liked: 'A terraced garden, above it a vineyard, below it an orchard, facing it was a little chestnut plantation.' Life at Les Charmettes was all simplicity and happiness: 'Here begins the short period of my life's happiness; here I come to those peaceful but transient moments that have given me the right to say that I have lived'.

A PLACE OF PILGRIMAGE
During the French Revolution Rousseau was a cult figure. Among visitors to Les Charmettes at this time was the political writer Arthur Young and Hérault de Séchelles, a member of the Committee of Public Safety. Later, the Romantics came to the wooded valley to 'remember the smallest details in the precise and complete way that enables us to possess certain places as we possess our own homes' (George Sand).

'A charming, intelligent woman'

Françoise Louise de La Tour, Baroness de Warens (1699–1762), whom Rousseau affectionately called 'Mamma', had been given the task of converting the Genevan Protestants to Catholicism. This 'charming, intelligent and graceful woman', whose 'demeanor, looks [and] gestures all expressed a strong compassion', gave Rousseau his first taste of happiness, an introduction to society and an insight into his true nature: 'Loved by a gentle and indulgent woman, I did what I wanted, I was what I wanted'. Although this happiness was short-lived, the last lines that Rousseau ever wrote, in the tenth *promenade* of the *Reveries*, were dedicated to Madame de Warens.

LES

CONFESSIONS

DE J.-J. ROUSSEAU

SUIVIES DES RÊVERIES DU PROMENEUR SOLITAIRE

NOUVELLE ÉDITION

VIGNETTES

PARIS

GARNIER FRÈRES, LIBRAIRES-ÉDITEURS

1876

'A store of ideas'

During his time at Les Charmettes Rousseau read avidly. With the enthusiasm of the self-educated he used the libraries of his friend François Joseph de Conzié and the Jesuit college in Chambéry. He wrote his first essays (*Mme de Warens' Orchard* and *Discovery of the New World*) and built up 'a store of ideas'. Rousseau also loved music and organized concerts, taught music to the young ladies of Chambéry's polite society, and invented a new system of musical notation.

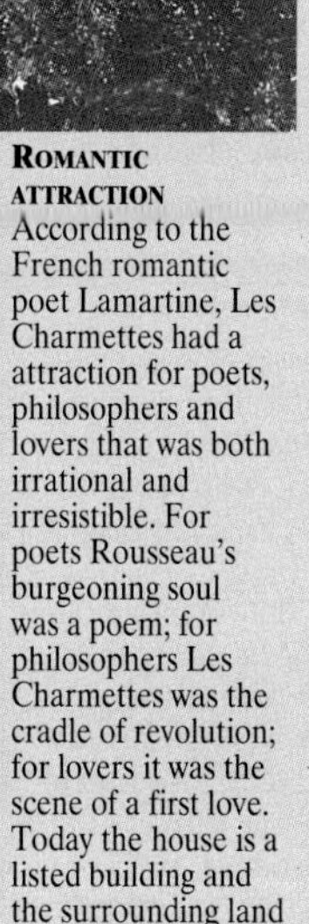

Romantic attraction

According to the French romantic poet Lamartine, Les Charmettes had a attraction for poets, philosophers and lovers that was both irrational and irresistible. For poets Rousseau's burgeoning soul was a poem; for philosophers Les Charmettes was the cradle of revolution; for lovers it was the scene of a first love. Today the house is a listed building and the surrounding land a protected site.

The Combe de Savoie has always been a major communications route and, because of its strategic importance, was guarded by such châteaux as Cruet and Miolans. These former feudal residences surrounded by vineyards are still impressive sights.

The itinerary follows the *cluse* (steep gorge) of Chambéry to Montmélian and then the Combe de Savoie. These broad valleys were gouged out by glaciers during the Quaternary period. The first, formed by a tongue from the Rhône glacier, runs between the Bauges and Chartreuse massifs and widens out at Montmélian, where it joins the valley of the Grésivaudan. The second, running between the Massif des Bauges and morainic hills, was hollowed out by the Tarentaise and Maurienne glaciers, which converged at what is now the confluence of the Arc and Isère rivers.

CLUSE DE CHAMBÉRY, MASSIF DE LA CHARTREUSE

APREMONT ● *59*. (*D201*) Apremont marks the beginning of the Abymes de Myans, an area of geological chaos resulting from the Mont Granier landslide of 1248. This area of scattered rocks, bogs and small lakes was long abandoned. It was eventually cleared and planted with vines. Today the Jacquère variety of white grape produces the famous Vins de Savoie, the AOC Abymes and Apremont wines.

MYANS. The village of Myans been an important place of Marian pilgrimage ever since popular belief attributed to the Black Madonna its escape from disaster during the Mont Granier landslide The CHURCH OF NOTRE-DAME (Our Lady), built in the 15th century and restored in the 19th and 20th centuries, consists of two superimposed places of worship. The lower (the crypt) houses the miraculous statue of the Black Madonna while the upper church was run by the Franciscans until the French Revolution.

THE MONT GRANIER LANDSLIDE
During the night of November 24–25, 1248, thousands of tons of rock and mud slid down the mountain, engulfing the town of Saint-André and several of the surrounding villages. The disaster gave rise to a number of mystical interpretations, but it was traditionally believed that the Black Madonna of Myans brought the landslide to a halt. A monumental gilt-bronze statue of the Virgin was therefore erected on the belfry of the church of Notre-Dame (Our Lady) in 1855.

CLUSE DE CHAMBÉRY, MASSIF DES BAUGES

CHALLES-LES-EAUX. This has been a famous spa town since the 19th century. Its cold waters have a high sulfur content and are used in the treatment of gynecological and respiratory diseases. The baths and casino, in late-19th-century style, stand in a beautiful park. The 17th-century castle has been converted into a hotel.

CHIGNIN. (*D21*, via *la Boisserette*) In the Middle Ages an outer castle wall, set with ten towers and enclosing an area of just under 10 acres, dominated the valley. The Carthusians converted the Tour de la Biguerne, the only well-preserved part of the fortress, into a chapel dedicated to Saint Anthelm, who was born in Chignin in 1105. On its way to Torméry the D21 crosses the Chignin vineyards which produce AOC Chignin and Chignin-Bergeron, white wines renowned since the 11th century.

Montmélian

This ancient town stands on the right bank of the Isère, at the foot of a rocky knoll which was once surmounted by one of the most powerful forts of the dukes of Savoie. The medieval citadel, which withstood two long sieges (1690–91 and 1703–5), was demolished in 1706 on the orders of Louis XIV. The town still has several interesting buildings, including the Maison du Gouverneur (governor's house), rebuilt in the 18th century, and the Pont Cuénot (1682), a magnificent ten-arched bridge that is now a listed monument. The Musée d'Histoire, which occupies a Renaissance mansion in the old town, has maps of the two sieges and a copy of the relief-plan of the citadel.

The Bastille de Miolans
The Château de Miolans was used as a state prison between 1694 and the French Revolution. Its most famous inmate was the Marquis de Sade, who was imprisoned there in 1772 but who managed to escape the following year.

Right bank of the Isère

The road that crosses the vineyards planted on the scree slopes of the Massif des Bauges is the old Roman road that linked Italy with the Dauphiné via the Petit-Saint-Bernard Pass ● *42*.

Arbin. This is the home of the famous Mondeuse grape, descended from the Roman *allobrogica*, which produces a light, fragrant red wine. In 1486 the young Pierre Terrail, lord of Bayard (1473–1524), then in the service of the dukes of Savoie, stayed in the fortified Maison de la Pérouse at the entrance to the town. The house was badly damaged during the siege of Montmélian and was replaced by a bourgeois residence in the 18th century.

Château de Miolans ● *84*. This stronghold on the Dent d'Arclusaz dominates the confluence of the rivers Isère and Arc. From the 10th to the 15th centuries it belonged to the lords of Miolans. The castle, built on the site of a Roman *oppidum* (town), was extensively fortified in the 13th century; an access ramp protected by three gateways, ramparts and rampart walks, towers and dungeons were added. When the Miolans dynasty died out in 1523, the castle passed to the dukes of Savoie who fortified it further before turning it into a prison.

The casino at Challes-les-Eaux (*top*) and the Château de Miolans (*above*).

The Chignin vineyards (*below*).

▲ The Parc Naturel Régional de Chartreuse

The Parc Naturel Régional
The 52 *communes* of Chartreuse, supported by the Rhône-Alpes region and the *départements* of Isère and Savoie, joined forces to protect and promote the natural wealth of the Massif de la Chartreuse. The project came to fruition in 1995, when it was classified as the Parc Naturel de Chartreuse. The park, with its 32,000 inhabitants, is an experimental and innovative area that aims to:
◆ preserve, manage and promote the wealth of its natural, cultural and human heritage;
◆ develop the economy and social life of the region;
◆ welcome and inform visitors and increase public awareness.

The park, which approximately encompasses the pre-Alpine Massif de la Chartreuse, is bounded by three major towns: Grenoble, Voiron and Chambéry. The mountainous landscape of this limestone mass is very varied: there are deep, precipitous gorges and sheer cliffs but also gently sloping pastures and hillsides, and attractively forested slopes. The Carthusian order, founded in 1084 by Saint Bruno, played a decisive role in the cultural life of the massif, and the traditional activities of the monks (livestock, woodcutting, metallurgy and distilling the famous Chartreuse liqueur) made a major contribution to its prosperity up until the 20th century. Today the economy is based mainly on agriculture and 'green' tourism.

Saint-Pierre-d'Entremont. The D912 links Entremont-le-Vieux, a village perched high up the valley, with Saint-Pierre-d'Entremont, divided by the Guiers river, which straddles the Isère and Savoie. The 12th-century Château de Montbel, a listed monument, towers above the village. The castle originally belonged to the Carthusians. It was later ceded to the lords of Montbel, masters of the Entre-Deux-Guiers, who were responsible for the division between Dauphiné and Savoie.

Cirque de Saint-Meme. The Guiers-Vif river rises above ground and cascades from a cave in the 1300-foot cliff face in spectacular shimmering falls.

Pas-du-Frou. At Pas-du-Frou the mountain road between Saint-Pierre-d'Entremont and Les Échelles runs 500 feet above the impressive gorges carved by the Guiers-Vif river.

Les Échelles. The valleys of Les Échelles and Chambéry are separated by a sheer limestone wall pierced by galleries. The Romans were the first to use these natural tunnels to open up a road. In the Middle Ages a pathway cut in the form of flights of steps (*échelles*) made the slope of the pass easier to climb. In 1667 Charles-Emmanuel II had a terraced ramp built so that carriages could cross the pass. This road fell into disuse when Napoleon built a tunnel (through which the N6 now passes) to facilitate links with Italy.

Saint-Pierre-d'Entremont (*right*).

Gorges de Chailles
'At a place called Chailles, not far from a precipitous mountain wall called the Pas des Échelles, there runs boiling through hideous gulfs below the high road – which is cut into the rock – a little river which would appear to have spent thousands of centuries excavating its bed.' (Jean-Jacques Rousseau)

The Préalpes de Savoie, bounded by the Rhône river to the north and west, the Guiers-Vif to the south and the Massif de la Chartreuse and the Montagne de l'Épine to the east, is a lush region of mid-altitude mountains that stands at the gateway to the High Alps. The former region of Petit Bugey, a major communications route and crossroads, was for a long time fought over by the states of Savoie and Dauphiné. The castles that once controlled access to the dukedom of Savoie and the bridge-towns built on the Guiers, the natural boundary between the two states, signal the importance of this strategic location. Besides this rich historic heritage, the region also has a number of tourist attractions: the wide, winding Rhône; the Lac d'Aiguebelette, a favorite place for fishing, swimming and rowing; and the Lacs de Chevelu. Local traditions are also very much alive: specialties include the praline-filled *brioches* of Saint-Genix-sur-Guiers and the furniture of Pont-de-Beauvoisin.

LAC D'AIGUEBELETTE

AN 'EMERALD IN A GREEN MOUNTAIN SETTING'. The calm waters of the Lac d'Aiguebelette lie at the foot of the Montagne de l'Épine. It is owned jointly by the De Chambost family and the EDF (Électricité de France). This 'emerald in a green mountain setting' (as Henry Bordeaux described it) has attracted tourists since the early 20th century. The waters of the lake teem with fish, and fishermen in boats can be seen fishing for lavaret (whitefish) throughout the year. Because it is sheltered from wind, the lake is also a swimmer's paradise and a famous rowing center. The church of SAINT-ALBAN-DE-MONTBEL, on the eastern shore, commands a beautiful view across the water.

COL DE L'ÉPINE. From Novalaise the D921 winds its way – past the flower-filled village of Nances with its picturesque church square – to the Col de l'Épine. The pass, at an altitude of 3240 feet, offers serene views of the Lac d'Aiguebelette and the Lac du Bourget.

YENNE AND THE 'ROUTE DES VINS'

SAINT-JEAN-DE-CHEVELU. The forest road between the Col de l'Épine and Saint-Jean-de-Chevelu is punctuated with many viewpoints. From Verthemex on the Vacheresse plateau the view sweeps down to the Rhône. The town and the jade waters of its two small lakes are dominated by the Dent du Chat (4600 feet).

A PRODUCTIVE REGION
The lakes and rivers of the region have allowed traditional metalworking and woodworking crafts to prosper. Thanks to the rich pastures of the Préalpes, it is also a cheese-producing region. And to complement the cheese, the picturesque Jongieux vineyards, which flourish on the slopes of the Mont du Chat, produce some high-quality AOC (*appellation d'origine contrôlée*) wines.

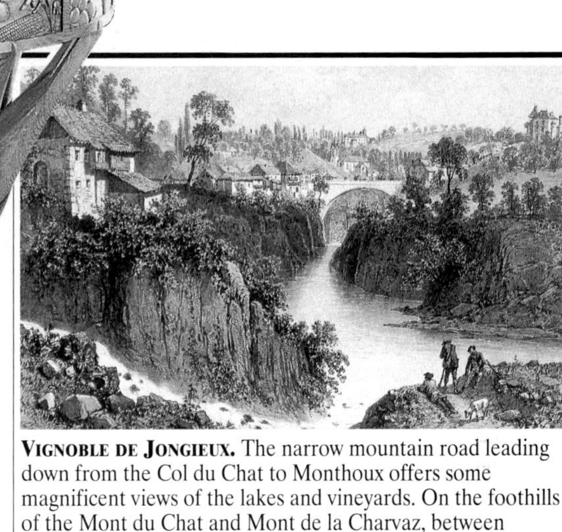

VIGNOBLE DE JONGIEUX. The narrow mountain road leading down from the Col du Chat to Monthoux offers some magnificent views of the lakes and vineyards. On the foothills of the Mont du Chat and Mont de la Charvaz, between Monthoux and Jongieux, lies the Jongieux vineyard, one of the *département*'s most picturesque. It sunny slopes produce dry, fruity white wines and a range of high-quality red wines.

YENNE. The former Roman town of Etanna, on a broad curve of the Rhône, became Savoie's first free town in 1215. Within the impressive ramparts of the medieval town center are arcaded houses and narrow streets. The listed CHURCH, originally attached to a priory, has some beautiful 12th-, 13th- and 16th-century features, including two Romanesque capitals at the doorway and some magnificent Gothic choir stalls.

DÉFILÉ DE PIERRE-CHATEL. As it leaves Yenne the N516 enters the gorge known as the Défilé de Pierre-Châtel, through which the Rhône flows away from the Alps. The gorge is dominated by the fortress of Pierre-Châtel, built in the 13th century to defend the main point of entry into Savoie. It was converted into a Carthusian monastery by the Green Count, Amadeus VI, in the 14th century, and served as a prison during the French Revolution. It was sold to a private buyer in the early 20th century.

THE TOWNS OF THE GUIERS

SAINT-GENIX-SUR-GUIERS. This attractive tourist town, with its picturesque cobwork houses and rounded-tile roofs, stands at the confluence of the Rhône and the Guiers, which flows down from the Massif de la Chartreuse. The town is famous for the cake that bears its name, a *brioche* made with eggs and filled with red praline whose legendary origins can be discovered in the local *pâtisseries*.

THE PONT-DE-BEAUVOIS. Beyond SAINT-MAURICE-DE-ROTHERENS, the highest point in the Guiers region, and Rochefort, where the legendary smuggler Louis Mandrin was captured, lies Le Pont-de-Beauvoisin. This former Franco-Sardinian border post is unusual in that it lies in the *départements* of Savoie and Isère. The stone bridge (*above*) built across the Guiers by François I and Charles III of Savoie marked the boundary between the two states. The bridge was entirely rebuilt in 1941.

FURNITURE CAPITAL
In the past the proximity of the forests of Chartreuse to Pont-de-Beauvoisin and the surrounding villages drew cabinetmakers of the Italian school to the region. Today many local craftsmen still make and exhibit high-quality hand-crafted furniture.

IN MEMORY OF SAINT AGATHA
According to tradition the *brioches* of Saint-Genix are associated with the legend of Saint Agatha of Sicily, who was martyred in the 3rd century. Because she rejected his advances the Roman governor had her breasts cut off, but they grew back the next day. Savoie adopted the legend when Sicily became part of the dukedom in 1713. On February 5, Saint Agatha's day, the women would bake breast-shaped brioches in honor of her memory.

Aix-les-Bains and the Lac du Bourget

Geneviève Frieh

▲ AIX-LES-BAINS

'I remembered that month, spent so agreeably, as the happiest time of my life… I was entirely alone in Aix taking the waters, which are excellent for the chest and so beneficial for my health that had I not felt the need to be reunited with my children, I would have prolonged my stay.'

Hortense de Beauharnais, *Mémoires*

'The little town of Aix, in Savoie, pervaded by the steam, sound and smell of its hot, sulfurous springs, occupies a series of terraces on a broad, steep hill covered with vines, meadows and orchards... In the distance, through the vistas beneath the walnut trees and vines, lies the blue lake that sparkles or pales in sunlight or beneath a cloudy sky, and depending on the time of the day' (*Raphaël*, 1849). This was how the French romantic poet Alphonse de Lamartine (1790–1869) described Aix in October 1816 when he was advised by his doctor to take the waters as a cure for his romantic melancholy. Aix-les-Bains – known in the 19th century as the 'spa town of queens and the queen of spa towns' – has been renowned for the curative properties of its hot springs since antiquity. Today the town on the eastern shores of the Lac du Bourget is famous for its thermal treatments, its architectural heritage, its prestigious past and its magnificent setting.

HISTORY ● 33

VICUS AQUENSIS: 'TOWN OF WATERS'. Around the 4th century BC a Celtic community left the shores of the lake to settle near the hot, sulfurous springs whose fame had already spread beyond the borders of Allobrogia. The springs were entrusted to the protection of Borvo (an epithet of Belenus, the Celtic 'Apollo'), the god of healing, and surrounded by a sacred wood. In the 1st century BC the same sulfurous springs led the Roman conquerors to endow the *vicus* (village) with monumental and luxurious *thermae*. This was initially a place to meet and relax but, because of the high temperature of the waters (116° F) and their therapeutic properties, the baths soon became a cure center. The town, which lay on the strategic route between the Po and Rhône valleys, across high Alpine passes, extended its baths and acquired a temple and villas. It went into decline in the 4th century, at the time of the first Germanic invasions, and later was partially engulfed by a mudslide.

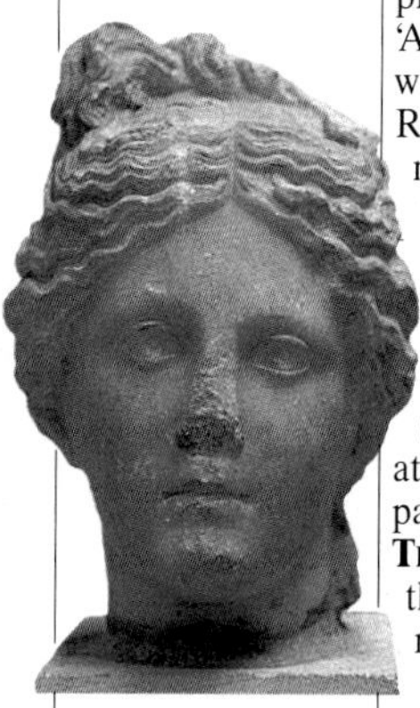

This head of Venus or of a muse, dating from the 2nd century and discovered in the baths in 1935, can be seen in the town's Musée d'Archéologie et de Préhistoire.

THE MIDDLE AGES. During the Middle Ages Aix was part of the kingdom of Transjuran Burgundy. Rudolph III had a residence in the town which he gave to his wife Ermengarde in 1011. On her husband's death she entrusted its administration to Humbert I (White Hands), Rudolph's successor ● 40. In 1057 the estate devolved to the De Seyssel family, who were vassals of the counts of Savoie. The town lay on the road between Chambéry and Geneva, and was protected by ramparts pierced by four gates which survived until the 19th century. Although it had a feudal castle and a priory, the town's thatched houses maintained its essentially rural character. It appears that, during this period, the therapeutic properties of the water were forgotten.

THE BIRTH OF A SPA TOWN. In 1600 Cabias, a physician from the Dauphiné, described how King Henri IV 'dismounted from his horse at the Grand Bain, where, with several princes of the royal court, he bathed and washed for an hour, with as much pleasure and contentment as if he had been enjoying one of the greatest delights in the world' (*Les Merveilles des*

bains d'Aix-en-Savoye). The town regained some of its former prestige, playing host to the High Constable of Lesdiguières and the dukes of Savoie. While the ordinary people bathed in the source itself or in the old Roman baths, people of rank preferred to have the spring water brought to their rooms. In 1775 Victor-Amadeus III decided to build new baths. The Établissement Royal des Bains (royal baths), which opened in 1783, had two public baths, including one for the poor, as well as rooms reserved for the royal family. After the French Revolution, the Bonaparte family revived the fortunes of the spa town. In 1813 Hortense de Beauharnais subsidized the foundation of a hospital to enable the poor and needy to take the waters. In 1824 the Cercle Royal des Étrangers (a club for visiting royalty), with a ballroom, gaming rooms and a theater, was installed in the castle of the marquises of Aix.

A bird's-eye view of the Roche du Roi in the 19th century.

THE VICTORIAN ERA. Although extended after 1830 at the instigation of Charles-Albert, the baths were soon unable to meet the needs of an increasingly demanding clientele. The Pellegrini baths, completed in 1860, doubled the extent of the bathing facilities. When Savoie became part of France that year ● *44* the springs were nationalized.

THE BONAPARTE FAMILY IN AIX
Aix was little more than a village when, in 1808, Pauline Borghèse, Napoleon's favorite sister, came to take the waters under the watchful eye of their mother, Maria Letizia Bonaparte. In 1810 the de Beauharnais family followed their example and the former Empress Josephine, accompanied by her entourage, came to Aix, where she was joined by her daughter Hortense, queen of Holland. Hortense grew extremely fond of the town where she recovered her health, returning in 1811 with her lover, Charles de Flahaut. In 1812 Maria Letizia Bonaparte was joined in Aix by her daughters Pauline and Caroline, her daughter-in-law Julie, and Julie's sister Désirée. They were soon followed by Josephine and Hortense de Beauharnais. In 1814 the Empress Marie-Louise visited the town while her husband went into exile on Elba.

The Marlioz baths, opened in 1861, used alternative methods of treatment for respiratory disorders and skin diseases. Enlightened doctors introduced the 'shower-massage' and 'Scottish shower', and experimented with mud cures and the 'Berthollet' treatment, a steam bath that used steam from the hot springs. Their publications and the foundation of a school of thermal techniques established the town's reputation as a treatment center for rheumatic complaints. The same doctors accompanied rich foreign visitors to salons, the theater and on excursions, for by now there were as many tourists as there were *curistes*. People were coming to Aix to enjoy themselves, to 'see and be seen'. In 1879 the casino of the Grand Cercle (1849) was joined by the casino of the Villa des Fleurs. From 1885 Queen Victoria's regular visits to the town launched an 'English' fashion and the British community began to impose a lifestyle in which hotels, mansions and villas vied with each other in luxury.

A MEDICAL AND SOCIAL ROLE. During the interwar years the town continued to be extremely popular. A new bath was built, a vast complex that met the health requirements of the period and included an Olympic swimming pool and mechanotherapy facilities. Cures became more medically oriented and, with costs reimbursed by the state from 1947, the spa attracted a clientele of more modest means. Numbers rose sharply, reaching their peak in 1986 with a total of 52,000 *curistes*. Aix-les-Bains had become France's leading spa town.

AIX, TOWN OF WATERS

THE AIX-MARLIOZ BATHS. The cold, sulfurous waters of the Marlioz baths originally rose in meadows to the south of Aix-les-Bains. In the 18th century doctors became aware of their

astringent properties. Plans for the construction of the Marlioz baths were approved in 1860 and they were built by the architect Pellegrini, around three springs known as Esculape, Bonjean and Adélaïde. The waters of the Marlioz baths were used primarily to treat respiratory disorders and, from 1986, infections of the mouth and tongue. Today the privately run Marlioz estate is an ultramodern complex, with two hotels, residential accommodation and a balneotherapy center, all set in a rolling 24-acre park. Apart from traditional cures, it offers special cures for children, antismoking cures and an innovative treatment for certain pulmonary infections and other disorders of the respiratory tract.

THERMES NATIONAUX. The hot, curative waters of the Thermes Nationaux (National Baths) rise discreetly in a natural cave in the hillside. In 1992 the sinking of a well to a record depth of more than 7200 feet made it possible to draw the waters as required while maintaining their excellent quality.

THE ROMAN BATHS. The remains of the old Roman baths have been preserved inside the Thermes Nationaux. Several of the pools still have their original marble cladding and pipework, as well as the small piers of an elaborate hypocaust system that heated the floors and walls of the various rooms.

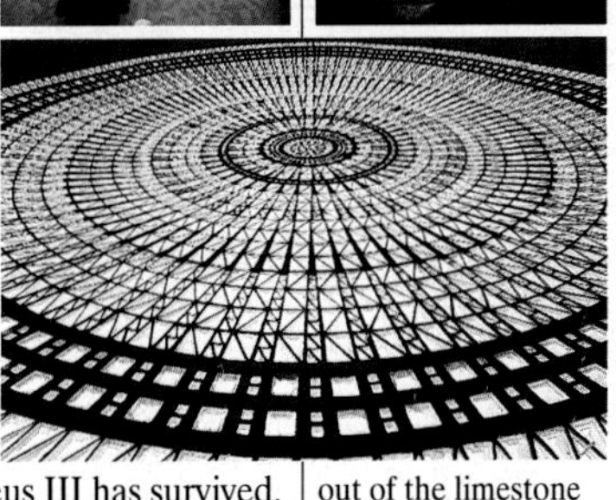

THE 'OLD' BATHS. Only part of the building founded in 1776 by Victor Amadeus III has survived. Particularly noteworthy among the successive extensions are the triple-arched façade with its decorative metalwork, the monumental staircase, the Neoclassical glass-roofed pump room, the treatment rooms with their ceramic tiles and floral decoration, and the huge oval pools. The baths are lit by natural light, which creates an atmosphere both of grandeur and privacy.

PÉTRIAUX BATHS. In 1936 Roger Pétriaux, one of the town's leading architects, was given the task of enhancing the buildings. He added the spacious Art Deco entrance hall, which is built in concrete and glass, the materials in vogue at the time.

CHEVALLEY BATHS. With the construction of the Chevalley baths, designed by the architect Stanislas Fiszer, the range of treatments and cures that Aix-les-Bains had to offer was complete. Traditional thermal cures, preventive treatment and balneotherapy were all available here, especially as part of individual fitness and revitalization programs.

SOURCE OF THE MINERAL SPRINGS
(*Place de l'Ingénieur-François*)
A narrow tunnel almost 110 yards long leads to the source of the hot mineral springs. Visitors can see the caves that, over thousands of years, were hollowed

out of the limestone rock, their strange forms enhanced by subtle lighting. Recent investigations have revealed the origin of the springs: the rainwater that filters down through the Massif de la Charvaz, on the western shores of the Lac du Bourget, lies at a depth of more than 6500 feet where it becomes saturated with mineral salts before rising via natural chimneys.

CULTURE
Aix is not only a spa town but also a center of art and culture, and the venue for festivals. For more than a century, since the French première of Wagner's *Tristan and Isolde*, it has hosted many cultural events. The Théâtre du Casino and the Centre des Congrès present a wide-ranging program of opera and music. The *Festival des Nuits Romantiques*, in October, includes a series of prestigious concerts; at *Navigaix* history boats are exhibited; and the *Fête des Fleurs* is a traditional procession of floral floats. The Musée Faure, which occupies a beautiful private mansion, has a major collection of paintings, including works by Pissarro, Jonkind, Degas and Marquet, as well as some twenty bronzes by Rodin.

EDWARDIAN AIX

Aix-les-Bains, known as 'the spa town of queens and the queen of spa towns', enjoyed a golden age between the late 19th century and the 1930s. The aristocracy and moneyed classes of Europe made this little Savoyard town one of the smartest resorts of the Edwardian era.

CASINO GRAND CERCLE. When the casino was built in 1847 the elegance of the spa town was complemented by a fashionably feverish atmosphere of gaming and gambling. Since then the building has been embellished by various additions; today it has an opera-house façade, a red-and-gold theater with a delightfully old-fashioned atmosphere, an Edwardian 'Raphaël Room', a traditional gaming room with baize-covered tables and an impressive domed ceiling decorated with mosaics signed by the Italian glassmaker Antonio Salviati (1816–90) in 1883.

LUXURY HOTELS. The Splendide, Beau Site, Royal and Mirabeau, on the hillside above the shores of the lake, were all built as luxury hotels. They were designed by the great architect families of Aix (Bernascon and Rossignoli) and were patronized not only by most of the crowned heads of Europe but also by Indian maharajas. These magnificent buildings fell into decline and, apart from the Hotel Astoria, most have been converted into flats. Some retain vestiges of their original neo-Baroque or Art Deco style. They can be visited as part of the *Au fil de l'eau* guided tour.

VILLAS. Several villas, which *curistes* rented by the season or the year, attest to the town's former prosperity. The oldest, the VILLA CHEVALLEY, where the rich and famous, including the French romantic poet Alphonse de Lamartine, once sojourned, is currently awaiting restoration. Unfortunately the richly decorated Edwardian interior of the Villa de Solms, named for Marie de Solms, Napoleon's great-niece, is not open to the public. Nor is the CHALET CHARCOT, built by the family of the French Antarctic explorer Jean Charcot (1867–1936) and whose wooden scalloped moldings give it the appearance of a Swiss chalet. The CHÂTEAU DE LA ROCHE DU ROI, overlooking the Marlioz baths, is more like an Art Nouveau fairy-tale castle with its finely worked carriage awning, angle turrets and decorative metalwork in the style of Hector Guimard (1867–1942).

THE GARDENS OF AIX

Aix, which won a European 'floral town' award in 1992, has a fine tradition of urban gardens that is more than 200 years old. The Promenade du Gigot is a broad poplar-lined avenue

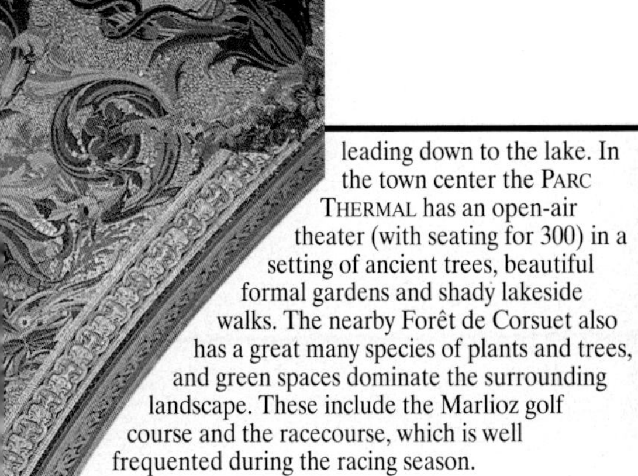

leading down to the lake. In the town center the PARC THERMAL has an open-air theater (with seating for 300) in a setting of ancient trees, beautiful formal gardens and shady lakeside walks. The nearby Forêt de Corsuet also has a great many species of plants and trees, and green spaces dominate the surrounding landscape. These include the Marlioz golf course and the racecourse, which is well frequented during the racing season.

MONT REVARD

Mont Revard (5085 feet) lies on the eastern shore of the lake, on the edge of the Massif des Bauges. It is a plateau of mountain pastures and forests which, until the late 19th century, was accessible by a mule track. In 1890 the great wall of rock overlooking Aix-les-Bains fired the imagination of a Swiss engineer named Riggenbach who built a 5¾-mile cog railroad from the town center to the plateau.

LE REVARD. From 1908, thanks to the railroad, the inhabitants of Aix were among the trendsetters in the new fashion for winter sports. However, although the line proved extremely successful (it carried 32,000 passengers in 1920), it was replaced in 1935 by a spectacular cableway, which in turn fell into disuse some thirty-four years later. Today a road leads up to the plateau, which is France's leading cross-country ski resort with 90 miles of marked ski routes. It also has two modestly sized Alpine ski resorts: La Féclaz and Le Revard, which also offers magnificent views of the Lac du Bourget and the Alps. Visitors to the resort can walk the theme trails (geology on the 'ridge trail'), go botanizing in the Alpine garden (planted in 1913) or visit an Alpine farm that makes the Tome des Bauges cheese, typical of the massif.

THE VILLAGES OF MONT REVARD. The villages on the slopes of Mont Revard offer a wide range of open-air leisure activities as well as spectacular views of the lake. You can also visit the Domaine des Corbières at Pugny-Chatenod (exhibition of pottery and icons by the Sisters of Bethlehem), follow the ecological and educational trail of Montcel or, at the end of July, enjoy the Gruyère festival of SAINT-OFFENGE.

LEISURE

The Grand Port was built in the early 19th century as a commercial port for salt, stone and wood. The Petit Port has been used as a marina since 1865 and today has 1420 berths for all kinds of pleasure craft. Beaches of fine (imported) sand and a nearby Olympic pool are ideal for swimming or simply relaxing. At the sailing club would-be sailors can learn how to harness the light breezes or gusting winds that skim the lake. The golf course hosts the Semaine Internationale (international week), the most important amateur championship in the golfing calendar.

NAVIGATION ON THE LAC DU BOURGET
Since the Bronze Age navigation on the Lac du Bourget has facilitated trade and communications with Lyons and the Mediterranean. In the 11th and 12th centuries trade increased and local craft, including *sapines*, *seysselandes* and *savoyardes*, transported salt, coal, wood and corn. In 1837 the first steam navigation company was formed and the *Abeille* sailed from Aix to Lyons in 12 hours, and from Lyons to Aix in 30 hours. Today several companies offer cruises on the Lac du Bourget, the Canal de Savières and the upper Rhône, as well as trips to the Abbaye de Hautecombe.

The Lac du Bourget is framed by the final foothills of the Jura (Montagne de l'Épine, Mont du Chat, Mont de la Charvaz, Massif de la Chambotte) and the first limestone cliffs of the Préalpes, whose bleakness is softened by such vast plateaus as that of Mont Revard. This romantic lake, surrounded by mountains, is a place of great natural beauty. Its waters seem to reflect its rich history and the great love stories that have been played out upon its shores.

LE BOURGET-DU-LAC

Le Bourget-du-Lac is situated on the Roman road that once led into Switzerland along the Rhône valley. It was one of the major ports on the lake to which it gave its name.

ÉGLISE SAINT-LAURENT. The church was built in the 11th century by Benedictine monks, on the site of a Roman temple, and rebuilt in the 13th and 15th centuries by two priors from a distinguished family from the Bugey, Aymard and Odon de Luyrieux. The Gothic church is built in 13th-century Savoyard style, with a single nave, no transept and a polygonal chevet (exterior of the apse). In the choir is a remarkable series of 13th-century relief sculptures illustrating scenes from the life of Christ. They were originally part of the rood screen separating the monks in the chancel from the congregation in the nave. Vividly and realistically capturing physical movement and emotional expression, they are remarkable portraits and detailed depictions of everyday life. The CRYPT beneath the apse is a

FISHING
Eight professional fishermen share fishing rights on the Lac du Bourget. The catch consists mainly of lavaret (whitefish), char, perch and pike.

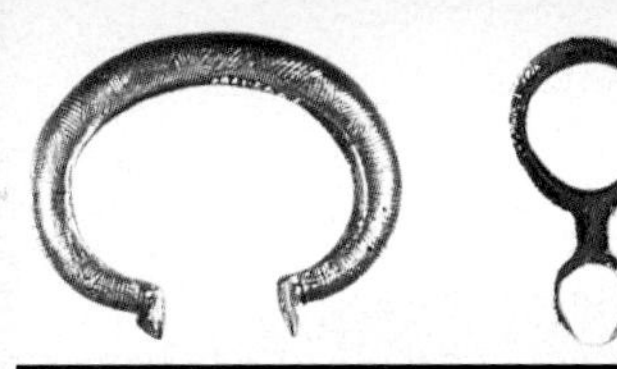

At the end of the Bronze Age, c. 1000 BC, potters and metalworkers settled on the shores of the lake. Many objects of the period, evidence of their presence there, can be seen in the Musée Savoisien in Chambéry

vestige of the Romanesque building and incorporates stones reused from the Roman temple that once stood on the site. The CHATEAU-PRIEURÉ (priory) (*below*), restored from 1912 onward, is arranged around the cloister that services a chapel, the chapter house, a library (whose ceiling is lined with 17th-century Cordoba leather) and a refectory adjoining the kitchen. The monastery gardens are built around a long central vista giving access to the terraces.

THE CASTLE. In 1248 Thomas II, count of Savoie and brother of Amadeus IV, built a castle on former monastic land. The building, regarded as one of the most beautiful examples of a medieval castle, was originally a simple hunting lodge for members of the House of Savoie and only later assumed the appearance of a fortress. It stands on what is today protected marshland at the southern end of the lake and has been the subject of an extensive excavation and restoration program. Its four towers, which have been rebuilt, frame a spacious central area where concerts and historic festivals are held. A bird-watching observatory is being installed in the east tower.

CHÂTEAU DE BOURDEAU

This impressive 11th-century castle stands in a lush setting overlooking the lake. For a long time it was owned by the de Seyssel family and, according to the French writer Montaigne (1533–92), housed a weapons factory in the 16th century. Damaged during the French Revolution and restored in the 19th century, the castle (*right*) is today privately owned. Near the delightful port of Bourdeau is the entrance to the GROTTE DE LAMARTINE, where the poet and his beloved Julie Charles ▲ *148* wanted to die.

THE ABBAYE DE HAUTECOMBE

THE SITE. In 1121 Benedictine monks from Aulps-en-Chablais settled on the Montagne de Cessens, between the northeastern shore of the Lac du Bourget and the road to Aix-les-Bains. They called the valley 'Haute Combe' (high valley) because of its location high above the valley of Rumilly. It was a strategic location, with two mountain passes – controlled by two castles, whose ruins can still be seen today – giving the monks access to the lake and the lands of the House of Savoie. In 1135 the community moved to the opposite shore of the lake and a monastery was built on the site of a small chapel, which could only be reached by boat.

SAVOIE-TECHNOLAC
In 1988 this former military site on the shores of the Lac du Bourget was converted into an urban research center: Savoie-Technolac. The buildings and green spaces of the landscaped complex, designed by Jean-Louis Chanéac, cover

a total area of 615 acres. The modern businesses, high-tech companies, training and research centers are devoted to the economic growth of Savoie and Haute-Savoie.

The gardens of the Château Prieuré of Le Bourget-du Lac (*below*).

LAC DU BOURGET

With a surface area of 17 square miles the Lac du Bourget is France's largest natural lake. Stretching for 11 miles between two mountain ranges, it fills a depression formed by the folding of the Alps during the Tertiary period and filled with soft rocks deposited by glaciers during the Quaternary period. Before it became polluted, the lake was renowned for the purity of its waters. However, a diversity of aquatic plants and waterfowl have now returned to the lake.

MUTE SWAN
The lake has a permanent population of swans. In winter their numbers are swelled by swans arriving from the east.

GREAT CRESTED GREBE
In spring these birds perform spectacular mating displays. In winter they tend to congregate near the Abbaye de Hautecombe.

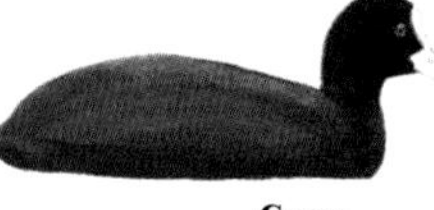

COOT
The resident population nests in the reedy marshland on the shores of the lake. Numbers are at their highest in winter, when birds from northern regions spend winter on the lake.

TUFTED DUCK
Over one thousand of these ducks, many from eastern Europe, overwinter on the lake.

MARSH-HARRIER
The marsh harrier frequents the reedy marshland and lake shores, where it preys on wounded birds and small mammals.

Plant belt
The reedy marshland colonized by tall plants (reeds) tends to be found at either end of the lake. It forms a dense plant belt that provides protection for nesting birds. The plants grow in layers determined by the depth of water.

Reed warbler
This small insectivorous member of the sparrow family nests deep in the reedy marshland where it build its nest among reed stems.

Water milfoil
(*Myriophyllum*)
Water milfoil, water spike (pondweed) and hornwort provide underwater vegetation that acts as a spawning ground for fish.

Common reed
These are the predominant plants in the lake's reedy marshland. Their dense habit makes them fairly impenetrable.

Lavaret
The lavaret or whitefish, with its delicately flavored flesh, was once extremely common. n recent years its numbers have declined and is currently being reintroduced into the lake.

Char
The char frequents the deep, oxygen-rich waters of the lake. In early winter it spawns in gravel pits known locally as *omblières*. Its flesh is particularly succulent.

A PROSPEROUS ABBEY. Before it was transferred to the opposite shore of the lake, the abbey was inhabited by some 200 monks. It became extremely prosperous during the 13th century. The community took part in the Crusades, founding several missions in the East, and provided two popes: Celestine IV (1294), and Nicholas V (1277–80). At the time its possessions extended to the Rhône and included Chautagne, Lucey, Yenne and the Mont du Chat. In the 14th century the abbey reached the height of its material and spiritual power, and the Chapelle des Princes was built to house the remains of the members of the house of Savoie, who until then had been buried near the church.

CENTURIES OF DECLINE. The establishment of the commendam in the 15th century marked the beginning of a long period of decline. In 1738, on the death of the last commendatory abbot, the abbey devolved to the senate of Savoie and then to the Chambre des Comptes. By the time of the French Revolution it was inhabited by eight monks. The buildings had fallen into disrepair and were used as a pottery works before being abandoned in 1807.

RENAISSANCE. The Sardinian restoration (1816) ● *38* and the accession of Charles-Félix injected new life into the abbey. The king bought the monastery and, in 1824, gave the Italian architect Ernesto Melano the task of restoring the church that housed his ancestors to its former 16th-century glory. On August 7, 1826, Charles-Félix entrusted the abbey to the Cistercians of La Consolata from Turin, reserving royal apartments for his personal use. On his death the king's widow, Marie-Christine, continued his work: the east wing was completed, and the Chapelle Saint-André and Tour du Phare (whose beacons guided boatmen on the lake) were built. The decorative work was entrusted to famous artists and sculptors from northern Italy, including Cacciatori, the Vacca brothers and Gonin.

A CHARISMATIC COMMUNITY. In a testament dated March 13, 1981, Humbert II (1904–83), king of Italy until 1946, required his heirs to renounce their patronage of Hautecombe, thus making the archbishop of Chambéry the guarantor of the foundation. In 1992 the Benedictines who had occupied the

ROMANCE
When the Abbaye de Hautecombe was abandoned in 1807, its ruins became a place of rendezvous for the Romantics. The poet Alphonse de Lamartine made the abbey the setting for *Raphaël* and referred to it in his *Méditations poétiques*. Visitors can relive the turbulent love affair of Lamartine and Julie Charles at Hautecombe, where he saved her from drowning; on the Plage des Adieux, at Saint-Innocent, where they swore their eternal love; and at Tresserve where he wrote the desolate lines of *Le Lac*.

'LES AMANTS DU LAC'
(The Lovers of the Lake) is a nocturnal cruise which retraces this romantic idyll, accompanied by chamber music and extracts from the writings of Lamartine.

abbey since 1922 left Hautecombe. They were replaced by the charismatic Communauté du Chemin Neuf, part of the Renouveau Charismatique movement, founded in 1973.

THE CHURCH. The church, restored in 1824, has an exuberant neo-Gothic façade (1837) with statues representing the three theological and four cardinal virtues. Inside, more than 300 statues in Carrara marble and soft Seyssel stone watch over the cenotaphs and tombs glorifying the forty-three members of the house of Savoie buried there. Three of the marble statues are particularly fine: a Pietà (*right*), a statue of Charles-Félix, by the Milanese sculptor Cacciatori, and the group depicting Queen Marie-Christine flanked by a young prince and a child in rags, by Albertoni.

THE WATER BARN. Near the landing stage is a beautiful building in the Romanesque style that exemplifies the simplicity of Cistercian architecture. This was the water barn (*grange batelière*) where salt and other goods brought to the abbey by boat were stored.

THE MONASTERY
The refectory, kitchen and parlor are arranged around the cloister on the first floor, while the monks' cells are on the second floor. The royal apartments, whose ceilings were richly decorated by the Vacca brothers, occupied two pavilions and the wing at the western end of the monastery. The stained-glass windows of the adjoining Chapelle Saint-André are by the Bernese Muller brothers. There is a spectacular view from the terraced garden overlooking the lake.

CANAL DE SAVIÈRES

THE PORTOUT POTTERY WORKS. The refuse dump of a 4th-century pottery works was discovered at the mouth of the Canal de Savières. The pottery made at this prolific workshop was traded all over southeastern Gaul and along the Mediterranean coast. A display of the underwater excavations and a reconstruction of a workshop can be seen on the site.

THE CANAL. The canal acts as an outlet from the Lac du Bourget into the Rhône and as an overflow channel for the river's floodwaters. According to legend it was dug by a princess from the neighboring village of Lavours so that she could go to meet her lover. However, the canal in fact existed since Roman times. Its banks are a botanist's and bird-watcher's paradise.

CHANAZ. This delightful little town has a turbulent political history. It has marked the limit of navigation on the Rhône and canal since the Middle Ages and, as a border-village belonging to the dukedom of Savoie, was given to France by the Treaty of Lyons (1601) and was restored to Piedmont in 1760. For the last fifteen years efforts have been made to promote the town's historic

The Canal de Savières at Chanaz.

heritage. Today visitors can admire the MAISON DE BOIGNE (16th–18th century), which houses the town hall and tourist office, and a restored walnut-oil mill.

CHÂTEAU DE CHATILLON. The castle stands on the site of what in Roman times was the residence of the commander of the fleet of boatmen on the upper Rhône. The fortress, built in the 13th century, controlled the Chautagne region and the entire length of the lake. From 1477 to 1756 it belonged the De Seyssel family of Aix. It is now a listed building and its gardens command a magnificent view of the lake.

THE CHAUTAGNE VINEYARDS

THE CHAUTAGNE VINEYARDS ● *59* were cultivated originally by the Allobrogi ● *34* and then by the Romans. They were significantly improved in the 12th century with the introduction of two grape varieties: the Altesse, or Roussette, brought back from Cyprus, and the Mondeuse, or *savouëtta*, from the Holy Land. The southwest-facing vineyards slope gently toward the Rhône and the Lac du Bourget. The light and heat reflected from the white rocks of the Montagne du Gros Foug, and the tempering influence of the lake, allows the cultivation of varieties of red grape (unusual in Savoie) which produce the subtle and original red Chautagne wines.

THE MARAIS DE CHAUTAGNE. The Chautagne marshland, now much reduced, is confined to the northern end of the lake. It is planted with poplars covering an area of 1850 acres.

THE EASTERN SHORES

BELVÉDERE DE LA CHAMBOTTE. A restaurant established in 1833, and owned by the Lansard family, offers magnificent views over the Lac du Bourget. The menu includes tea and scones, in the purest English tradition, in memory of the visits made by Queen Victoria.

BRISON-SAINT-INNOCENCE. Mediterranean vegetation covers these sunny slopes. Visitors can climb up to the Chapelle de Brison, bathe at the Pointe de l'Ardre, or visit the former Maison Despine (now the town hall), which still houses the collections and library of this 19th-century family of doctors.

BIRDS ON THE LAC DU BOURGET
Some 110 species of nesting birds live in the marshland on the northern and southern shores of the lake and along the banks of the upper Rhône. Rare species include the curlew, short-toed eagle, corn bunting, bluethroat, little bittern and great crested grebe. The lake also attracts less desirable species: from August to April the great cormorant catches between 10 and 17 oz of fish per day.

THE WINES OF CHAUTAGNE
The Chautagne vineyards ● *59* produce AOC 'Vin de Savoie Cru Chautagne' wines. The most typical red wines are made from the Mondeuse, Gamay and Pinot grapes, and the most typical whites from the Roussette, Chautagne and Aligoté varieties. Wine-tastings in the *cave-coopérative* and the five vineyard cellars are highly recommended.

Massif des Bauges and Albanais

▲ Massif des Bauges

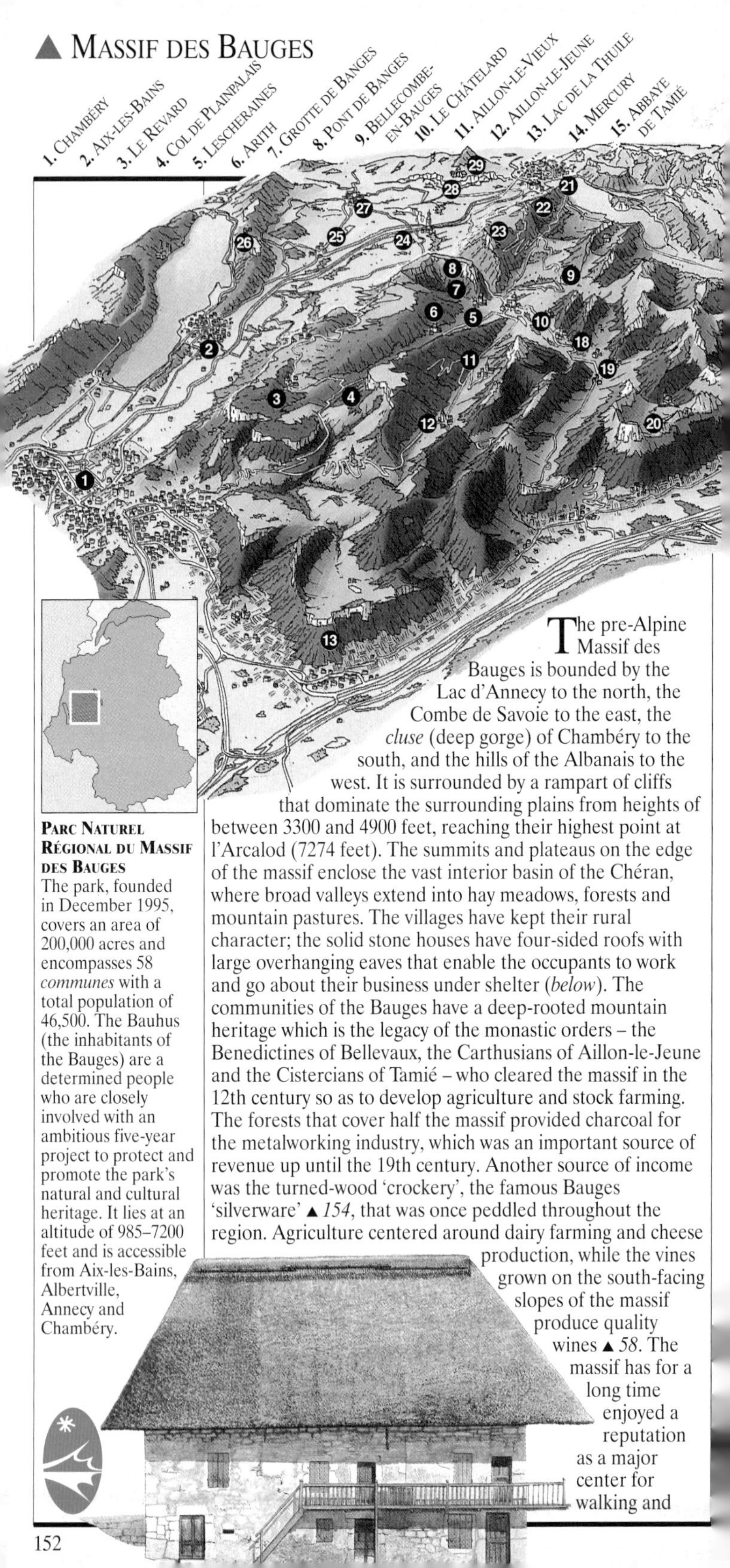

The pre-Alpine Massif des Bauges is bounded by the Lac d'Annecy to the north, the Combe de Savoie to the east, the *cluse* (deep gorge) of Chambéry to the south, and the hills of the Albanais to the west. It is surrounded by a rampart of cliffs that dominate the surrounding plains from heights of between 3300 and 4900 feet, reaching their highest point at l'Arcalod (7274 feet). The summits and plateaus on the edge of the massif enclose the vast interior basin of the Chéran, where broad valleys extend into hay meadows, forests and mountain pastures. The villages have kept their rural character; the solid stone houses have four-sided roofs with large overhanging eaves that enable the occupants to work and go about their business under shelter (*below*). The communities of the Bauges have a deep-rooted mountain heritage which is the legacy of the monastic orders – the Benedictines of Bellevaux, the Carthusians of Aillon-le-Jeune and the Cistercians of Tamié – who cleared the massif in the 12th century so as to develop agriculture and stock farming. The forests that cover half the massif provided charcoal for the metalworking industry, which was an important source of revenue up until the 19th century. Another source of income was the turned-wood 'crockery', the famous Bauges 'silverware' ▲ *154*, that was once peddled throughout the region. Agriculture centered around dairy farming and cheese production, while the vines grown on the south-facing slopes of the massif produce quality wines ▲ *58*. The massif has for a long time enjoyed a reputation as a major center for walking and

Parc Naturel Régional du Massif des Bauges
The park, founded in December 1995, covers an area of 200,000 acres and encompasses 58 *communes* with a total population of 46,500. The Bauhus (the inhabitants of the Bauges) are a determined people who are closely involved with an ambitious five-year project to protect and promote the park's natural and cultural heritage. It lies at an altitude of 985–7200 feet and is accessible from Aix-les-Bains, Albertville, Annecy and Chambéry.

'ecotourism'. The diversity of flora and fauna make this a patchwork of ecological environments. The 600 recorded plant species include the European cyclamen (*below*), and such rare species as Perier's iris, the slipper orchid, marsh gentian and Alpine sea-holly. The national hunting and wildlife reserve of the Bauges takes in the massif's highest peaks, in the heart of the park, and is the preserve of nesting birds and mountain mammals ▲ *157*.

Savoie-Grand-Revard
Mont Revard became a major tourist resort, in 1880, and one of France's first winter ski resorts, in 1905, as a result of the popularity of Aix-les-Bains ▲ *143*. The spa town was linked to the plateau by a cog railroad, which opened in 1892, and by a cableway from 1936 ● *67*. The resort experienced a revival in the late 1960s when cross-country skiing became fashionable.

The Central Bauges

From Chambéry and Aix-les-Bains the D913 climbs, via Mouxy, to the Plateau du Revard. From the plateau, in clear weather, there is an extensive view of the Lac du Bourget and the surrounding mountains.

Col de Plainpalais. The pass, which overlooks the village of Les Déserts and the basin of the Leysse river from a height of 3870 feet, is one of the principal points of access to the central Bauges. On the other side are meadows, orchards and copses.

Lescheraines. In the Middle Ages Lescheraines lay on the road linking Chambéry and Annecy via Plainpalais and the Pont du Diable ('devil's bridge'). Today the village stands at a crossroads in the heart of the massif. Its watersports center is popular with summer visitors.

Arith. Because of its excellent situation this delightful village is known as the 'Nice of the Bauges'. There is a pleasant walk from Montagny to Mariet d'Arit, a picturesque valley dotted with mountain chalets which are occupied in summer when farmers come to graze their flocks and cut the hay. The little Lac du Mariet nestles in a secondary fold of Mont Revard at an altitude of 3280 feet.

Grotte de Banges. The cave forms the entrance to a major network of underground lakes and sumps at the sheer southern edge of the Montagne du Semnoz, overlooking the Gorges du Chéran (2360 feet). Traces of human occupation dating from the Magdalenian period (including a 12,000 year-old harpoon carved out of a reindeer antler) have been discovered along with vestiges from the Gallo-Roman times and the Middle Ages.

Pont de Banges. The bridge, built on Roman foundations, spans the Chéran, the principal river of the Bauges, which is traditionally believed to contain gold. However, trout fishermen tend to have better luck than gold prospectors.

Bellecombe-en-Bauges. It is well worth making a detour via the Pont du Diable, on the old road. The bridge crosses the Nant de Bellecombe, which roars through the deep gorge.

The Chéran, with its perpetual roar, crashes down deep gorges and reemerges at the Pont de l'Abîme (*above*). The bridge, built in 1887, is 215 feet long and is suspended 330 feet above the water by cables attached to the rock. The bridge and the Tours Saint-Jaques, vertical outcrops of rock that rise like needles out of the forest at an altitude of 3250 feet (*below*), are an impressive sight.

This turned maple wood 'crockery' seems to have originated in the 12th century, when the monastic orders settled in the Massif des Bauges. It was made during the winter months by the farmers of the Bauges and then peddled on the plains of eastern France. In 1645 the bishop of Geneva ironically referred to this shining white rustic 'crockery' as 'silverware'. The term was adopted by the general population, who traditionally mocked and jeered at peddlers. Today only the artisans of the Bauges perpetuate this ancient craft.

Vessels and implements
Vessels and implements were made in all shapes and sizes, including knives and forks, cream ladles, plates, dishes, bowls and mortars. The most highly prized pieces of this ancient craft were the ladle (*pôche*) and gourd (*boteillon*).

La Magne, village of wood turners
The village of La Magne had the highest concentration of wood turners. In 1850 sixty farmers in the village produced wooden 'crockery' during the winter months, each 'signing' their work. Today only one man continues this traditional craft and ancient tradition.

The 'plane'
The sycamore (*plane* in the local dialect) is a dense, smooth-grained wood that does not taint food. The trees are felled at the end of August, a process that requires great care since any splits in the timber or damage to the bark leave marks on the sycamore's pearly white wood.

The 'pôche'
This highly symbolic object was bought from peddlers at Easter, to mark the beginning of the new agricultural year. A bridegroom's mother would give a ladle (and an apron) to her future daughter-in-law to show that she was accepted by her new family.

The 'boteillon'
Farmers used gourds as containers for the wine or cider that they would take with them when they worked in the fields. Wood is a good insulator and kept the contents cool.

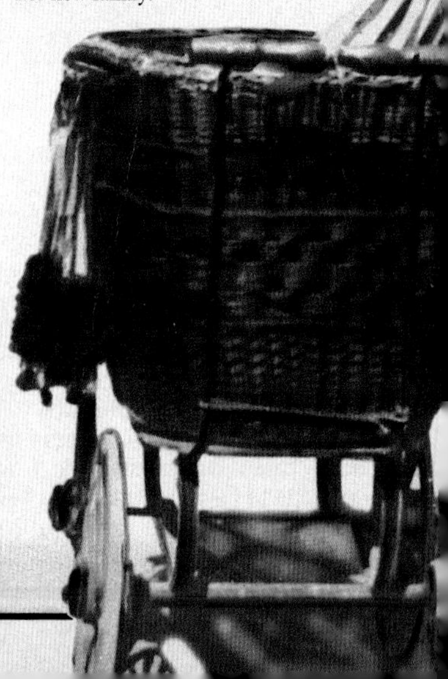

'It is born of the forest of La Magne and is also a winter occupation; it has always been an additional source of income, an item exported by peddling and a remedy against emigration.'

Abbé Gex

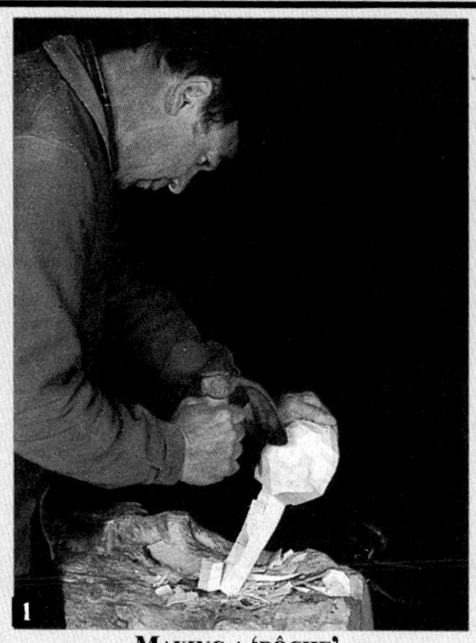

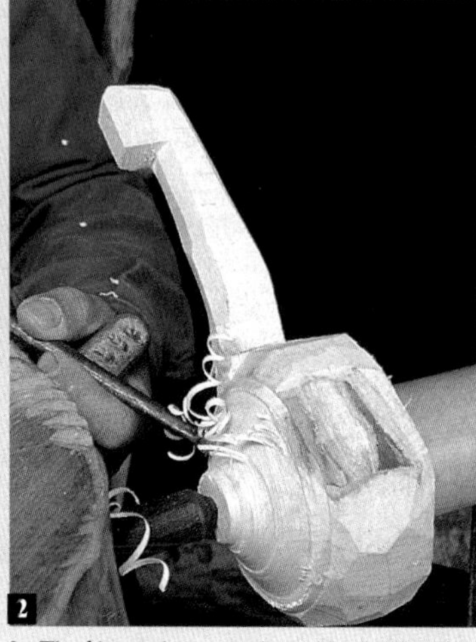

MAKING A 'PÔCHE'

The ladle (*pôche*) is made from one piece of wood. It is a very delicate item to make.

1. The log is split in half, giving two identical rough shapes (*lévo*). The shaping is done with a saw and an adze. The *lévo* is then fixed onto a wooden cylinder (*clavière*) which is rotated by a pedal-operated strap.

2. The *lévo* and *clavière* are held in place by lathe centers. The interior and exterior of the bowl is turned by depressing the pedal so that the piece makes more than a full turn. The handle of the *pôche* is shaped by varying the pedal's movements so that the handle does not rotate completely. When tensioned, the bar of the lathe reverses the direction in which the piece is rotating and brings the pedal back up.

A SYMBOL
The apprenticeship of a young craftsman is complete when he has turned a *pôche.*

3. The *garé* – the cone of wood left inside the piece to make it rotate – is broken off. A curved knife is used to remove the marks left on the inside by the *garé* when it is broken off, and by the lathe center on the outside, by carving the signature. The handle and its hook (another 'signature') are finished with a knife. The wood is very carefully dried so that it keeps its whiteness without splitting.

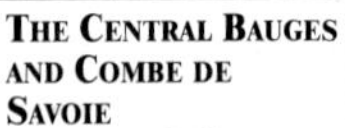

In the past farmers from the Bauges used sleds to transport fertile soil to their plots of vines in the Combe de Savoie.

THE CENTRAL BAUGES AND COMBE DE SAVOIE
In terms of climate and agriculture, the center of the Massif des Bauges and its foothills, the Combe de Savoie, are diametrically opposed. Even so, these two regions have maintained close relations. Growing vines on plots on the slopes of the Combe de Savoie has always provided an additional source of income for farmers from the Bauges, while those who lived in the foothills would go up into the mountains to collect wood and to buy the famous Bauges cheeses. The creation of the Parc Naturel Régional, which has united the center and foothills of the massif into one dynamic commune, has revitalized these relations.

The village of Bellecombe still has its traditional houses, as well as a sawmill with a HUGE FRAME SAW, which is worked by the hydraulic power of the mountain torrent.
LE CHÂTELARD. (*Via la Motte-en-Bauges.*) The village of Le Châtelard, the historic capital and seat of the Parc Naturel Régional, is perched on a rocky spur. It has been a trading center since Roman times, as evinced by coins discovered there in the late 19th century and by the statue of Mercury now in the Musée Savoisien ▲ *126*. The former CORN EXCHANGE (*grenette*) houses an art gallery and the ÉGLISE SAINT-JEAN-BAPTISTE (1834) has some interesting wall paintings. Its parvis offers a magnificent view across the valley.
VALLÉE DES AILLONS. (*Via the D206*) The village of AILLON-LE-VIEUX, which has a strong pastoral tradition, is dominated by the Dent de Rossanaz (6200 feet). AILLON-LE-JEUNE bears traces of the presence of the Carthusian order between the 12th century and the French Revolution (1789–99). The hamlet of LA CORRERIE still has the chapel that received visitors to the convent. All that remains of the vast Carthusian monastery is the façade, which is currently being restored.
LEYSSE BASIN. The village of Thoiry, perched on a sunny ledge above Chambéry, is reached via the Col des Prés (3725 feet). The LAC DE LA THUILE, which the monks of Aillon once exploited for its fish, makes a delightful excursion.

FROM THE FOOTHILLS OF THE MASSIF TO THE HEART OF THE NATIONAL HUNTING RESERVE

MERCURY. The village was named after the ruined temple of Mercury on whose site the church was built. The church houses fifty gilt wooden statues, some dating from the 17th century, while in the belfry hangs one of the largest bells in France. The 14th-century castle is also well worth a visit.
ABBAYE DE TAMIÉ. The monastery was founded (1132), on land donated by the De Chevron family, by the local Cistercian community, together with the Carthusians of Aillon and the Benedictines of Bellevaux. The present buildings, which date from the 17th century, have been occupied by Trappist monks since 1860. Only the church is open to the public, but visitors can buy cheese made by the monks and see an audiovisual presentation of the life of the community.
CLÉRY. The ÉGLISE SAINT-JEAN-BAPTISTE is a beautiful 12th-century Romanesque building with a square belfry. It houses a magnificent sculpted marble altar and a Baroque retable. (*At Saint-Pierre-d'Albigny take the D911.*)
PLAIN OF LA COMPÔTE. The largest plain in the massif owes its charm to its *grangettes*, the barns where hay was left to dry until the beginning of winter.
LA COMPÔTE. Many of the houses that border its narrow winding streets still have *tavalans*, curved wooden uprights positioned beneath the eaves to support the balcony on which firewood was stored.

JARSY. (*Via Doucy-Dessous, Sur-Roche and Belleville.*) For a long time this village, perched below the Dent de Pleuven, had the largest population on the massif. This was why its huge church was known as the 'cathedral of the Bauges'. (*Take the D60, which follows the valley of the upper Chéran.*)
NOTRE-DAME-DE-BELLEVAUX. A footpath leads to the chapel built (1839) on the site of the former priory, which was founded between 1050 and 1090 and occupied by the Benedictines until the French Revolution (1789–99). The chapel, where the last priors of Bellevaux are buried, is the focal point of a pilgrimage held on Whit Monday. As it follows the Chéran upstream the forest road passes through shady woodland, emerging at Nant-Fourchu on the edge of the Réserve National de Chasse et de Faune Sauvage des Bauges (national hunting and wildlife reserve).

From Le Semnoz there is a sweeping view from the Bauges to the Chartreuse.

THE TOME DES BAUGES ● *62*
This famous unpasteurized cheese is matured in damp cellars. Unlike Tomme de Savoie, Tome des Bauges is written with a single 'm'. This idiosyncratic spelling matches the strong, distinctive flavor of the cheese, the legacy of an ancient tradition.

RÉSERVE NATIONALE DE CHASSE DES BAUGES

A 13,340-acre area in the steepest part of the massif has been a national hunting and wildlife reserve since 1950. The area is inhabited by large numbers of chamois, the emblem of the Bauges, roe deer, wild boar, marmots and Corsican mouflon, which were reintroduced in the 1950s. There are also a great many birds, including such rare species as the black grouse, golden eagle, and short-toed eagle ■ *22*. The reserve is a unique environment for the study and conservation of wildlife.

LE SEMNOZ TO THE VALLÉE DU CHÉRAN

FOREST OF SEMNOZ. Leaving Annecy ▲ *159* the D41 enters a forest where deer and mouflon can be glimpsed, but where the more timid marmot is rarely seen. Gradually fir and spruce are interspersed with beech. The Montagne du Semnoz is 10 miles long and almost 3 miles wide. At the Maison du Semnoz and the Jardin Alpin (Alpine garden) is an exhibition of mountain life and local flora and fauna. The great yellow gentian, the pride of the forest, is still gathered for its roots, which are used to make alcohol according to a traditional recipe.
CRÊT DE CHÂTILLON. At the summit of the massif, the great Alpine pastures that were cleared by the monks come into view, against the backdrop of the Massif du Mont Blanc ▲ *226*, the Jura, Bauges and the Lac du Bourget. An orientation table (5575 feet) identifies the surrounding peaks.

Woodland in the Forest of Semnoz.

The Albanais, bounded by the Lac du Bourget in the south and the Lac d'Annecy in the north, is a little-known region of contrasting landscapes: lush hills and green valleys, deep gorges carved out by the Chéran and Fier rivers, and the cliffs of the Bauges, Semnoz, Sapeney, Clergeon and Chambotte mountains. The Albanais, once famous for tobacco-growing, is today a rich agricultural region.

ALBY-SUR-CHÉRAN. This medieval village is dominated by the CHAPELLE SAINT-MAURICE. The triangular square, the PLACE DU TROPHÉE (*above*), is lined with 16th-century arcaded workshops. At the bottom of the narrow street the Pont-Vieux spans the Chéran.

ÉGLISE NOTRE-DAME-DE-PLAINPALAIS. The church, designed by the Savoyard architect Maurice Novarina, was built in 1954. It has a remarkable stained-glass wall by Manessier.

LAKES OF BEAUMONT AND CROSAGNY. (*West of Alby.*) These lakes were dug in the Middle Ages for fishing and hunting and as a source of energy to work mills and tilt hammers. They were restored in the 1990s as part of a nature reserve.

LA CHAMBOTTE. This vantage point beyond Albens commands a panoramic view, taking in the Lac du Bourget and the Chautagne vineyards.

RUMILLY. In the old part of Rumilly, capital of the Albanais, are the former HALLE AUX BLÉS (corn exchange or *grenette*, rebuilt in 1869), the town-hall square with its arcaded mansions (some dating from the 16th and 17th centuries) and the ÉGLISE SAINTE-AGATHE (1937), with a 12th-century belfry. Its industry (Nestlé, Tefal, Salomon), the legacy of tobacco production, has brought Rumilly economic prosperity. The MUSÉE DE L'ALBANAIS, in a former tobacco factory, traces the history of the town and the region from the 17th century.

GORGES DU FIER. These impressive gorges were carved out by the Fier, a mountain stream that rises in the Chaîne des Aravis ▲ *177*. Visitors can walk along the galleries built (1869) above this narrow corridor, which is 330 yards long and almost 200 feet deep. There is a view of the MER DES ROCHERS, a mass of boulders through which the Fier has carved a passage.

CHÂTEAU DE MONTROTTIER. The fortress was built between the 13th and 15th centuries on a rocky spur above the Gorges du Fier. Renovated in the 19th century, it still exemplifies traditional Savoyard military architecture, with a keep, towers, turrets, stairways and gardens. It was bequeathed to the Académie Florimontane ▲ *170* in 1910 and today houses pottery, lace, armor, ivory, Oriental and African artifacts, and 16th-century bronzes by Peter and Hans Vischer.

ALBY SHOEMAKERS
Shoemakers have a long tradition in Alby: as far back as 1325 there were around twenty shoemakers and leather-workers in the village. In 1880 Alby became the regional capital of their guild. The shoemakers would walk to Geneva, Lyons and Paris to sell their wares and all the carriers and horsemen in the Alps had their shoes made in Alby. The tools and machines used in the industry over the centuries are exhibited in the Musée de la Cordonnerie, under the watchful eye of Saint Crispin, patron saint of shoemakers.

The Château de Montrottier has all the appearance of an impressive medieval Savoyard fortress.

Annecy

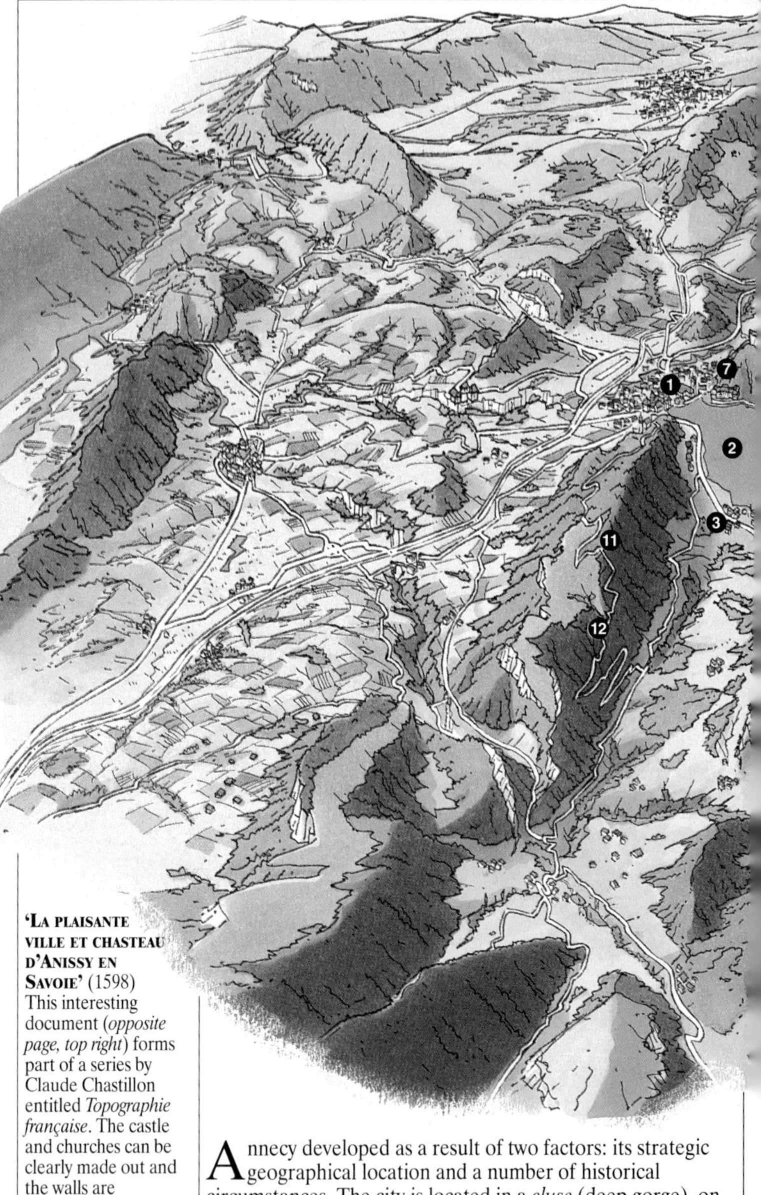

'LA PLAISANTE VILLE ET CHASTEAU D'ANISSY EN SAVOIE' (1598)
This interesting document (*opposite page, top right*) forms part of a series by Claude Chastillon entitled *Topographie française*. The castle and churches can be clearly made out and the walls are accurately depicted. This panoramic view of 'the pleasant town and castle of Annecy' gives an excellent impression of the town on the shores of the lake, the surrounding mountains and the broad external sweep of its many canals.

Annecy developed as a result of two factors: its strategic geographical location and a number of historical circumstances. The city is located in a *cluse* (deep gorge), on the Thiou river at the northern end of the Lac d'Annecy, and at a junction of the principal routes between Italy and Geneva. It is also within easy reach of the mountainous Préalpes of the Chaîne des Aravis ▲ *178* and the plain of the Albanais foreland ▲ *158*. The location has many assets, including a lake that has become legendary; the Thiou, an industrial route that is now a tourist attraction; the great unspoiled forest of Le Semnoz; the extensive Plaine des Fins, which has allowed the town to expand unhindered; and the

hillside on which stands Annecy-le-Vieux and which forms a pleasant northern boundary. Historically, Annecy's proximity to Geneva was the reason why the town rose to power, first as the new capital of the counts of Geneva and later as the diocese of the bishop of Geneva, following the victory of Calvinism (1535). It was chosen as the state capital of the house of Savoie in the 15th century. In the 19th century it was fundamentally developed when it became a busy industrial center. Its industry expanded further in the 20th century, without however adversely affecting tourism, which resulted from the discovery and gradual popularization of this truly grandiose site.

'[The waters of the lake] counterbalance the dark mass of the mountains that surround the lake and which, instead of overlapping and overlying in chaos, form a natural and orderly succession of terraces up to the crenelated peaks of La Tournette which an intangible light renders even more inaccessible, more elevated.'
Léandre Vaillat, *Paysages d'Annecy*

COLUMN OF BOUTAE
This column shaft, seen today on the Place des Romains, once stood in the Roman town of Boutae, which was destroyed by invaders in the late 3rd century and which was finally abandoned in the 5th

century. Boutae, with a population of around 2000, had a forum, a basilica, baths and a theater.

HISTORY

● 33

EARLY SETTLEMENTS. Annecy was probably the first town to be established in the northern Alps. Recent excavations carried out by the French department of underwater and submarine archeology have dated the submerged lakeside settlement off the shore of Annecy-le-Vieux ▲ *172* to 3041 BC. The harbor site, located near the Ile des Cygnes and discovered in 1884, is thought to date from as early as 2500 BC. In c. 50 BC Boutae, a Gallo-Roman *vicus* (town), with a population of about 2000, was established on the Plaine des Fins. The town's triangular layout suggests that it lay at a junction where several roads converged. The extremities of the triangle point toward Faverges (Roman Casuaria), Aix-les-Bains (Aquae) and Geneva (Geneva).

THE MIDDLE AGES. When Boutae was abandoned in the 5th century the population moved to the surrounding hillsides and into the caves, fragmenting into rural communities centered around the old Gallo-Roman *villae* (country estates). One of these communities was named Anicius, the possible root of the name Annecy. The population gradually colonized the banks of the Thiou, a natural outflow from the lake. The settlement, which inevitably became the crossing point over the river near the Ile des Cygnes, on the main north-south

AN EARLY DEPICTION OF ANNECY
The *Heures du duc Louis de Savoie*, an illuminated manuscript of c. 1450 by Jean Bapteur and his school, includes an interesting Nativity scene. The townscape in the background has been identified as Annecy: the central feature is the castle, which bristles with spires, and several streets lead down to the river in the foreground. Another significant detail is the steps leading to the river, a characteristic feature of Annecy and one which the town's inhabitants have always found very convenient.

This statue of a young man (24 inches high), known in antiquity as Bonus Eventus, was excavated at Clos Bonetti, in the Plaine des Fins, in 1867.

route, soon became the seat of a feudal lord, and a toll was levied. From then on the medieval town was enclosed by ramparts and became more homogeneous. It enjoyed unexpected prosperity in the 12th century when the counts of Geneva transferred their capital to Annecy and built a castle which became the royal residence. When the dynasty came to an end with the death (1394) of Robert of Geneva, Annecy devolved to Savoie.

THE 15TH CENTURY. During the 15th century, Annecy, stripped of its status as capital of the Genevois, experienced a period of decline, not least as a result of a series of devastating fires that destroyed the greater part of the town. Amadeus VIII of Savoie, aware of its plight, helped Annecy to rise from its ruins by rebuilding the castle and helping the town to recover from disaster. As a final mark of his esteem he established the Genevois as an appanage (grant of land) in favor of his son Philip (1434). Annecy rose from the ashes and resumed its role as capital of a region that covered most of what is now the *département* of Haute-Savoie.

THE GOLDEN AGE. This brilliant dynasty of princes endowed with an appanage married into the French royal family and received the duchy of Nemours from François I, king of France (r. 1515–47). This period greatly influenced the history of Annecy, which became the seat of the bishop of Geneva following his expulsion from that city, together with a number of monastic institutions, after the triumph of Calvinism in 1535. This reinforced the religious character of Annecy, which became known as the 'Rome of Savoie'. The city enriched its heritage with the construction of the Logis Nemours ▲ *164*, the Cathédrale Saint-Pierre ▲ *169*, the Maison Lambert and the belfry of Notre-Dame-de-Liesse. With the episcopate of Saint François de Sales ▲ *169*, the establishment of the Collège Chappuisien and the foundation of the literary Académie Florimontane ▲ *170*, it would be no exaggeration to say that this was the town's golden age.

THE REVOLUTIONARY PERIOD. The occupation of Savoie by the French Revolutionary army (1792) disrupted Annecy's established order, which was suddenly opened up to new ideas. These were reflected in the development of new industrial techniques and the establishment of many different kinds of factories driven by the hydraulic power of the Thiou, which in turn gave rise to a strong upward trend in the economy. The urban development plans drawn up by Thomas Dominique Ruphy in 1794 were also inspired by Revolutionary vision. Thus the early 19th century witnessed the emergence of an industrial impetus that was to exploit all available resources: customs protection, hydroelectric power and, more recently, postwar industrial decentralization.

EARLY TOURISM. At the same time an increasing awareness of the beauty of Alpine towns and landscapes opened the region to the new fashion for tourism, attracting ever greater numbers of visitors to the lake.

URBAN DEVELOPMENT AHEAD OF ITS TIME

In 1793 the local authorities gave Thomas Dominique Ruphy the task of drawing up the first urban development plan for Annecy. Nine months later the plan was approved by the Paris Commune's departmental council. The plan reflected the genius of its author, who came up with new, forward-looking ideas while taking account of the existing urban fabric. Ruphy wanted to create an extensive road system whose layout would have been excessive for a town with a population of no more than about 4500. He opened up the town by laying out a straight, central thoroughfare that followed the axis of the Rue du Pâquier, an idea well in advance of its time. Extending westward to join the Rue Neuve (now the Rue Royale) and the Avenue de Chambéry, and eastward to join the present Avenue d'Albigny, this central thoroughfare was about 1½ miles long. After a hesitant start during the Revolutionary period, the Ruphy plan was implemented some years later, when Annecy was under Sardinian rule (1815–60).

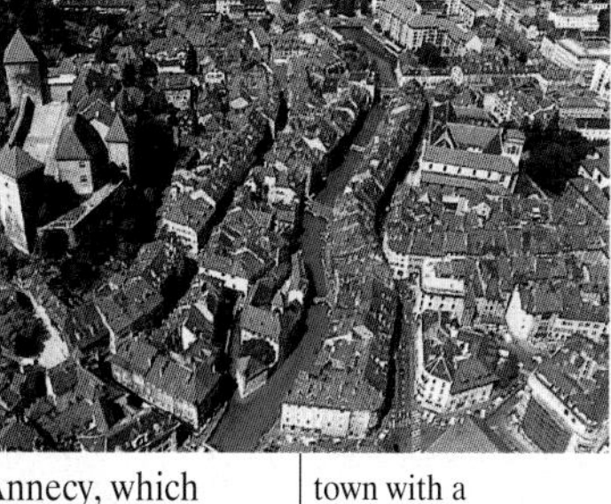

MUSÉE-CHATEAU D'ANNECY
Founded in 1842 at the instigation of the Académie Florimontane ▲ *170*, the museum's purpose was to give an account of Annecy's regional and natural history. From 1934, as the rural life of the region began to decline, greater emphasis was placed on ethnography. Radical changes were made in the 1970s, when these collections were transferred to the castle and replaced by collections of contemporary art. Today the museum presents an innovative combination of traditional heritage and modern art.

TOUR DE LA REINE
The Tour de la Reine (Queen's Tower) stands at the southern corner of the castle. The 12th-century tower, with walls over 13 feet thick, is the oldest part of the castle complex. It was originally part of the sturdy and austere fortress from which rose high walls surmounted by a rampart walk.

THE CASTLE

The castle's impressive outline blends harmoniously with the landscape around Annecy, rising against a mountain setting or serving as a backdrop for the shores of the lake. Its history is closely linked to that of the town of which it is both a faithful reflection and a constant reminder. A visit to the castle readily evokes the history of Annecy and the Genevois. The very structure of the fortress attests to the functions that it fulfilled at the various stages of its history: it was the residence of a sophisticated court, the seat of a dukedom and a vast garrison, and is today a museum of regional history and one of the town's main cultural centers.

THE MAIN COURTYARD. Entering the main courtyard, the visitor will discern four centuries of history in the successive development of the façades. On the left, beyond the former guard house (now the caretaker's lodge), the carefully dressed white stone of the early Renaissance façade and watchtower of the LOGIS NEMOURS (1565) is reminiscent of the architecture of the Ile-de-France region. This is hardly surprising since it was built to the specifications of Charlotte d'Orléans, wife of Philip, Duke of Genevois-Nemours. The Logis Nemours is extended by the earlier LOGIS VIEUX. This part of the castle dates from the 13th century, when the counts of Geneva transferred their capital to Annecy and built their residence between the two ancient towers – the Tour Saint-

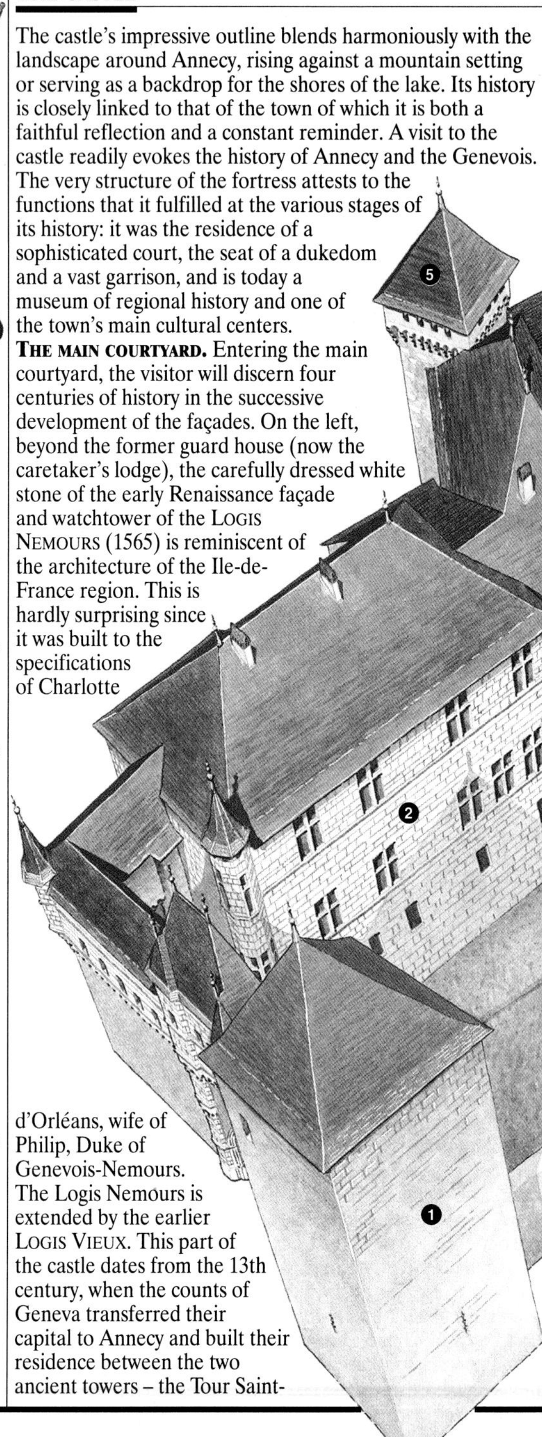

The castle, acquired by the town in 1953, was restored with the help of the Monuments Historiques in order to house the museum.

1. Tour de la Reine
2. Logis Nemours
3. Logis Vieux
4. Logis Neuf
5. Tour Saint-Pierre
6. Tour Saint-Paul
7. Logis Perrière
8. Tour Perrière
9. Cistern

Pierre and the Tour Saint-Paul – which overlook the town. The kitchens, fronted by a great arcade and a well 130 feet deep, still have their two chimneys, which would have smoked as food was prepared for the feasting and banqueting that took place in the great hall. Next to the kitchens is the GRAND PÊLE whose fourteen stone pillars support the GRANDE SALLE situated on the second floor and reached via a spiral staircase. The great hall (82 feet by 43 feet) is on a truly royal scale. Indeed, such royal guests as Henri IV (1600) and Louis XIII (1630) were welcomed there when they visited Annecy. With its magnificent coffered ceiling, the great hall now provides the ideal setting for municipal receptions and cultural events. The more austere façade of the LOGIS NEUF, built as a garrison in 1570, lies at the end of this series of buildings and overlooks an esplanade that offers a sweeping view of the lake and surrounding mountains. The late-15th-century LOGIS PERRIERE stands against the Tour Perrière, on the opposite side of the main courtyard from the Logis Neuf. The tower overlooks the Porte Perrière, which for centuries was one of the main gateways into the town, on the main route to Faverges and Italy.

OBSERVATOIRE RÉGIONAL DES LACS ALPINS

The observatory's informative and instructive exhibitions aim to promote and protect the natural environments of the mountain lakes. Nine rooms in the Logis and Tour Perrière illustrate the different aspects of the lakes' ecosystem.

MUSÉE LAPIDAIRE

The museum of stoneworking is housed in a former circular cistern thought to be the foundations of the original keep. It is reached via a flight of steps on the outer wall of the castle.

CITY OF WATERS
Visitors are often surprised by the amount of water in Annecy: it flows beneath churches, alongside galleries, through parks and along disused mill courses. The focal point of the old town is the Grand Thiou river, the natural outflow from the Lac d'Annecy. For many centuries the river was the nerve center of the town and the only source of energy for its crafts industry. In the 19th century the mills and workshops along the riverbank gave way to quays. The old sluices perpetuate the memory of the town's past prosperity as a crafts center.

OLD ANNECY

The old town was crossed from east to west by a broad, curving thoroughfare – the Grande Charrière – which followed the base of the cliff on which the castle was built. The Porte Perrière was one of the town gates through which traffic arrived from Italy via Faverges and the western shore of the lake.

RUE PERRIÈRE. The Porte Perrière still has its hinges, guardhouse (to the left) and tower. The tower is perfectly integrated into the old town wall, which ran between the gate and the castle, where it joined the Tour Perrière. Beyond the gate lie the arcaded streets that are one of the most typical features of Old Annecy. Unfortunately the short Rue Perrière lost some of its arcades in a large clearance operation that uncovered the impressive façade of the castle.

RUE DE L'ÎLE. The street, named for the nearby Palais de l'Île ▲ *167* on the right, is lined with old houses. Across the street from a beautiful wall fountain, and a little way beyond, is the carriage entrance of the HÔTEL DE CHARMOISY, at no. 1. The mansion was named for its former occupant, Louise du Châtel, wife of Jean-Claude Vidonne de Charmoisy. It was to this pious woman, whom he called Philothée ('friend of God'), that François de Sales, her spiritual adviser, wrote a series of letters which were later included in his *Introduction à la vie dévote*. The gateway, in the late Gothic style, leads into a large courtyard with stables, a vaulted first-floor cellar and a huge watergate that, typically of Annecy's old mansions, give direct access to the Thiou river.

TOWARD THE PORTE SAINTE-CLAIRE. At the intersection on the right ignore the Rue du Pont-Morens and turn down the arcaded RUE SAINTE-CLAIRE. This brings you to the heart of Old Annecy, whose active commercial life was carried on under these very arcades. The HÔTEL BAGNOREA, at no. 18, is well worth a visit. A Renaissance gateway, surmounted by a triangular pediment supported by a pair of fluted columns, marks the entrance to this mansion built in 1563 by Mgr Gallois de Regard, bishop of Bagnorea. It was subsequently bought by Antoine Favre (1557–1624), future president of the senate of Savoie. The literary institution known as the Académie Florimontane ▲ *170* was founded here in 1607 and in 1610 the mansion

The winding Rue Sainte-Claire, lined with arcades, follows the outline of the cliff on which the castle was built.

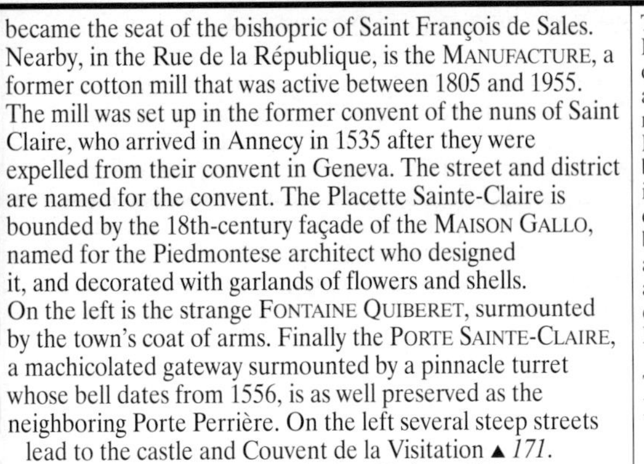

became the seat of the bishopric of Saint François de Sales. Nearby, in the Rue de la République, is the MANUFACTURE, a former cotton mill that was active between 1805 and 1955. The mill was set up in the former convent of the nuns of Saint Claire, who arrived in Annecy in 1535 after they were expelled from their convent in Geneva. The street and district are named for the convent. The Placette Sainte-Claire is bounded by the 18th-century façade of the MAISON GALLO, named for the Piedmontese architect who designed it, and decorated with garlands of flowers and shells. On the left is the strange FONTAINE QUIBERET, surmounted by the town's coat of arms. Finally the PORTE SAINTE-CLAIRE, a machicolated gateway surmounted by a pinnacle turret whose bell dates from 1556, is as well preserved as the neighboring Porte Perrière. On the left several steep streets lead to the castle and Couvent de la Visitation ▲ *171*. Beyond the gateway, the district of Sainte-Claire leads to the Porte du Sépulcre, named for the convent of Saint-Sépulcre that once stood on the road to Chambéry and Aix-les-Bains. (*Return to the Rue Sainte-Claire.*)

PALAIS DE L'ÎLE. This intriguing stone building stands in the middle of the Thiou river like a huge stone ship with its prow cleaving

THE MANUFACTURE
For 150 years the life of the town was based around the old cotton mill known as the Manufacture, founded by Jean-Pierre Duport in 1805. After it was closed in 1955, it was bought by the town and replaced by an apartment block designed by Éric Kasper in 1978.

The steeply sloping Rue Perrière.

THE FAÇADE OF SAINT-FRANÇOIS
The classic façade was inspired by that of Il Gesu in Rome, the mother church of the Jesuit order, designed by Giacomo da Vignola in 1568. The style was later widely adopted.

MUSÉE DE L'HISTOIRE D'ANNECY
Since 1986 the Palais de l'Île (*below*) has housed a museum that traces the history of Annecy and the surrounding region. The former law courts, jailer's quarters, prison cells and chapel are also open to the public.

the waters. Its position on the north-south route that passed through Annecy on the way from Geneva to Italy helps to explain its role as a bridge and key point in antiquity. In the 12th century the Palais de l'Île was the modest fortified residence of a local lord. It became an administrative building when the counts of Geneva moved their capital to Annecy, serving as a prison, law courts, a mint, archives and the seat of the chief justice of the Genevois. Its presence soon attracted lawyers, attorneys and notaries, who built the *banches* (single-story shuttered cobwork buildings) around the Cour de l'Île. This function was reinforced when the House of Savoie transferred its capital to Turin ● *36* and Annecy became the capital of the Genevois appanage. During the French Revolution (1789–99) the Palais de l'Île reverted to its medieval role as a prison. This continued until 1864, when a prison was built in the Rue Guillaume-Fichet (it was demolished in 1970). In the late 19th century the building became the subject of a bitter political controversy when a proposal for its demolition was made for public health reasons. Its classification as an historic monument in 1900 saved it at the eleventh hour. The former mansion was carefully restored and housed the trade union center and the French philanthropic society until 1947, when it became the property of the museum conservation department which founded the Musée de l'Histoire d'Annecy. (*Take the Passage de l'Île.*)

ÉGLISE SAINT-MAURICE. The parish church, formerly the chapel of the Dominican convent, is named for Annecy's first church, built in the 12th century near the castle. The building of the new church was financed by Cardinal Jean de Brogny, and was consecrated in 1445. It is a fine example of the regional architectural style known as Savoyard Flamboyant ● *81*. The surprisingly large nave has ribbed vaulting with keystones decorated with the arms of Jean Magnin, an illustrious benefactor. The aisles have various irregularities that betray the fact that the church was built in stages over a period of

The tomb of Philippe de Monthouz
The skeletal, naked figure of Philippe de Monthouz is shown lying on a large tomb surrounded by mourners. The painting, attributed to a Rhenish artist of the school of Konrad Witz ● *96*, is unusual in that it is a *trompe-l'oeil* that replaces the sculpture traditionally used in the 15th century, possibly for reasons of economy.

almost a century. The most interesting feature of the church is the huge *trompe-l'oeil* wall painting that decorates the last left-hand bay of the chancel. It represents the tomb of Philippe de Monthouz, duke of Savoie and Burgundy who, as indicated by a long inscription, died in 1458.

Église Saint-François. The church, which stands on the river at the far end of the bridge leading to the Palais de l'Île, has a particularly rich history. As the Église de la Sainte-Source it was the first church of the Couvent de la Visitation (1610) ▲ *171*, the cradle of a still very active order which today has 163 communities throughout the world. It was here that the Visitants buried their founders, Saint François de Sales and Saint Jeanne de Chantal, whose tombs rapidly became a place of European pilgrimage. The magnificent religious ceremonies held for the beatification and canonization of the town's patron saints went down in the annals of Annecy's history. Royal gifts were bestowed on the church, which was chosen by Charles-Emmanuel II of Savoie to celebrate his marriage to Françoise Madeleine, the daughter of Gaston d'Orléans, in 1663. Restored as a place of worship after housing a textile factory, Saint-François was given to the Italian community in 1922, which is why it is also known as the 'church of the Italians'. (*Follow the Quai de l'Île along the banks of the Thiou to the Passage des Célestins, which leads to the cathedral.*)

François de Sales
François de Sales was born on August 21, 1567 into an old aristocratic family. Rejecting a brilliant political career, he chose to follow another calling that led him to take holy orders (1593) and become a bishop (1602). His preaching and the simplicity of his lifestyle won the hearts of the people of Savoie, Paris and France. He was entrusted with diplomatic missions that made him an ambassador for peace in Europe. In 1610, with Jeanne de Chantal, he founded the Order of the Visitation and, between 1610 and 1700, some 145 convents were established. Saint François de Sales died on December 18, 1622, in Lyons. He was buried in the church of the first Couvent de la Visitation ▲ *171* and became the object of great popular devotion.

THE DECOR OF SAINT-PIERRE (*right*)
The cornice of the chancel is surmounted by an attic story punctuated by acroteria and four flame ornaments, the statues of four evangelists and the pontifical arms (*left*) and episcopal arms (*right*), carved by the Turin sculptor Aguisetti. The center of the composition is dominated by a remarkable *Deliverance of Saint Peter* (Joseph Mazzola de Valduggia) in which the 'supernatural light coming from the angel's body, as if radiating from within, floods into the cell leaving Peter and his guards in the shadows'.

THE ACADÉMIE FLORIMONTANE
The Académie Florimontane was founded in the Hôtel Bagnorea, in 1607 (twenty-seven years after the Académie de Richelieu), as a result of the friendship between François de Sales and Antoine Favre, president of the senate of Savoie. It was a literary institution inspired by the Italian academies and was well received in Annecy due to the presence of these two spiritual leaders. The academy, housed in the former bishop's residence, still thrives.

PONT DES AMOURS
The bridge spans the Canal du Vassé, which runs from the Jardins de l'Europe to Le Pâquier. There is a fine view of the canal from the bridge.

CATHÉDRALE SAINT-PIERRE. The cathedral, originally the modest chapel of a Franciscan convent founded in Annecy in the early 16th century, has a strange history. The triumph of Calvinism in Geneva (1535) led to the departure of a major part of that city's former religious community: firstly the cathedral chapter, then the Maccabean chapter and finally the bishop himself. The warm welcome extended by the Franciscans in Annecy soon gave way to disagreements arising from cohabitation, to the point that a separation had to be envisaged that could only be to the bishop's advantage. The latter gained the support of Rome in ousting the Franciscans and obtaining sole use of the church and convent, on whose site the new bishop's palace was built in 1782. The church became a cathedral in 1772 and was refurbished in a manner befitting its new role.
Its decoration was entrusted to the Turin artist Joseph Plaisance who, in 1787, was given the task of creating a stuccowork border for the chancel, with a Baroque decor of composite orders in which twelve columns were arranged in pairs.

LE PÂQUIER

LE PÂQUIER. Before turning right down the Rue du Pâquier, which leads invitingly to the nearby lake, it is worth taking a look at the 17th-century HÔTEL DE SALES, whose façade is decorated with four busts allegorically representing the four seasons.
CENTRE BONLIEU. The modern concrete and glass building of the Centre Bonlieu stands opposite the extensive lawns of Le Pâquier. The center, opened in 1981, is primarily a cultural center, with a theater, library and tourist office, and also contains shops and service facilities and restaurants. They are arranged around a large central forum that provides an ideal setting for cultural events and popular entertainments.

TOWARD LE SEMNOZ

Before it became the location of the departmental Conservatoire d'Art et d'Histoire, the Grand Séminaire d'Annecy had a turbulent history. Built in 1648 by Mgr Jean d'Arenthon d'Alex, the bishop of Geneva who was resident in Annecy, this fine edifice served as a seminary, a hospital during the French Revolution, a factory and garrison, and from 1922 as a hotel. It was not until 1923 that the Church could afford to recover its property. When it was put on the market fifty years later the seminary aroused a great deal of interest from property developers. However it was acquired by the departmental council of Haute-Savoie and was used to house the departmental archives and the Conservatoire d'Art et d'Histoire. This new cultural institution, opened on July 25, 1980, enabled the *département* to bring the collections of Paul Payot, General Chastel and Evariste Jonchère (1892–1956), winner of the first Grand Prix de Rome, together under one roof. The Conservatoire organizes regular temporary exhibitions relating to the history of the Alps.

BASILIQUE DE LA VISITATION. The white belfry, which has stood on the edge of the forest of the Crêt du Maure for about sixty years, marks the site of the new Couvent de la Visitation. Each year the church, where lie the tombs of Saint François de Sales and Saint Jeanne de Chantal, cofounders of the Order of the Visitation, welcomes pilgrims from all over the world. In 1909 work began on the new convent, which was built to replace the one on the Rue Royale (the latter was impeding urban development). On August 2, 1911, the remains of the two saints were transferred to the new convent in a ceremony attended by a crowd of some 150,000 people. Although it was completed in 1930 the church was not consecrated until 1949. The 236-foot belfry is surmounted by a 23-foot bronze cross. It houses a peal of twenty six bells and a great bell weighing 4 tonnes. The spacious nave is lit by stained-glass windows depicting scenes from the lives of the two saints who founded the order.

This pectoral cross, which once belonged to Saint François de Sales, is today kept in the Couvent de la Visitation.

THE COLLECTIONS OF PAYOT AND CHASTEL
The Conservatoire d'Art et d'Histoire houses the collections of Paul Payot, the former mayor of Chamonix (15,000 volumes, 3000 prints and paintings relating to the Alps) and General Chastel (17th- and 19th-century paintings), an enlightened art lover whom Napoleon entrusted with the task of enriching the museums of France.

PACCARD BELLS
From the 'Savoyarde' of the Sacré Coeur (Paris) and the 'Jeanne d'Arc' in Rouen Cathedral to the American Liberty Bells and the Peace Bell of Hiroshima, bells made in the Paccard foundry – great bells, peals and little bells for announcing matins – ring out across the world. This, the oldest and largest bell foundry in France, was established in 1796 by Antoine Paccard and, some 80,000 bells later, is run by Pierre Paccard, a member of the sixth generation of this dynasty of bell-founders.

PACCARD: 200 YEARS OF EXPERTISE
First a plaster cast of the bell is made, to be used as a mold. The interior of the mold is lined with a layer of clay and horsehair, and the outside decorated with motifs made of wax. The mold is then covered with a layer of sand and clay and fired in a kiln. The plaster is removed and molten bronze poured between the walls of the clay mold casing. Although it takes eight to ten hours for bronze to reach a temperature of 1800°F, when it becomes molten, pouring into the mold is a process that takes only minutes.

This magnificent 3rd-century bronze cauldron, almost 2 feet in diameter, was discovered in the villa at Thovey. It can be seen in the Musée Archéologique of Vuiz-Faverges.

The shores of the Lac d'Annecy stretch for a distance of 23 miles and offer a succession of views in which the landscapes, in the foreground close by the road or in the distance, blend harmoniously. Shady orchards, extensive forests and high peaks silhouetted against the sky are interspersed with villas, towns, villages and hamlets. Above the western shore of the lake the dark bulk of the Montagne du Semnoz contrasts with the turquoise waters below, pinched at their narrowest point by the Duingt peninsula (*above*). Overlooking the eastern shore the steep slopes of La Tournette catch the evening light. The scene is completed by the Dents de Lanfon, Le Veyrier and Le Taillefer.

THE WESTERN SHORE

According to the French geographer Raoul Blanchard (1877–1965) 'Tourism has undoubtedly been promoted by the concept of beauty made fashionable by the Romantics, but more so by the development of the railroad. It has been popularized by the private automobile and public vehicles that bring in crowds of people.' Indeed, a railroad line once followed the western shore of the lake between Annecy and Albertville (1901). Now abandoned, part of it (the Sévrier-Doussard section) has been converted into a cycle track.

SÉVRIER. The collections and slide shows at the MUSÉE DE LA CLOCHE trace the history of bell-making and of the FONDERIE PACCARD, which was moved from Annecy-le-Vieux to Sévrier in 1989. Opposite the church the ÉCOMUSÉE DU COSTUME SAVOYARD, housed in a 19th-century Sardinian-style building that was once a girls' school, displays fine traditional costumes.

SAINT-JOROZ. Saint-Joroz, which lies between the lake and the Laudon river, is the most densely populated of the lakeside villages. To fully appreciate the sights, sounds and atmosphere of the lake, take the footpath from the beach that runs along the edge of the reedy marshland. You can also follow the Laudon upstream to the Parc Naturel Régional du Massif des Bauges ▲ *152*.

DUINGT. The Duingt peninsula, a projection of the rocky outcrop of Le Taillefer, separates the Grand Lac from the Petit Lac. Perched on a promontory overlooking the strait, the 11th-century CASTLE (not open to the public) was restored in the 18th century by the marquises de Sales.

DOUSSARD. The village of Doussard, set back from the southern shore

of the lake, has fine examples of well-to-do rural architecture. The marshland of the RÉSERVE NATURELLE DU BOUT DU LAC ▲ *174* is an overwintering and breeding ground for waterfowl. A colony of beavers also lives there. A marked footpath leads to the marshes and the medieval tower is used for bird-watching.

FAVERGES. There is evidence to suggest that the site, situated some distance from the lake, between the Massif des Bauges ▲ *152* and the Chaîne des Aravis ▲ *177*, has been occupied since the Bronze Age. The MUSÉE ARCHÉOLOGIQUE of Viuz-Faverges houses a collection of artifacts found in the region: flint axes, bronze jewelry, iron tools, Gallo-Roman jewelry, Roman coins and pottery. It also has exhibits relating to the Alemmanni, an itinerant people who arrived on the site of Thovey some 1700 years ago and torched the 1st–2nd century Gallo-Roman villa (only part of the baths survive). The castle, perched beneath the Dent-de-Cons and the Montagne de la Sambuy, is dominated by a 13th-century keep. Henry IV (1553–1610), king of France, once came here. It is now a holiday center. In summer Faverges hosts the Musik Alpes, a festival of Alpine music.

SOUTH OF FAVERGES. In a valley south of Faverges lies the GROTTE (cave) and CASCADE (waterfall) DE SEYTHENEX, the only underground site open to the public in Haute-Savoie. Working models of watermills show how water was used in traditional industries, to power oil-mills and sawmills and to work machinery for making tools. A little further on lies the Cistercian ABBAYE DE TAMIÉ (Savoie), where only the church is open to the public ▲ *156*.

THE EASTERN SHORE

ANNECY-LE-VIEUX. Many tourists end up in the hills above the bay of ALBIGNY without realizing that the Canal du Thiou and the old town of Annecy ▲ *166* are less than two miles as the crow flies from the town they are visiting. Annecy-le-Vieux has its own history and some real architectural treasures. To visit the Romanesque belfry next to the ÉGLISE SAINT-LAURENT, knock at the door of the town hall. The huge bronze bell, founded in 1796 and weighing 1540 pounds, today hangs silent. Opposite the belfry is the Villa Dunand, where the composer Gabriel Fauré (1845–1924) lived from 1919 to 1924. The Petit Port, in the lower town, offers a view of the privately owned Villa de la Tour, where the writer Eugène Sue (1804–57) ended his days. The author of *Les Mystères de Paris* enjoyed an unrivaled view of the bay of Albigny.

FAVERGES, AN INDUSTRIAL TOWN
The production of Dupont lighters and pens, Staubli weaving machines and Bourgeois industrial furnaces and ovens attests to the industrial nature of the town, which spawned the innovative idea of incorporating a wood-fueled boiler-room into its ecofriendly waste-treatment plant. This unusual installation provides heating for one third of the town's inhabitants.

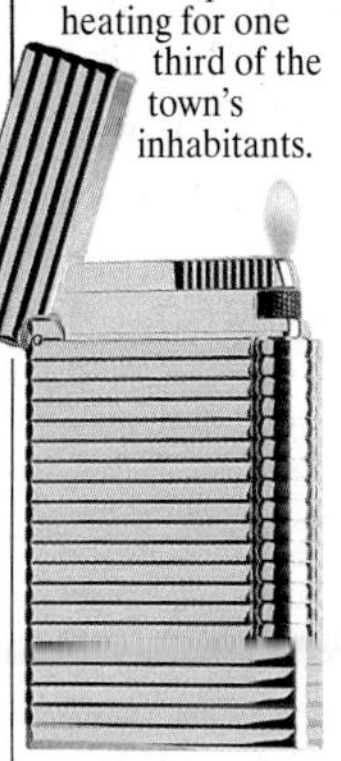

EUGÈNE SUE IN EXILE
After the *coup d'état* of December 2, 1851 the author of *Les Mystères de Paris* (1842–3), in which he expressed his social and democratic ideas, sought refuge in Haute-Savoie. In a villa perched 650 feet above the lake, the popular novelist wrote his last novel, *Cornélia d'Alfy*. He died in 1857 and was buried in the cemetery at Loverchy.

With a surface area of 10 square miles, the Lac d'Annecy is France's second-largest natural lake. By the 1960s the waters and bottom of the lake had become badly polluted as a result of the increased amounts of waste flowing into the lake from its shores. An unprecedented joint initiative on the part of the local authorities led to the construction of an underwater drainage system and installation of a filtering plant.

AN UNPRECEDENTED INITIATIVE

Pollution of the lake caused a build-up of organic sludge that threatened all forms of life. The alarm was raised by Dr Servettaz, a doctor from Annecy who was aware of the health hazards of this situation. Together with local fishermen and specialist agencies, and at the instigation of Charles Bosson, mayor of Annecy, an association of lakeside authorities was formed on July 15, 1957. As a result, an underwater drainage system was build around the edge of the lake.

DRAINAGE SYSTEM

The system has 280 miles of pipes and forty three pumping stations. Waste water from the twenty two municipalities in the association is channeled through the underwater pipes laid around the lake shores, and into the filtering plant located at the downstream end of the lake.

FISH

Today the Lac d'Annecy has a large population of lavaret (whitefish), char and trout. As the result of a joint initiative, natural spawning grounds have been improved, the lake has been restocked by fish farming and the fish population has been monitored. Today, around 30 tons of fish are caught in the lake each year.

THE LAKE THROUGH THE SEASONS

In winter, when the temperature of the lake is about 40°F, its waters are at their clearest. In very harsh winters the lake may partially freeze over. In spring the presence of plankton clouds the waters, giving them their emerald-green color. In late summer surface temperatures can reach 75° F.

Briar, spring onions, meadowsweet and mountain avens are just a few of the plants in the herbal of the botanist and gastronomic chef Marc Veyrat.

PANORAMIC VIEW OF THE LAKE
At a height of 3795 feet the Col de Forclaz is the perfect starting point for hang-gliding, and fine weather the sky is dotted with these silent craft. For those who prefer to keep their feet firmly on the ground, the pass offers a panoramic view across the lake.

VEYRIER-DU-LAC. The village is dominated by Mont Veyrier which, at a height of 4265 feet, forms a natural observatory. It is particularly popular with those attending the magnificent firework display of the widely publicized FÊTE DU LAC, held on the first Saturday of August. The vantage point was once reached by a cableway, which is no longer in operation. Still very much alive, however, is the AUBERGE DE L'ÉRIDAN, owned by Marc Veyrat, one of the virtuosos of French gastronomy.

MENTHON-SAINT-BERNARD. Towering over this peaceful town is a mysterious castle that appears to have come straight out of *Sleeping Beauty*. According to local tradition Walt Disney, who was staying in Talloires in the 1930s, fell in love with this eyrie perched high on the mountainside. It is reputed to have provided the inspiration for his impregnable baroque castles. Since the 12th century the castle has been the home of the Menthon family, whose famous son, Saint Bernard, founded the hospices of the Grand- and Petit-Saint-Bernard passes. In more recent times François de Menthon was minister of justice during the Liberation and a prosecutor at the Nuremberg trials. Another of the town's famous residents was the French philosopher and historian Hippolyte Taine (1828–93), who would entertain the intellectual elite of the time in his manor house at the foot of the Roc de Chère. His tomb is located on the slopes of one of the town's parks.

TALLOIRES. After Annecy, Talloires (*reached via the D24*) is probably the most famous resort on the shores of the lake. It nestles at the foot of the Roc de Chère, on a bay overlooked by the Dents de Lanfon and the Massif de la Tournette. In the summer of 1896 the post-Impressionist painter Paul Cézanne (1839–1906) stayed here after a cure and painted several views of the lake ● *97*. For several centuries Talloires was a major center of pilgrimage. It has an important religious heritage: the 11th-century priory, now the cultural center of Tufts University, Boston, and the BENEDICTINE ABBEY (rebuilt in the 17th century), now a hotel. The CHAPELLE SAINT-GERMAIN was built above the town in 1829 in honor of the abbey's first prior, who lived as a hermit in a nearby cave (reached by a footpath) from 1033 to 1060. The more secular Auberge du Père Bise offers gastronomic delights for the more discerning palate.

The Château de Menthon-Saint-Bernard.

Chaîne des Aravis

Michel Voisin

André Trabut and Michel Germain

▲ CHAÎNE DES ARAVIS

FIVE PASSES AND THREE GORGES
The Pays de Thônes is delimited to the north by the Col de la Colombière (5300 feet) and the Défilé des Étroits; to the west by the Défilé de Dingy-Saint-Clair and the Col de Bluffy (2070 feet); to the south by the Défilé des Essérieux and the Col de l'Épine (3100 feet); and to the east by the Col des Aravis.

The Pays de Thônes is situated between Arve and the *cluse* (deep gorge) of Annecy, in the Massif des Bornes-Aravis, a straight mountain range rising to an altitude of 9030 feet at its highest point, the Pointe Percée. Within this region, bounded by five *cols* (mountain passes) and three *défilés* (gorges), the mountain landscapes are dominated by peaks ranging from 6560 to 8860 feet: Le Lachat du Châtillon, Le Lachat des Villards, La Tournette, Le Charvin and l'Étale. There are several mountain streams and four main rivers: the Nom, which flows from the Col des Aravis; the Fier, which rises in the Lac du Mont-Charvin; the Borne, which flows from the Col des Annes; and the Chaise, from Le Charvin. The local economy is based on traditional crafts, timber (Mobalpa has been in Thônes for fifty years) and agriculture, especially dairy produce and cheeses: Reblochon ▲ *180* and the blue cheese and goat's cheeses of Les Aravis ● *62*.

9. Thônes 10. Les Clefs 11. Manigod 12. Morette 13. La Balme-de-Thuy 14. Dingy-Saint-Clair 15. Alex 16. Thorens-Glières 17. Plateau des Glières

Les Aravis near La Clusaz.

Col des Aravis

A divine furrow. The Col des Aravis (4915 feet) straddles the *départements* of Savoie and Haute-Savoie. According to legend it was the scene of a divine manifestation that put an end to the rivalry between the villages of La Giettaz and La Clusaz, which both laid claim to the chapel built on the pass in the 17th century. One day, at dawn, a strange furrow appeared (said to have been traced by angels during the night) which divided the pass in two and placed the chapel in the territory of La Clusaz. Traces of the furrow can still be seen today, near the chapel.

Chapelle Sainte-Anne. The chapel was founded in 1687 by Pierre François de Riddes de Belletour, lord of Flumet, and dedicated to Saint Anne, as indicated by the inscription on the façade. For a long time it provided shelter for travelers caught on the pass in bad weather.

Year-round tourism With such village-resorts as La Clusaz, Le Grand-Bornand, Manigod and Saint-Jean-de-Sixt, the pleasant valley of the Pays de Thônes enjoys the benefits of tourism in summer as well as in winter.

The home of Reblochon
Reblochon is a farmhouse cheese made from the milk of the Abondance breed of cow. The Pays de Thônes accounts for most of the 3500 tons that are produced each year. The cheese is made by some 250 farms in the low valleys between October and April, and in the chalets of the mountain pastures after transhumance (*emmontagnée*) in May.
1. After milking, rennet is added to the milk, which is then gently heated.
2. The resulting curd is cut into pieces and pressed by hand into molds.
3. The cheeses are removed from the mold, salted and placed on boards. They are turned each day for 8 to 10 days.

The village of La Clusaz under snow and the chapel of Chinaillon.

LA CLUSAZ

This village-resort occupies a unique site at the mouth of the *cluse* (*clusa* in the Savoyard dialect) of the Nom, a turbulent mountain stream which has carved this narrow gorge as it flows down the mountainside. Originally built in the valley bottom, the village expanded outward in concentric circles around its church and square, now a pedestrian precinct. The ÉGLISE SAINTE-FOY, which replaced a Sardinian Neoclassical church (1821–2), was entirely rebuilt in the mid-1970s. It combines freestone and wood to good effect, including a resolutely modern framework of wood core plywood, while the spire of the belfry (1797) has a slightly bulbous base. The Lac des Confins nestles in a delightful setting (*right*) and offers some beautiful walks at the foot of the Chaîne des Aravis and the Pointe Percée.

LE GRAND-BORNAND

Le Grand-Bornand, on the D4, is a truly delightful village which has preserved its authenticity in a harmonious blend of tradition and modernity, stone and wood. It stands against a background of forests surmounted by the majestic Chaîne des Aravis. The village still has a strong pastoral tradition based on the success of its famous Reblochon cheeses.

MAISON DU PATRIMOINE. The chalet, built in 1830, has been entirely restored and furnished in traditional style. Its three stories offer an insight into local history and tradition: the architecture centered around the famous *pointe d'âne* (central pillar) has been meticulously reconstructed, while the living accommodation and rustic furniture have been restored to recreate the atmosphere of everyday village life.

VALLÉE DU CHINAILLON. Beyond the little hamlet of Bois-Bercher, whose chalets and barns are roofed with shingles and wooden tiles, the old village of Chinaillon nestles around the CHAPELLE NOTRE-DAME-DES-NEIGES (1677). With its stone façade and finely carved pinnacle turret, this charming and beautifully proportioned chapel is the most admired and photographed monument in Les Aravis. (*Return to the village and follow the signs to the Vallée du Bouchet.*)

THE 'POINTE D'ÂNE'
The chalets of Le Grand-Bornand ● 77 are characterized by a structure known as the *pointe d'âne*. It consists of a central pillar that stands on stone plinth and supports the ridge-pole. Two sloping crossbeams (the *bras d'âne*) run from the top of the pillar to the side walls, forming an inverted V. This pillar strengthens the framework of the chalet, enabling it to withstand the weight of snow.

TOWARD LE PETIT-BORNAND-LES-GLIÈRES

DÉFILÉ DES ÉTROITS. The gorge is little more than a gash between two steep cliffs, just wide enough for the road and the Borne. This turbulent mountain stream is notorious for its violence, especially when spring rains combine with melting snows to devastating effect, as in 1987 when its rate of flow was multiplied one-thousand-fold.

ENTREMONT. The delightful village of Entremont lies at the junction of a small valley and the larger Vallée du Borne, into which it has had ample room to spread. Its agricultural and pastoral activities are carried on between the valley and mountain pastures, depending on the season. The village became famous when a religious community was founded on the left bank of the Borne (1115) by the canons of the Abbaye d'Abondance ▲ *202*. Today all that remains is the church (1680), which has changed very little and whose interior has some notable features: 15th-century wooden choir stalls, a chancel with a double Baroque retable and a treasure that includes several reliquaries (a 12th-century shrine and three 13th-century 'blessing arms' (*left*) inlaid with precious stones).

LE PETIT-BORNAND-LES-GLIÈRES. This large agricultural village occupies a middle-altitude location where rural life has always depended on the exploitation of the forests and meadows: there are sawmills along the Borne, factories where buckets and bowls (*bachals*) are made from solid tree trunks, and nurseries where conifers and mountain species are grown. Dairy produce is also important. Le Petit-Bornand, which was given parish status in 1152 by the monks who cleared the pastures of Entremont, embraces eleven hamlets and six mountain pastures. In the past men and animals went up to the summer pastures (*emmontagnée*) ● *56* in time for Midsummer's Day. The lower meadows were meanwhile left for the production of winter hay, since making Reblochon ▲ *180* requires cows to be fed and grazed in the traditional manner. In 1947 the words 'les Glières' was added to 'Le Petit-Bornand' in memory of the role played by the village during World War Two ● *46* ▲ *186*. (*Return to Saint-Jean-de-Sixt and take the D4 toward Thônes.*)

SHINGLES AND WOODEN TILES
Roofs made of shingles and wooden tiles are beginning to reappear in the Pays de Thônes. *Tavaillons* are wooden tiles about 15½ inches long. They are nailed onto the roof, and five or six layers are needed to make the roof weatherproof. *Ancelles* (shingles) are exactly twice the size of *tavaillons* and are used to cover low-pitched roofs.

TOWARD THÔNES

LES VILLARDS-SUR-THÔNES. The village, which nestles at the foot of Mont Lachat (6650 feet) on the banks of the Nom, still has a great many wood craftsmen. The church (1795) has a beautiful organ (1978) built by a local craftsman, Louis Mermillod-Gossemain, according to the technique of the 18th-century monk Dom Bedos.

THÔNES. Thônes, a popular summer resort since the late 19th century, is now also a winter resort. The town, which nestles at the foot of the cliffs of the Roche (tawn) de Thônes after which it is named, has existed for over a thousand years. It lies at an altitude of 2050 feet, at the confluence of the Fier and Nom rivers, on the road between Annecy ▲ *160* and most of the villages in the valley.

THE FOREST
An estimated 40 percent of the Vallée de Thônes is covered by forest. It consists of three main species: spruce (60 percent); broad-leaved deciduous trees, including beech, (20 percent); and conifers (pine and fir), which grow at middle altitudes and on north-facing slopes.

In the town center a series of late-15th-century arcades form a semicircle around the fountain of the Place Bastian, a gift from the Thônains of Paris (1867–69). The CHURCH, with its tall onion-shaped spire (138 feet), was built in 1697 under the direction of the Milanese architect Pietro Chiesa. Unfortunately it was badly damaged during the French Revolution (1789–99) and the bombing raids of August 1944. It has a freestone façade with a neo-Romanesque entrance that contrasts with the more sober architecture of the rest of the building. Inside are several altars and retables, including the 17th-century retable of the Sacré-Coeur. This 'wall of faith' is a pictorial catechism on three levels: the Trinity, the Incarnation and the Redemption – the Church, its Fathers and its doctors. In the center is the martyrdom of Saint Maurice, the town's patron saint. Beyond the church is the MUSEUM, installed in 1939 in the former Asile Avet, which served as a calefactory for the older inhabitants and a school for the younger generation. It traces the history of the valley from prehistoric times to the present day. Its most prized pieces include the stained-glass window representing local flora, from the tympanum of the church; a 15th–16th century Pietà (*right*), from the Chapelle de la Bossonaz; a 17th-century carved wooden beehive; and a game of chance, also in carved wood.

AROUND THÔNES

ÉCOMUSÉE DU BOIS ET DE LA FORÊT DES ÉTOUVIERES (*1¾ miles west of Thônes*). The museum is laid out in a restored sawmill on the banks of the Malnant in the Vallée du Montremont. The abandoned mill, more than 100 years old, was donated by its former owners.

THE 'ROI DU MONT'
From the Place Bastian take the Chemin des Addebouts and then the Chemin du Mont. The latter passes through a larch wood which soon gives way to ancient spruces. After the orientation table, follow the signs for the Circuit du Roi du Mont (1½ hours' walk). The Roi du Mont (King of the Mountain) is a tree 180 high and with a circumference of more than 17 feet. It stands at an altitude of 3345 feet and is said to be more than 300 years old.

The ancient standing stone on the Col de la Croix-Fry.

LES CLEFS. (*South of Thônes.*) This is the second-oldest village in the valley after La Balme-de-Thuy. During the 11th and 12th centuries the lords of Les Clefs extended their jurisdiction to the shores of the Lac d'Annecy and to Ugine and Faverges ▲ *173*. Between 1310 and 1350 their influence decreased, to the benefit of the neighboring town of Thônes.

VALLÉE DE MANIGOD

Manigod, Les Clefs, Serraval and Le Bouchet-Mont-Charvin form an association of villages – LE VAL-SULENS – to the southeast of Thônes. Serraval and Le Bouchet lie on the region's southern boundary, which is formed by the Essérieux and the Col de l'Épine.

LA TOURNETTE. A ramp carved out of the rock gives easy access to the circular outcrop at the summit (7730 feet). From this vantage point there is a magnificent view of the Lac d'Annecy ▲ *172* and Lake Geneva ▲ *192* to the north and the Lac du Bourget ▲ *144* to the southwest.

MANIGOD. The village of Manigod is situated in the upper valley of the Fier, in a vast area of traditional agriculture dominated by l'Étale (8150 feet). The valleys' many hamlets are characterized by their traditional chalets, oratories and chapels. Further up the valley, at a place known as Sous l'Aiguille ('beneath the needle'), is the STONE OF SAINT FRANÇOIS DE SALES against which the saint is said to have rested and left the impression of his back. At the side of the old road leading up to the COL DE LA CROIX-FRY, near the Chapelle de Mont-Pellaz, is a spring with miraculous powers which is also associated with the saint. On the *col*, at an altitude of 4845 feet, is a standing stone which was once the focus of pagan worship. In 1607 Bishop François de Sales traced a line at right

THE CHALET AT MANIGOD
Typically of the region, the chalet is fronted by a *nova*, a broad terrace sheltered by overhanging eaves which acts as the entrance. People pass through to enter the living quarters, and animals to reach their stables or byres. The harvest is brought in through the wide barn. A ladder leads up to the second-floor of the barn. Bales of hay are carried to the top of the ladder and thrown down to the first floor.

LA TOURNETTE
The name of this mountain, meaning 'The Reel', probably derives from the circular shape of its summit.

The Dents de Lanfon (5950 feet).

angles to an earlier sword mark, thereby sanctifying the stone with a cross. In the village the ÉGLISE SAINT-PIERRE, built between 1688 and 1690 by a master-craftsman from Samoëns ▲ *214*, is one of the earliest Savoyard churches to be based on the 'hall-church' principle: the nave and aisles are covered by a one double-pitched roof. The church stands on a very steep slope and the entrance has a broad canopy to give shelter when the congregation gathers after the service. (*Return to Thônes and take the D909 toward Annecy.*)

MORETTE

About 2½ miles outside Thônes, on the road to Annecy, lies the NÉCROPOLE NATIONALE DES GLIÈRES. Together with the monument on the Plateau des Glières ▲ *186*, the cemetery is one of the major sites commemorating the famous episode of Les Glières in March 1944 ● *47*.
MUSÉE DÉPARTEMENTAL DE LA RÉSISTANCE. Not far from the cemetery, the museum nestles among trees on the edge of the forest. It is housed in an Alpine chalet from Le Grand-Bornand ▲ *181*, which was dismantled and reassembled at Morette. It is devoted to the events of 1940–43, 1944, Les Glières and the Liberation ● *46* ▲ *186*. The nearby MÉMORIAL DÉPARTEMENTAL DE LA DÉPORTATION is a poignant memorial to the human tragedy of the death camps and the suffering of victims from Haute-Savoie. (*Continue in the direction of La Balme-de-Thuy, turning right just after the Cascade de Morette.*)

THE HEROS OF MORETTE CEMETERY
As Resistance fighters withdrew following the German assault on the Plateau des Glières, twenty-two *maquisards* were cut down by enemy artillery units. The Germans wanted to bury their bodies in a mass grave, but the mayor of Thônes, Louis Haase, objected and was permitted to bury them individually. Over the following months the bodies of many more victims of the Nazi regime were buried at Morette. After the Liberation the bodies of the other *maquisards* of Les Glières were transferred to Morette cemetery.

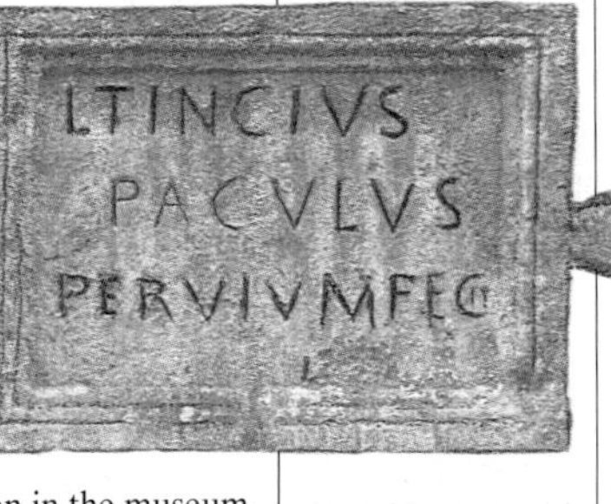

TOWARD DINGY-SAINT-CLAIR

LA BALME-DE-THUY. Excavations, begun in 1970, have revealed evidence of human habitation going back 10,000 years, from the earliest human presence in the region to the late Bronze Age (2500 years ago). Artifacts from the excavations can be seen in the museum in Pays-de-Thones ▲ *183*. (*On leaving, take the D216.*)
DINGY-SAINT-CLAIR. The village stands on the right bank of the Fier, at its confluence with the Mélèze. Beyond the bridge the ROMAN ROAD linking Albertville with Geneva is carved into the rock. There is an inscription dedicated to L. Tincius Paculus (*above*), who appears to have financed the road. The village may also have been named for him, 'Tincius' becoming 'Dingy'. The ÉGLISE SAINT-ÉTIENNE has a 15th-century chancel and stained-glass windows in the apse (1531), which were inspired by the Flemish and Germanic schools.
ALEX. The town is located in a wide valley surrounded by three mountain ranges: the Dents de Lanfon, the Dent du Cruet and the cliffs of the Parmelan Mountain. The focal point of the town is the ÉGLISE NOTRE-DAME (1864) and a 16th-century cross in the square.

A MIRACULOUS SPRING AND A HEALING ROCK
The water that rises in the fountain of Saint-Clair, near the Roman road, is said to cure conjunctivitis. A little higher up, just before the stone with the Roman inscription (*above*), is a rock-cut niche known locally as the Saint Bernard's Chair. According to legend Saint Bernard sat down to rest in the niche; it restored his strength and now, so it is claimed, will cure back pain in anyone who sits there.

Top to bottom: the first parachute landing on the Plateau des Glières, on February 14, 1944; the funeral cortege of Lieutenant Tom Morel ● *47*; parachute drops of arms and ammunition.

PLATEAU DES GLIÈRES

CHÂTEAU DE THORENS. The castle stands on the edge of the Plateau des Glières, overlooking the Ravin de la Filière. Despite restoration, its buildings, whose foundations date from the 11th century, are still impressive. Not far from the castle a small oratory dedicated to Saint François de Sales is all that remains of the place where the saint was born in 1567. When it was demolished in 1630, on the orders of Louis XIII (r. 1610–43), the de Sales family moved to the Château de Thorens. The castle is still owned by the family and houses artifacts and documents relating to the life of Saint François. Two rooms have been refurbished with furniture belonging to Count Cavour (1810–61), champion of the unification of Italy and a relative of the de Sales family.

PLATEAU DES GLIÈRES. The plateau, at an altitude of 4600 feet, stands as a symbol of national honor, embodied by the motto of its 460-odd Resistance fighters: *Vivre libre ou mourir* ('freedom or death') ● *46*. At the end of March 1944 more than 150 *maquisards* gave their lives for freedom when they faced the black-uniformed militia and the 12,000 soldiers of the 157th Alpine division of the German army, supported by airplanes and artillery. Their sacrifice, which left its mark on the spring snows, finally convinced the British government that the Resistance was more than a mere symbol. On August 1, 1944, 2000 *maquisards* gathered on the Plateau des Glières to receive a parachute drop of arms and ammunition (*left: top and bottom*). A fortnight later their leaders launched an attack against the Nazis and on August 19 the Annecy garrison surrendered unconditionally. The *maquisards* of Les Glières had finally won recognition.

TAKING FLIGHT
The sculpture *Envol* ('Taking Flight'), by Émile Gilioli, commemorates the *maquisards*. It was unveiled in 1973 by André Malraux (1901–76).

The Genevois

Georges Hyvernat

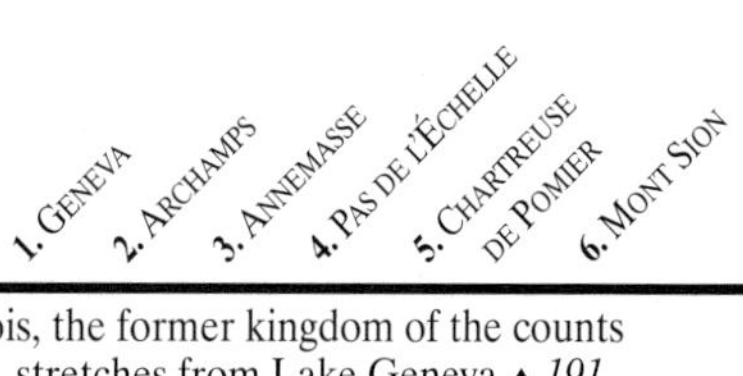

The Genevois, the former kingdom of the counts of Geneva, stretches from Lake Geneva ▲ *191* to the Massif des Bornes, between the Rhône and the Préalpes de Savoie. It consists of a patchwork of different

landscapes: there are limestone outcrops such as Mont Salève and the Montagne de Vuache, meadows and wooded valleys bisected by rivers, vast Alpine pastures that have been cleared in the forest, and cultivated areas in which market garden produce and flowers are grown. These landscapes are interspersed with heavily industrialized towns, whose economy thrives on account of their border location, and delightfully peaceful villages, hamlets and tourist resorts.

IBP at Archamps
The economic growth of 1950–70 led to the creation of new industrial estates and business parks. The most recent example is the International Business Park at Archamps, devoted to the international service sector and new technologies. It stands at the cross-roads of the Alpine freeways, in a free zone reestablished in 1934 according to the terms of the Treaty of Turin (1816) ● *38, 45*.

Annemasse

It is hard to imagine that, when the Sardinian land register ● *37* was drawn up in 1730, the present town of Annemasse was a small agricultural village surrounded by a scatter of tiny hamlets. For a long time this border town was the object of dispute between Savoie and Geneva. However, the fact that it lay at the crossroads of major railroad and road routes brought it prosperity, and since World War Two it has been the capital of the Genevois (Haute-Savoie). Today Annemasse, with a population of 60,000, has its own developed economy, based on commerce, and is throwing off its image as a dormitory town.

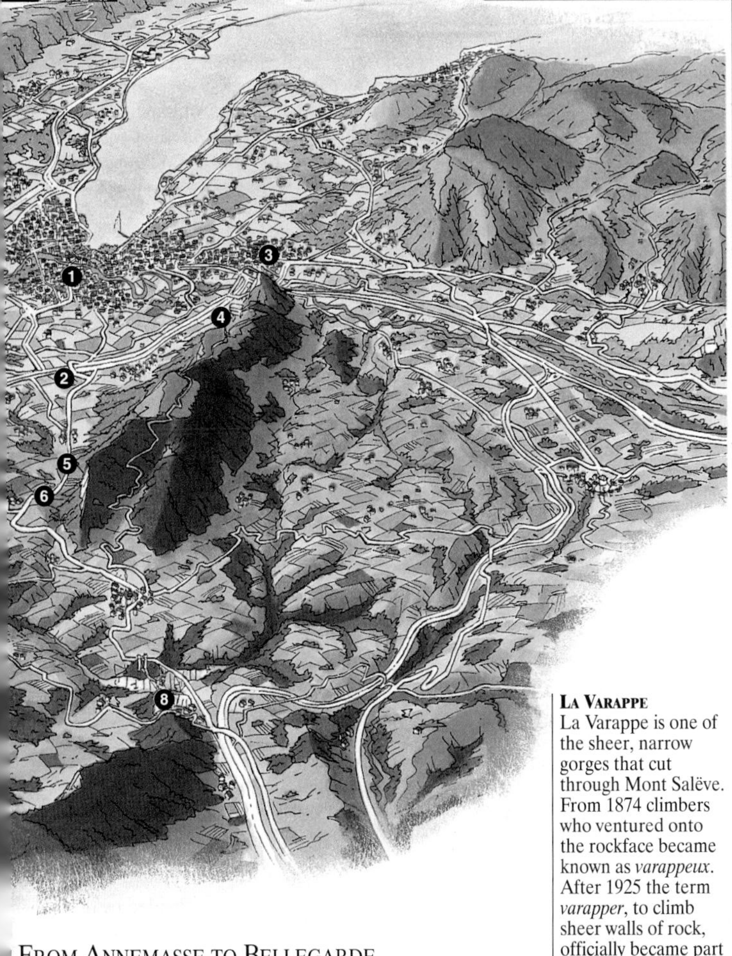

La Varappe
La Varappe is one of the sheer, narrow gorges that cut through Mont Salève. From 1874 climbers who ventured onto the rockface became known as *varappeux*. After 1925 the term *varapper*, to climb sheer walls of rock, officially became part of the French language.

From Annemasse to Bellegarde

Pas de l'Échelle. During the Middle Ages a flight of rock-cut steps, after which the village is named, gave access to the neighboring village of Monnetier-Mornex. Today a cableway carries visitors to a summit which offers a magnificent view of Geneva, Lake Geneva ▲ *192* and the Jura.

Chartreuse de Pomier. The Carthusian order, founded in 1084 by Saint Bruno, gradually migrated into Savoie and the Dauphiné. In about 1170 a community founded the monastery at Pomier, which lay on the route to Santiago de Compostela and which flourished until the French Revolution (1789–99). The monumental entrance (1179) and ruins of the 16th–17th century monastery can still be seen today.

Chevrier. The site was inhabited from the Neolithic period (4125 BC). Today the land around the village, which lies at the foot of the eastern slopes of the Montagne de Vuache, is given over to orchards, pasture and red-fruit cultivation. The CHAPEL, with an ogival entrance, is today incorporated into a house. The nave has some remarkable 18th-century murals.

Today the Château de Clermont belongs to the *département* of Haute-Savoie. It is used as an exhibition and concert center.

ROUSSETTE GRAPES
The Altesse variety of grape that produces Roussette wines was brought from Cyprus in the 14th–15th centuries. Since 1973 the AOC (*appellation d'origine contrôlée*) Roussette de Savoie wine has been attributed to dry white wines with a sharp, fruity flavor. Each year, on the first Saturday in August, the town of Frangy holds a Roussette festival.

A DIFFICULT CROSSING
For a long time spanning the Gorges des Usses was something of a challenge. Up until the 18th century a path led down to the bottom of the gorge where the river was spanned by the Pont Vieux. In 1780 Victor-Amadeus III had a new bridge built further upstream. It was replaced 60 years later by the present suspension bridge. The last bridge to be built across Les Usses (1924–28) was at the time regarded as the very latest in French technology ● *90*.

VALLÉE DES USSES

Les Usses, a fast-flowing mountain trout stream in the northwest of the Genevois, winds its way eastward to join the Rhône at Seyssel. The Vallée des Usses, untouched by the main communication routes, is dotted with mills, fortified residences, houses and castles. Every effort is being made to preserve its historic and natural heritage.

PONTS DE LA CAILLE. Near Allonzier-la-Caille the Gorges des Usses are spanned by two bridges ● *90*. One is an elegant suspension bridge (*below*), regarded as a feat of technology when it was built in 1838. The other (1924–8) is a single-arched bridge with a span of 460 feet, which was classified as a historic monument in 1966.

MARLIOZ. The privately owned Château de Sallenôves, which stands on the road to Bonlieu, was once the home of one of the oldest vassal-families to the counts of Geneva. This 11th-century feudal fortress, defended by an impressive square keep, also has some Renaissance buildings and outbuildings dating from the 16th century.

CHAUMONT. Chaumont was a staging post on the Roman road that linked Vienna and northern Italy and later lay on the route to Santiago de Compostela. Its former prosperity is reflected in its fine buildings and the remains of its hospital (destroyed in 1482), law courts and CASTLE. The vineyards below the village produce the famed Roussette de Savoie.

FRANGY. The church is typical of the Sardinian Neoclassical style ● *86* and has an elegant onion-shaped spire (1843). It stands next to an impressive presbytery (1637).

CHÂTEAU DE CLERMONT. The late-16th-century castle (*left and above*) reflects the influence of the Italian Renaissance, as shown by the double tier of galleries that line the courtyard. Inside is a huge staircase and the chapel where Saint François de Sales ● *36* is said to have taken holy orders.

SEYSSEL-SUR-RHÔNE. In 1760 Seyssel was divided by the border between France and Savoie, which was marked by the river. When Savoie became part of France in 1860 ● *44* it still straddled the *départements* of Ain and Haute-Savoie. With the construction of the Vieux Pont and the modern bridge ● *91*, the two *communes* became one town, with two town halls and two schools. The old town has medieval squares and narrow streets.

Lake Geneva and the Chablais

Paul Guichonnet, Bruno Gillet

The Chablais comprises two distinct regions: the mountainous pre-Alpine massif of the Haut-Chablais and, below, the plateaus and plains of the Bas-Chablais that stretch to the shores of Lake Geneva (Lac Léman). The lake is bounded by the Massif du Chablais and its foreland to the south, and the Préalpes and the Vaud plateau to the north. It is fed by the waters of the Rhône and Dranse rivers and is the largest expanse of water in France. Like a vast inland sea it tempers the climate of the Bas-Chablais in which thrives a luxuriant vegetation usually associated with more southerly latitudes. The shoreline of the Chablais, punctuated by resorts and marinas and dotted with villas and parks, curves and winds its way between the Pointe d'Yvoire and Saint Gingolph.

THE POINTE D'YVOIRE

The promontory known as the Pointe d'Yvoire divides the Grand Lac from the Petit Lac. The latter, forming part of the western end of Lake Geneva, is almost entirely in Switzerland. This tiny, shallow part of the lake lies almost parallel to the folds of the Jura and was attached to the main expanse of water relatively late in its history.

YVOIRE. Perched on a rocky outcrop on the edge of the Grand Lac, Yvoire, one of the most beautiful medieval villages in Savoie, is known as the 'pearl of Lake Geneva'. Its narrow streets lead down to the lake in a cascade of flower-covered balconies. In the early 14th century Amadeus V's military architects

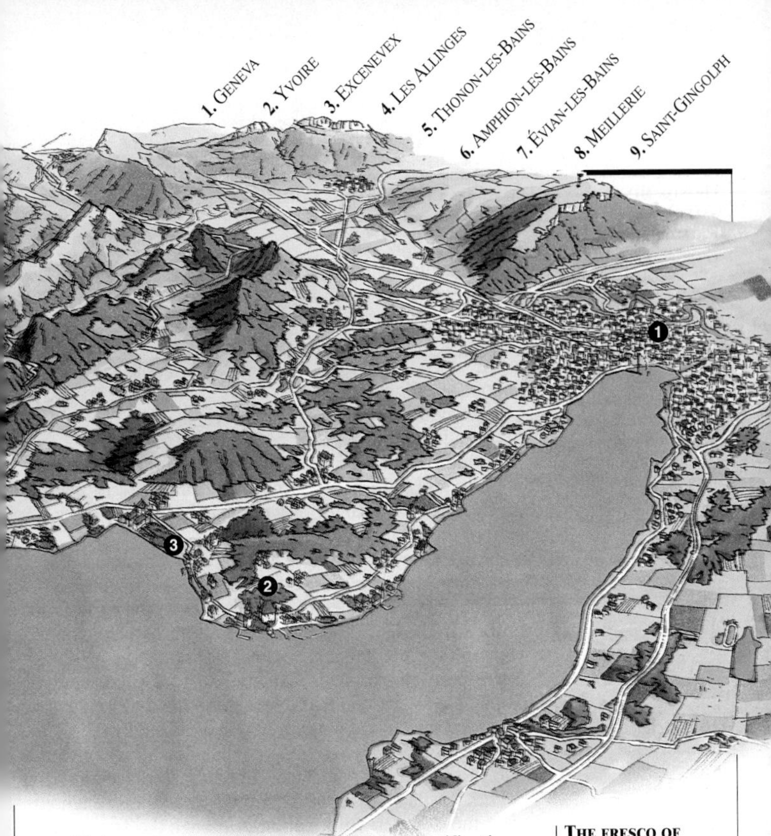

turned it into a fortified village. The surviving fortifications include two Gothic gateways (1322) and the 14th-century CASTLE (*not open to the public*), which with its impressive keep overlooks the lake like the prow of a great ship.

EXCENEVEX. The broad bay of Excenevex, in the Golfe de Coudrée, is the most oceanlike bay on the lake. Northerly and southwesterly winds whip up waves whose breakers carry fine sediment that has formed coastal dunes, unique in western Europe. This charming resort has the largest sandy beach on the French shore of Lake Geneva.

CHÂTEAUX DES ALLINGES

The hill (Colline des Allinges) overlooking Thonon-les-Bains and the estuary of the Dranse is dominated by the ruins of two castles that stand only a few yards apart, testimony to the bitter disputes between the houses of Faucigny and Savoie. The older of the two, ALLINGES-LE-VIEUX (10th century), was inherited by the Fucigny family in the 11th century, while ALLINGES-LE-NEUF was built by the House of Savoie. By 1355, after three centuries of conflict, the counts of Savoie became sole masters of the site. Allinges-le-Vieux was abandoned in favor of Allinges-le-Neuf, which played a major role during the Wars of Religion before being demolished in 1703. In 1836 the site became a center of pilgrimage for followers of Saint François de Sales. The barrel-vaulted apse of the chapel ● *78* survived to be incorporated into the new church. It has an 11th-century fresco of Byzantine inspiration which is one of the oldest wall paintings in Savoie. Part of the curtain wall of the newer castle and the keep of the older castle still stand. The site commands a panoramic view of Thonon-les-Bains, Lake Geneva and the Préalpes.

THE FRESCO OF ALLINGES-LE-NEUF
The fresco inside the chapel depicts Christ in Glory, flanked by the Evangelists, a scene evocative of the Apocalypse as St John decribed it. The seraphim recall the prophecies of Isaiah and Ezekiel.

JARDIN DES CINQ SENS
The former market garden at the Château d'Yvoire has been turned into a medieval walled garden such as was cultivated by monks. The herbs and plants grown there appeal to all five senses.

THONON MINERAL WATER
The springs of Thonon, which rise on the Plateau de la Versoie, were first discovered by the Romans. Analyses were carried out in 1859 and in 1882 the French Académie de Médecine authorized the commercial exploitaton of the springs. The building of Thonon's first baths began in 1886 and the town was officially renamed Thonon-les-Bains in 1890. The waters of La Versoie, which have diuretic and detoxifyng properties, are recommended for kidney and bladder complaints. Since 1989 various fitness programs have been offered in conjunction with cures.

THE 'CLAIRIÈRE DES JUSTES'
A national monument dedicated to the memory of those who gave their lives to the cause of freedom and justice ● *46* lies in a clearing between the oak wood and arboretum of the Ripaille forest. It was commissioned by the Central Consistory of the Jewish communities in France and was unveiled on November 2, 1997. The monument, by Nicolas Moscovitz, conveys a strong message of solidarity, hope and tolerance.

THONON-LES-BAINS

Thonon-les-Bains, the third-largest urban center in Savoie, occupies a high terrace overlooking the Grand Lac, the vast central basin of Lake Geneva. It is renowned for its climate and mineral waters, and is today a dynamic town where industry, commerce and tourism are successfully combined. Its energy, character and rich architectural heritage have made it the capital of the Chablais.

HISTORY. The town's history was shaped by the spread of Christianity during the Early Middle Ages, and by the fact that it belonged to the House of Savoie from the early 11th century. In the late 13th century the counts of Savoie made Thonon their permanent residence, fortifying the medieval town, granting it franchises and building the Château de Ripaille ● *79*. During the Reformation the developing town suffered various tribulations: it was occupied by the Bernese (1536–64) and much of the population converted to Protestantism. After the Catholic backlash led by Saint François de Sales ▲ *169* Thonon became the stronghold of the Counter-Reformation. Although the Treaty of Saint-Julien (1603) put an end to conflict with Geneva, the peace remained fragile. Until the early 18th century the town was disputed by the passage of the French armies and then the occupation of Savoie by the Spanish army ● *37*. Union with France ● *45*, in 1860, gave the town's economy a much-needed boost. Prosperity in the 1930s also led to various developments: the industrial estate, the thermal baths and the Maison des Arts et de la Culture all date from this time.

COUVENT DES MINIMES. The former convent, built (1649–86) by an Italian architect from Como, is the most beautiful building in Thonon and the only building in the Tuscan style in Savoie. Its classic cloister and elegant façade pierced by a Baroque entrance and blazoned windows give it a modest and reserved charm. It was not completed until the 18th century.

MONASTÈRE DE LA VISITATION. Exhibitions are held in the monastery's Gothic chapel, while the restored buildings off the cloister serve as a public library and house the Académie Chablaisienne and other associations. The monastery forms part of what is known as the Renovation district, which has a subtle blend of modern and historic architecture.

ÉGLISE SAINT-HIPPOLYTE. This Romanesque church is Thonon's main place of worship. Although the exact date of its foundation is unknown, the triple-naved crypt dates from the 11th century. In the 17th century the church's vaults and columns were rendered with stucco by Piedmontese artists, and the chancel was decorated with frescos depicting scenes from the life of Christ and the Holy Trinity. Thus what was basically a Romanesque church was turned into a remarkable and exuberantly decorated Baroque building.

PLACE DE L'HÔTEL DE VILLE. The town hall square and fountain (1736) are surrounded by a series of buildings that form a composite but well-balanced whole. THE HÔTEL DE VILLE (town hall), in Sardinian Neoclassical style • *86*, contrasts with older buildings whose uneven roofs are covered with pantiles. The nearby PALAIS DE JUSTICE (law courts) occupies the former castle of the lords of Bellegarde, which dates from the 16th century. The 17th-century CHÂTEAU DE SONNAZ has been converted into a museum. The Clos de Sonnaz has been recently opened up and now gives easy access from the square to a terrace overlooking the port of Rives and the Grand Lac.

RIVES. As the port of Thonon, Rives has always been closely involved with the town's development. In the late 13th century it became the 'new town' of Thonon and is today one of its liveliest districts. A funicular linking the port with the upper town offers some spectacular views of the lake. For a pleasant walk along the waterfront, follow the Quai de Ripaille, from which the DOMAINE DE RIPAILLE can be reached.

CHÂTEAU DE RIPAILLE • *58*, *79*. The Château de Ripaille, which stands among vineyards on the edge of the Dranse estuary, played a key role in the history of Savoie. It was originally a simple hunting lodge built by Amadeus V, and was extended and embellished in the 15th century by Amadeus VIII • *40*, who added seven residential wings and seven defensive towers. The castle was badly damaged during the Wars of Religion. It was later given to the Carthusian order, who built a large Baroque church on the site in 1762. It was sold in 1809 and extensively altered, and the Carthusian monastery was demolished in 1893. The part of the castle built by Amadeus VIII was restored in the 19th century. It is still flanked by four of its towers and makes an impressive sight. The castle's exhibition rooms trace the history of the first duke of Savoie. Its vineyards produce a wine described by the Thonon-born writer Henry Bordeaux (1870–1963) as 'subtle and sometimes treacherous'.

'As for me, Lake Geneva, I am a swan in winter/Lost upon your shores, returning to brave/Your stormy skies; O that I may sometimes bathe/My soiled plumes in your crystal waters.'
Alphonse de Lamartine

FONDATION RIPAILLE
The foundation, established in 1976, organizes conferences and sponsors research on the ecology, the geography and the natural resources of Lake Geneva. It also organizes visits to the Réserve Naturelle du Delta de la Dranse.

ANNA DE NOAILLES (1876–1933)
Of all the poets to have extolled the beauty of Lake Geneva, Anna de Noailles was among those who wrote the most moving lines. The little town of Évian, on the edge of the lake, enjoyed its golden age during the Edwardian era. In 1875 Anna's father, Prince Bassaraba Brancovan, bought the summer residence of Count Walewski at Amphion, where he entertained some illustrious guests, among them the Prince of Wales, Prince Edmond de Polignac, Paderewski, Maurice Barrès, and Marcel Proust. His daughter Anna, later Comtesse Mathieu de Noailles, combined a life in high society with a major literary career. Her health was fragile and she was bedridden for the last twenty years of her life, only leaving her room to stay at Amphion. She died at the age of 56.

TOWARD ÉVIAN-LES-BAINS

AMPHION-LES-BAINS. Amphion, on the shores of the lake between Thonon and Évian, is today a popular tourist resort and marina. It inspired a great many poets, including Anna de Noailles, who spent much of her childhood and youth at the Villa Bassaraba. In 1966 a bottling factory for Évian mineral water ▲ *198* was established at Amphion, whose ferruginous waters, although discovered before those of Évian, were at that time untapped.

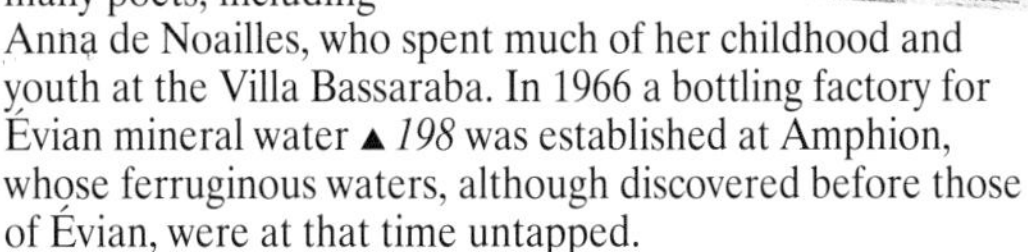

ÉVIAN-LES-BAINS

Évian-les-Bains, which occupies a privileged site on the shores of Lake Geneva, has retained all the elegance of an Edwardian spa town. As well as being a resolutely modern resort, renowned for its tourist facilities and sophisticated entertainments, it also has a rich history.

HISTORY. The site was originally inhabited by the Celts and then by the Romans. During the Middle Ages the town of Évian was one of the favorite residences of the House of Savoie. It was devastated by the Wars of Religion, and later developed as a tourist resort as the result of the discovery and subsequent use (from 1789) of the waters of a spring that rose in the garden of a gentleman by the name of Mr Cachat ▲ *198*. This discovery marked the beginning of the history of the famous Évian mineral water. However the resort's real development came after 1860, when Savoie became part of France. The construction of the port and quay, and the subsequent influx of a fashionable clientele, forced the expansion of the town. Palace-hotels, huge public buildings and luxurious apartment blocks sprang up and, in the space of a few years, Évian-les-Bains had become an international resort frequented by the aristocracy and members of high society. The golden age of Évian-les-Bains lasted until 1929.

ÉGLISE NOTRE-DAME-DE-L'ASSOMPTION. This 13th-century church is a fine example of early Gothic architecture in Savoie. Its square belfry is surmounted by a steeple flanked by four turrets. To the right of the chancel, the Chapelle Notre-Dame-de-Grâce houses a polychrome relief of the Virgin and Child (1493).

BUVETTE DE LA SOURCE CACHAT. The Art Nouveau pavilion (1903) is crowned by a dome of glazed tiles with semicircular stained-glass windows decorated with plant motifs. It is a masterpiece of spa architecture. In 1956 it was replaced by a new *buvette.* It now houses the offices of the Société Cachat.

Villa Lumière. The villa (*below*) was acquired in 1890 by the industrialist Antoine Lumière. His two sons, Louis and Auguste, the inventors of the cinematograph and color photography, commissoned the Genevan architects Chevalliers and Pelissier to transform it into a sophisticated if costly residence. In 1927 the villa was acquired by the municipality and today houses the town hall.

Palace-hotels. In 1880 the Grand Hôtel des Bains (1859) was renovated and renamed the Hôtel du Parc (now closed). It was here the Treaty of Évian, marking the end of the Algerian War, was signed on March 18, 1962. The Hôtel Splendide (1898), which commanded fine views of the town and lake, was the largest palace-hotel on the French shore of Lake Geneva. Marcel Proust (1871–1922) recalled it when describing the Grand Hôtel de Balbec in *Remembrance of Things Past* (1913–27). When the hotel was demolished in 1983 its gardens were opened to the public. The Hôtel Royal (1909), one of the most beautiful in Évian, is very popular with international visitors.

The casino. With the thermal baths and the theater, the casino is one of Évian's most important public buildings. In 1878 Baron Louis Ennemond de Blognay bequeathed his 17th-century castle to the town. However, the authorities decided to open a gaming house and the castle was demolished in 1911 to make way for the new casino, the last great piece of Edwardian architecture to be built in Évian. While the exterior remains unaltered, the interior has been refurbished.

Villa Lumière
The rooms of the villa are richly furnished and decorated with works of art. The walls are lined with lacquered and gilt wood paneling or hung with Lyons silk. The main staircase (*below*) is guarded by a bronze lioness.

Toward Valais

Beyond Évian the landscapes change as you enter the old glacial valley occupied by the Haut Lac. On both sides of the lake the mountains are much closer to the shore and give the waters a darker hue.

Meillerie. The old village of Meillerie, built against a rocky cliff, was once one of the busiest villages on the lake. Stone from the quarries there was transported to construction sites in Geneva and Lausanne by lateen-rigged ships. The village, where the French writer and philosopher Jean-Jacques Rousseau (1712–78) set part of *La Nouvelle Héloïse*, has lost none of its old charm. The active little fishing port is currently being renovated.

Saint-Gingolph. The village of Saint-Gingolph is divided between Haute-Savoie and the Swiss canton of Valais by the Morge river, which, since 1569, has marked the French-Swiss border. It has two schools and two town halls, but still forms a single parish within the diocese of Annecy.

Novel. This traditional mountain village, over which towers Le Gramont (7125 feet), is like a little corner of the Alps. There is a sweeping view down the valley to the Swiss canton of Vaud, on the far side of the lake.

The Pays Gavot
The hinterland behind Évian-les-Bains is an integral part of the landscape of Lake Geneva. It rises in broad terraces between the shore and the Préalpes du Chablais. Each level has a different type of vegetation. The vines that grow on the lower slopes give way to chestnut trees at higher altitudes. Higher still the slopes are covered with stands of beech and ancient lime trees. Rare plants are found in the wet zones of the peat bogs.

In 1789 the Marquis de Lessert, a nobleman from the Auverge who suffered from kidney stones, went to take the waters at Amphion. However, he found that the town's ferruginous water had little effect. Out walking in Évian he stopped to drink at Saint Catherine's spring, which rose just below the garden fence of a certain Mr Cachat. Finding the water 'light and refreshing', he began to drink it regularly. It alleviated his condition, and he extolled the virtues of this 'miraculous' water. Doctors began to prescribe it for similar complaints. It proved so successful that Mr Cachat fenced off the spring and began to sell the water. The history of the famous Évian mineral water had begun.

A GEOLOGICAL MIRACLE

The natural mineral water of Évian is the product of a rare set of geological conditions. In the foothills of the Chablais, rainwater and meltwater collect in a layer of sand, formed by glaciers, sandwiched between two layers of clay-rich moraine. As the water filters through the sand its mineral content is reduced. The water filters down through the sand at a rate of 330–985 feet per year, emerging fifteen years later at the spring at a constant temperature of 52.8° F.

THE HISTORY OF THE SOURCE

The first baths at Évian were opened in a private house in 1824. Two years later the king of Sardinia authorized the bottling of the water, and construction of the first public baths began in 1827. The Société des Eaux d'Évian, formed in 1869, drilled new collection channels, acquired new springs and developed the town's architectural heritage ▲ *196* by financing the construction of hotels, *buvettes* (refreshment pavilions), a theater and a casino. In 1878 the Académie de Médecine gave its seal of approval and in 1902 the beneficial effects of pure mineral water on the kidneys was proven. In the same year a new thermal establishment was opened. The Cachat spring was classified as a site of public interest in 1926.

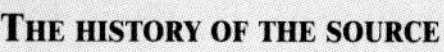

The *Apothéose de la source Cachat*, by Louis Charles Beylard, which became a meeting place for *curistes*.

THE GOLDEN AGE OF SPA BATHING

In the late 19th century the extension of the railroad from Annemasse to Évian brought an influx of *curistes* to the town. Officially renamed Évian-les-Bains in 1864, it became the resort of aristocrats and the international elite, who could enjoy various social events as well as taking cures. The resort became extremely fashionable, and all the 'best people' were to be seen there. To attract a fashionable clientele all kinds of entertainments were organized, including concerts in the gardens of the Cachat spring, plays, firework displays and festivals on the lake. In 1904 the Royal Golf Club was opened for the benefit of the large numbers of English visitors. Aristocrats, artists, writers and politicians rubbed shoulders on the greens, in the Royal Hotel and Hôtel Splendide, in the Casino and in the *buvettes*. Visitors included the future Edward VII, the writers Marcel Proust and Jean Cocteau, and the politician Maurice Barrès.

A COMMERCIAL REVOLUTION

Initially Évian mineral water, which was claimed to cure kidney trouble, digestive complaints and nervous disorders, could be bought only in pharmacies. In 1960 Évian entered the age of mass marketing and the famous bottles with their pink label made their appearance on supermarket shelves. Today, with four million bottles of water per day produced at the Amphion factory (*below*), Évian has become the world's leading exporter of mineral water.

▲ The Haut-Chablais

Origins
The origin of the name Chablais is based on the root *cab,* from the Latin *cadere* meaning 'to fall'. It is probably is associated with the idea of the 'fall' or 'descent' of the *chables*, the steep mountain corridors down which wood-cutters once slid the trunks of pine trees.

Names such as Roc d'Enfer, Dent d'Oche and Hauts Forts suggest a harsh, mineral environment, but the Haut Chablais is in fact very reminiscent of the gently curving shores of Lake Geneva ▲ *192*. During the folding of the Alps, a layer of soft, crumbly soil was deposited in the region. This soil was easily eroded by the strong currents of the Dranse river and the valleys widened out into broad basins. Today the Haut-Chablais is a region of Alpine meadows and chalets, where mountain passes are softened by forest-clad slopes, where the even flow of rivers is occasionally interrupted by barriers of more resistant rock, where the horizon is bounded by strongly defined ridges, and where the green patchwork of plateaus and mountain pastures is scored by gorges, vertiginous paths and steep mountain tracks. From the Val d'Abondance to the Vallée d'Aulps, and the resorts of the Portes du Soleil to the secluded valleys of the Brevon and Ménoge, chalets and herds reflect the pastoral nature of the Chablais.

10. Châtel
11. Dents du Midi
12. Montriond
13. Les Lindarets
14. Morzine
15. Avoriaz
16. Les Gets
17. Abbaye d'Aulps
18. Gorges du Pont du Diable
19. La Forclaz
20. Bellevaux
21. La Chèvrerie
22. Boëge
23. Les Habères

Amadeus VIII.

History

● 33

From the prehistoric lakeside settlements until the arrival of Christianizing monks in the Middle Ages, the Haut-Chablais was a virgin land. Cleared and cultivated, it saw the flowering of influential abbeys and a rich culture. It was a powerful and aristocratic land, which brought prosperity to the House of Savoie and witnessed the finest hours of the reign of Amadeus VIII. In the 16th century invasions and the Wars of Religion brought this golden age to an end. Emerging victorious but devastated it remained obscure until 1860, when its people voted for it to become part of France.

The boundaries of medieval Chablais
During the Middle Ages the Chablais covered a much wider area than it does today. Before they were reduced by the conflicts of the late 16th century, its boundaries extended to the lower Valais and the strip of land in the canton of Vaud, east of Lake Geneva.

CHALET OF THE VAL D'ABONDANCE
The opulence of these chalets ● *75* echoes the richness of the valley's mountain pastures. Everything about them reflects the close family ties that characterize the Chablais. Their generous proportions recall the well-to-do farms of Switzerland and the Tyrol. The chalets are often perched on steep slopes, and their highsided wooden framework on stone foundations give them stability. The broad roof is covered with slates from Chatel or with *tavaillons*, the wooden roof tiles that are shorter than the more commonly used *ancelles*. A *cort'na*, the open area along the side of the chalet, allows the occupants to move between the living quarters and the barn under the shelter of the eaves. The openwork balustrades are hand-carved in the winter, when the wood is harder. These chalets are often inhabited by two families; such friendships are symbolized by the famous doves of Abondance, carved at L'Opinel.

With its soft contours, great cirques, and gentle landscape in which the mountains do not exceed 8200 feet: it is easy to see why a visitor to the Val d'Abondance in 1860 described it as a 'perpetual Sunday'. Access to the valley is via the D22, built during the reign of Napoleon III. It is worth leaving the road to walk in the Alpine pastures and along the footpaths that border mountain streams and waterfalls.

THONON TO LA SOLITUDE

TOWARD THE MOUNTAIN PASTURES. Beyond Bioge the road leaves the turbulent Gorges de la Dranse and winds its way between broad-leaved forests. Near the Chapelle du Villard, in the village of VACHERESSE, a footpath leads up into the mountain pastures of Bise, with its lake and its chalets built of the blocks of gray limestone that lie scattered across the meadows. Across the valley are the snowy peaks of the CORNETTES DE BISE.

APPROACHING THE GLACIAL THRESHOLDS. The road continues along the Dranse. The first fir trees begin to appear and the woods become more dense as the road nears La Solitude and its sawmills. Here the rocks are closer together, announcing the glacial thresholds of Les Portes du Soleil beyond Sous-le-Pas. The road leaves the open valley and enters a narrower corridor, beneath the cliffs of Mont Jorat with their Mediterranean vegetation, and the mountain pastures of Mont de Grange (7980 feet).

ABBAYE D'ABONDANCE

The Abbaye Notre-Dame-de-l'Assomption nestles at the foot of Mont Jorat. The convent, with its austere façade, and the church are in a Gothic style ● *81* that is rare in the region. They also contan fine paintings and sculptures.

HISTORY. In the 11th century Abondance was a priory attached to the great Abbaye de Saint-Maurice-d'Agaune. It became

The church of Abondance, with its rounded apse, viewed from the southeast.

an Augustinian abbey in 1139, and its influence soon spread throughout the diocese of Geneva. The establishment of the commendam in the 15th century dampened this religious fervor and the canons became increasingly lax, to the great indignation of the population. François de Sales tried in vain to reestablish the order. In 1606 Pope Paul V replaced the canons by Feuillants (Reformed Cistercians), but the golden age of the abbey has passed and it was dissolved in 1761.

The abbey church. All that remains of the 13th-century church are the Gothic chapels and the great apse, which is supported by massive flying buttresses, the only examples of their kind in the *département*. In the apse the intersecting ribs of the strongly defined arcades rise to a height of 60 feet.

The cloister. The ribbed vaults of the only two galleries to have survived from the 14th century are inspired by the same Gothic rhythm. Here the more modest arcades form pointed arches, but they are less austere and decorated with marble colonnettes and sculpted capitals.

The spirituality of Abondance
The abbey not only exerted its influence on the valley but reflected its location. The local gray sandstone from which it was built expresses the religious fervor of a mountain people accustomed to hardship. Inside are a 15th-century abbot's chair and walnut choir stalls, 18th-century gilt retables, and 19th-century *trompe-l'oeil* decor.

Abondance to Châtel

La Chapelle-d'Abondance. The houses of this popular family village-resort stretch along the D22 as it winds through the broad valley. The 15th-century church, restored in the 18th century, has an onion-shaped belfry. From the village a path leads up Mont Chauffé, through forests and pastures to the Chalets de Chevenne (4095 feet). The path, known as the *Sentier des Cornettes*, follows a mountain stream where Abondance trout may sometimes be seen.

The frescos of the cloister
In their mellow tones and their detail, the frescos in the abbey's cloister reflect the influence of the 15th-century Piedmontese master Giacomo Jacquiero. A blend of folk art and high art, they depict the daily life of Savoie no less vividly than scenes from the life of the Virgin Mary.

Châtel. On the rim of the vast amphitheater of Châtel the road is bordered by chalets as it skirts round the Mont de Grange (7980 feet). Rising to the east is the snow-covered range of the Dents du Midi. Although, together with its many hamlets, Châtel has a strong pastoral tradition, it is also a resort and is in fact regarded as the most 'Swiss' of the French Alpine resorts. The *pistes* of Super-Châtel, on the Massif du Morclan (6465 feet), and the Tête du Linga (6980 feet), to the south, have some excellent slopes with magnificent views of the Dents du Midi and Mont Blanc.

The upper valley. As it approaches the source of the Dranse the D228 traverses an area of forest paths, torrents, mountain streams and chapels. It passes the Cascade de l'Essert and the impressive Chalets de Plaine-Dranse, as it winds its way up to the Col de Bassachaux (5835 feet).

Like many mountain regions Haute-Savoie has a history of emigration. Between the 16th century and World War One seasonal and then permanent emigration changed the character of the region and reduced the number of mouths to be fed during the winter months. The younger, stronger men left for Paris, Lyons and Germany to work as stonemasons, chimney sweeps, peddlers, servants, coach drivers, waiters, unskilled laborers, odd-job men or tinkers. In 1789 it was estimated that between 30,000 and 40,000 men left Savoie during the winter months.

LITTLE CHIMNEY SWEEPS
Among the seasonal migrants, Savoyard chimney sweeps played a major role in Parisian life until the early 20th century. Parisian society found them a picturesque and touching subject that was widely used in artistic imagery and songs. Far from home, wretched, poor, exploited, reduced to begging or becoming street entertainers, they were either represented in the manner of Victor Hugo's *Les Misérables*, as the dirty but honest hero in the vein of the worthy peasant, or as a mischievous mountain ragamuffin. With the 20th-century developments in heating children no longer worked in these conditions.

PEDDLERS
Boys as young as twelve would accompany their fathers on their travels. The boy would often play the viol to attract customers while his peddler-father unpacked his wares on the village square.

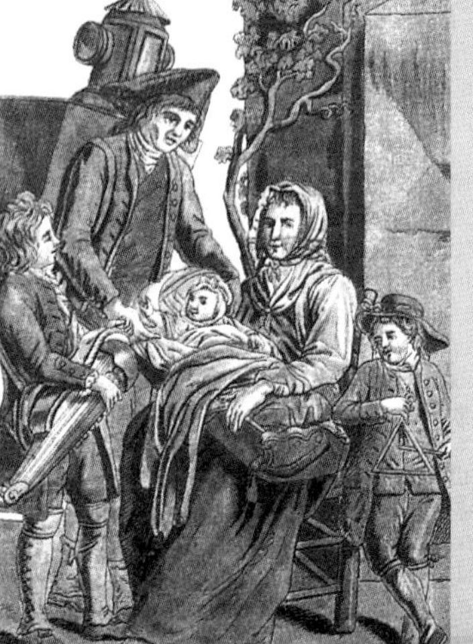

DISTANT HORIZONS
From the 1850s an increasing number of Savoyards, especially from the Haut-Chablais, emigrated to South America and Argentina in particular. They were encouraged by emigration agencies and by the success stories of those who had gone before.

Returning home

As a mark of their success migrant merchants renovated their homes and added freestone door and window frames. Some engraved the figure 4 – the symbol of totality (the Holy Trinity plus one) – by way of a coat of arms, accompanied by the letter I.H.S. ('heart of Christ'). Until 1914 the 'Savoyards de Paris', who made their fortune and returned home, often had political ambitions and played a major role in the social life of their community.

The 'café-restaurant du Mont-Blanc'
Coach drivers and taxi drivers from Haute-Savoie would meet each day in the café-restaurant of Ernest and Emma Bibollet, at 9 rue du Dragon in Paris.

Generous donations
Successful Savoyard emigrants never forgot their origins: many of them set up charitable foundations, built chapels and donated sumptuous church ornaments. To combat the problem of illiteracy some, such as the haberdasher Antoine Violland from Nancy-sur-Cluses, bequeathed their wealth to the village schools.

Leaving the homeland

After the French Revolution (1789–99) emigration became more widespread and tended to be permanent. Although Geneva attracted large numbers of Savoyards, Lyons and Paris were the principle destinations. In 1860 there were an estimated 10,000 Savoyard emigrants in Lyons and almost 60,000 in Paris. They worked as street-porters, commissionaires, shop assistants, servants and coach drivers, while some owned their own cafés and restaurants. Those already in business often employed or found work for their compatriots and set up a number of mutual assistance organizations.

Departure for America.
Joachim Dumax-Baudron left the Val d'Arly for New York in 1908. He made his fortune in San Francisco as a laundryman.

ÉGLISE SAINTE-MARIE-MADELEINE AT MORZINE
This is a fine example of the Neoclassical churches built during the Piedmontese period of Savoie's history. Like many others of its kind it replaces an earlier building, in this instance a chapel (1690) that had been damaged during the French Revolution (1789–99). The generous proportions of Sardinian architecture – in stark contrast to the Baroque style of older rural chapels – express a conservative faith combined with authoritarian urban power. At Morzine the restorers were at pains to respect local traditions, to be seen, for example, in the beautifully carved wooden choir stalls dating from the 16th century.

The 'imperial crown' of the church of Montriond.

With its rocky peaks and high mountain pastures, the southern Chablais, wedged between the Roc d'Enfer and the Dents du Midi, provides a striking contrast to the undulating valleys of the north. The Pointe du Chésery (7430 feet), Hauts Forts (8090 feet), Pointe de Nyon (6625 feet) and Mont Chery (5990 feet) foreshadow the higher mountain ranges that lie to the east. The Haut-Chablais, always a region of exchange and pilgrimage, was quick to adapt to tourism, while preserving its traditional crafts and social structures. The Portes du Soleil, currently one of the largest skiing areas in the world, comprises twelve ski resorts (eight of them in France) which not only offer 350 miles of *pistes* and slopes but also a wide range of traditional art and culture.

ON THE ROAD TO LES LINDARETS

MONTRIOND. The village, which retained its pastoral economy until the 1960s, is now a modest tourist resort. It has some original features, including an early-18th-century Baroque church whose belfry is surmounted by a strange openwork imperial crown. Inside is a 14th-century wooden Virgin and Child and a magnificently restored Baroque retable. From the village the D228, bordered by old chalets, leads up to the Lac de Montriond, which lies in a steep-sided valley. Just above the lake the Cascade d'Ardent drops 165 feet down the north-facing slope. The road continues to climb to Les Lindarets, whose Alpine chalets are roofed with *tavaillons* ▲ *182*.

MORZINE

In 1900 Morzine was still a large pastoral village whose economy also relied on local wood and slate. By 1930, after rapid expansion and modernization, it had become the tourist capital of the Haut-Chablais.

FROM VILLAGE TO RESORT. In the early 20th century those who came to Morzine were mainly rich tourists from Switzerland. Children's summer camps were also to be seen. In 1934 the opening of the Le Pleney cableway boosted its potential as a mountain resort. The hamlets with their 19th-century chalets were soon overwhelmed and a disjointed network of houses and hotels began to encroach on the valley. In 1960, when Jean Vuarnet, born in the Haut-Chablais, won a gold medal at the 1960 Winter Olympics in Squaw Valley, California, the village received a further boost. Morzine's mountain pastures were turned into ski slopes and the Nyon and Super-Morzine cableways were built.

ECOTOURISM. Morzine's ski slopes have a moderate gradient, and many of the footpaths in the area offer beautiful walks. The VALLON DES ARDOISIÈRES (D338) is also well worth a visit. The slate quarries opened on the slopes of the Montagne de Séraussaix in 1743 brought prosperity to the village. There is a magnificent view of Mont Blanc from the Col de Joux-Plane, and the view from the summit of Le PLENEY (5130 feet) stretches as far as Lake Geneva.

Avoriaz

Before entering the resort, the D338 passes an unusual prow-shaped chapel. Designed in 1960 by Maurice Novarina, the stone and *lauzes* (roofing stones) building is dedicated to the memory of the deportees of 1940–5. Although built of traditional materials, in outline and color it anticipates the style of the futuristic resort of Avoriaz.

A virtual paradise. The resort stands on a vast plateau once occupied by mountain pastures and owned by an aristocratic Chablais family, the counts of Rovorée. The plateau, acquired by the commune of Morzine and renamed Avoriaz, caught the attention of Jean Vuarnet, who envisioned creating a high-altitude resort in which the streets would be ski tracks. With an eye to the future, Morzine's municipality endowed the resort with the latest and most sophisticated equipment, and a young real estate agent, Robert Brémond, decided to invest in the project.

The 'Brasilia of the snows'. This was how the two buildings that were opened in the 1966 ▲ *94* were described in the press. One was an irregular skyward-pointing building, and the other appeared to be flattened against the ground. Other buildings were subsequently built in the same style. With its irregular lines, steep slopes and roofs tiled with red cedar, Avoriaz was designed to integrate with its natural surroundings. The innovative architecture was combined with intelligent urban planning.

Les Gets

In this 14th-century village, now a holiday village and ski resort, sports facilities and culture are artfully combined. It is ideal for more cultured skiers and well-educated gourmets.

Musée de la Musique Mécanique. The museum is housed in a 16th-century building. Its collection of 400 musical instruments includes carillons, clocks, barrel organs, music boxes, animated scenes, automata, player-pianos and gramophones. The pieces are displayed in their historical context, be that a music room, a fairground or a 1900-style bistro. Music is also to the fore in the neighboring church, where a philharmonic organ with 1000 pipes reproduces the sound of violins, flutes, trumpets and human voices.

Portes du Soleil
The name of this ski-resort complex might well have been thought up for the purposes of publicity. It is in fact named for a pass (Gates of the Sun) which, because of its situation on south-facing slopes, is exposed to the sun throughout the day. On the north-facing slopes is the pass known as the Portes de l'Hiver (Gates of Winter), where shadow prevents the snow from melting.

Modern architecture at Avoriaz (*top, left and right*) and the music of bygone days at Les Gets (*above*).

EARLY GOTHIC ARCHITECTURE
The west end, pierced by a rose window and an entrance with arch molding, and part of the north wall of the nave are all that remains of the 13th-century Abbaye d'Aulps, built in the early Gothic style. The double tier of arches, the triforium and the high windows in the walls draw the eye up to the ribs of the vaults. The focal point, the quatrefoil rose window of the west end, reflects the structure of the choir. For all that they are runs, these vestiges seem to envelop the visitor in the warmth of the Christian faith.

The Vallée d'Aulps – deeper, narrower and less peaceful than its neighbor – follows the turbulent course of the Dranse de Morzine. Here the river becomes a torrent, the wooded slopes are replaced by cliffs, the churches are perched on promontories and the road runs through gorges. Even the ruins of the Abbaye d'Aulps, which survived insurrection and vandalism, reflect the violence and harshness of the valley.

ABBAYE D'AULPS

In 1092 two Benedictine monks from the Abbaye de Molesmes in Burgundy founded a community at the foot of the Rocher de la Chaux, in the wooded depression at the head of the Vallée d'Aulps. The community flourished under the protection of Count Humbert of Savoie.

INDUSTRIOUS MONKS. The monks were quick to realize the potential of the hitherto unexploited natural resources, and cleared the woods to make way for pasture. They soon acquired other lands and their jurisdiction spread to the Genevois and Faucigny. Saint Guérin, their second abbot, used his popularity in Savoie to obtain autonomy for the abbey from the Pope and incorporate it into the Cistercian order. Appointed bishop of Sion in 1138, he returned to Aulps in 1150, where he ended his days. This latter period was marked by the construction of the monastery and church that housed his relics.

ABBATIAL DISPUTES. The abbey's great wealth inevitably aroused jealousy and disputes. The monks had to contend with the envy of the neighboring Abbaye d'Abondance ▲ *202*, quell a popular rebellion in 1311 and overcome their own tendencies. The early ideal of poverty and love was being gradually eroded and it took all the authority of Saint François de Sales to return the monks to the Rule of Saint Benedict.

Scattered relics

The reliquary of Saint Guérin, once kept in the Abbaye d'Aulps, can today now be seen in the Église de Saint-Jean-d'Aulps.

Other pieces, such as the copper reliquary bust of Saint Félicule, dating from the 14th century, are housed in the village presbytery.

Punishment. On August 24, 1702 the Abbaye d'Aulps was struck by lightning. During the French Revolution (1789–99) the monks were driven from the abbey. In 1813 the neighboring church of Saint-Jean-d'Aulps was destroyed by fire, and it was rebuilt with stones taken from the abbey. The demolition was completed by vandals using dynamite. In 1902 the only surviving remains – the façade, entrance and part of the north wall – were classified as an historic monument. The rubble that lay all around them was cleared by the Abbé Couttin with a shovel and wheelbarrow.

A romantic valley

The powerful torrents, stark rocks, secret woods and steep pathways that fired the imagination of the writer and philosopher Jean-Jacques Rousseau (1712–78), held a similar fascination for the Romantics. For these artists, writers and poets, the wilderness of the Gorges du Pont du Diable and the emaciated silhouette of the Abbaye d'Aulps symbolized the omnipotent force of nature, which constantly wreaked revenge on feeble human endeavors. Many of their writings and paintings reflect this fascination.

Pont du diable to Thonon

Gorges du Pont du Diable. The Dranse, which elsewhere flows through a debris of relatively fragile rocks, here encounters a more resistant barrier of gray marble. It has carved out a narrow fissure through which the waters plunge with a deafening roar. On the left of the road a pathway leads to this rockface, 200 feet high, in which the river has carved huge potholes. The rock is tinged with green and blue, and ocher and gray limestone deposits are interspersed with luxuriant vegetation. Landslides from the cliffs above have deposited great piles of boulders in the gorges. One of these boulders, wedged 130 feet above the torrent, forms a natural arch known as the Pont du Diable (*above*).

La Forclaz. 'It's so steep in your village that even the chickens wear crampons!' The inhabitants La Forclaz are used to such jokes. The D122 winds its way up to the little village perched high on the south-facing slopes above the valley, where the houses seem to be balanced precariously on the mountainside. The church, which once overlooked vineyards, was built in 1829 and was restored in 1960 by Maurice Novarina. Its restrained apse and the small spire of its Baroque belfry express the ambivalence of an austere and joyous faith. Above the village are the mountain pastures of Tréchauffex, where a viewpoint (3820 feet) offers sweeping views of Lake Geneva and the vineyards of the Bas-Chablais.

Gorges de la Dranse. Leaving the peace and tranquillity of these high pastures, the road crosses the Pont de l'Église, which marks the entrance to the Gorges de la Dranse. The Dranse de Morzine joins the Dranse d'Abondance and the Brevon to form the Dranse (*above right*), a torrent that flows between tree-capped pillars – rocky sentinels surmounted by firs and beeches – and gray-tinged cliffs carved out of a matrix of drift boulders and limestone. This stretch of the river is popular with white-water rafters. The Grotte Jean-Jacques Rousseau is reached by a steep path on the left of the road, which then continues to Thonon via the Pont de la Douceur.

The slender belfry of the church towers over La Forclaz.

THE BLACK MADONNA OF BOËGE
On July 2 each year pilgrims gather before the strange figure of the Black Madonna of Boëge.

A WRITER'S RETREAT
The French writer Michel Butor came to live at Lucinges, on the lower slopes of the Montagne des Voirons. Butor, the author of *Passage de Milan* (1954) and *La Modification* (1957), on the theme of spatial and temporal journeys, exchanged the constant changes and exchanges of train journeys, the interplay of sound-track and rail track, role reversal and masked balls for walks through the forest, where it is in fact just as easy to lose your way. His incisive style marked out the enigmatic landscape of the *nouveau roman.*

Although not very deeply scored, these two valleys have a complex topography. One follows the course of the Brevon along a narrow channel running from the Roc d'Enfer. The other follows the winding course of the Menoge from the Plateau des Moises to the Vallée du Giffre ▲ *212.*

VALLÉE DU BREVON

BELLEVAUX. The only *commune* on the upper reaches of the Brevon comprises some thirty hamlets scattered across the Alpine pastures. Even so the inhabitants are bound together by a strong sense of history. They still speak of the pipe-smoking women of the 19th century and of the monks who helped clear the region's pastures.
VALLON DE LA CHÈVRERIE. Above the gorge of La Clusaz and the tiny Lac de Vallon, the Brevon flows through the hamlet of La Chèvrerie, where the Carthusian monastery once stood. Resentful of the dominance of the *commune* of Bellevaux, the inhabitants of La Chèvrerie have always used the pastures collectively. A huge landslide in 1943 isolated the village, reinforcing its separate identity. The basin that was formed soon filled with water and the Lac de Vallon now laps at the foot of the 12th-century chapel dedicated to Saint Bruno.

VALLÉE VERTE

BOËGE AND ITS SURROUNDINGS. The neighboring villages of VILLARD, with its Sardinian Neoclassical church (1828), and BURDIGNIN, with its impressive 17th-century church, reflect the rural nature of this tree-covered valley. In BOEGE the square still has a *grenette* (covered corn market) ▲ *86,* with grain measures. The neo-Gothic church houses the Black Madonna that came from the hermitage of Les Voirons.
LES HABÈRES. The name of these former possessions of the Abbaye d'Aulps derives from the term *albergement*: a piece of land rented out for the duration of a harvest. Habère-Lullin, which once stood on the border between the Chablais and the Faucigny ▲ *218,* is now the home of the famous Duret skis.
BEYOND THE MOUNTAIN PASSES. The Vallée Verte is bounded to the east and north by mountain passes above rolling hillsides. Between the Col de Terramont (3600 feet) and the Col de Cou (3800 feet) the landscape changes completely, from wooded hilltops and the murmuring course of the Menoge to Lake Geneva and the ranges of the Jura.

Vallée du Giffre and The Faucigny

Jean-François Tanghe

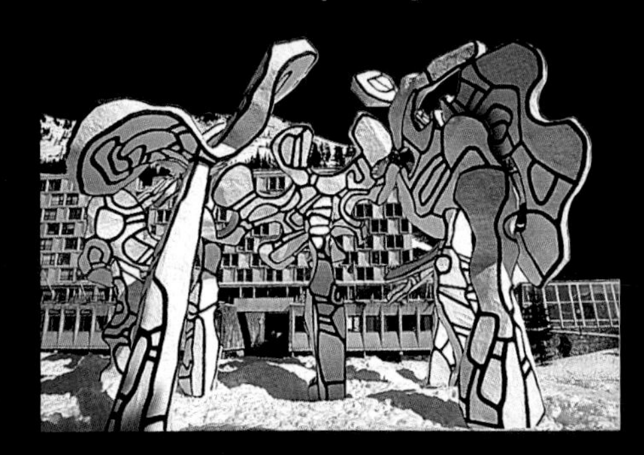

JOHN BERGER
Born in England in 1926, John Berger – man of letters, poet, art critic, essayist and novelist – has lived in Mieussy since the 1970s. The life of the farmers of Savoie has formed the subject of several of his novels and he pays them special tribute in his trilogy *Pig Earth*, *Once in Europa* and *Lilac and Frog* (published in French as *La Cocadrille*, *Joue-moi Quelque Chose* and *Flamme et Lilas*).

The Vallée du Giffre lies between Geneva and Chamonix. It starts just outside Mieussy (2165 feet) and rises gently to the glacial cirque of the Fer-à-Cheval (3440 feet), last bastion of the limestone Préalpes, before veering off toward the granite peaks of the Massif du Mont-Blanc. According to François-Joseph Martin's *Itinéraire Descriptif de la Vallée de Sixt* (1821), 'this part of the valley is the most picturesque and fertile of all; whichever way you look, all you can see are beautiful meadows, fruit trees, chalets and romantic houses half-hidden in the trees.'

MIEUSSY

Mieussy – the cradle of paragliding, which was invented here in 1978 by three local *montagnards* – comprises about a dozen rural hamlets whose solid farmhouses have traditional carved wooden balconies. The church, on the edge of the village, is

one of the most remarkable examples of the strange late Gothic style in which the pointed arch was retained until the late 16th century. Its elegant onion-shaped belfry is reminiscent of the Savoyard Baroque style ▲ 82, while the entrance (1535) is decorated with two colonnettes, a pointed arch and foliage motifs.

Taninges

The town. The old town, dominated by the Pointe de Marcelly (6560 feet), lies on either side of the Foron river, which flows down from the Col des Gets. The arcaded streets, vaulted bridge, fountain and well-to-do houses echo the town's prosperity in the 17th and 18th centuries, when its copper foundries and forges earned it a reputation as a busy and prosperous town. Today Taninges' economy is based on furniture and salt-cured meats. The Église Saint-Jean-Baptiste, built in Sardinian Neoclassical style, is the largest in the diocese: it is almost 130 feet high, 190 feet long and 88 feet wide.

Fruits of yesteryear

As it climbs up to Mieussy the road is bordered by a specialist orchard in which old varieties of mountain fruit trees are grown: there are pears, such as Jacques Lebel, *rambours d'hiver* and *maudes* (*below*), and apples, such *croizons blancs,* that are no longer seen in mountain orchards. Grown in the past by farmers for their own consumption, these varieties have been replaced by other less hardy varieties that are grown on a large scale. No less than 235 old mountain varieties grow in this conservation orchard.

LA JAŸSINIA
This house, at the entrance to the Jardin Botanique Alpin, was given to the *commune* by its founder. It became an information and exhibition center in 1997.

CHARTREUSE DE MÉLAN. The convent, founded by Béatrix de Faucigny for Carthusian nuns, was largely destroyed by fire in 1967. Only three elements of the original buildings (1262) remain: the majestic church (1290), in which the five bays are covered with ribbed vaulting; the solid, rustic cloister (1528), a fine example of the late Gothic style; and the 17th-century farm buildings. These sober buildings, built from massive blocks of tuff stone and gray limestone, are now used for concerts and exhibitions.

ILLUSTRIOUS STONEMASONS
Samoëns is the capital of the *frahans*, the famous stonemasons who worked for the French military engineer Vauban (1633–1707), the philosopher, poet and historian Voltaire (1694–1778) and Napoleon Bonaparte (1769–1821). From the 14th century the *frahans* developed great skill and artistry in working with the locally quarried limestone. They were responsible for many works of art and public buildings throughout Savoie, France and Europe.

MORILLON

Morillon is situated on the southern slopes of the valley, above the road leading to the skiing area of the Grand Massif. In the ÉGLISE SAINT-CHRISTOPHE, with its tuff stone belltower (1500), the ribbed vaulting above the naves and aisles is reminiscent of the late Gothic style of Morillon. In the 1950s a resort was built on the Plateau des Esserts (3600 feet). The restaurant *La Cashta* has an interesting a gallery of portraits of such great artists as Cocteau and Picasso, friends of the site's developer, Ivan Bettex.

SAMOËNS

Samoëns lies at the bottom of a wide valley dominated by the sheer cliffs of Le Criou (7200 feet). The town and its flower-decked houses are centered around the Place du Gros-Tilleul, with its FONTAINE AUX BORNEAUX (1763). The entrance to the ÉGLISE NOTRE-DAME-DE-L'ASSOMPTION is flanked by a pair of couched lions, vestiges of the church's Romanesque origins. Near the entrance is the Chapelle Saint-Claude (1437), in the Flamboyant Gothic style. The north aisle (1555) and the rest of the entrance are characteristic of the late Gothic period. The area around the 19th-century *grenette* (covered corn market) ▲ *86* and the 17th-century CHÂTEAU DE LA TOUR are enlivened by cafe terraces and a variety of shops, as are the town's narrow streets and small shady squares.

THE CONFRÉRIE DES QUATRE-COURONNÉS
The stonemasons of Morillon broke away from the strongly Republican guild of Samoëns (founded in 1659) in 1830 forming the Confrérie des Quatre-Couronnés.

OPENWORK MOTIFS PROVIDE VENTILATION
The openwork motifs on the wooden façades of the barns provide ventilation and enable the hay to dry. As well as being decorative, these motifs also express religious and political beliefs. Farmers with strong religious convictions believed that hearts, doves and crosses protected their crops against fire. Republicans, on the other hand, chose playing-card symbols or secular motifs. The swastika-based motifs (commas, mustache or horns) are said to have been brought back by the stonemasons of the Vallée du Giffre, after their travels in Europe

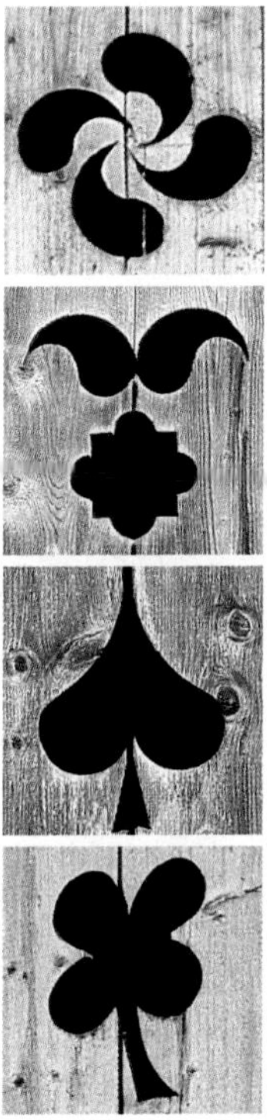

THE GOOD SAMARITAN AND LA JAŸSINIA.
Marie-Louise Jaÿ (*below*), who with her husband Ernest Cognacq founded the famous Parisian department store La Samaritaine, was born in Le Villard in 1838. In 1906 she created a botanical garden for her village. It covers 8 acres and contains 5000 species of mountain plants, trees and shrubs from all over the world. The JARDIN BOTANIQUE ALPIN, in the heart of Samoëns, is now run by the Musée National d'Histoire Naturelle.

GOUFFRE JEAN-BERNARD. The Gouffre Jean-Bernard, to the northeast of Samoëns, near the Réfuge de Folly, was discovered by potholers from Lyons in 1963. Reaching down 5255 feet, it is one of the deepest chasms in the world.

SIXT-FER-À-CHEVAL ▲ *216*

The village of LES VALLONS has many attractive traditonal buildings, which have door lintels that bear the mark of the stonemason who carved them. Beyond the village the Vallée du Giffre narrows for a short distance as it passes through the Gorge des Tînes (formed by a glacial threshold) before widening out toward Sixt and the village of Salvagny, dominated by the summit of Mont Buet (10,170 feet).

THE ABBEY. The crosses, oratories and chapels that line paths and dot the landscape attest to the influence of the canons of the Swiss canton of Valais who in 1144 built an abbey on the banks of the Giffre. Following their departure in 1793 the main abbey building served as a foundry, a warehouse and finally a hotel. The ÉGLISE SAINTE-MADELEINE, restored in 1997, consists of part of the 13th-century Gothic abbey, with characteristc groin vaulting, but it is also a parish church, and this part was once separated from the rest of the building by a rood screen. The black marble tomb of Ponce de Faucigny, the founding abbot, is the focus of a popular cult.

THE VILLAGE. The main square, with its attractve fountain, contains the presbytery and the 16th-century MAISON ALLAMANS. The MAISON DE LA RÉSERVE NATURELLE DE SIXT traces the history of the valley, abbey and village with special emphasis on the natural environment. As you leave the village a track leads up to the Alpage de Salvadon, where visitors can see the famous chevrotin cheeses being made.

'Visit the valley of a thousand waterfalls, the valley of beautiful horrors.' When Louis Duboin, a former bellhop in New York, devised this publicity slogan for his Hôtel du Fer-à-Cheval in 1887, little did he suspect that, just over a century later, it would be heard by more than 400,000 people a year. The Cirque du Fer-à-Cheval (Horseshoe Amphitheater), in the *commune* of Sixt-Fer-à-Cheval, is a huge glacial amphitheater. Rising to a height of 6560 feet, its steep slopes are among the highest in Europe. The amphitheater is made up of sedimentary rocks. The cliffs, composed mainly of superimposed strata of limestone, alternate with terraces and grassy banks consisting of marl or clay that has been turned into schist.

THE FIRST VISITORS

From 1770 the Vallée de Sixt was visited by naturalists such as the Deluc brothers, who were probably the first foreigners to climb Le Buet (10,170 feet), the highest point in the valley and the high limestone Alps. There followed a number of published works, in particular the *Itinéraire Descriptif de la Vallée de Sixt* (1821), by François-Joseph Martin. In 1857 Alfred Wills (*below*), a London barrister and founder member of the Alpine Club, discovered and fell in love with the valley. He became an ardent pioneer and chronicler of this 'little paradise' and encouraged a number of his compatriots to come and see it for themselves. A cafeteria was built near the Fer-à-Cheval (*top right*) and in 1899 Pierre Moccand, known as Pierre au Merle, built a café-museum – *Aux Merveilles de la Nature* – in the village of Molliet. The museum displayed stuffed animals, pottery and unusually shaped roots. It also had a carousel powered by a mountain stream.

A MINING DREAM

Iron ore had been known to be present in the valley since the 14th century but it was not exploited until 1655. Extraction was hampered by the location of the seam, which lay between the Cirque du Fer-à-Cheval and the summit of Le Tenneverge. From the open-cast mine on the slopes above the Fond de la Combe, the ore was carried by men or transported by mule to the furnaces of Molliet (*above*) in the 17th century, and to the depot in Sixt in the 19th century. At the foundry the ore was turned into ingots and then used for cast-iron firebacks and agricultural implements. In 1850 a bylaw prohibiting the tipping of ore down the path of Le Boret to the foundry marked the end of a dream for Sixt.

A LA MÉMOIRE
DE JACQUES BALMAT
VAINQUEUR DU MONT BLANC
DÉCÉDÉ ACCIDENTELLEMENT
AU GLACIER DU RUAN
EN SEPTEMBRE 1834

THE GOLD LEGEND
In September 1843 Jacques Balmat ▲ *235*, the first mountaineer to climb Mont Blanc, died on the Glacier du Ruan while prospecting for gold. His obsession with gold led him to his last resting place deep in the mountains of the Cirque du Fer-à-Cheval. Well before Balmat, there had been many legends about the existence of gold in the valley. The Fontaine de l'Or, below the Corne du Chamois, one of the many waterfalls in the cirque, was named after a seam of gold that was discovered by a local man and soon exhausted! The tale of the treasure of Le Tenneverge, the leaves in the Fond de la Combe that changed into gold, the ibex with hooves covered in gold dust were all legends that contributed to the magic of these mountains.

SIXT-FER-À-CHEVAL: A NATURE RESERVE
The beautiful mountains of Sixt, and especially the Fer-à-Cheval, now have the protection they deserve. In 1977 the Réserve Naturelle de Sixt ▲ *215*, an area of 22,730 acres which covers three quarters of the *commune*, was created. Under the care of the municipality and the French Ministry for the Environment, the region is protected and the continuation of its traditional activities guaranteed. Together with the reserves of Passy and Les Aiguilles Rouges, the Réserve Naturelle de Sixt constitutes an area of more than 34,595 acres that is a paradise for Alpine fauna and hikers.
In 1993 overuse of certain parts of the *commune* of Sixt-Fer-à-Cheval led to their being declared sites of national interest. In the same year the Région Rhône-Alpes region classified the *commune* as a site of regional interest.

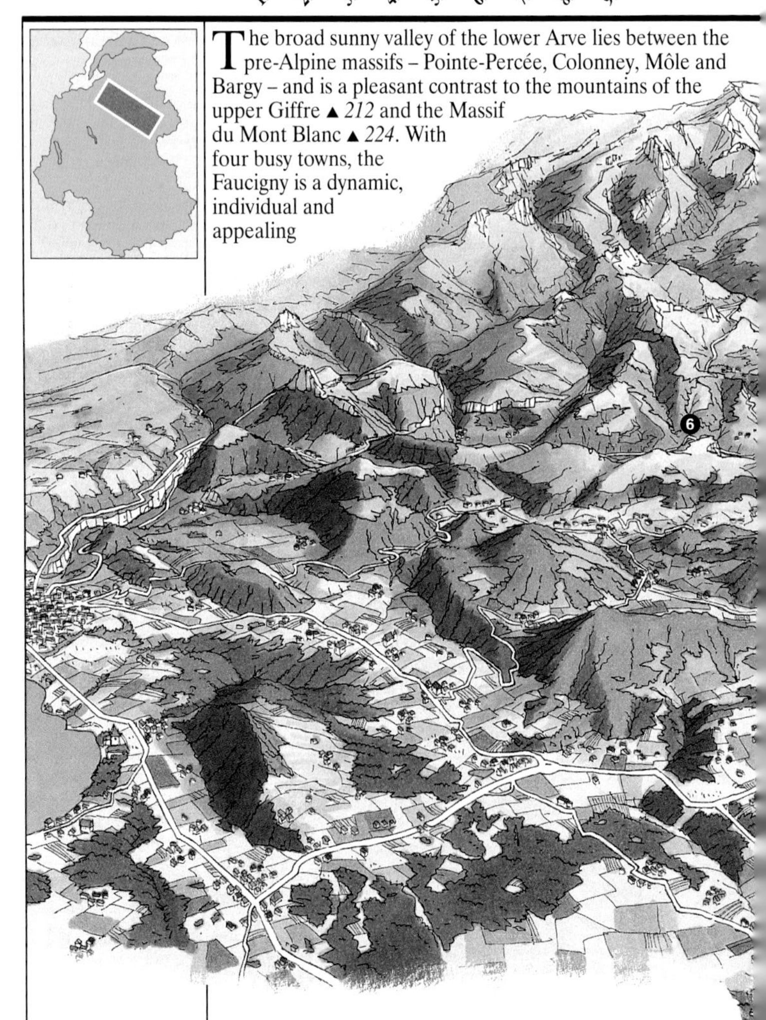

The broad sunny valley of the lower Arve lies between the pre-Alpine massifs – Pointe-Percée, Colonney, Môle and Bargy – and is a pleasant contrast to the mountains of the upper Giffre ▲ *212* and the Massif du Mont Blanc ▲ *224*. With four busy towns, the Faucigny is a dynamic, individual and appealing region. The Faucigny family for whom the region was named were originally vassals of the counts of Geneva ● *35*. When the family joined the House of Savoie in 1355, the Faucigny region became part of the dukedom of Savoie.

LA ROCHE-SUR-FORON

From the top of a rocky spur, the old town of la Roche-sur-Foron overlooks the lower valley of the Arve and the route over the Col d'Évires to Annecy. In the 12th century the counts of Geneva fortified the town and encouraged the development of trade with Savoie and northern Switzerland. La Roche has long been dependent on trade and commerce, as evidenced by its *grenette* ▲ *86* (1816), its active shopping streets, and two international events: the Foire de Haute-Savoie-Mont-Blanc and the Salon du Décolletage (a machine tools and mechnical parts fair).

HOSPICES, COLLEGES AND CONVENTS
Several of the religious communities who established hospices, colleges and convents in La Roche are still active today. They have made the town a center of private education. Colleges in La Roche include the national school of the meat and dairy industry.

Quartier de Plain-Chateau. In 1320 the district – the residence of the counts of Geneva – was enclosed by a trapezoid rampart. Today all that remains of the counts' three castles is the Tour Ronde, which houses a museum of local history. The tower offers an all-round panoramic view, from the Jura to Mont Blanc. The narrow streets of the district are lined by tastefully restored 15th- and 16th-century shops and houses such as the Maison Adhémar-Fabri, in the Rue du Silence, and the Maison de la Grange, in the Rue Perrine.

Église Saint-Jean-Baptiste. The onion-shaped steeple was added to the square belfry (1575) after the French Revolution (1789–99). The church, which stands on a slope, is built on two levels linked by a flight of steps. The first level has a neo-Gothic nave, while the second consists of a polygonal chancel in the late Gothic style and two side chapels (1530).

Commanderie de Moussy
(1¾ miles outside La Roche, on the D2 toward Geneva.)
The former commandery of the Knights Hopitallers (1278) stands alone in a lush setting. The beautiful doorway in the Romanesque façade is flanked by two pairs of columns whose capitals are decorated with plant motifs. The original chapel survives and has been used as a house since 1836.

Statue of Saint François de Sales: 'I am here in Viuz, the land of my diocese,' he wrote in a letter of July 1607.

TOWARD VIUZ-EN-SALLAZ

Viuz-en-Sallaz, dominated by the Pointe des Brasses (4930 feet) and Mont Vouan (3205 feet), lies on the road between the Vallée du Giffre ▲ *212* and the Vallée Verte ▲ *210*.

CONTAMINE-SUR-ARVE. The Cluniac priory of this agricultural and wine-growing commune was founded in 1083 by Guy de Faucigny, bishop of Geneva. Until 1268 it was the burial place of the lords of Faucigny. The church, destroyed several times and rebuilt in 1295, is in a Gothic style reminiscent of English Perpendicular.

VIUZ-EN-SALLAZ. The former estate of Viuz-en-Sallaz is now a commercial and industrial town. It is surrounded by hamlets with neat, flower-decked farmhouses. The MUSÉE PAYSAN, in a converted dairy cooperative, well deserves its high reputation. Objectively and unsentimentally, it documents traditional life in the mountains and explains the need to adapt to the modern world. Just outside Viuz, on the road to Samoëns, one can go trout fishing in the artificial Lac du Môle (*above*) in a setting of willows, reeds, swans and ducks.

GLAZED POTTERY
Pottery has been made in Savoie since Neolithic times, but glazed pottery did not come into its own until the 19th century. Today the potting tradition is continued at three workshops. The oldest, owned by the Guyot family of Marnaz, near Cluses, has existed for 200 years. The Rybczynski pottery in Saint-Jorioz ▲ *172* was established in 1963, and that of Jean-Christophe Hermann, which produced the wedding plate shown below, was founded in Évires in 1972. Jean-Christophe Hermann also set up a museum of Savoyard pottery.

SAINT-JEOIRE-EN-FAUCIGNY

The Saint-Jeoire triangle is formed by three valleys which run between Geneva and Samoëns, toward the Chablais ▲ *200* and toward the Vallée de l'Arve ▲ *222*. The medieval village of Saint-Jeoire is dominated by the 13th-century CHÂTEAU DE BEAUREGARD, which has been restored by Viollet-le-Duc. The village was transformed under the Sardinian government following the restoration of Savoie to Victor-Emmanuel I in 1815.

MÉGEVETTE. The chalets, the former cooperative cheese dairy and the peaceful pastoral landscapes mark the agricultural traditions of the village. Beyond the Col de JAMBAZ, the D26 enters the Chablais, whose lower slopes gently descend toward Lake Geneva ▲ *192*.

BONNEVILLE

At the bridge over the Arve, a statue of Charles-Félix, king of Sardinia and duke of Savoie, looks down on Bonneville from the top of a 95-foot COLUMN erected in 1826 to commemorate the harnessing of the Arve. The town was founded by Béatrix de Faucigny in 1283 and became the capital of the Faucigny. It expanded in the 16th century due to its administrative and judicial activities. Beyond the bridge the PLACE DU PARQUET lies at the intersection of the town's

The Lac du Môle.

main access roads. It is a fine example of monumental Neoclassical architecture. As well as 17th-century arcaded houses and a fountain (1786), it has an elegantly symmetrical town hall (1853).

Maison des Têtes. The 'house of heads' (1731), which also stands on the square, is the Faucigny's only example of German Baroque architecture. The lintels of the windows are decorated with masks of angels and grimacing monsters.

Église Sainte-Catherine. The church is another fine example of Sardinian Neoclassicism ▲ *86*. Its façade is reminiscent of a classical temple, while its furniture and interior decoration, painted in *trompe l'oeil*, attest to the Piedmontese influence in vogue at the time.

The castle. The castle stands high above the town to the north of the Place du Parquet. It was built by the counts of Savoie in the 13th century and subsequently altered. The two turrets on the east side of the ramparts allowed the castle to control the surrounding area. In the 18th century the residential wings served as a prison. Today these rooms are used for meetings and exhibitions. The nearby Musée Départemental de la Résistance (Rue Sainte-Catherine) traces the history of the Savoie Resistance.

Toward Cluses

Aÿze. The vineyards of Aÿze cover an area of some 50 acres on the right bank of the Arve, at the foot of Le Môle. They produce an unusual sparkling wine using a vine (le gringet) probably imported from Cyprus by the counts of Savoie.

Mont-Saxonnex. The chapel (1664) in the hamlet of Pincru has a strange gilt marrow-shaped bulb and a retable depicting the marriage of the Virgin Mary (1665). The promontory (3280 feet) of the Église Notre-Dame-de-l'Assomption offers a sweeping view of the slopes of Aÿze, the Vallée du Giffre ▲ *212*, the mountains of the Chablais ▲ *200* and the Jura.

Le Reposoir. The Chartreuse du Reposoir nestles in the forest beneath the Pointe Percée (9030 feet). The Carthusian monastery was founded in 1151 by monks of the order of Saint Bruno. It was abandoned in 1901 and later occupied by the Carmelites. The Maison du Gypaete nearby has details of a project to reintroduce the bearded vulture to the Alps.

Germain Sommeiller
(1815–71)
Germain Sommeiller, born in Saint-Jeoire, was the inventor of the pneumatic drill that was used to build the very first Alpine tunnel – the Tunnel de Mont-Cenis ● *43* ▲ *279* – in 1862. He also worked on extending the rail network in Sardinia.

Return of the 'bone breakers'
In 1986 the bearded vulture, which had disappeared from the Alps in the early 20th century, was reintroduced to the Massif du Bargy. August 1997 saw the first hatching of a chick in the wild as a result of the project. The bearded vulture is also known as the 'bone breaker' because of its habit of dropping the bones on which it feeds from a great height, so as to break them into pieces on the rocks.

Fresco (*right*) by Casimir Vicario, from the Église Saint-Jacques in Sallanches.

Sallanches.

CLUSES

The town stretches across the plain, protected by the glacial threshold of the Arve. It has become the French capital of mechanical parts and, together with its neighbors, Magland, Scionzier, Marnaz and Marignier, forms the 'Silicon Valley' of Haute-Savoie.

MUSÉE DE L'HORLOGERIE ET DU DÉCOLLETAGE. The museum, opened in 1933 in the Maison Carpano (a pioneer of the mechanical parts industry), traces the history of clockmaking and its industrial development, from traditional clockmaking to state-of-the-art and futuristic techniques of the mechanical parts industry.

ÉGLISE SAINT-NICOLAS. The 16th-century church is a fine example of Flamboyant (late Gothic) style, but was badly renovated in 1930. The finely carved font (c. 1520) is one of its major features. At the foot of the large cross that rests in the octagonal basin, the keeling figure of Mary Magdalene looks up at Christ surmounted by a pelican (symbolizing nurture). On the other side is the Virgin Mary, holding Jesus.

BETWEEN CLUSES AND SALLANCHES

FLAINE. The resort of Flaine was built in the early 1960s, on a sheltered site at an altitude ranging from 4920 to 6560 feet. Based on an idea by Éric Boissonas and developed by Marcel Breuer, the American architect and designer of the Bauhaus school, this integrated resort is an architectural tour de force ● *94*. Sculptures by Jean Dubuffet, Véra Cardot, Pablo Picasso and Victor Vasarely are displayed around the resort.

DÉSERT DE PLATÉ ■ *16*. A cableway – the *Téléphérique des Grandes Platières* – runs from Flaine to the Désert de Platé, an extensive limestone plateau that covers an area of 15½ square miles and rises to a height of 8200 feet. Cracked and fissured in all directions, it looks like a huge stone glacier.

SALLANCHES

Mont Blanc suddenly comes into view at the end of the valley, so near and yet inaccessible. Sallanches' location at a crossroads offers easy access to the surrounding beauty spots. It also has a thriving industry (Dynastar skis are made here). After the great fire of 1840, the town was rebuilt by the engineer Justin in the Sardinian style: arcaded streets, colored façades, an imposing town hall, *grenette*, and fountains ● *86*.

ÉGLISE SAINT-JACQUES. After the great fire, only the church's interior was restored; Piedmontese artists and master-plasterers working under the direction of Casimir Vicario. Medallions, *trompe l'oeil* and paintings create a profuse decor in delicate colors. Beyond the entrance, on the left, are a collection of 15th-century religious objects, among the richest treasures in Savoie. Nearby, a station or temporary altar, serves as a font. Very finely worked, it is reminiscent of the holy-water stoup at Cluses and appears to date from the same period.

A CLOCKMAKING TRADITION
Claude Ballaloud, born in Saint-Sigismond, above Cluses, emigrated to Nuremberg, where he learned the art of clockmaking. In 1715 he returned to his native region, where he introduced the skills that he had learned. Clockmaking establishments multiplied, providing a new source of winter employment. The opening of the royal school of clockmaking in 1848 revived the clock-making tradition and marked the transition to industrial methods of production. In 1860 it was renamed the 'imperial school' and in 1864 received a grant from Napoleon III which enabled it to provide free training for the next two years.

The Pays du Mont-Blanc, Val d'Arly and Beaufortain

FROM SERVOZ TO CHAMONIX

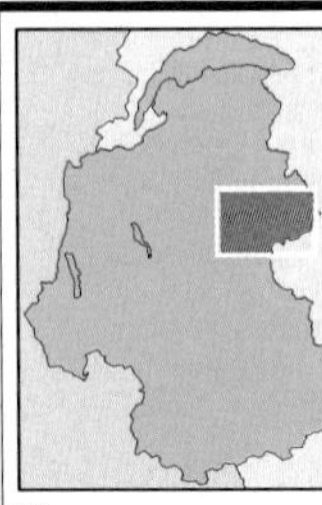

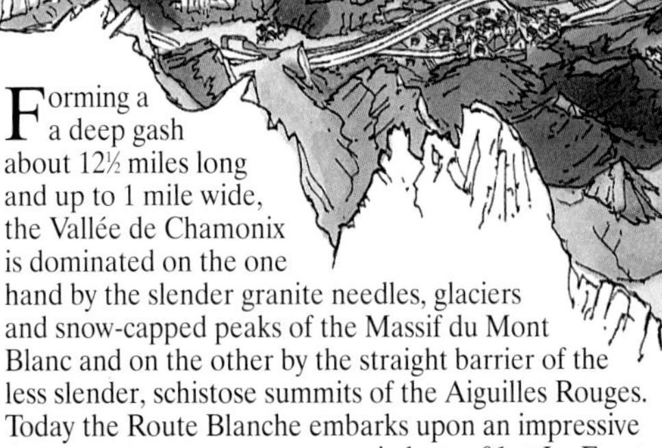

THE VILLAGE THAT ROSE FROM A LAKE
2500 years ago the site of Servoz, which today nestles at the foot of the huge limestone cliffs of Les Fiz, was covered by a huge lake. The lake was fed by the Arve and Diosaz rivers and was contained by a barrier of boulders brought down by landslides from Les Fiz. When this natural dam collapsed, the level of the lake was lowered; it was later completely filled by a second landslide.

A DANGEROUS APPROACH
In the early 19th century, to facilitate access to the valley, a transport service from Sallanches was organized. However, the tracks were so narrow that the carriages sometimes had to be dismantled and carried piece by piece by porters. Horses would also often slip on the ascents of Pélissier.

Forming a a deep gash about 12½ miles long and up to 1 mile wide, the Vallée de Chamonix is dominated on the one hand by the slender granite needles, glaciers and snow-capped peaks of the Massif du Mont Blanc and on the other by the straight barrier of the less slender, schistose summits of the Aiguilles Rouges. Today the Route Blanche embarks upon an impressive viaduct ● *91* at Le Fayet, at the very point which marked the beginning of the arduous 'voyage à Chamouny'.

GORGES DE LA DIOSAZ. The Diosaz rises on the southern slopes of Le Buet and descends toward Servoz in a series of seven waterfalls along the bottom of a narrow gorge. Since 1847 galleries have enabled visitors to walk along the gorge in complete safety.

LES HOUCHES

The name Les Houches is derived from the Celtic word *olca*, meaning 'cultivable land'. To this day the *commune* maintains an agricultural and pastoral tradition, as proven by the presence of about 200 cows, some of the last in the valley.
ÉGLISE SAINT-JEAN-BAPTISTE. The church, with its metal steeple, stands on the left bank of the Arve. It is the only Baroque church in the region to have kept its original façade.

It was built by artisans from northern Italy who could withstand the harsh climate of the mountain villages. Features include three retables and a rood beam with an18th-century Crucifixion.

Toward Charousse. The hamlet of Les Chavants offers an impressive panoramic view of the Aiguille du Gouter, one of the classic ascents of Mont Blanc, which starts from Les Houches. The Oratoire Notre-Dame-des-Voyageurs stands on the old mule and carriage route to the 'ice fields'. Further up the mountain, a pleasant track through woodland leads to Charousse and its Alpine chalets.

Right bank of the Arve. At Merlet, opposite Mont Blanc, is a nature reserve that extends over an area of almost 57 acres. Here live mouflon, chamois, ibex, deer, marmots and llamas.

Les Bossons

The hamlet lies at the foot of the Glacier des Bossons, the longest icefall in Europe (10,830 feet). It forms on the summit of Mont Blanc and, although it has retreated significantly in recent years, it extends almost to the valley and has the lowest glacial tongue in the Alps.

The Kandahar (AK)
The Arlberg Kandahar takes place on the famous Piste Verte (green run) (*below*) of Les Houches. First run in 1928, this combined descent and slalom is the oldest traditional skiing event.

Mont-Blanc: panorama from l'Index

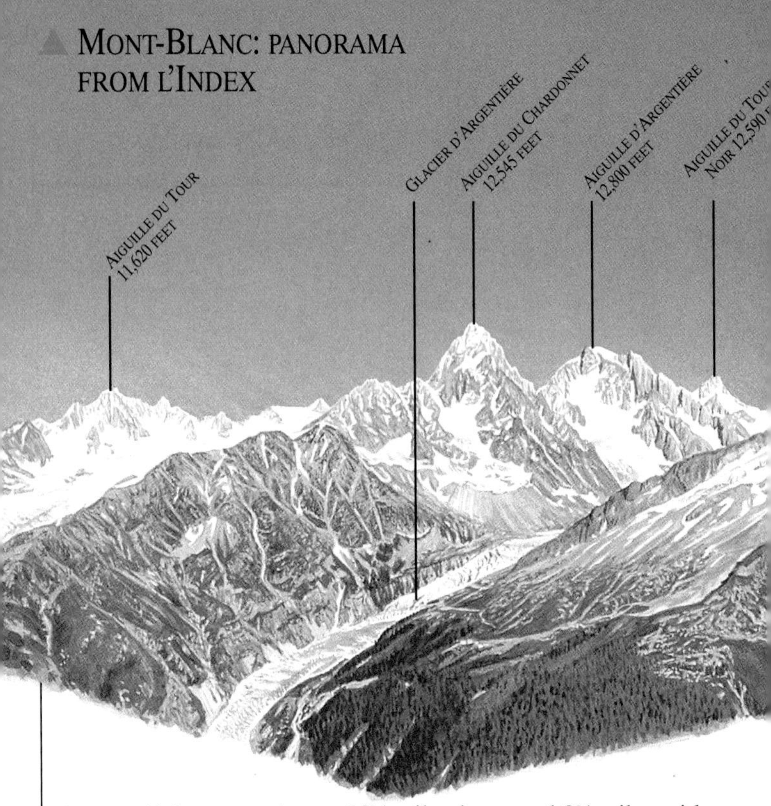

The massif du Mont-Blanc – 18½ miles long and 9¾ miles wide – occupies a relatively small area within the Alps. Visually, however, it is without equal anywhere in Europe: here are forests of slender needles, majestic pyramids, impressive glacial domes, granite cliffs and vast glaciers. Until the 18th century only a few adventurers, in search of rock crystal, had dared go near these 'accursed mountains' as it was believed that they were the preserve of monsters and evil spirits. With Windham, Pococke and Saussure, the age of mountaineering arrived. The massif ceased to be a terrifying place; it was now fascinating and irresistible. By the end of the 19th century all the major summits had been conquered. The era of great exploration is past, but climbers are still achieving first ascents, and sometimes the summits that they conquer are named for them.

Windham and Pococke
In 1741 two tourists, ignoring warnings, set off to see the 'icefields'. Windham and Pococke became the first tourists from the valley to set eyes on a 'sort of agitated sea that seemed suddenly to have frozen'. This was the Mer de Glace ('sea of ice') on Le Montenvers.

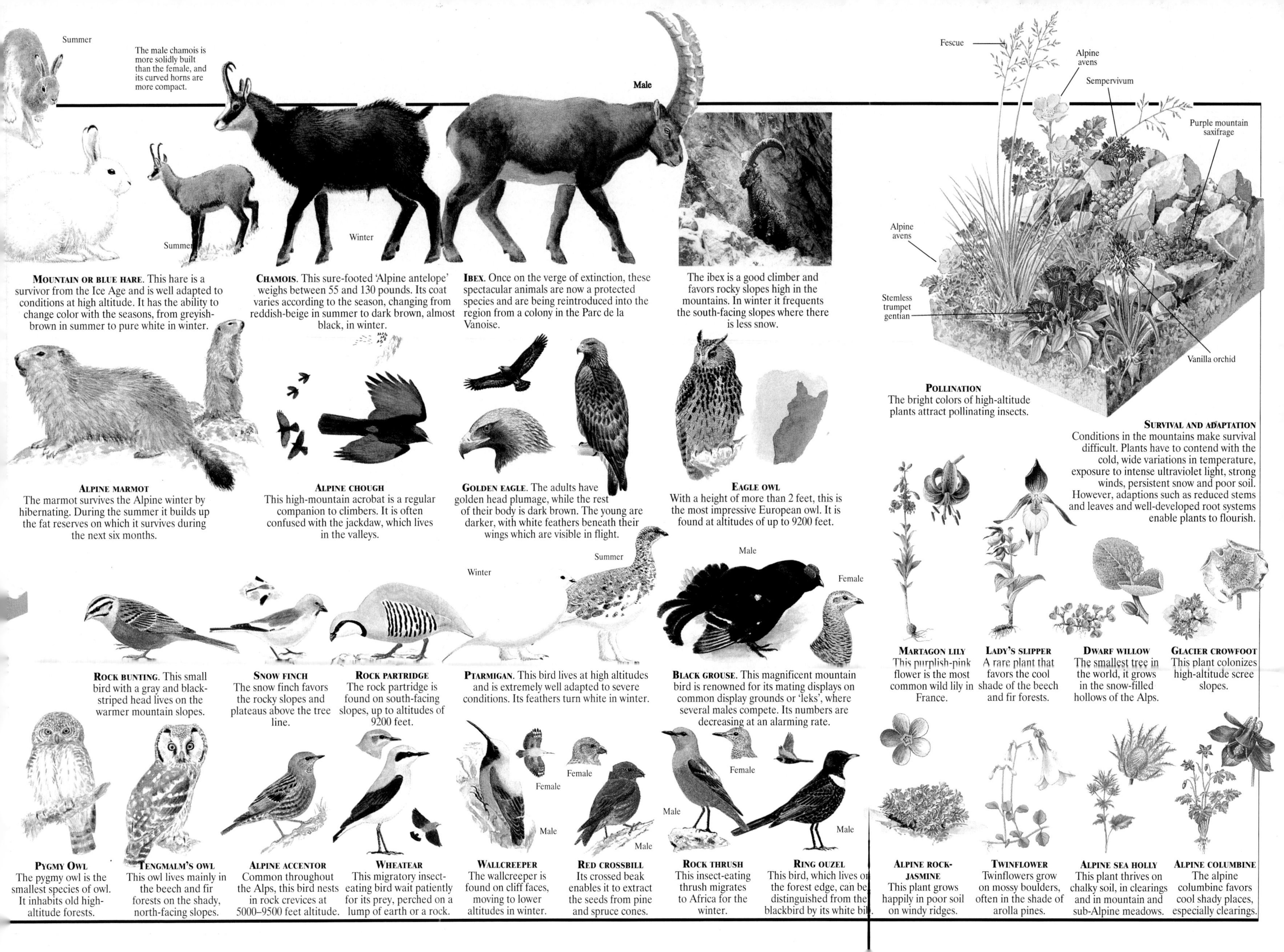

Mountain or blue hare. This hare is a survivor from the Ice Age and is well adapted to conditions at high altitude. It has the ability to change color with the seasons, from greyish-brown in summer to pure white in winter.

Chamois. This sure-footed 'Alpine antelope' weighs between 55 and 130 pounds. Its coat varies according to the season, changing from reddish-beige in summer to dark brown, almost black, in winter.

Ibex. Once on the verge of extinction, these spectacular animals are now a protected species and are being reintroduced into the region from a colony in the Parc de la Vanoise.

The ibex is a good climber and favors rocky slopes high in the mountains. In winter it frequents the south-facing slopes where there is less snow.

Pollination
The bright colors of high-altitude plants attract pollinating insects.

Survival and adaptation
Conditions in the mountains make survival difficult. Plants have to contend with the cold, wide variations in temperature, exposure to intense ultraviolet light, strong winds, persistent snow and poor soil. However, adaptions such as reduced stems and leaves and well-developed root systems enable plants to flourish.

Alpine marmot
The marmot survives the Alpine winter by hibernating. During the summer it builds up the fat reserves on which it survives during the next six months.

Alpine chough
This high-mountain acrobat is a regular companion to climbers. It is often confused with the jackdaw, which lives in the valleys.

Golden eagle. The adults have golden head plumage, while the rest of their body is dark brown. The young are darker, with white feathers beneath their wings which are visible in flight.

Eagle owl
With a height of more than 2 feet, this is the most impressive European owl. It is found at altitudes of up to 9200 feet.

Martagon lily
This purplish-pink flower is the most common wild lily in France.

Lady's slipper
A rare plant that favors the cool shade of the beech and fir forests.

Dwarf willow
The smallest tree in the world, it grows in the snow-filled hollows of the Alps.

Glacier crowfoot
This plant colonizes high-altitude scree slopes.

Rock bunting. This small bird with a gray and black-striped head lives on the warmer mountain slopes.

Snow finch
The snow finch favors the rocky slopes and plateaus above the tree line.

Rock partridge
The rock partridge is found on south-facing slopes, up to altitudes of 9200 feet.

Ptarmigan. This bird lives at high altitudes and is extremely well adapted to severe conditions. Its feathers turn white in winter.

Black grouse. This magnificent mountain bird is renowned for its mating displays on common display grounds or 'leks', where several males compete. Its numbers are decreasing at an alarming rate.

Pygmy Owl
The pygmy owl is the smallest species of owl. It inhabits old high-altitude forests.

Tengmalm's owl
This owl lives mainly in the beech and fir forests on the shady, north-facing slopes.

Alpine accentor
Common throughout the Alps, this bird nests in rock crevices at 5000–9500 feet altitude.

Wheatear
This migratory insect-eating bird wait patiently for its prey, perched on a lump of earth or a rock.

Wallcreeper
The wallcreeper is found on cliff faces, moving to lower altitudes in winter.

Red crossbill
Its crossed beak enables it to extract the seeds from pine and spruce cones.

Rock thrush
This insect-eating thrush migrates to Africa for the winter.

Ring ouzel
This bird, which lives on the forest edge, can be distinguished from the blackbird by its white bill.

Alpine rock-jasmine
This plant grows happily in poor soil on windy ridges.

Twinflower
Twinflowers grow on mossy boulders, often in the shade of arolla pines.

Alpine sea holly
This plant thrives on chalky soil, in clearings and in mountain and sub-Alpine meadows.

Alpine columbine
The alpine columbine favors cool shady places, especially clearings.

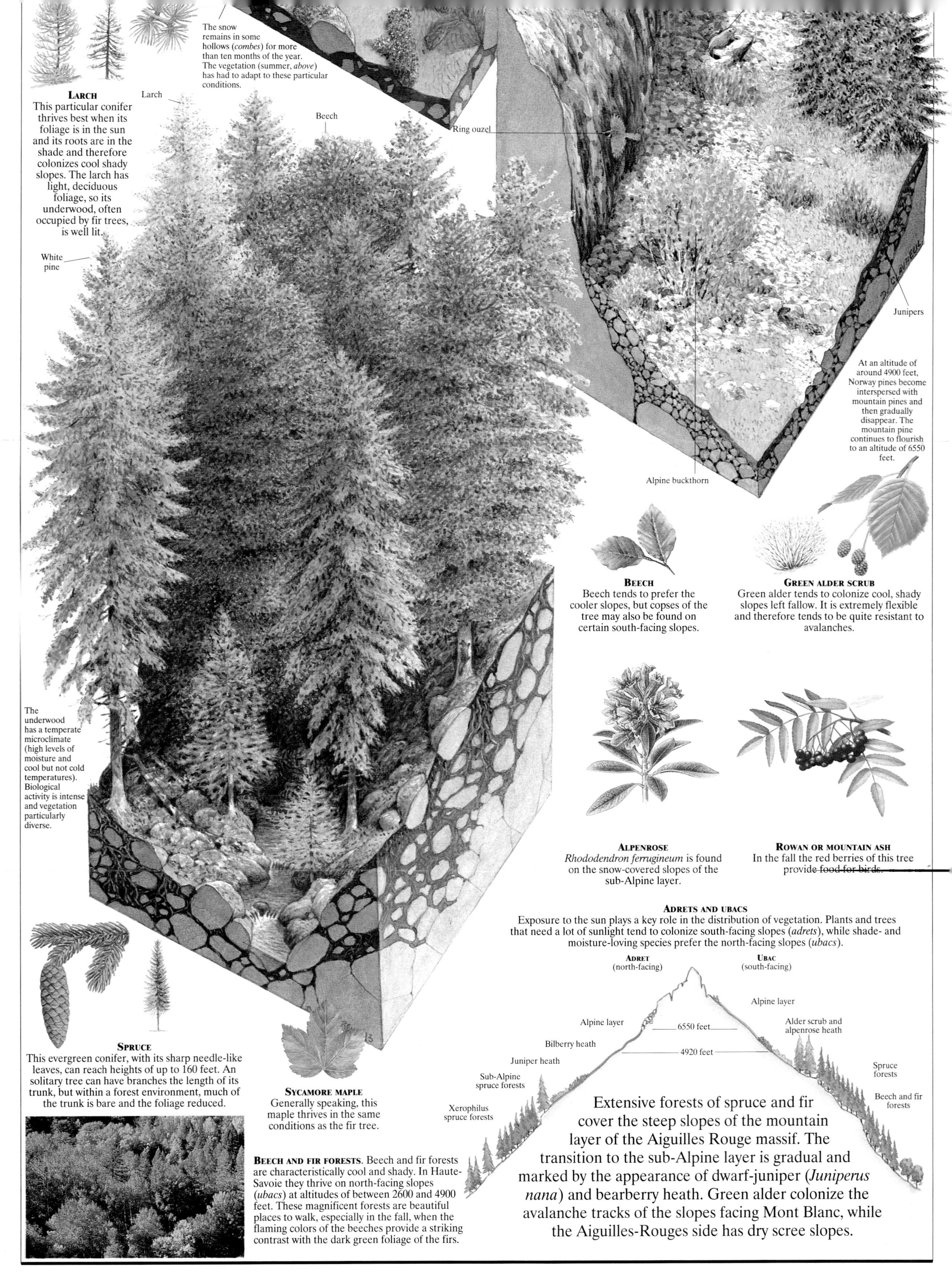

The snow remains in some hollows (*combes*) for more than ten months of the year. The vegetation (summer, *above*) has had to adapt to these particular conditions.

Larch
This particular conifer thrives best when its foliage is in the sun and its roots are in the shade and therefore colonizes cool shady slopes. The larch has light, deciduous foliage, so its underwood, often occupied by fir trees, is well lit.

At an altitude of around 4900 feet, Norway pines become interspersed with mountain pines and then gradually disappear. The mountain pine continues to flourish to an altitude of 6550 feet.

Beech
Beech tends to prefer the cooler slopes, but copses of the tree may also be found on certain south-facing slopes.

Green alder scrub
Green alder tends to colonize cool, shady slopes left fallow. It is extremely flexible and therefore tends to be quite resistant to avalanches.

The underwood has a temperate microclimate (high levels of moisture and cool but not cold temperatures). Biological activity is intense and vegetation particularly diverse.

Alpenrose
Rhododendron ferrugineum is found on the snow-covered slopes of the sub-Alpine layer.

Rowan or mountain ash
In the fall the red berries of this tree provide food for birds.

Adrets and ubacs
Exposure to the sun plays a key role in the distribution of vegetation. Plants and trees that need a lot of sunlight tend to colonize south-facing slopes (*adrets*), while shade- and moisture-loving species prefer the north-facing slopes (*ubacs*).

Spruce
This evergreen conifer, with its sharp needle-like leaves, can reach heights of up to 160 feet. An solitary tree can have branches the length of its trunk, but within a forest environment, much of the trunk is bare and the foliage reduced.

Sycamore maple
Generally speaking, this maple thrives in the same conditions as the fir tree.

Beech and fir forests. Beech and fir forests are characteristically cool and shady. In Haute-Savoie they thrive on north-facing slopes (*ubacs*) at altitudes of between 2600 and 4900 feet. These magnificent forests are beautiful places to walk, especially in the fall, when the flaming colors of the beeches provide a striking contrast with the dark green foliage of the firs.

Extensive forests of spruce and fir cover the steep slopes of the mountain layer of the Aiguilles Rouge massif. The transition to the sub-Alpine layer is gradual and marked by the appearance of dwarf-juniper (*Juniperus nana*) and bearberry heath. Green alder colonize the avalanche tracks of the slopes facing Mont Blanc, while the Aiguilles-Rouges side has dry scree slopes.

REFUGE DES COSMIQUES
The refuge, near the Aiguille du Midi, was designed by Paul Parisey, an architect and mountain guide from Chamonix. It is used by climbers on their way up to Mont Blanc and skiers who want to enjoy a night at high altitude before making the descent via the Vallée Blanche ▲ 238. It is named for the research that Louis Leprince-Ringuet carried out on cosmic rays. His observatory was located there.

GERVASUTTI (1909–46)
Two ascents via the northeast face of Mont Blanc du Tacul are named for Gervasutti: the great glacial corridor by which he made the first ascent in 1934, and the central chimney rock where he died without reaching the summit. Beaten by bad weather, he was killed as he was roping down during the descent.

DESTIVELLE
After a career in competition climbing, Destivelle, known as the Danseuse de Roc ('rock dancer'), abandoned artificial rockfaces to concentrate on the mountains. She spent twelve days on Les Drus, the most legendary rockface of the entire massif, and carved her name next to the famous Bonatti chimney rock.

GABARROU
Most of the 250 ascents pioneered by Gabarrou, a climber eager for firsts, are in the Massif du Mont-Blanc. They include the Super-Couloir on Mont Blanc du Tacul, Divine Providence and Tibet Libre

For a long time Mont Blanc was known as the Montagne Maudite ('the accursed mountain'). The inhabitants of the mountain valleys were terrified of the 'icefields', which were said to be haunted by the souls of the dead. Only a few smugglers and hunters were prepared to brave the seracs and act as guides for the occasional tourist. However the Enlightenment allayed these fears and explorers took to the slopes of the magic mountain in ever greater numbers. The outlaws of the past became experienced guides and, their clients being affluent, they began to build refuges. These were places in which the guides felt at home, where they shared experiences and formed friendships. Their solidarity was further strengthened when the Compagnie des Guides de Chamonix was formed in 1821. Refuges were also a place to rest after their exploits. The age of discovery came to an end and was replaced by the age of sport and competition mountaineering.

JOSEPH MARIE COUTTET (1792–1877)

Joseph Marie Couttet was a botanist who had an intimate knowledge of the mountains. In 1820 he was asked by a certain Dr Hamel to lead a team of scientists to the summit of Mont Blanc. The weather was changing but the client insisted. An avalanche proved fatal. The 'Dr Hamel disaster' highlighted the need for an organization that could resolve the ambiguities of the guides' occupation. In 1821 Couttet was involved in the formation of the Compagnie des Guides de Chamonix. It had three main aims: to ensure the safety of clients by training competent guides; to create a welfare fund to help guides who were the victim of an accident; and to give guides certain rights when faced with unreasonable demands. The company was officially recognized in 1823. The status of guides had evolved from enlightened amateur to qualified professional.

LE MONTENVERS

Liszt, Hugo and Goethe were among the many famous people who stayed overnight in this legendary refuge. In 1775, when the Mer de Glace was attracting its first visitors, Charles Blain decided to build a shelter near the glacier. Made more permanent, it became a very fashionable rendezvous. At an altitude of 6275 feet, it was easily reached by mule and after 1908 by train ● *66*. More of a society hostelry than a refuge, it symbolized the golden age of 'mountaineering' when, in the words of Leslie Stephen, the ascent was an outing rather than a sport.

Bureau des Guides

Les Grands Mulets

The refuge of Les Grands Mulets is perched on a rocky spur near the treacherous crevasses of La Jonction, at an altitude of 10,010 feet. Until 1853 it was no more than a bivouac, set up by the first conquerors of Mont Blanc in about 1790. The decision of the Chamonix authorities to build a more permanent structure marked the beginning of a large-scale construction program. Refuges had become an essential part of mountaineering both for climbers and tourists. Most are owned by the *communes*. They are run by mountaineering clubs and associations of mountain guides.

From father to son

The guide, with a bushy beard and gnarled body, was waiting in front of the hotel. He was really a farmer but to supplement his income he had offered his services as a guide. As a child he had climbed up to the mountain passes with his father. Later he became a porter and then a guide. The Compagnie des Guides de Chamonix was a real community and it only recruited guides who were raised in the valley. But things were changing. In the 19th century, less bucolic guides with a taste for adventure challenged the family hierarchy that governed the association. It was only recently that the associaton admitted the first guides not born in Chamonix, for example the first woman guide, Sylviane Tavernier.

The conquest of Mont Blanc

Mont Blanc was conquered for the first time at 6.23pm on August 7, 1786, not by an experienced guide but by a crystal hunter. Jacques Balmat (1762–1834), accompanied by Dr Paccard, succeeded where other attempts over the previous twenty years had failed. He was attracted by the reward offered by the naturalist Horace Bénédict de Saussure. Balmat succeeded because he was the first climber to dare to sleep out on the mountain, defying ancient fears and proving that it was possible to survive the cold and solitude. His success was due not so much to his technical skill as to that spirit of discovery and conquest that in the 18th century drove men to 'conquer' nature ▲ *217*.

ACT OF DONATION
'I, Aymon, count of Geneva, and Gérold, my son, do hereby give and concede to the Lord God our Saviour, and to Saint Michael the Archangel of La Cluse, the whole of Chamonix with its dependencies, from the river known as Diosa and the rock known as Blanc to Les Balmes ... keeping nothing for ourselves, except the alms and prayers for our souls and those of our family so that Saint Michael the Archangel may lead us with them into the joy that is Paradise...'
Departmental archives of Annecy

ENSA
The Compagnie des Guides de Chamonix, founded between 1821 and 1823, met a need for solidarity. It also helped to give guides a professional status by defining the level of competence required and by providing training approved by a panel of fellow guides. In 1945 the Collège d'Alpinisme et de Ski was founded in Chamonix, and the École National de Ski at Val d'Isère. They were amalgamated in 1949 to form ENSA (École Nationale du Ski et d'Alpinisme).

Chamonix, which lies at the foot Mont Blanc, is the international capital of skiing and mountaineering. More than a resort, it is a real town, inhabited by people of forty different nationalities, which has managed to preserve the rebellious spirit of the Chamoniards of yesteryear and the first pioneers of the summits. The mountains that frame the town like two huge walls are an invitation to liberty and freedom, while each street and each summit enshrines the memory of prestigious challenges and ascents.

HISTORY

AN ACT OF DONATION. In 1091 Count Aimon I of Geneva gave the Vallée de Chamonix to the monastery of SAINT-MICHEL-DE-LA-CLUSE, in Piedmont. The first prior, Pierre, and several of his monks settled in the valley in the 13th century.
FREE MEN. The few inhabitants that they encountered were 'free men' who were fiercely proud of their independence. The monks built a priory, a farm and mills on the Arve river, and cleared the south-facing slopes of the valley. In 1326 the priory had 76 communities, increasing to 250 in 1471 and 500 in 1606. It passed to the collegiate church of Sallanches (1519) and, together with Savoie, became part of the kingdom of Sardinia in 1713. The Chamoniards were always rebellious, often refusing to pay tithes, abusing official representatives and dispensing their own justice. The priory ceased to exist in 1786, the year in which Mont Blanc was conquered.
MOUNTAIN TOURISM. On July 6, 1860 the guides of the Compagnie des Guides de Chamonix ● *234* raised the French flag on the summit of Mont Blanc. Increasing numbers of visitors were coming to Chamouny, as it was known, and were awed by the sight the 'icefields' despite the difficult access to the valley. Having experienced these discomforts for himself, Napoleon III provided funds for a road to be built. The valley was made more easily accessible in 1901 when an electric cog railroad was installed. The international reputation of Chamonix was secured when the Winter Olympics ● *64* were held there in 1924.

'Mont Blanc shines on high; that is where the power is, a peaceful and solemn power with a thousand faces, a thousand sounds, that contains life and death.'

P.B. Shelley

THE TOWN

PLACE DE L'ÉGLISE. The Place de l'ÉGLISE SAIN-MICHEL, on the edge of the ascent of La Mollard, is the real heart of Chamonix. Although the belfry is dated 1119 the church's façade and onion-shaped belfry date from the 18th and 19th centuries. The retable, by the northern Italian artist Pandrini, was a gift from the Compagnie des Guides de Chamonix in 1838. Two stained-glass windows dating from the 1920s depict Saint Bernard killing the dragon and Saint Christopher, patron saint of mountaineers. The church shares its parvis with the priory, now the Maison de la Montagne, headquarters of the Compagnie des Guides de Chamonix ▲ *234*. Also on the square are the weather station, the ski school and the high-mountain center. The bar has always been a favorite meeting place for guides. Roger Frison-Roche was one of its regulars.

PLACES BALMAT AND SAUSSURE. As you make your way down to the Arve you come to the Place Balmat. In front of La Terrasse, a bar in the Art Nouveau-style, is a bronze statue (*below*) of the pioneers Saussure and Balmat, who is pointing toward Mont Blanc. On the far side of the river is the PLACE SAUSSURE and the HOTEL ROYAL (1848), where Napoleon III's entourage stayed in 1860. It is now the casino.

MUSÉE ALPIN. The large white building of the former Chamonix-Palace today houses the Musée Alpin, which documents major events in the development of the valley, the conquest of the massif and the scientific epic played out on its slopes. During the winter of 1999 a fire damaged the museum and destroyed a number of paintings by Gabriel Loppé ● *102*.

THE ENGLISH IN CHAMONIX. Many British visitors once stayed at the Hôtel Couttet. Its most prestigious guest was Edward Whymper, who conquered the Aiguille Verte in 1865 and who died in the hotel in 1911. English mountaineers, artists and poets were so numerous in the valley that in 1857 an Anglican chapel was built. Beside the Lac à l'Anglais, near the Rocher des Gaillands, are the ruins of one of the meeting places favored by the Romantics during the golden age of British tourism in Chamonix.

MONT BLANC IN THE MOVIES
Many films and documentaries have been shot on these mountains. They include three short films by Max Linder (1883–1925), Theodore Tetzlaff's *The White Tower* (1950), with Glenn Ford and Alida Valli, Edward Dmytryk's *The Mountain* (1956) with Spencer Tracy (Paramount spent an entire summer there), Philippe De Broca's *Les Tribulations d'un Chinois en Chine* (*Up to his Ears*, 1965), with Jean-Paul Belmondo, and John Huston's *The Man Who Would be King* (1975), with Sean Connery and Michael Caine. Guides were trained or doubled for the actors. The mountaineer Gaston Rebuffat ▲ *230* worked for Walt Disney Productions in this capacity.

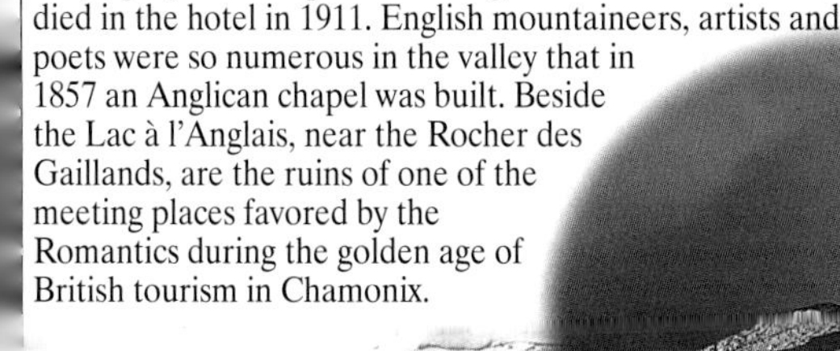

THE OBSERVATORY
The Observatoire Vallot (*above*) is owned by the CNRS (Centre National de la Recherche Scientifique). It is used as a base by the glaciology research center in Grenoble.

Top to bottom: Le Montenvers railroad, with the Aiguilles Rouges in the background; the Aiguille du Midi; the Aiguilles de Chamonix (Blaitière and Les Ciseaux); the seracs of the Mer de Glace, some of which are 100–165 feet deep.

LE MONTENVERS RAILROAD ● *67*. Plans for this rack-and-pinion railroad between Chamonix and the Mer de Glace were initially rejected by the local inhabitants, who feared competition and pollution from the steam train. Today no one has any regrets about the line, opened in 1910.
MER DE GLACE. The glacier came to be known as the 'sea of ice' after it was described by the Englishman William Windham in 1741 as a 'sort of agitated sea that seemed suddenly to have frozen'. It became extremely popular with artists and writers. It provided Mary Shelley with inspiration for harrowing scenes in *Frankenstein*, and was the setting for Eugène Labiche's *Voyage de M. Perrichon*. It also inspired Goethe and Byron, and more recently Gaston Rebuffat's *Les Cent Plus Belles Courses du Massif du Mont-Blanc*. This constantly moving valley glacier is over 8½ miles long. It retreated by 670 yards between 1925 and 1960 but began to advance again in 1975.
THE AIGUILLE DU MIDI CABLEWAY ▲ *67*. The cableway links the Plan du Midi (7600 feet) with the Aiguille du Mid (12,605 feet) over a distance of almost 3300 yards and a rise in altitude of 4920 feet, without pylons. The cable, divided into coils weighing 66 pounds each, was physically carried part of the way. The ascent now takes about 8 minutes at a speed of 28 miles per hour with 66 passengers on board.
AIGUILLE DU MIDI. Its twin peaks are linked by a footbridge. It offers an all-round view, with Le Cervin and the Jura mountains in the distance, and the Grandes Jorasses, Mont Maudit, Les Drus and the Aiguille Verte ▲ *226* in the foreground. Another cableway runs from the Aiguille du Midi to the Pointe Helbronner in Italy, above a breathtaking panorama of glaciers.
VALLÉE BLANCHE. The Aiguille du Midi is the starting point for the ski descent of the Vallee Blanche. The route runs for about 12 miles, passing Les Grandes Jorasses, Le Grepon, Les Grands Charmoz and l'Aiguille du Dru. Although this extremely popular run does not require a high level of technical skill, it is inadvisable to attempt it without a guide since it traverses an area of glaciers where snow conceals treacherous crevasses.

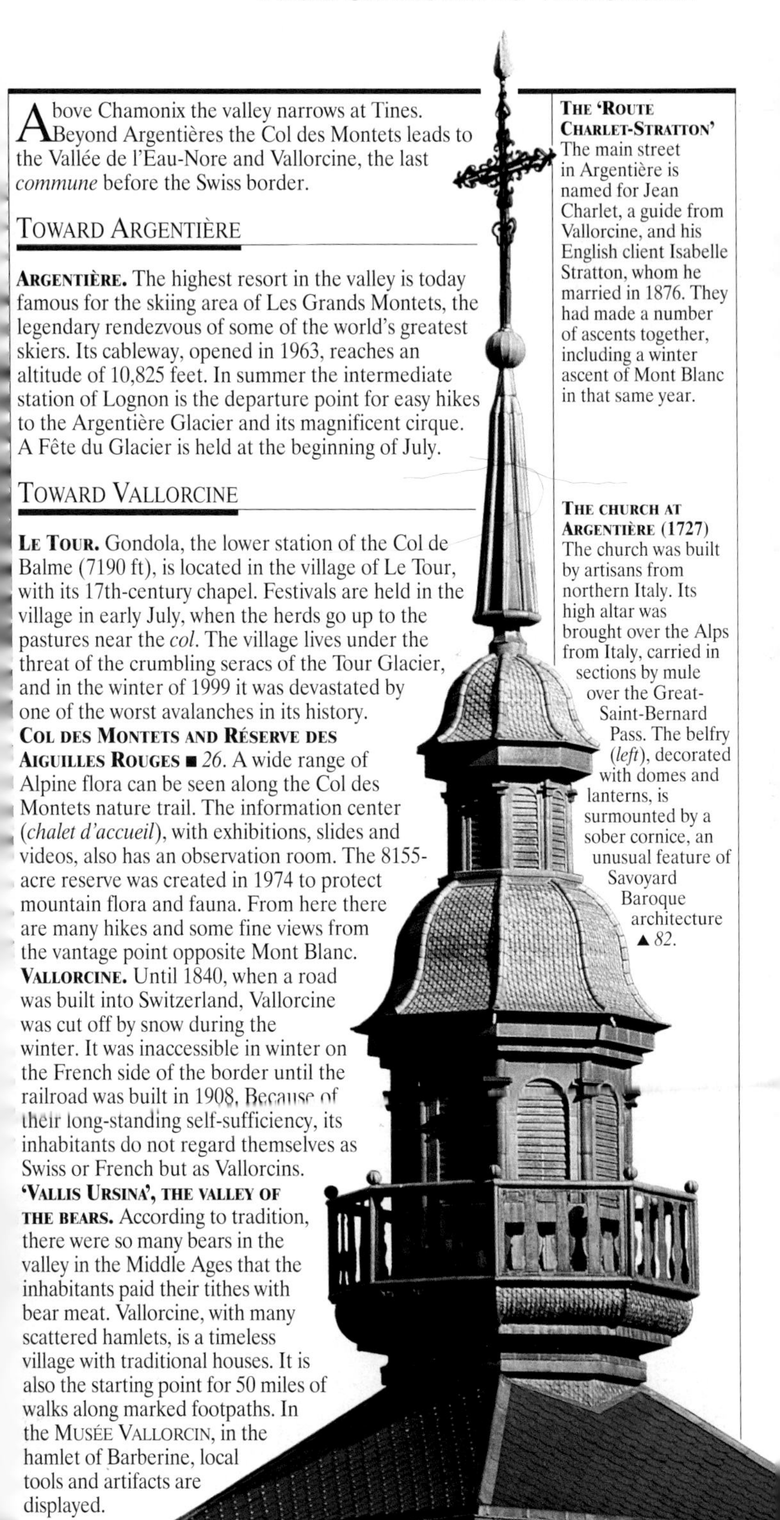

Above Chamonix the valley narrows at Tines. Beyond Argentières the Col des Montets leads to the Vallée de l'Eau-Nore and Vallorcine, the last *commune* before the Swiss border.

TOWARD ARGENTIÈRE

ARGENTIÈRE. The highest resort in the valley is today famous for the skiing area of Les Grands Montets, the legendary rendezvous of some of the world's greatest skiers. Its cableway, opened in 1963, reaches an altitude of 10,825 feet. In summer the intermediate station of Lognon is the departure point for easy hikes to the Argentière Glacier and its magnificent cirque. A Fête du Glacier is held at the beginning of July.

TOWARD VALLORCINE

LE TOUR. Gondola, the lower station of the Col de Balme (7190 ft), is located in the village of Le Tour, with its 17th-century chapel. Festivals are held in the village in early July, when the herds go up to the pastures near the *col*. The village lives under the threat of the crumbling seracs of the Tour Glacier, and in the winter of 1999 it was devastated by one of the worst avalanches in its history.

COL DES MONTETS AND RÉSERVE DES AIGUILLES ROUGES ■ *26*. A wide range of Alpine flora can be seen along the Col des Montets nature trail. The information center (*chalet d'accueil*), with exhibitions, slides and videos, also has an observation room. The 8155-acre reserve was created in 1974 to protect mountain flora and fauna. From here there are many hikes and some fine views from the vantage point opposite Mont Blanc.

VALLORCINE. Until 1840, when a road was built into Switzerland, Vallorcine was cut off by snow during the winter. It was inaccessible in winter on the French side of the border until the railroad was built in 1908. Because of their long-standing self-sufficiency, its inhabitants do not regard themselves as Swiss or French but as Vallorcins.

'VALLIS URSINA', THE VALLEY OF THE BEARS. According to tradition, there were so many bears in the valley in the Middle Ages that the inhabitants paid their tithes with bear meat. Vallorcine, with many scattered hamlets, is a timeless village with traditional houses. It is also the starting point for 50 miles of walks along marked footpaths. In the MUSÉE VALLORCIN, in the hamlet of Barberine, local tools and artifacts are displayed.

THE 'ROUTE CHARLET-STRATTON'
The main street in Argentière is named for Jean Charlet, a guide from Vallorcine, and his English client Isabelle Stratton, whom he married in 1876. They had made a number of ascents together, including a winter ascent of Mont Blanc in that same year.

THE CHURCH AT ARGENTIÈRE (1727)
The church was built by artisans from northern Italy. Its high altar was brought over the Alps from Italy, carried in sections by mule over the Great-Saint-Bernard Pass. The belfry (*left*), decorated with domes and lanterns, is surmounted by a sober cornice, an unusual feature of Savoyard Baroque architecture ▲ *82*.

THE 'ROUTE DE LA SCULPTURE' AND THE LAC VERT
Sculptures by Gosselin, Féraud, Calder, Semser and Cardenas line the road leading from the plain to the Plateau d'Assy and the Col de Plaine-Joux, where there is a sculpture by Gardy-Artigas. From the *col* the road runs down to the Lac Vert (4490 feet), a small lake set among fir trees, with the reflection of Mont Blanc shimmering in its waters. A path known as the Chemin des Alpagistes leads from the lake to the Réserve Naturelle de Passy (4940 acres).

The Val Montjoie is a hanging valley that stretches from the town of Saint Gervais to the Col du Bonhomme and separates the Massif du Mont-Blanc ▲ *226* from Mont Joly. The Bon Nant flows along the valley, which consists of middle- and high-altitude landscapes. Spas, skiing, Baroque architecture and hiking have made this a year-round tourist resort to suit every taste.

VAL MONTJOIE

PASSY. Passy was originally a center of trade between the Allobrogi and Ceutrons, and its sunny slopes were later colonized by the Romans. Evidence of their presence includes three votive offerings dedicated to Mars, Roman god of war, beneath the porchway of the church.
PLATEAU D'ASSY. The hamlet on the Plateau d'Assy, renowned for its climate, was important in the fight against tuberculosis. Several medical establishments, built between the wars and now converted, still stand. Just before World War Two, Canon Devémy, who was involved in the treatment of TB patients, commissioned Maurice Novarina to design a church for the hamlet. NOTRE-DAME-DE-TOUTE-GRACE, decorated by some of the greatest artists of the period, is a masterpiece of modern religious art. The façade has a mosaic, based on the litanies of the Virgin Mary, by Fernand Léger; Lurçat decorated the chancel with a scheme on the theme of the Apocalypse; Bonnard and Picasso decorated the side altars, dedicated to Saint François de Sales and Saint Dominic; and Braque designed the front of the tabernacle. *Le Passage de la Mer Rouge*, by Chagall, in ceramic and stained glass, uses the theme of the crossng of the Red Sea to symbolize the font. Among other artists who contributed were Rouault and Bazaine (stained-glass windows), Jabob Lipchitz (*Vierge*), Kijno (fresco) and Germaine Richier (*Christ*). The church is a truly unique spiritual and cultural center.
LE FAYET. The spa town is situated at the mouth of the Bon Nant and linked to Le Nid d'Aigle (7830 feet) by the Mont-Blanc tramway ● *66*. The tramway offers a magnificent view of massif and the Chamonix valley, the mountain pastures of Le Prarion, Bellevue (5885 feet) and the Col de Voza (5420 feet). Since the 19th century the springs of Le Fayet have been used to treat skin diseases and respiratory disorders.
SAINT-GERVAIS-LES-BAINS. Renowned for its sulfurous waters, Saint-Gervais has been a summer resort since the 19th century and a winter sports resort since the late 1930s.

MODERN ART GLORIFIES RELIGION
A mosaic by Fernand Léger covers the façade of Notre-Dame-de-Toute-Grâce, designed by Maurice Novarina. Inside there is an Apocalypse by Lurçat and paintings by Bonnard and Matisse.

The *commune* of Saint-Gervais includes Mont Blanc, the symbol of international tourism, and the town is also the departure point for the Mont-Blanc tramway ● *66*. The springs of Saint-Gervais were discovered at the bottom of the Gorge du Bon Nant in 1806, and the first baths were built in 1820. In 1892 they were destroyed by a flash flood on the Bon Nant but were rebuilt and reopened several years later, when the railroad reached the town (1898). The CHURCH (1698) is a fine example of Baroque architecture. Paintings decorate the main façade and the onion-shaped belfry is one of the finest of its kind.

LES CONTAMINES-MONTJOIE. Les Contamines is a high-altitude ski resort. In summer hikers come to enjoy the adjacent nature reserve and walk on the footpath (GR5) that skirts the lower slopes of Mont Blanc.

CHAPELLE NOTRE-DAME-DE-LA-GORGE. *(2½ miles from Les Contamines.)* For centuries the chapel (1699) has been a center of pilgrimage. Although the exterior appears modest and simple, the interior houses a remarkable Baroque decor, including a polychrome retable on the high altar. According to Jacques Lovie it embodies the wonder of Savoie, its wooden-tiled roof blending with the setting of rocks, firs and snow, and pervaded by the spirit of the pilgrims of the past.

MEGÈVE AND THE VAL D'ARLY

The broad Val d'Arly is the only communication route between the valleys of the Arve and Isère. The development of tourism, which began in the 1880s and 1890s, was favored by the construction of the road linking north and south Savoie and which runs through the Gorges de l'Arly. Associated with the resort of Megève, the Val d'Arly combines broad, sunny valley bottoms with wooded slopes that are ideal for skiing, against the spectacular backdrop of Mont Blanc.

COMBLOUX. Combloux – *combe aux loups* ('valley of the wolves') – lies at an altitude of 3280 feet. Its position high above the valley of the Arve, opposite the Massif du Mont-Blanc and the Chaîne des Aravis, has made it a tourist center renowned for its climate and the truly exceptional panoramic view of the 'roof of the Alps'. In winter it is a ski resort and in summer 50 miles of marked footpaths through forests and mountain pastures can be explored. Despite modern developments, the village has kept its charm and its thirty farms maintain a strong pastoral tradition. The ÉGLISE SAINT-NICOLAS-DE-COMBLOUX is famous for its belfry whose double onion-shaped dome and octagonal galleries enhance its elegance. This is a fine example of an 18th-century Alpine church in Baroque style. The façade has a sundial (1756) and an inscription glorifying the sun: Soli-So-Li-Soli ('the land belongs to the sun'). Inside is a beautiful 18th-century retable.

'SENTIER BAROQUE'
The 'Baroque' path, leading from Combloux to Notre-Dame-de-la-Gorge via Saint-Gervais and Saint-Nicolas-de-Véroce, offers an opportunity to visit four churches, six chapels and a number of oratories.

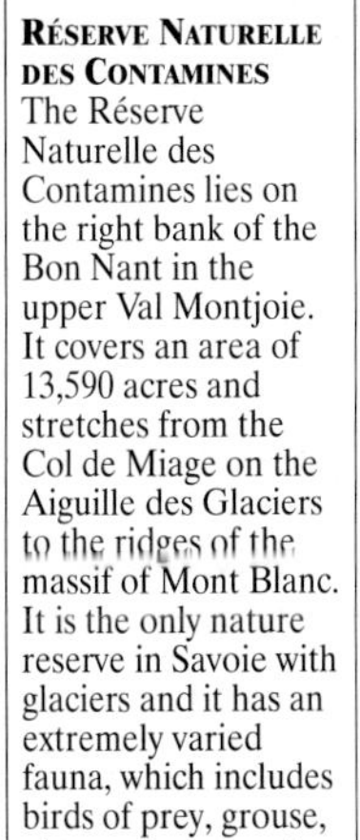

RÉSERVE NATURELLE DES CONTAMINES
The Réserve Naturelle des Contamines lies on the right bank of the Bon Nant in the upper Val Montjoie. It covers an area of 13,590 acres and stretches from the Col de Miage on the Aiguille des Glaciers to the ridges of the massif of Mont Blanc. It is the only nature reserve in Savoie with glaciers and it has an extremely varied fauna, which includes birds of prey, grouse, pheasants, marmots (*above*) and chamois.

1. ALBERTVILLE
2. UGINE
3. GORGES DE L'ARLY
4. SAINT-NICOLAS-LA-CHAPELLE

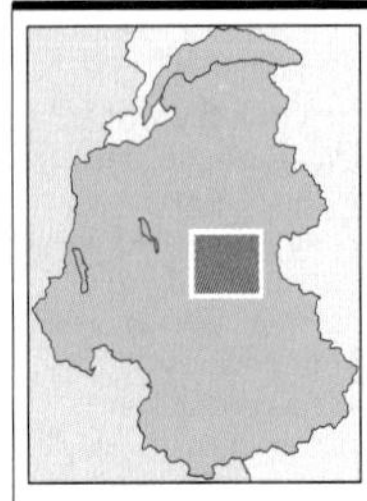

MEGÈVE. Megève, lying at an altitude of 3600 feet and framed by the Massif du Mont-Blanc and the Chaîne des Aravis, stands above the Val d'Arly and the Vallée de l'Arve. Famous for its *après-ski* and carnival atmosphere, Megève was modernized gradually while preserving its traditions. Its buildings draw their inspiration from traditional farms and the carriages that glide silently through the streets are a great improvement on motorized vehicles. The first tourists came to Megève in the 1880s, when it was little more than a large village. In the 1890s it became a popular resort for the inhabitants of Lyons and Paris. In 1921 Baroness Noémie de Rothschild ● *65* decided to make it a high-status resort and today Megève is the best known and liveliest of the French ski resorts. The architecture of the ÉGLISE SAINT-JEAN-BAPTISTE, founded in 1805, reflects the styles of three periods: the chancel with its tuff pillars is typical of Flamboyant Gothic (16th century); the nave (1692) has a number of sculptures and paintings by the Italian artist Mucegno (1830); and the onion-shaped spire of the belfry dates from 1809. The tabernacle (1443), the retable (1731) and the organ (1842) reflect the progressive embellishment of the church. The CROSS – based on the Italian *sacri monti* – that stands outside the village, on the slopes of the Mont d'Arbois, was erected between 1840 and 1878. In the 19th century it was a popular place of pilgrimage.

PRAZ-SUR-ARLY. For a long time Praz-sur-Arly was part of the *commune* and parish of Megève. It became a parish in its own right in 1803 and an independent *commune* in 1907. This village resort benefits from a double tourist season: in winter it has a skiing area linked to those of Flumet and Notre-Dame-de-Bellecombe and in summer walkers can follow a network of footpaths. The Plan de l'Are footpath, for example, offers a sweeping view of Mont Blanc. Today traditional cheeses are still produced on the many farms of the *commune*: Tomme de Savoie, the blue-veined cheeses of Les Aravis, Reblochon, Beaufort ▲ *247* and Abondance.

ÉMILE ALLAIS

This triple world ski champion (1937) was born in Megève in 1912 and made the resort's reputation. He invented the 'French method' (parallel turn), imported ski run layouts from the United States and launched the legendary Allais 60 skis. He was director of the Megève ski school until 1955.

A FREE ZONE

From 1860 until 1923 much of Haute-Savoie was a free zone. The customs boundary between Flumet and Praz-sur-Arly corresponded to the present departmental boundary. During this time many smugglers would travel back and forth across the border, frequently accompanied by their wives, wearing suspiciously loose clothing!

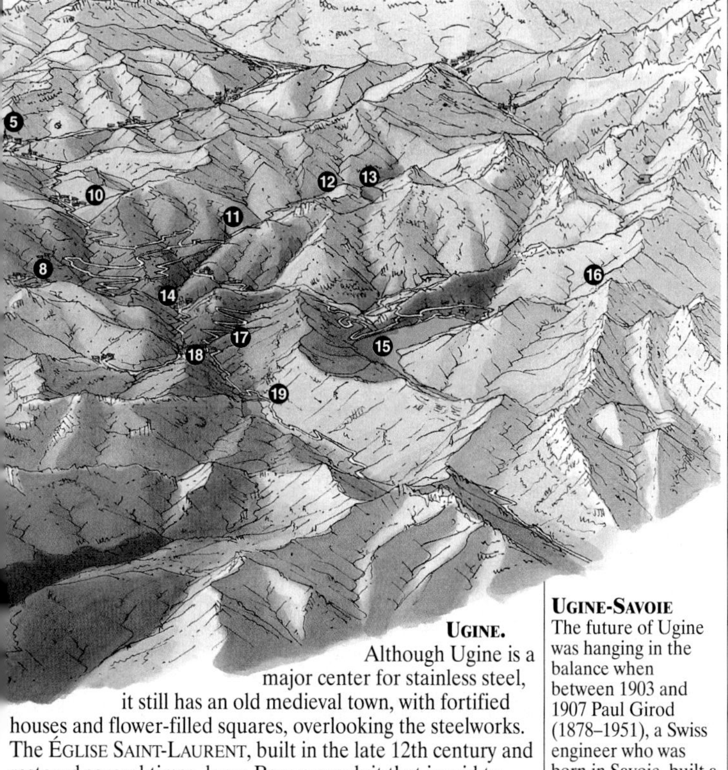

Ugine. Although Ugine is a major center for stainless steel, it still has an old medieval town, with fortified houses and flower-filled squares, overlooking the steelworks. The Église Saint-Laurent, built in the late 12th century and restored several times, has a Baroque pulpit that is said to have come from the refectory of the Abbaye de Tamié ▲ *156*. The Château du Crest-Cherel, built in 1200, once controlled the main routes to Annecy, the Val d'Arly and Conflans ▲ *248*. It was rebuilt in 1984 and today houses the Musée d'Arts et Traditions Populaires du Val d'Arly.

Saint-Nicolas-la-Chapelle. The Baroque church (*below right*), one of the treasures of the Val d'Arly, has three magnificent altars with 18th-century retables by artists from northern Italy. The retable of the high altar has a rich canopy supported by wreathed columns and decorated with garlands, vine leaves and cherubs. The 18th-century organ is identical to that in the church at Chaucisse, a hamlet perched high up the valley opposite the massif of Mont Blanc.

Flumet. This large village stands at the confluence of the Arly and Arondine rivers, at the intersection of the roads from the Col des Saisies and the Col des Aravis. In the 12th century the strategically located village was chosen by Aymon II, lord of Faucigny, as his capital. The dominant role played by Flumet in the development of a region that stretched from Lake Geneva to the Vallée de Chamonix, made it one of the first *communes* in Savoie to be granted municipal franchises (1228). Although it was devastated by fire in 1678, the village still has an interesting medieval heritage: the church with its tower-belfry, the ruined castle of the lords of Faucigny, the fortified residence of the counts of Bieux and the picturesque houses whose wooden balconies overlook the Arly.

Ugine-Savoie
The future of Ugine was hanging in the balance when between 1903 and 1907 Paul Girod (1878–1951), a Swiss engineer who was born in Savoie, built a ferroalloy factory in Flumet. The factory started production in 1910 and, twelve years later began producing stainless steel. Over the years the factory made its mark on the village and throughout the valley. Renamed Ugine-Savoie in 1976, it now exclusively produces long stainless steel, of which it is the world's leading producer.

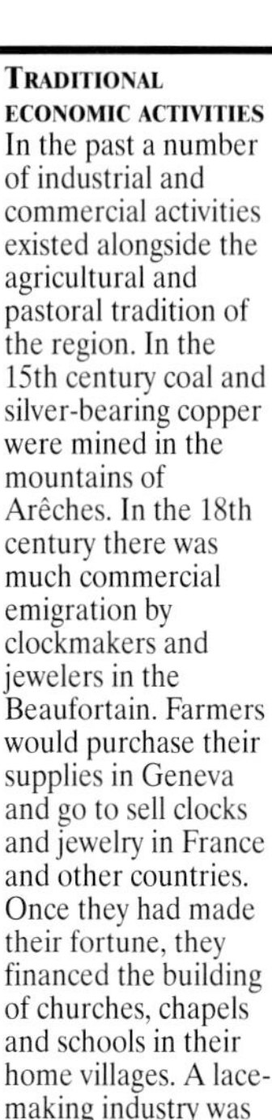

TRADITIONAL ECONOMIC ACTIVITIES
In the past a number of industrial and commercial activities existed alongside the agricultural and pastoral tradition of the region. In the 15th century coal and silver-bearing copper were mined in the mountains of Arêches. In the 18th century there was much commercial emigration by clockmakers and jewelers in the Beaufortain. Farmers would purchase their supplies in Geneva and go to sell clocks and jewelry in France and other countries. Once they had made their fortune, they financed the building of churches, chapels and schools in their home villages. A lace-making industry was established at Villard in the early 20th century. By 1906 it employed 150 women but declined after World War One.

The Beaufortain lies between the Val d'Arly, Val Montjoie and Tarentaise. It is a middle-altitude region whose cirques and valleys were hollowed out by Quaternary glaciations. The small crystalline massif, which reaches its highest point at the Aiguille du Grand Fond (9480 feet), is covered with fir forests and mountain pastures. The pastures are grazed by the Tarine cattle ● *57* whose milk produces Beaufort cheese ▲ *247*. For a long time the local economy was based on forestry, livestock and cheese-making but, in the early 20th century, the huge hydraulic potential of the Doron basin enabled the Beaufortain to develop hydroelectric power. The architectural heritage of the village resorts and their unspoilt surroundings have also favored tourism.

QUEIGE

ÉGLISE SAINTE-AGATHE. The austere façade of the church (1674) is in striking contrast to its richly decorated interior. The vaulting is covered with polychrome paintings (1856) and a large wooden painted and gilt retable stands at the far end of the chancel. The lower level of the retable, made by Guy Parraud in 1677, was extended by the sculptor Durant in 1753. The church also houses a notable carved wooden Pietà (late 15th or early 16th century), the base set with the coat of arms of the lords of Beaufort. From Queige the road leads to Ugine ▲ *243* and the Val d'Arly via the Col de la Forclaz.

VILLARD-SUR-DORON

The village lies on the road leading to the resorts of Villard-1500 and Les Saisies. It is dominated by the brow of the Signal de Bisanne (6370 feet), which offers a magnificent view of the Combe de Savoie ▲ *132*, Les Aravis ▲ *178*, the Massif du Mont-Blanc ▲ *224* and the whole of the Beaufortain.
ÉGLISE SAINT-PIERRE. The church was built in 1672 on the site of an earlier church dating from 1171. The interior has an interesting painted decor and the marble-effect pillars found in all the Baroque churches in the region. Its furniture includes a beautiful rood beam and a 17th-century retable.

‘The Beaufortain [is] a peaceful and friendly region, probably the last blessed valley in the Alps.’

Roger Frison-Roche

VALLÉE D'HAUTELUCE

HAUTELUCE. Perched midway up the south-facing slope of a glacial valley (Hauteluce), with its stone houses and Mont Blanc as a backdrop, is one of the most beautiful villages in Savoie. THE ÉGLISE SAINT-JACQUES-D'ASSYRIE dates from 1558, but the upper section of its onion-shaped belfry, with its turret and lantern, was rebuilt in 1830. The façade, restored in 1987, has a beautiful *tromp-l'oeil* decoration (*below*): on the pediment the patron saint of the parish, the first archbishop of the Tarentaise, is flanked by Saint Peter and Saint Paul. The high altar (1728) is surmounted by a canopied retable by Joseph Albertini and Joseph Gentil (1749), and the early 18th-century statues on the pulpit are attributed to Jacques Clérant. The Écomusée, in the center of the village, documents the traditional life and economy of Savoie. From Hauteluce the road continues to the resort of Les Saisies, on a vast plateau at an altitude of 5415 feet, between the Beaufortain and the Val d'Arly.

BELLEVILLE. The hamlet of Belleville nestles at the bottom of a valley, below the Lac de la Girotte reservoir. Its attractive CHAPELLE DES DOUZE-APOTRES probably dates from the 12th century. The road winds its way up to the COL DU JOLY (6526 feet), from where there is a spectacular view of the valley of Hauteluce and the southwestern slopes of the Massif du Mont-Blanc.

THE PULPIT OF SAINT-MAXIME DE BEAUFORT
The stained walnut pulpit was carved by Jacques Clérant in 1722. On the main body four fathers and doctors of the Latin Church are carved in high relief: Saint Gregory the Great (Pope Gregory I); Saint Augustine, bishop of Hippo; Saint Jerome as a cardinal; Saint Ambrose, bishop of Milan. The angel carved on the top of the sounding board is blowing a trumpet to summon the dead to the Last Judgment.

BEAUFORT-SUR-DORON

The village of Beaufort is perched on rocky spur above the confluence of the Doron and Argentine. It has given its name to the ‘prince of gruyères’ ▲ *247* produced at the COOPÉRATIVE LAITIERE (dairy cooperative) (*open to the public*).

THE OLD TOWN. The old town huddles on the left bank of the Doron, which is spanned by a stone humpbacked bridge (1832). It has retained some interesting medieval features: narrow winding streets bordered by the solid, turreted houses of wealthy citizens, façades painted in *trompe l'oeil* and entrances and shop fronts with carved wood cladding.

ÉGLISE SAINT-MAXIME. The church was rebuilt in 1666 and all that remains of the original church (1171) is the Romanesque base of the belfry. Its richly furnished interior includes a retable, whose central section was made by François Cuenot in 1657–9, a pulpit (1722) in Savoyard Baroque style, and a silver reliquary statue of the Virgin and Child (17th century).

The listed village of Boudin.

ROSELEND

DÉFILÉ D'ENTREROCHES. Soon after Beaufort the road enters the Défilé d'Entreroches, where the waters of the Doron have hollowed out impressive potholes known as 'giant's kettles'.
LAC AND CORMET DE ROSELEND. A series of hairpin bends leads to the Col du Méraillet and a reservoir-lake in which the outline of the Roc du Vent (7740 feet) is reflected. The road continues along the north shore of the lake and across meadows dotted with the colorful rhododendrons from which the lake takes its name (*rose lande*). Beyond the Cormet de Roselend (6600 feet) lies the Haute-Tarentaise region.
THE DAM. Double back and follow the road along the west shore of the lake and across the dam to the Col du Pré (5590 feet). A viewpoint offers a sweeping panorama of the dam, with the Vallon de Treicol and the PIERRE MENTA (8895 feet) in the distance. According to local legend the giant Gargantua, disappointed at not being able to cross Mont Blanc into Italy, angrily kicked the ridge of the Chaîne des Aravis, sending this great 655-foot monolith flying across the Gorges d'Arly into the heart of the Beaufortain.
CHAPELLE SAINTE-MARIE-MADELEINE. The tuff and limestone chapel was built before the 15th century. It originally stood in the valley that is now the basin of the Lac de Roselend. It was taken down and reassembled on the shores of the lake.

HYDROELECTRIC POWER
Completed in 1946, the multivaulted dam on the LAC DE LA GIROTTE is the oldest of the four reinforced concrete dams in the Beaufortain. The waters are harnessed at Belleville. Together with the BARRAGE DE SAINT-GUÉRIN (1960) and BARRAGE DE LA GITTAZ (1967), which each hold about 3434 million gallons, the impressive BARRAGE DE ROSELEND (1961) supplies the underground power station at La Bâthie, in the Basse-Tarentaise region.

ARÊCHES

BOUDIN. The hamlet, a listed site since 1943, is a fine example of a traditional village in the Beaufortain. The chalets are built in tiers on the hillside, at an altitude of 4035 to 4530 feet, on a steep sunny slope.
ARECHES. Ignore the road on the left that follows the valley of the Pontcellamont to the Barrage de Saint-Guérin, and continue to Arêches. The village stands at the confluence of the Pontcellamont and the Argentine rivers, at the foot of the Massif du Grand-Mont (8620 feet). The Église Saint-Jean-Baptiste (1829) has a distinctive stained-glass window and abraded bays. The gilt wooden retable and paintings on the vaulting and walls date from the 19th century.

The huge dam on the Lac de Roselend is 875 yards long and 490 feet high.

Immediately after milking the milk is heated to a temperature of 91° F (**1**) and curdled in 30 minutes by the addition of natural rennet, a process known as *emprésurage*. The rennet contains the lactic fermenting agents required to produce and mature Beaufort cheese.

The curdled milk is cut into tiny pieces about the size of a grain of corn using a curd cutter. The grains of curd are stirred for 30–45 minutes to accelerate the separation of the curd from the whey, and then hardened at temperatures of 127–129° F (**2** and **3**).

The cheese-maker presses the grains in a linen cloth (*soutirage*) (**4**) and then molds and presses the cheese into beechwood hoops known as *cercles à beaufort*. The hoops give the cheese its characteristic concave heel.

The cheeses have to be turned several times during pressing (*retournage* and *pressage*) to ensure that all the liquid is drained off. The round is left to rest for 24 hours, then plunged into brine. This first salting helps the rind to form and aids the fermenting agents.

The rounds of Beaufort are placed in a cellar (**5** and **6**) on spruce boards known as *tablards*. The temperature of the cellar is maintained at 53° F and the humidity at a level of at least 92 percent. The maturing process lasts for five to twelve months.

The rounds, weighing almost 88 lbs, are turned, salted and rubbed with linen at least twice a week until the end of the maturing process. The rind turns reddish brown, while the smooth cheese, which ranges from ivory to pale yellow, develops its distinctive flavor.

AOC (*appellation d'origine contrôlée*) Beaufort can be recognized by its concave heel and characteristic blue stamp. It is ideal for serving on the cheese board, but can also be used in cooking: including in salads, fondues (*raclettes*), cooked dishes (gratins and soufflés) and fondue Savoyarde.

Albertville was founded in 1836 when Conflans, a medieval town, perched on a rocky spur, was amalgamated with L'Hôpital, a small village that lay on the plain. The newly formed town was named for its founder, Charles-Albert of Sardinia. Today it is at the center of the winter tourist industry and is a major staging post on the summer tourist routes. It gained international recognition when it was chosen to host opening and closing ceremonies of the 16th Winter Olympics in 1992.

PANORAMAS
Conflans offers some impressive views across Albertville and the Combe de Savoie from the Esplanade de la Grande-Roche and the gardens of the 12th-century Tour Sarrasine, the oldest and highest building in the town.

CONFLANS

Conflans stands on the site of an old Roman town, Confluentem, at the confluence of the Arly and Isère rivers. During the Middle Ages, as a large fortified town and a prosperous trading center, it was a major staging post on the routes between Milan and Vienne. Its crenelated ramparts, fortified gates and the shops on the RUE GABRIEL-PÉROUSE have remained unchanged since the time of the Green Count, Amadeus VI. On the Grande-Place, the heart of the medieval city, the 14th-century MAISON ROUGE houses a small museum of archeology and ethnology. Its arcades and gemel windows show the Italian influence on the work of the architect, Pierre Voisin, formerly treasurer to the Green Count.

ÉGLISE SAINT-GRAT
Conflans's church has a remarkable pulpit (1718) by Jacques Clérant. The front is decorated with high-relief sculptures of Saint Peter and the four Evangelists with their symbols. On the back are images of the Good Shepherd and the Virgin Mary.

ALBERTVILLE

Albertville was modernized for the 1992 Winter Olympics: the Dôme built on the Place de l'Europe is a cultural complex incorporating a modern Italian-style theater, a mediatheque and a film theater. Various Olympic installations were built on the western edge of the town.

MAISON DES JEUX OLYMPIQUES. Designed as a 'living memory of the Olympic experience', the Maison des Jeux Olympiques aims to recreate, through the medium of photographs, films and ceremonial costumes designed by Philippe Decouflé, the spectacular ceremonies and sporting achievements of the 16th Winter Olympics.

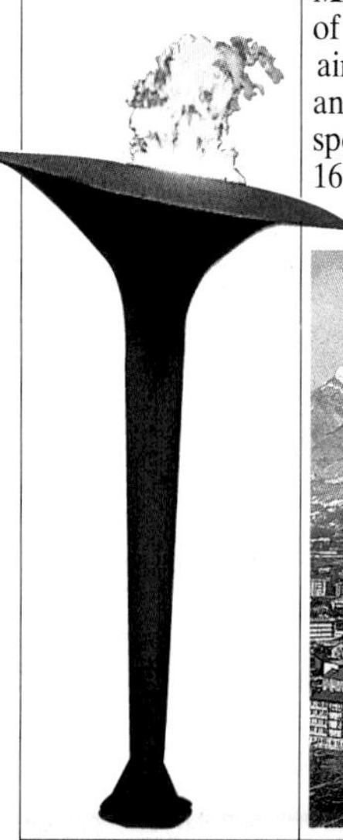

The Tarentaise, The Maurienne

Jean-Pierre Duc, Marthe and Pierre Dompnier

1. ALBERTVILLE
2. CEVINS
3. COL DE LA MADELEINE
4. LA LÉCHÈRE-LES-BAINS
5. AIGUEBLANCHE
6. MOÛTIERS
7. SAINT-JEAN-DE-BELLEVILLE
8. SAINT-MARTIN-DE-BELLEVILLE

The Tarentaise lies on either side of the winding valley through which runs the Isère, extending northward into the Beaufortain ▲ *244* and the Pays du Mont-Blanc, and southward onto the Massif de la Vanoise, dominated by the Pointe de la Grande Casse (12,645 feet). A main valley of deep corridors, clearings, basins, narrow passages, depressions and gorges gives way to serried ridges scored by series of transverse valleys and extensive slopes colonized by different layers of vegetation. Finally, rising above the ridges, valleys and slopes are the sheer, ragged outlines of the high summits: peaks, *dents* (teeth), *aiguilles* (needles), cirques and glaciers. Today the Tarentaise – which has the largest skiing area in the Alps – is known as the region of WHITE GOLD, but, away from the ski slopes, charming mountain villages and Baroque churches reflect its rich history and cultural heritage. A large part of the Tarentaise is also occupied by the PARC NATIONAL DE LA VANOISE ▲ *264,* a paradise for Alpine fauna and hikers.

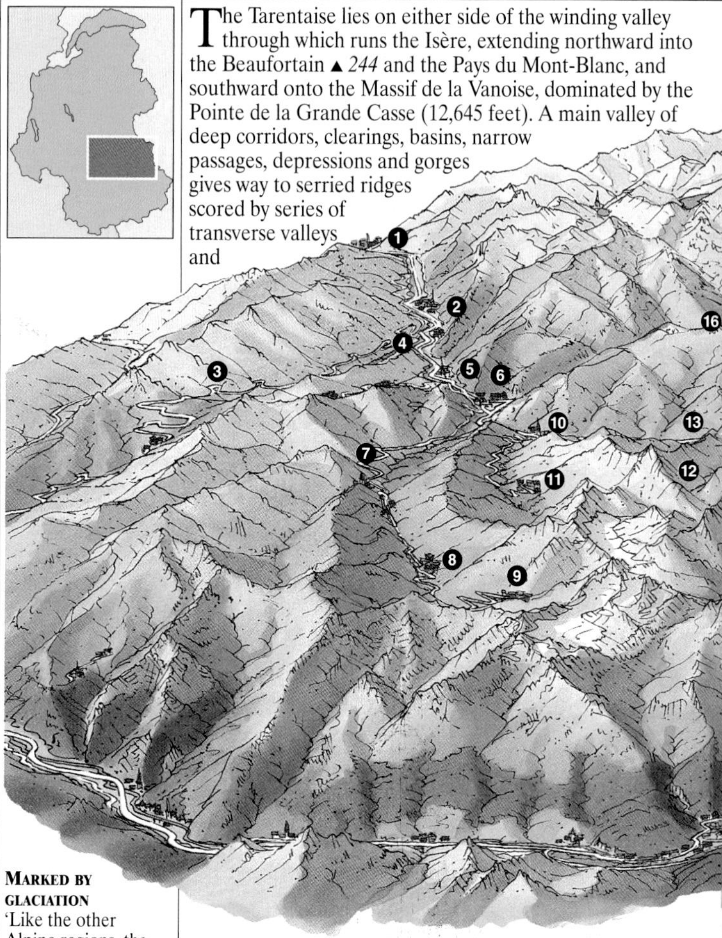

MARKED BY GLACIATION

'Like the other Alpine regions, the Tarentaise was marked by the last glacial phase, which is partly responsible for its present relief: wide, flat glacial valleys, glacial thresholds, shoulders, hanging valleys with waterfalls in their connecting gorges, cirques cut into the upper slopes and sometimes filled by lakes, moraine filling the valley bottoms, roches moutonnées which, in the high mountains, take on strange shapes in the light of the setting sun.'

Marius Hudry

HISTORY

● *33*

The first inhabitants of the high valley arrived from the Val d'Aoste via the Col du Petit-Saint-Bernard in about 3500 BC. However, the mountains were not permanently settled until the end of the Bronze Age. The rich burial sites left by the powerful local Iron Age civilization, for example the cemetery at SAINT-JEAN-DE-BELLEVILLE, contained many decorative objects. The Ceutrons occupied the Tarentaise until the

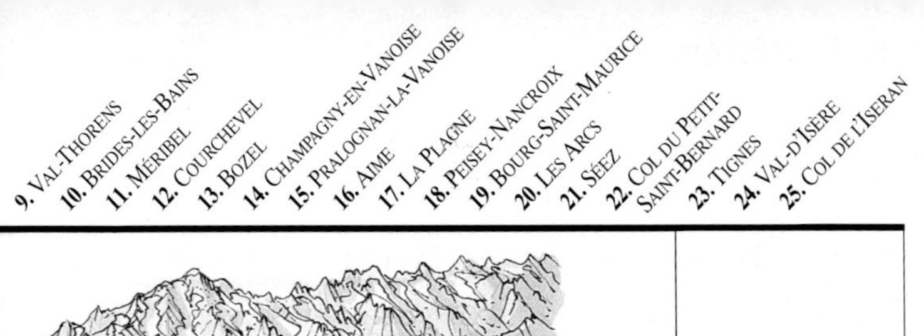

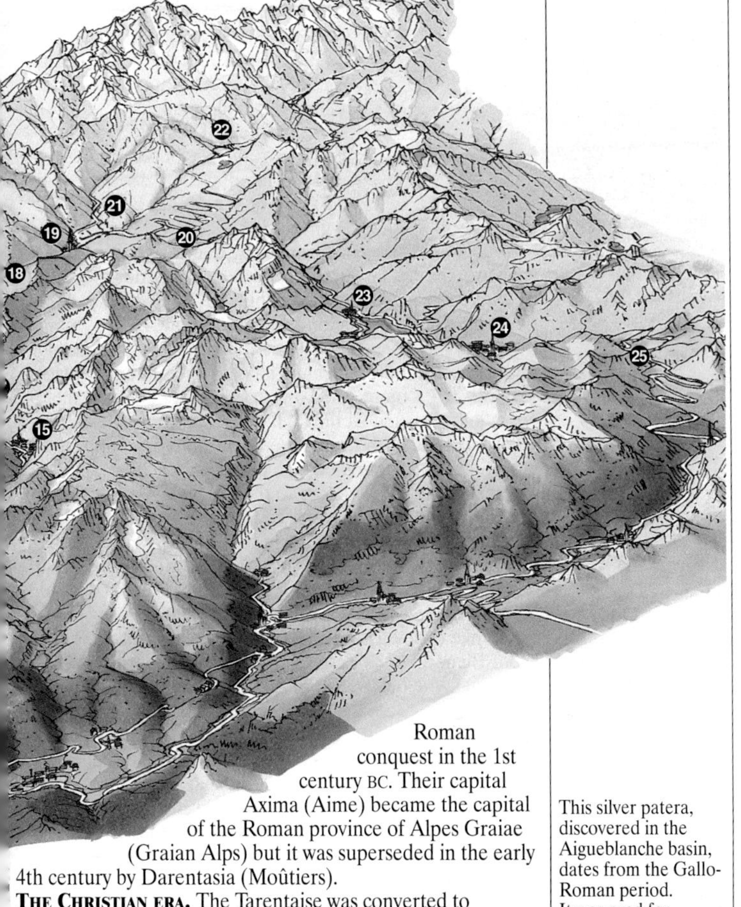

Roman conquest in the 1st century BC. Their capital Axima (Aime) became the capital of the Roman province of Alpes Graiae (Graian Alps) but it was superseded in the early 4th century by Darentasia (Moûtiers).

The Christian era. The Tarentaise was converted to Christianity in the early 5th century. The Burgundians settled in the region, establishing their dynasty within a Romanized population. From the 6th to the 8th centuries the various Frankish kingdoms installed counts at Salins who enjoyed a certain degree of autonomy. With the Treaty of Verdun (843) the Tarentaise became part of the kingdom of the Frankish emperor Lothair I. In 995 Rudolph III, king of Burgundy, limited the counts' power by devolving temporal power to the archbishops of the Tarentaise. Moûtiers was their capital.

From the House of Savoie to the French Republic. In the 13th century Philip I consolidated the state of Savoie by redeeming the feudal rights of the counts, including those of the Tarentaise. From the castellany at Salins, he controlled the upper part of the Étroit de Siaix, the narrowest passage of the Isere valley. Having lost its independence in the 16th century the Tarentasie regained a certain importance in 1814–15 when the House of Savoie installed the administrative seat of the dukedom at Conflans. In 1860 Savoie became part of France and was divided into two *départements*.

This silver patera, discovered in the Aigueblanche basin, dates from the Gallo-Roman period. It was used for serving wine or religious drink-offerings.

ALBERTVILLE TO MOÛTIERS

CHANTEMERLE. About 3 miles from Albertville ▲ *248*, on the D990, the Château de Chantemerle (*left*) stands high above the road, its towers rising like sentinels. The castle was the former residence of the archbishops of the Tarentaise.

FEISSONS-SUR-ISÈRE. Beyond the impressive hill of Cevins, the site of a former slate quarry and a famous vineyard, the road enters a deep wooded corridor overlooked by hamlets perched high on the hillside. The Château de Feissons, which once belonged to the Briançon d'Aigueblanche family, was rebuilt by an enthusiast and now houses a restaurant. The main hall has its original fireplace.

TOWARD THE COL DE LA MADELEINE. Before entering the gorge known as the Défilé du Pas de Briançon – the former territory of the lords of Briançon, notorious extortionists whose manor was perched high on the rocky cliffs – nature lovers should make a detour to the Col de la Madeleine. The opening of the pass linking the Tarentaise and Maurienne ▲ *270*, which is often included in the Tour de France, led to the discovery of this austere high valley. Beyond a beautiful chestnut forest, the village of PUSSY occupies the last shoulder before the gorge, where BONNEVAL and Celliers cling to the slopes like eyries. The magnificent view of the massifs of Mont-Blanc and Les Écrins from the viewpoint on the COL DE LA MADELEINE (6540 feet) makes the climb worthwhile. The famous Tarine cattle graze the pastures near the pass, which for inhabitants from both sides of the pass is also the venue for celebrations held at the Feast of the Assumption (August 15).

BASSIN D'AIGUEBLANCHE. The basin, known as the 'garden of the Tarentaise', opens northward onto the Beaufortain ▲ *244*, via the hanging valley of Nâves and the Vallée de la Grande-Maison, and southward onto the Maurienne ▲ *270*, via the resort of Valmorel. The Grand Pic de la Lauzière (9280 feet) rises above the peaceful slopes of Les Avanchers-Valmorel, which are covered with meadows, copses and hamlets, not far from the forest of Doucy.

SLATE QUARRIES
Cevins and the Col de la Madeleine had the largest slate quarries in the Tarentaise. The high altitude (6235 feet) made extraction difficult and they were closed during World War One.

THE DOUCY RETABLE
The retable in the parish church of Doucy consists of a central panel depicting the martyrdom of Saint Andrew (by Gnifetta, 1859), and side panels with Saint Andrew and Saint Peter. The whole is surmounted by a Crucifixion.

The baths of La Léchère-les-Bains (*below*).

DOUCY. The 17th-century parish church of Saint-André has a magnificent interior by the 19th-century Piedmontese artist Casimir Vicario, the master of *trompe l'oeil* in Savoie. The retable of the high altar, dedicated to Saint Andrew, combines the exuberance of Clérant (columns, caryatids and angels) with the classicism of Marin.

LA LÉCHÈRE-LES-BAINS. The thermal baths (*above*) opened by the French writer and politician Édouard Herriot (1872–1957) in 1930 were completely renovated for the 1992 Winter Olympics. The sulfated, calcic waters of the hot springs are used to treat vascular diseases and rheumatism.

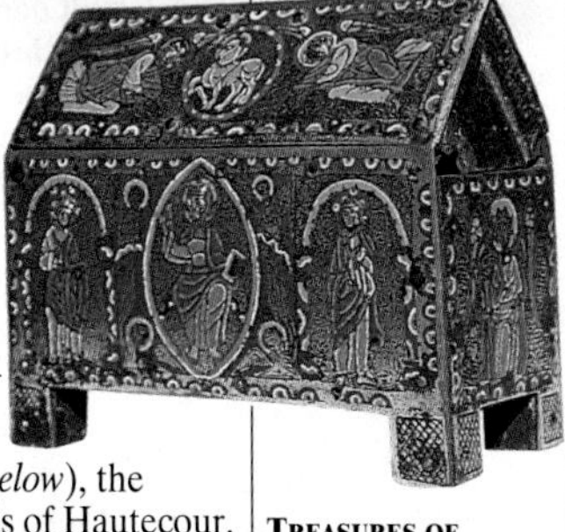

MOÛTIERS

Beyond Les Échelles d'Hannibal – also known as the Défilé de Siboulet – Moûtiers (*below*), the capital of the Tarentaise, nestles at the foothills of Hautecour. The town is dominated to the north by the summit of Le Quermoz (7560 feet) and to the east by Mont Jovet (8380 feet), one of the most beautiful viewpoints in the Alps.

HISTORY. The original town of Darentasia (which became Monasterium and then Moûtiers) occupied a strategic position at the crossroads of the region's most populated and busiest valleys. In the 4th century Moûtiers eclipsed Aime ▲ *257* as the episcopal, administrative and commercial capital of the region. Originally situated near the Pont de Saint-Pierre, the ramparts of Moûtiers were demolished by Aimon 'the Peaceful' in 1335 and rebuilt as a barrier against the plague in the 16th and 17th centuries. The town developed with the establishment of the salt works in the 15th century, but did not expand beyond the banks of the Isère until the 19th century. With the advent of the railroad in 1893 and the gradual abandonment of agriculture, Moûtiers began to spread onto the slopes of Champoulet and Hautecour. Today the town, which has lost its bishop's palace, subprefecture and industry, is primarily the gateway to the resorts of the valley.

TREASURES OF THE CATHEDRAL
Inside the cathedral are two notable polychrome sculptures, one depicting the Entombment (16th century) and the other the Crucifixion (17th century), both life size. The treasure, one of the riches of the cathedral, includes the 12th-century ivory cross from the abbot's staff of Saint Pierre de Tarentaise, and a 13th-century reliquary decorated with Limoges enamel (*above*).

CATHÉDRALE SAINT-PIERRE
The cathedral combines several architectural styles: the chancel and apse date from the 11th century, the entrance forms part of the rebuilding program in the Gothic style, and the transept and dome date from the 17th century. Further alterations were made in the 19th century by the Italian architect Ernesto Melano.

MUSÉE DE L'ACADÉMIE DE LA VAL D'ISÈRE. The Académie de la Val d'Isère, founded in 1865, occupies the former bishop's palace in Moûtiers. It houses a collection of documents tracing the history of the Tarentaise and, in the synodal chamber, a small museum with exhibits ranging from protohistoric flint axes, bracelets and fibulae to Gallo-Roman vases and other artifacts, and medieval illuminated manuscripts.

LES TROIS VALLÉES

These high valleys – Courchevel, Méribel and the Vallée des Belleville – form the largest skiing area in the world.

VALLÉE DES BELLEVILLE. Just before the village of Saint-Jean-de-Belleville, which was rebuilt after being almost entirely destroyed by fire in 1927, the CHAPELLE DE NOTRE-DAME-DES-GRACES stands above the gorge at the confluence of the Nant-Golet and Doron rivers. The rich furniture of this chapel, built between 1734 and 1741, includes three 18th-century polychrome retables. The vaults are decorated with paintings by the early 19th-century Piedmontese artist Giovanni Arienta. An Iron Age cemetery dating from 500–300 BC, one of the largest in the Alps, was discovered nearby, above the road.

Bozel, a regional capital.

DECOR OF NOTRE-DAME-DE-LA-VIE
Of the three retables inside this church, that above the main altar (*detail, right*), by the northern Italian sculptor Jean-Marie Molino (1676), is notable for being one of the most homogenous in the Tarentaise. Apart from the painting of the Assumption, it is made entirely of painted and gilt wood. The central panel is arranged around the niche housing the statue of the Virgin, to whom miraculous powers are attributed, while chubby angels in high relief form the shape of a cross. The four Evangelists are depicted in cartouches at each corner of the retable.

ÉGLISE DE SAINT-MARTIN-DE-BELLEVILLE. The 17th-century retable of the high altar, by Jacques-Antoine Todescoz and Guillaume Moulin, is a major work of art: its proportions are particularly well balanced – the three sections of the lower register are of equal width – and it has variety of columns. The colors and gilding have recently been restored to their original brightness.

NOTRE-DAME-DE-LA-VIE. The chapel, perched on a rocky spur in the upper valley of the Doron de Belleville, has been a place of popular worship since the 13th century. It is the most highly venerated chapel in the Tarentaise, which doubtless explains the richness of its retables. The chapel was extended in the early 17th century, and rebuilt and further extended by Nicolas Deschamps between 1633 and 1680. Today Notre-Dame-de-la-Vie is the focus of pilgrimages on Feast of the Assumption (August 15) and the first Sunday in September.

MÉRIBEL. The discreetly chic resort of Méribel has made every effort to integrate its whitewood and stone buildings into its natural surroundings. It has turned this low-key development to its advantage by offering an alternative to the strongly individualistic style of the neighboring resorts

VALLÉE DE SAINT-BON. The late 17th-century ÉGLISE DE SAINT-BON lies on the road to Courchevel. Its has an unusual gold and polychrome retable depicting souls in purgatory and illustrates two of the Counter-Reformation's favorite themes: the universality of death and the deliverance of souls by prayer. In the central panel a priest officiates before the souls in purgatory; only their heads are visible, carved in low relief.

In 1819 work was carried out at Brides-les-Bains to protect the spring from further flooding.

MOÛTIERS TO PRALOGNAN-LA-VANOISE

SALINS-LES-THERMES. The saline waters of Salins were used by the Romans. During the Middle Ages they were diverted in order to extract the salt. In 1820 the discovery that salt water was beneficial for skin diseases and rheumatism led to the construction of thermal baths and the development of cures. Given the strength of the spring – it produces 1.3 million gallons of water a day – it has been possible to develop baths with running water, which have earned the spa the reputation for providing 'sea bathing in the Alps.'

BRIDES-LES-BAINS. About 2½ miles further up the valley, toward Méribel and Courchevel, is Brides, which lies in the lush valley of the turbulent Doron river, at the foot of beautiful fir forests with the Glaciers de la Vanoise as a backdrop. The thermal waters of Brides cross the extravasated gypsum along the brow of the Briançonnais fold and rise at a temperature of 90° F. The waters were known to the Romans, but disappeared in the 18th century during a period of flooding and landslides, reappearing in June 1818 when the Doron-de-Champagny glacier broke up. Brides, which became Brides-les-Bains when it was amalgamated with La Saulce in 1947, specializes in treatments for obesity and general fitness cures. Chosen as the site of the Olympic village for the 16th Winter Olympics (1992), the spa had to extend its tourist infrastructures and provide a cable-car link with Méribel and the Trois Vallées.

BOZEL. The village of Bozel is situated on the dejection cone of the Bonrieu, at the confluence of the Doron de Pralognan Doron de Champagny. The TOUR SARRASINE (*right*) on the banks of the Bonrieu evokes, if only by its name, the presence of the Saracens in the 10th century. Although they did in fact build many towers and castles during their 100-year occupation of the region, local legend often misattributes to them the exploits of the Romans, Burgundians, Visigoths and Huns. The tower in Bozel is thought to have been built in the late 12th century on the site of a Saracen building. The PARISH CHURCH OF SAINT FRANÇOIS DE SALES (1732) is surmounted by an onion-shaped belfry that replaces the one destroyed during the French Revolution (1789–99). Most of its original furniture also disappeared and was replaced by 19th-century artifacts, including the great retable and the pulpit.

The Tour Sarrasine was the home of the Bozel family, who were influential in the Tarentaise in the 12th and 13th centuries.

FROM PASTURE TO CHEESE
Champagny upholds two interdependent traditions: grazing cattle on the Alpine pastures ● 56 and producing Beaufort cheese. The cycle of production and maturing ▲ 247 takes place between the *emmontagnée* (when the cattle go up to the mountain pastures in spring) and the time when the round cheeses are brought down by sled, assisted by the entire village.

CHAMPAGNY-EN-VANOISE. In summer Champagny's exceptionally beautiful natural setting makes it an ideal base for hiking on the slopes of the highest mountains in the Vanoise ▲ *264*. In winter it offers a vast skiing area on the southern slopes of the Massif de Bellecôte and the Vallon de Champagny-le-Haut. The economy of CHAMPAGNY-LE-BAS, a traditional mountain village nestling on a sunny shoulder, was boosted when it was linked by cableway (1970) to the large resort of La Plagne. The village has successfully integrated its modern tourist infrastructure with its traditional architectural heritage. The Église Saint-Sigismond, built on a gypsum hillock that was gradually disintegrating under the effects of water, was nevertheless rebuilt on the same site in 1683 by Calcia and Graullo, master masons from northern Italy. The retable of the high altar, by Jacques Clérant (1710), is a masterpiece of exuberant Baroque art in which wreathed columns, the broken lines of the curved pediments, and a profusion of cherubs and gilt wood figures constitute a catechismal lesson on the themes of the Assumption and the Crowning of Christ. Beyond the impressive Gorges de la Pontille – a glacial threshold scored by the torrent – the road enters the basin of CHAMPAGNY-LE-HAUT (4725 feet), dominated by the high ice walls of La Grande Motte (11,920 feet) and La Grande Casse (12,645 feet) ▲ *257*. Although isolated in these 'awful mountains', 'Le Haut' was inhabited all year round due to the efforts and ingenuity of its inhabitants, who would dry unripe grains of rye by the fire. Today, although Champagny-le-Haut has opened up to tourism, its traditional environment, culture and identity survive intact. The Col du Palet – a pass covering 4 miles, with chalets, meadows, waterfalls, streams and forests and other classic features of an Alpine landscape – links the valleys of Peisey-Nancroix ▲ *259* and Tignes ▲ *262*.

PRALOGNAN-LA-VANOISE. Pralognan, a mountaineering and hiking center and winter ski resort, stands at the gateway to the Parc National de la Vanoise ▲ *264*. Its elegance, style and character are reminiscent of Tyrolean resorts. The village stands at an altitude of 4595 feet, at the confluence of two streams, looking

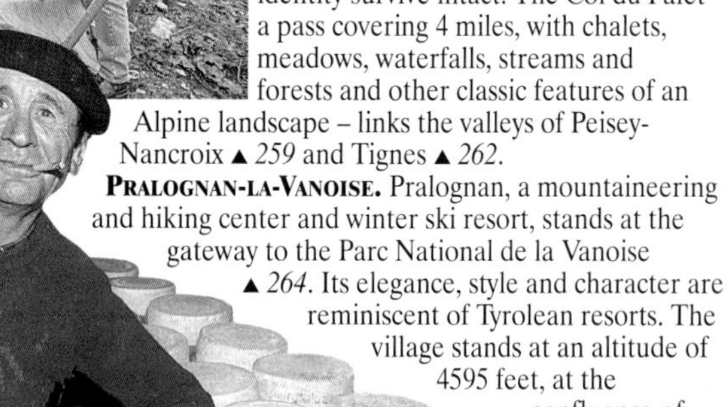

downstream to a broad corridor dotted with hamlets, upstream to the Vallon de la Vanoise, and southwest to the Val de Chavière. Pralognan was once a staging post on the 'salt road'. However the first ascent of the Pointe de la Grande Casse, by the Chamonix guide Michel Croz and the British mountaineer William Mathews, on August 8, 1860, earned the village an international reputation as a mountaineering center and placed it on a par with the famous resort of Chamonix. The foundation of the Club Alpin de Tarentaise, in 1875, a year after the Club Alpin Français, marked the beginning of a period of development that radically altered the face of the village. Hotels, refuges – including the famous Refuge Félix-Faure (*above*) in 1902 – and roads were built: from 1905 the village was accessible to motor vehicles. Pralognan also became a winter tourist resort with the creation of the Mont Bochor (6635 feet) cableway (1950) and the development of a skiing area at an altitude of 4595 to 7710 feet on the slopes of the same mountain.

The Refuge Félix-Faure (*top*) is today known as the Refuge de la Vanoise. Hiking in the Vanoise (*above*) with the Pointe de la Grande Casse in the distance.

The Moyenne Tarentaise

As it leaves Moûtiers the road to Aime and Bourg-Saint-Maurice climbs between sheer walls of rock: on the Roc Pupim, to the right, once stood the castle of the archbishops of the Tarentaise. Passing beneath a cliff surmounted by ruins of the 12th century manor of a notorious family of 'toll collectors', the road enters the Étroit de Siaix, a grayish-white barrier of crystalline limestone barely fissured by the glacier.

Bassin Tarin. Beyond the Étroit de Siaix lies the alluvial plain of Centron which precedes the depression leading to Bourg-Saint-Maurice. After skirting round the glacial threshold of Villette and the Saut de la Pucelle, the road leaves the narrow passages, rocky barriers and basins and enters a more open landscape. It runs for more than 65 miles between the sloping sides of the valley. This is a shady area with occasional clearings amid vast forests and many torrents, where the land is cultivated on an incline and the population moves according to the seasons. There are also extensive hillsides with a sparse vegetation on their sunny slopes, a few streams and villages huddled on sheltered shoulders.

Aime. Once the heart of the Tarentaise, the town is now a pale reflection of the fortified Roman encampment of Axima that preceded it. In the 5th century it was devastated by the

First ascent of La Grande Casse
Michel Croz and William Mathews, accompanied by Étienne Favre, a chamois hunter from Pralognan, had to cut 1100 footholds in the rockface before they were able to conquer the 'Grande Dame'.

WALL PAINTINGS
Scenes from Genesis, such as Adam and Eve expelled from Paradise (*below*), decorate the interior of the Basilique Saint-Martin. In the right-hand bay of the chancel are a striking depiction of Massacre of the Innocents and a badly deteriorated Flight into Egypt. On the ribbed vaulting the rivers of Paradise are personified by two old men holding vases representing the horn of plenty.

floodwaters of the Ormente and buried under an inch of mud and silt. A new, fortfied town was built on the Colline (hill) de Saint-Sigismond. Today this flourishing market town is the same size as the medieval town.

BASILIQUE SAINT-MARTIN. The basilica (*above*) is a masterpiece of Romanesque architecture ● *80* and one of the oldest monuments in Savoie. It was built on the foundations of a Roman edifice (possibly a basilica) and a Christian chapel (7th–8th century), and consecrated in 1019. Damaged by the ravages of time, it was rescued by the founders of the Académie de la Val d'Isère in 1865 and restored from 1905 onward. The church is centered around a nave with six bays, an apse and apsidal chapels. The chancel and apse have some wall paintings (thought to be 13th-century) which, although badly deteriorated, reflect Byzantine and Romanesque traditions: the former are expressed in the iconography (such as the personification of the rivers of Paradise) and the latter in the depiction of garments, the energy and dramatic emphasis of the scenes. The base of the building, the remains of the Roman edifice, houses a Musée Lapidaire which has a collection of ancient objects discovered in Aime and the surrounding area. The crypt of the earlier church is beautifully proportioned if somewhat austere.

TOUR DE MONTMAYEUR. The 13th-century tower was part of the castle of the Briançon-Montmayeur, the first viscounts of the Tarentaise (1097). Originally from Grésivaudan (Isère), this influential family countered the power of the archbishops.

CHAPELLE SAINT-SIGISMOND. *(North of Aime.)* The chapel was built on the site of an ancient Gallic oppidum in the 14th century and rebuilt in the late 17th century. Today it houses a museum of archeology and ethnography.

THE PARISH CHURCH. The church, which lies on the Chemin du Baroque (Baroque route), was rebuilt, reoriented and consecrated on May 18,

1681 to meet the demands of the Council of Trent (1545–63) and receive the increasing numbers of worshippers. The retable, by Jacques Clérant, above the high altar and a remarkable 18th-century pulpit survived the depradations of French Revolution (1789–99), although the church was entirely redecorated by the Artari brothers from the Val d'Aoste, who executed the paintings on the vaults of the nave, chancel and galleries. The vaults have been recently restored. South of Aime the D220E passes through the village of MACOT, dominated by its tall belfry, to the resort of La Plagne in the massifs of Bellecôte and Mont Jovet.

PEISEY-NANCROIX. Beyond Bellentre, with its distinctive onion-shaped belfry, the road winds its way up a series of hairpin bends to Peisey-Nancroix. At an altitude of 4430 feet the village, which huddles round its tall pointed steeple (the highest in the Tarentaise), is one of the gateways to the Parc National de la Vanoise ▲ *264*. Behind its sober façade the ÉGLISE DE LA TRINITÉ conceals a luxurious decor which includes no less than seven retables. The richly carved and gilded retable of the high altar is by Jacques-Antoine Todescoz and Jean-Baptise Guallaz. The three great mysteries of faith are magnificently evoked in a skillful composition in which the drapery of the statues and the breaking of the lines emphasizes the interplay of light and shadow that animates this vibrant composition. The village of LES LANCHES, perched higher up the valley, offers one of the most spectacular panoramic views in the Alps: Mont Pourri (12,400 feet) and the Sommet de Bellecôte (11,210 feet) with the Col du Palet in the distance. At an altitude of 5960 feet another of the region's Baroque treasures – the SANCTUAIRE NOTRE-DAME-DES-VERNETTES – stands in the heart of the mountain pastures, blending harmoniously with the surrounding cirque of impressive mountains. Renowned for its miraculous spring, it has been a popular place of worship since at least the 17th century and continues to be so today, especially for the pilgrimage of July 16. (*Retrace your journey, passing through the picturesque village of Landry and keeping to the left-hand side of the valley.*)

HAUTEVILLE-GONDON. The presbytery of the church houses the MUSÉE DE LA HAUTE TARENTAISE, an ethnographical museum in which is displayed a collection of costumes from the valley: dresses, embroidered shawls and headdresses, including the famous *frontière* ● *52*. The nearby Église Saint-Martin, the naves flanked by aisles and with a rectilinear apse, was built in 1691 under the direction of the master mason Pierre Arcin. It escaped destruction during the French Revolution, and its exceptionally rich interior decor has survived: two of its retables (above the high altar and the altar of the Rosary), by the northern Italian sculptor Joseph-Marie Martel, have been listed as historic monuments.

LE VERSANT DU SOLEIL

Although subsistence agriculture is dying out, the *montagnards* of the Tarentaise still have a strong pastoral tradition, and it is they who maintain the high mountain pastures. In 1982 the inhabitants of Le Versant du Soleil (on the right bank of the Isère) joined forces to promote their region. They devised a theme trail – the Sentier des Alpagistes – and opened the Maison du Versant La Côte d'Aime.

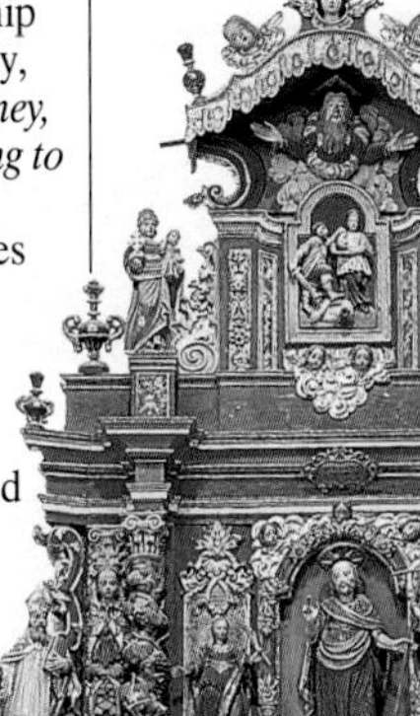

THE HAUTE TARENTAISE

BOURG-SAINT-MAURICE. Located at a valley crossroads and the foot of several mountain passes, the town has always occupied a strategic position. In the past, life in the town was regulated by the region's agricultural and pastoral economy (it was once famous for its cattle markets), but since the development of winter sports Bourg-Saint-Maurice has become a major tourist center in the heart of one of the most popular Alpine regions. Although linked to Les Arcs by a funicular railway, it is very much a winter and summer resort in its own right. It is particularly busy in July during the FETE DES EDELWEISS, the international folk festival of the Haute Tarentaise, when a colorful procession of floats fills the streets.
The PARISH CHURCH was rebuilt in 1845 after the Arbonne river flooded and destroyed all but the belfry of the original building. Although the exterior is in the Neoclassical style the interior has original Baroque furniture. No visit to Bourg-Saint-Maurice would be complete without a detour to the hamlet of VULMIX (3280 feet), whose chapel predates the 15th-century. The exterior is sober but the interior is covered with 15th-century wall paintings. The cycle consists of eighteen panels painted in distemper, in a delightfully naïve style. It tells how Saint Grat, the venerated protector of the harvest ● *54* to whom the chapel is dedicated, took the head of John the Baptist back to Rome.

THE QUEST OF SAINT GRAT
The Vulmix cycle begins on the south wall, near the choir. This scene (*above*) shows Saint Grat presenting the skull of John the Baptist to the Pope in exchange for the saint's jaw.

'LA CHANOUSIA'
The Abbé Chanoux laid out a botanical garden near the Hospice du Petit-Saint-Bernard in 1897 in order to cultivate rare Alpine plants. Abandoned after World War Two, the garden was renovated in 1976. Today more than 1200 species grow there.

SÉEZ: THE GREAT RETABLE (detail)
The four Evangelists depicted in low relief on the side panels of the retable and the statues of Saint Peter and Saint Paul (*left*) that they frame represent Writing and Tradition.

SÉEZ. The old Roman road between Bourg-Saint-Maurice and Séez was the route taken by pilgrims on their way to Rome. On the left a cylindrical 12th-century tower is all that remains of the former residence of the Rochefort dynasty. About ½ mile further on, on the steep promontory of Le Châtelard, stands a 12th-century square tower. As its name suggests Séez was the sixth milestone on the Roman road, and the tower was probably built on the foundations of a Roman lookout post. The town is situated on a vast alluvial plain, at the junction of the roads leading to the Col de l'Iseran and the Col du Petit-Saint-Bernard. The ARPIN MILL, the pride of the local craft industry, still produces the famous woolen cloth known as 'drap de Bonneval'.

ÉGLISE DE SAINT-PIERRE. The great retable in this 17th-century Baroque church, by the Maurienne sculptor Étienne Foderé, is centered around the intellectual bases of faith (Writing and Tradition). In a funerary niche to the left of the main entrance there is a 15th-century statue of a recumbent knight in armor, from the Val d'Isère.

COL DU PETIT-SAINT-BERNARD. This high, windswept plateau, which lies between the Tarentaise and the Val d'Aoste, is covered by snow for eight months of the year. It is said to have deterred even the most stout-hearted, yet travelers have used the pass since the earliest times. The region's prehistoric inhabitants erected a cromlech, a strange stone circle 230 feet across, which today straddles the border between France and Italy. The Romans built a road across the pass and entrusted it to the protection of Jupiter. The statue of the god that stood on a column that they erected was replaced in the 19th century by a statue of Saint Bernard. In the Early Middle Ages (1145) Saint Bernard de Menthon is said to have built a hospice to provide shelter for travelers. The hospice more than served its purpose and was rebuilt many times, enjoying its golden age under the Abbé Pierre Chanoux (1859–1909). In 1923 it was still welcoming 15,000 travelers a year, including 500 every month in winter. The hospice was bombed during World War Two and was left abandoned until enthusiasts devised a rescue plan. Since the summer of 1995 it has been renovated, refurbished and restored to its former role as the soul of the pass (*below*).

THE ARPIN MILL
In the 18th century the inhabitants of the Haute Tarentaise began to weave cotton and woolen cloth at home, using techniques from Piedmont. Among these pioneers were the brothers Jean-Louis and Alexis Arpin, dyers and weavers from Montvalezan. Jean-Baptiste, son of Jean-Louis, took over the family business, moving it to the banks of the Versoyen, where the torrent drove mechanical looms. The mill was moved to Séez in 1816 and was soon producing a woolen cloth ('drap de Bonneval') that was so durable that it was worn by mountain guides. The mill was fitted with electric machinery in the early 20th century. Production was hampered by the two World Wars and various economic crises but was booming again by 1960. In 1994 the mill was purchased by local enthusiasts who wanted to preserve the region's heritage. Although it has diversified, the mill upholds its reputation for quality.

The hamlets of La Gurraz and Le Monal (*above*) nestle in a delightful setting, dominated by the Montagne de Pierre d'Arbine and the glaciers of Mont Pourri.

MONTVALEZAN. The 12½ miles between Séez and the Col de l'Iseran consist of a series of steep rises and shelves between Mont Pourri and its glaciers and the Massif de la Sassière, which lies along the French-Italian border. In Montvalezan, situated at the foot of the Glacier du Ruitor, are 19th century houses with broad sloping roofs and a Baroque church with a 17th-century retable by Étienne Fodéré.

LE MIROIR (hamlet of Sainte Foy-Tarentaise). The stone-columned houses ● *76* built by Piedmontese masons in the 18th century now have listed status. Two to six columns support broad overhanging eaves; they are designed protect the balcony, which is used as a drying area, and keep a small farmyard area clear of snow in winter. The houses, which nestle around the chapel, are still inhabited. The occupants, some sixty people, have tended to abandon agriculture in favor of tourism.

LE MONAL (hamlet of Sainte Foy-Tarentaise). Le Monal is situated at an altitude of 6150 feet, between the permanent village and the mountain pastures where the communal herd is grazed in summer. It is a fine example of the *montagnette* (temporary hamlet) of the Tarentaise. Since the 1970s it has been used only in summer.

TIGNES. In 1952 the old village of Tignes-les-Boisses was submerge by the waters of the Lac du Chevril reservoir. In 1957 the community was recreated when the resort of Tignes was built higher up the mountain. The outer wall of the arch dam ● *88* is decorated with a huge fresco of a giant, painted in 1989 by Jean-Marie Pierret. The viewpoint (5930 feet) on the roof of the pumping station offers a view of the dam and the lake and, from left to right, the Glacier de la Grande Motte, the Dôme de la Sache and Mont Pourri, in the background.

VAL D'ISÈRE. Val d'Isère, situated at the bottom of a steep-sided valley, at the foot of the impressive ROCHER DE BELLEVARDE, the TETE DU SOLAISE and the high peaks of the RÉSERVE NATURELLE DE LA GRANDE SASSIÈRE, is the ultimate skier's paradise. The church in the old village has a Baroque retable on which the green of the vine branches and stems of the dog roses provides a striking contrast with the gold of the tabernacle.

COL DE L'ISERAN (9085 feet). Until the road was built in 1935 a mule track was the only way across the pass between the Tarentaise and Maurienne. Two years later the Route des Grandes Alpes, the highest road in Europe, which originally linked Thonon and Nice, was opened by Albert Lebrun (1871–1950), the president of France (1932–40). The Belvédère de la Tarentaise (8325 feet) offers a spectacular panorama across the massifs of La Vanoise, Mont Pourri and La Grande Sassière. From the top of the pass there is a sweeping view of the extensive mountain pastures and great glaciers of Le Mulinet and Levanna in the Haute Maurienne ▲ *278*.

'LA TRACE'
Bernard Favre chose Le Monal as the setting for his movie *La Trace* (*The Trace*, 1983). The movie follows the geographical and psychological journey of a peddler who sets out for northern Italy on the eve of union with France ● *44* and, in so doing, recounts an important chapter in the history of Savoie.

The retable is the dominant feature of the church altar, which celebrates the sacrifice of Christ and embodies his presence within the Catholic rite of transubstantiation. In Savoie's Baroque churches it is very evidently the principal element of the interior decoration. Following the Council of Trent (1545–63), and in the hands of skilled artists, it assumed a dual function: to present to the faithful an image of heaven that reflected its beauty and hierarchy, and to convey through imagery the basic teachings of the Catholic religion. In accordance with the principles of the Counter-Reformation, the retable glorified the worship of the Holy Trinity and the mediatory saints.

GREAT RETABLE (HAUTEVILLE-GONDON)
The profusion of figures in the retable reflects the desire to provide a realistic and complete catechismal lesson. The Eucharist appears in the upper section, in the relief carving of the Last Supper and the tabernacle. The three Christian mysteries (the Holy Trinity, the Incarnation and the Redemption) are also depicted. The foundations of faith are represented by the Evangelists in the side panels and the medallions in the upper section, while the tradition of the Church is expressed in the statues of the Church Fathers. The saint to whom this church is dedicated fills the central panel.

TABERNACLE (SÉEZ)
The tabernacle is the ornamented cabinet that is placed above the altar, in the central section of the retable, of which it is a reflection. It contains the Eucharist, the consecrated hosts that are the living body of Christ. A candle burning nearby indicates the presence of Christ in this form.

▲ Parc National de la Vanoise

The Parc National de la Vanoise, the oldest of France's national parks, was founded on July 6, 1963, by a decree signed by Georges Pompidou (1911–74), prime minister of France (1962–8), and fourteen ministers. This exceptional area of natural Alpine heritage is now a protected site in what is known as the 'central' zone, an area covering some 130,000 acres. The Massif de la Vanoise is bounded by the high valleys of the Maurienne and Tarentaise, which form a peripheral zone covering almost 360,000 acres and incorporating 28 mountain communes.

Objectives. The park – a public institution under the control of the French Ministry of the Environment – was initially created to protect the Alpine ibex ▲ *266*, which had become an endangered species in France. As well as the protection of this symbolic animal, the park has three main objectives:

La Vanoise
Parc National

◆ to protect the region's natural wealth and preserve an unspoiled legacy for future generations. To this end regulations protect the central zone from violation in any form. The park is also a

13. Grand Roc Noir
14. Refuge du Plan du Lac
15. Refuge du Col de la Vanoise
16. Champagny
17. Lac du Mont-Cenis
18. Termignon
19. Dôme de l'Arpont
20. Pralognan-la-Vanoise
21. Dent Parrachée
22. Courchevel
23. Aiguille du Froit
24. Sommet de Saulire
25. Col de Chavière
26. Modane
27. Aiguille de Peclet
28. Val-Thorens

'living laboratory' that facilitates the regular observation and scientific study of Alpine fauna with the purpose of improving knowledge of the various species and developing models for the management of natural resources that can be applied to other areas;

◆ to give public access to this natural heritage with the aim of heightening public awareness and nurturing a respect for nature. A network of 370 miles of marked footpaths and some 40 refuges (18 belonging to the park) enable visitors to explore this exceptional area in complete freedom. The park's warden-guides also offer a more in-depth insight into the park and its initiatives through guided excursions, talks and slide shows;

◆ to encourage a balanced and sensitive development of the environment on the part of the communes of the Parc de la Vanoise. By promoting ecotourism, supporting local agriculture and preserving traditional buildings, the park – in association with local partners and communities – aims to preserve the natural and cultural heritage of La Vanoise.

'Jumeller'
The expression *jumeller*, literally meaning 'to binocular', was invented by the park's warden-guides to describe the detailed observation and surveillance of the areas under their management and protection.

A PEACEFUL ANIMAL
The ibex spends part of its day slowly moving about in the sun.

In the 16th century France had a large population of Alpine ibex. With the development of firearms their numbers were decimated to the point that, by the late 19th century, there were only 100 or so individuals in the Italian Alps. The ibex is now a protected species. Following a number of initiatives to reintroduce this mountain goat into the Parc de la Vanoise, it is gradually repopulating the Alps. Today there are an estimated 3500 ibex in France, of which 1500 are in the Parc de la Vanoise and the rest in the massifs of Haute-Savoie, Le Vercors, Les Écrins, Le Queyras and Le Mercantour.

MOUNTAIN GOAT
The ibex is a sturdy mountain goat that usually frequents steep slopes, rockfaces and high mountain pastures but is sometimes also found at lower altitudes. Although this ungulate is remarkably resilient and sure-footed in a rocky environment, it is not as well-adapted to snow because its hooves do not have an interdigital membrane.

GAMES AND SPARRING
Young ibex are extremely playful and love to run about, slide down slopes, jump and perform all kinds of acrobatics. As they become aware of their strength they begin to spar. When they reach sexual maturity (from the age of two) their jousts become more serious and are sometimes violent as they establish their place in the male hierarchy.

The ibex gives a short, high-pitched call to indicate danger or excitement.

DISTINCT GROUPS
The females stay together in herds with the kids. Those born during the current year are called *cabris* and those born the previous year *éterlous*. Except during the mating season (December and January) the males also stay in herds, which may consist of up to 100 individuals.

The female (*étagne*) rarely weighs more than 110 pounds.

The females and kids tend to graze in the early morning and evening, spending the rest of the day ruminating and resting.

SUMMER COAT

In June ibex shed their thick winter fleece by rubbing against rocks and thorn bushes or scratching each other with their horns.

THE KIDS

The kids are born in May or June and weaned in September. While the young females remain with the female herd, the young males leave at the age of three.

The age of the male is indicated by the number of rings on its horns. These curved horns grow in summer, reaching a length of up to 3½ feet and a weight of up to 11 pounds.

A HARDY HERBIVORE

Ibex are herbivores, consuming up to 44 pounds of grass (especially new shoots), roots and lichens a day. They drink relatively little but are fond of salt. Heavy snowfalls may deprive them of food for weeks at a time and they may lose 30 percent of their weight in winter.

The horns of an adult female are usually about 10 inches long.

The male stands between 2¼ and 3 feet high at the shoulder and is about 5 feet long.

The male weighs between 165 and 220 pounds.

The lifespan of an ibex is 15 to 20 years.

Réserve Naturelle de Tuéda

- Departure point: Méribel-les-Allues; car park for the Réserve Naturelle de Tuéda.
- Duration: 2 hours (to reach the reserve).

This excursion starts in the Réserve Naturelle du Plan de Tuéda and continues into the Parc National de la Vanoise. It passes through an old forest of Arolla pines, rich in bird life (including the thick-billed nutcracker, *right*) and plants, before reaching the tongue of the Glacier de Gébroulaz. Three information tables at the start of the footpath give detailed information about the landscape. Established in July 1990, in the commune of Les Allues, France's 100th nature reserve covers an area of almost 2750 acres and lies at an altitude of 5580 to 10,335 feet. The path follows the edge of what was once an extensive wet zone. One million years ago the Glacier de Gébroulaz filled the Vallon de Tuéda. It began to retreat about 12,000 years ago, leaving a shallow lake on the Plan de Tuéda. Over the centuries the lake has been almost completely filled in and colonized by aquatic plants, which have created a marshland. The peat bog that remains today still supports several protected species of fauna and flora, including the Alpine newt, the Alpine cordulia (dragonfly) and the extremely rare wild lily-of-the-valley. However this wet zone on the edge of the reserve should not be confused with the lake, which is the result of a tourist initiative on the part of the commune. Beyond the forest lies the tongue of the Glacier de Gébroulaz, which is France's only privately owned glacier. Although its tip (tongue) is hidden, the glacier is still retreating and it is possible that, in years to come, an area of ice will stay trapped beneath the rocks and be separated from the tongue. With the benefit of research methods developed by scientists during the last 100 years, the Glacier de Gébroulaz is serving as a valuable case study. Its progress is being closely monitored by the glaciology research laboratory of Grenoble.

Le Plan du Lac

- Departure point: Bellecombe car park, above Termignon.
- Duration: ½ hour (to reach the lake)

This excursion climbs to the refuge of the Plan du Lac (7545 feet), one of the five gateways into the park on the edge of the central zone. The excursion offers some spectacular views of the principal summits of the Massif de la Vanoise: La Grande Casse, La Grande Motte, La Dent Parrachée and the glacial domes of La Vanoise. The Plan du Lac is also the starting point for hikes across the massif to Val-d'Isère, Tignes, Pralognan, Aussois and Lanslebourg-Mont-Cenis, while the broad, green valleys of the Rocheure and Laisse offer pleasant excursions through open high-altitude landscapes rich in mountain flora and fauna. The route is punctuated by little chapels and old Alpine chalets, discreet testimony to human presence high in the mountains.

MOUNTAIN PASTURES

Mountain agriculture has made the best use of the different Alpine zones by maintaining a balance between the grazing provided by the high pastures and the cultivable land of the valleys. By cutting the grass on these meadows, farmers enable the grasses to grow back, thereby helping to maintain their biodiversity. The park authorities are helping to restore agricultural buildings and to make high-altitude hamlets more accessible. They are also studying ways of improving the yield of mountain pastures.

MARMOTS

The marmot, which is widely found in the Vallon de la Rochure and in all the park's Alpine meadows, is the most commonly seen of its fauna. Marmots are easily located by the high-pitched whistle with which they sound the alarm at the approach of intruders.

Le Col de la Loza
- Departure point: Pont-Saint-Charles car park, Val-d'Isère.
- Duration: 2½ hours (to reach the col)

The Col de la Loza is accessed via the only footpath linking the Parc de la Vanoise and the Parc du Gran Paradiso, which share a common border for just over 8½ miles. The two parks were twinned in 1972 and today form the largest single protected area in the western Alps. The path has been used since very early times, between the end of spring and early autumn. In the Middle Ages it was used by pilgrims crossing the Alps on their way to the Holy Land. In their wake came merchants and peddlers. In the 19th century, the path was used by men in search of seasonal work. In the early 20th century shepherds from the Isère valley used the path every year in May when they went to buy goats at the fair held in Cuorgnè. They left the animals in Italy until summer, when they took them back over the pass. During World War Two people used the pass to move illegally between Canavese and France and, in 1945 and 1946, it was used by smugglers.

After following the steep-sided Gorges de Malpasset (which requires some care), the path passes the Refuge de Prariond on its way to the Col de la Loza (9185 feet), where an orientation table identifies the surrounding summits. Above the refuge the Cirque de Prariond provides mountain pasture for ibex in an ideal environment of rocks, cliffs and scree slopes. The animals are tagged and closely monitored by the warden-guides of the Parc de la Vanoise and Parc du Gran Paradiso with the aim of understanding their geographical distribution, their movements through-out the year and their social organization.

La Porte de l'Orgère
- Departure point: Modane.
- Duration: 3 hours (to reach the porte).

Because the Parc National de la Vanoise lies above 6560 feet, it has few forests. The excursion to the Porte de l'Orgère passes through one of the oldest and most remarkable larch forests in the Alps (some date from 1350). The carpet of alpenroses and bilberries attests to the age of the forest. Its hollow tree trunks provide shelter for a number of birds, including the shy Tengmalm's owl (*right*). A very rare three-toed woodpecker – there are only six pairs in the whole of France – was sighted in 1979. The Vallon de l'Orgère was originally a wooded valley that was gradually cleared and planted with the barley (*orge* in French) for which it was named. Fields are still patiently cleared and the stones and rocks piled in heaps. The best are then used to build Alpine chalets. For those who want to find out more about the valley, there is a nature trail – which starts and finishes at the refuge – through the Vallon de l'Orgère (2½ hours).

Chamois

As well as the many ibex in the Vallon de l'Orgère, chamois are also found on the slopes of the Aiguille Doran. The park has a population of about 4500 individuals, living in small groups and herds of varying size and composition.

Black grouse

The black grouse is found on the upper edge of the forest where the alpenrose and bilberry heath provides shelter and cover for the bird.

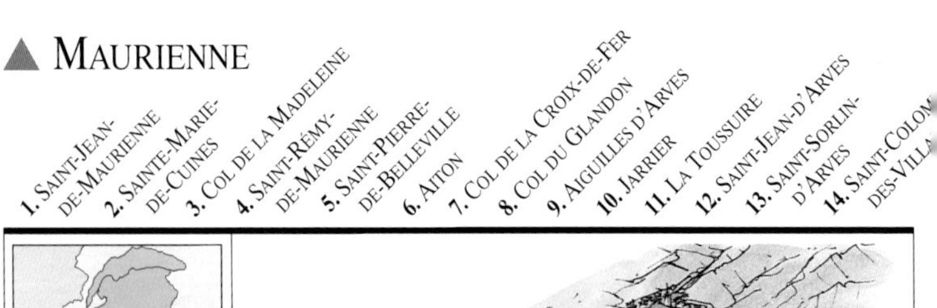

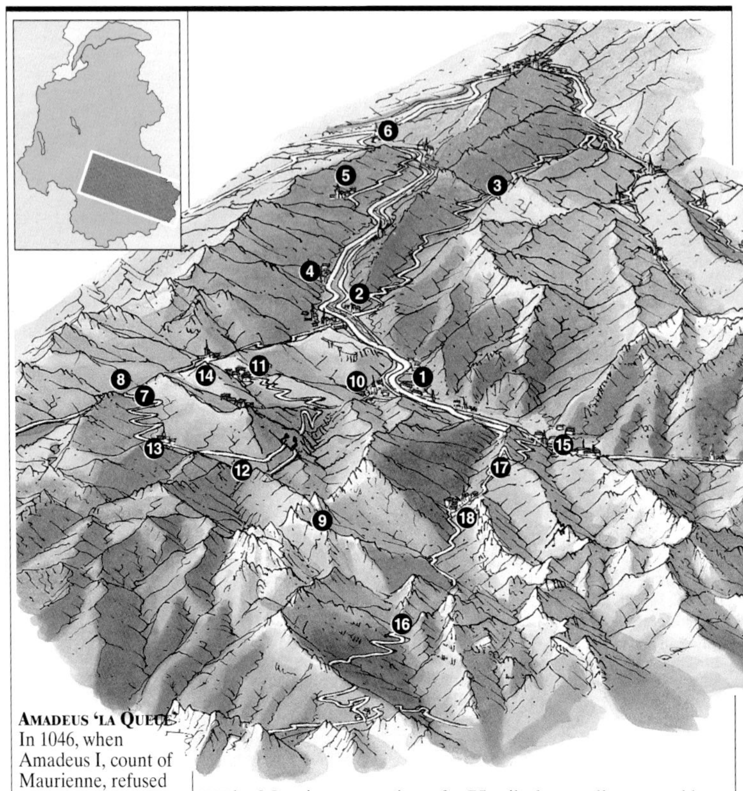

AMADEUS 'LA QUEUE'
In 1046, when Amadeus I, count of Maurienne, refused to be separated from his entourage when he was due to appear before emperor Henri III, uproar ensued. Told that the count wished to enter with his retenue (*queue*, which also means 'tail'), the emperor simply replied 'Then let him enter with his tail', after which the count was known as Amadeus la Queue.

The Maurienne consists of a 75 mile-long valley carved by the Arc river through the intra-Alpine zone and the central massifs, skirting the southern edge of the Massif de la Vanoise and running along the Chaîne de Belledonne before slipping between the Massif de la Lauzière and the Massif des Sept Laux. Broad navel-shaped depressions are bounded by glacial thresholds. The Haute Maurienne, above the fortifications at l'Esseillon, and the tributary valleys of Valloire, the Arvan, les Villards and the Bugeon have largely exchanged an agricultural and pastoral economy for tourism. In Moyenne and Basse Maurienne during the late 19th century large electrochemical and electrometallurgical plants sprang up in the valley, which was a major communications

route. Many of these have now closed down and only a few modern factory units are still operating. The last industrial wasteland disappeared under the freeway that has strengthened the Maurienne's position as a link between France and Italy.

History ● *33*

The valley has been inhabited since the late the Neolithic period. It entered the annals of history when Guntram (d. 592) incorporated it into the kingdom of Burgundy in 579. Such illustrious figures as Pepin the Short (c. 714–768) and Charlemagne (768–814), king of the Franks, trod its soil, and Charles II the Bald died there in 877. In the early 11th century it was given by Conrad II (c. 990–1039), Holy Roman Emperor and founder of the Salian dynasty, to Humbert White Hands ● *40,* who as lord of this major communications route became the 'gatekeeper of the Alps'. Plagues and wars strengthened the deep-rooted faith that is expressed in the Baroque art of the churches and mountain chapels. As the medieval towers gradually disappeared, the fortifications of a more modern age sprang up. From Montalembert to Maginot, via Séré de Rivières ● *85*, most of these forts can still be seen today.

General Ferrié
Thirty-five towns in France have a street or square named for General Ferrié. A bust at the foot of the Eiffel Tower bears the words: 'General Ferrié, member of the Institute, inventor of the military radiotelegraph, 1868–1932.' After World War One he became the second most decorated military man after Marshal Foch. He was born in the Maurienne, where he developed a taste for challenge and work well done.

OPINEL FRANCE

SAINT-JEAN-DE-MAURIENNE

The town stands at the confluence of the Arvan and Arc rivers, in a large navel-shaped glacial depression. It owes its prosperity to its commercial activity: during the 19th century peddlers from the town sold haberdashery the length and breadth of Europe. The advent of the railroad (1856) and the development of hydroelectricity ● *39* brought industrialization, which radically altered the landscape. The factory of Les Plans, in which electrolysis was used from 1907, became a flagship of the Aluminium-Préchiney company. In spite of this, an interesting architectural heritage survives in this former episcopal capital of the diocese of Morienna.

BISHOP'S PALACE. In the present building, which has been without a bishop since 1906, most of the 18th-century decor dating from the reign of Mgr de Martiniana is still in place. Themed exhibitions are held in the great Baroque hall, while the former chapel and various rooms house a museum of archeology, religious art and popular art and traditions. There is a tourist office on the first floor.

THE CATHEDRAL. Built in the 6th century to receive the relics of Saint John the Baptist, the episcopal complex still has its original layout: the Cathédrale Saint-Jean-Baptiste is flanked by the Église Notre-Dame whose bell tower (which now stands alone) may have replaced a baptistry. The shell of the present buildings dates from the 11th century and the roof timbers have been dated to 1075. During the 15th century powerful bishops added a cloister, vaults, a Gothic choir, a ciborium and choir stalls. Three centuries later the princes of the House of Savoie built the peristyle (1771) where lies the tomb of the dynasty's founder, Humbert White Hands.

SAINT-JEAN-DE-MAURIENNE TO AITON

THE HAIRPIN BENDS OF MONTVERNIER. Pontamafrey is the departure point for one of the most picturesque roads in the Maurienne: the famous hairpin bends of Montvernier, overlooked by the Chapelle de la Balme. The road leads to the sunny intermediate balcony of Montvernier and, higher up, to the upper balcony of Montpascal, which opens onto the extensive cross-country skiing area of the Col du Chaussy (5030 feet).

SAINTE-MARIE-DE-CUINES. The valley widens out onto the plain of Les Cuines, where the Glandon and Bugeon

1

THE OPINEL STORY

In 1890 Joseph Opinel was working with his father as a maker of edge tools, in Albiez-le-Vieux, when he decided to make a pocket knife in twelve different sizes. Twenty years later he registered his first trademark and chose a crowned hand as his emblem: the hand of benediction that features on the coat of arms of Saint-Jean-de-Maurienne is a reference to the relics of Saint John the Baptist, and the crown symbolized the dukedom of Savoie. The mountain knife, awarded a gold medal at the Alpine exhibition held in Turin in 1911, proved so successful that in 1916 a new factory was built at Cognin, on the outskirts of Chambéry. Thus the modest craftsman from the Maurienne became an industrial manufacturer. Opinel knives have an international reputation and are on display in the Victoria and Albert Museum in London and in the Museum of Modern Art in New York. The Musée Opinel in Saint-Jean-de-Maurienne, in a former factory that was closed in 1986, traces the history of the famous knife and describes the present production process.

CATHÉDRALE DE SAINT-JEAN-DE-MAURIENNE

1. Cloister
2. Crypt
3. Tomb of Ogier Moriset
4. Relics of Saint John the Baptist
5. Ciborium
6. Choir stalls

SAINT THECLE
In the late 6th century the bishop and historian Gregory of Tours (538–94) told how Thècle de Valloire brought three of John the Baptist's fingers back from Egypt. Today they are preserved in a reliquary (*below*) in the cathedral. The event was instrumental in the creation of the bishop's palace.

rivers join the Arc. The village, which lies at the foot of the ruined Château-Joli and Châtel-André, has a church whose apse and belfry date from the 11th century.
VALLÉE DU BUGEON. Just beyond Saint-Martin-sur-la-Chambre, the road branching off to the right leads to Montaimont, whose CHAPELLE NOTRE-DAME-DE-BEAUREVERS is an important chapel dedicated to the Virgin Mary and a chapel of grace: according to popular belief, stillborn babies brought there would come back to life just long enough to be baptized. The D213 continues to SAINT-FRANÇOIS-LONGCHAMP and the COL DE LA MADELEINE (6540 feet), from where it enters the Tarentaise ▲ *250*. This itinerary, made famous by the Tour de France, is extremely popular with cyclists. Just before Saint-François-Longchamp, on the opposite side of the valley, are some remarkable capped earth pillars, which were created by erosion.
SAINT-RÉMY-DE-MAURIENNE (D74). At the foot of the Grand Miceau (8590 feet), Saint-Rémy has a pleasant lake and an interesting neo-Gothic church decorated with blue and gray *trompe-l'oeil* paintings.

A MINING REGION
During the 19th century the iron and copper mines of Saint-Georges-des-Heurtières were only haphazardly worked. A concession was granted to the Grange family, who worked the mines in association with the Schneider brothers of Le Creusot. Exploitation declined at the end of the 19th century and the mines were finally closed in 1930.

SAINT-PIERRE-DE-BELLEVILLE. The village, situated on the far side of the valley, has a 13th-century iron bell struck with the cross of the Knights Templar. Few bells of this age exist; this one was probably made in a local foundry, as the iron mines of Les Heurtières were already being exploited at the time. According to legend it was here that Durandal, the famous sword of Roland in the *Chanson de Roland*, was forged. In the 16th century the Castagneri had foundries on the far side of the valley, at ARGENTINE, named for the silver mines that were opened there.

VERROU DE CHARBONNIERES. The valley narrows at this point. The rock (*verrou*), which overlooks a small lake, was once crowned by a castle that resisted François I in 1536, was captured by Henri IV in 1600 and was taken by the Spaniards in 1742. It was later demolished.

MONTSAPEY. From Randens the road climbs to a hanging valley between the Chaîne de la Lauzière and the Massif du Grand Arc. The village of Montsapey is known for its arts festival, which is devoted to classical music and which takes place in July.

AITON. Aiton, on the edge of the Maurienne, has an 18th-century church. The bishop's palace, however, built in 1669 by Mgr Valperga de Masin, survives only in legend; it is reputed to have had 365 windows. The fort of Aiton was built on the site of the palace in 1876. Together with the forts of Montperché and Montgilbert, it stands guard over the lower end of the Maurienne Valley.

THE ARVAN AND LES VILLARDS

MOUNTAIN PASSES. The valleys of the Arvan river and Les Villards, linked via the Col de la Croix de Fer and the Col du Glandon, today comprise ten communes. There are a number of possible itineraries. The road (D80) from Villargondran ascends steep forested slopes – with forty hairpin bends over a distance of 6¾ miles – to Albiez-le-Jeune, which perches 2625 feet higher up. The plateau occupied by Les Albiez can also be reached via Gevoudaz (the hamlet where Joseph Opinel ▲ *272* was born) and Albiez-le-Vieux. The Tour de France and other classic cycle races follow the picturesque 'tunnel' route, which offers some magnificent views of the Gorges de l'Arvan and the Combe Genin, a scree corridor framed by the sharp, leaflike layers of folia.

The Col de la Croix-de-Fer (*top*) and the Col du Glandon (*above*).

LES ALBIEZ. At an altitude of 4920 feet a vast balcony lies against the slopes of La Grande Chible (9620 feet). In the Combe de Claret, midway between Albiez-le-Jeune and Albiez-le-Vieux, stands the 'Moine [monk] de Champlon', an unusual example of a capped earth pillar.

MONTROND. With its backdrop of sharp needles Montrand's 17th-century church is one of the most photographed sites in the Maurienne. In the 19th century the impressive Aiguilles d'Atves were already attracting climbers.

JARRIER. Jarrier's thirty-odd hamlets and many chapels lie scattered across a sunny slope. In the less stable areas, an original building technique has been used: the framework is

supported by wooden beams set in the ground and held in place by flat stones. If the structure becomes distorted, the stones are simply readjusted. Jarrier's 17th-century church, which was not built using this technique, is lopsided.

FONTCOUVERTE-LA-TOUSSUIRE. The name evokes megaliths and vestiges of the Bronze Age and Iron Age, attesting to the origins of Fontcouverte. A church and chapels (17th and 18th centuries) and an artistic tradition perpetuated by the Pôterie de la Lune, add to the interest of the attractive resort of Toussuire, developed in the 19th century on the mountain pastures of this rural commune. Its sister village Villarembert followed its example when it created the purpose-built resort of Le CORBIER in the 1960s.

SAINT-JEAN-D'ARVES. The 17th-century parish church of Saint-Jean-d'Arves stands in the hamlet of La Tour, where the outline of a ditch recalls a Jacquerie (peasant uprising) that took place in 1326. The belfry of ENTRAIGUES has a strange sundial with a coded inscription giving the name of its creator, Giuseppe Gibellinno. It is surmounted by Masonic symbols.

SAINT-SORLIN-D'ARVES. In the hamlet of Belluard visitors can see a particularly good brand of Beaufort cheese ▲ *247* being made in the cooperative of Les Arves. In the main village of Saint-Sorlin, the 17th-century church of Saint-Saturnin (*below*) has some beautiful retables. The striking façade is covered with cast-iron and wrought-iron wreaths. The wreaths are set with glass beads that would not withstand the elements if the wreaths were placed on the tombs outside.

VALLÉE DES VILLARDS. The two communes in this valley are, unusually, dedicated to two Irish martyrs, Saint Columban and Saint Alban.The women wear a costume which, like that worn in the communes of the Arvan, is certainly among the most unusual in the Alps.

LES AIGUILLES D'ARVES

The famous Aiguilles d'Arves comprise the Tête de Chat (11,035 feet), La Centrale (11,525 feet) and La Méridionale (11,530 feet). For a long time their vertical sides awed even the most intrepid climbers. They were conquered in 1839 and 1878, by the American-born British mountaineer William Coolidge (1850–1926) and by an anonymous group of local chamois hunters who were well used to performing complex acrobatic feats.

THE COSTUME OF LES VILLARDS

This brightly colored and embroidered costume consists of a full, pleated skirt with bands of blue fabric. Women also wear a large cross ● *53*, up to 5½ inches long. The custom provoked a local priest to remark pessimistically: 'the weaker the faith, the larger the cross!'

Retable from Valloire
The side panels of the retable of the high altar, by François Rimelin, contain richly painted and gilded statues of Saint Peter (*below*) and Saint Thècle.

Col du Galibier
The col offers an all-round view, with the Aiguilles d'Arves and Mont Thabor (10,435 feet) to the north and the mountains of the Briançonnais and the glaciers and snowy peaks of Les Écrins to the south.

The Moyenne Maurienne

Saint-Julien-Mont-Denis. In the 16th century the vines of Saint-Julien were so precious that the inhabitants were ready to sue the insects that were destroying them. However the vines eventually disappeared and all that remains from this period is the octagonal Tour de la Rochelle and a few chapels. In the late 19th century the local slate quarries brought prosperity to the village and continued to be mined until 1980. At an altitude of 4710 feet, the hamlet of Saint-Denis, which is an interesting Iron Age site, lives by its pastoral activities and craft tradition. It was officially attached to Saint-Julien in 1965.
Montricher-Albanne. The picturesque villages of Montricher, ensconced on its sunny col, and of Albanne and Albanette, perched high on their slope, were revitalized by the creation of the original social tourist resort of Les Karellis in the 1970s.
Saint-Martin-la-Porte. The latter part of the name of this village refers to the narrow passage carved by the Roman road through the impressive glacial threshold of the Pas-du-Roc. Overlooking the passage, on the left bank of the valley, is the Fort du Télégraphe, built in 1888 on the site of one of the stations in the visual telegraph line invented by Claude Chappe (1763–1805).
Saint-Michel-de-Maurienne. The location of the town at a crossroads opened up the valley southward via Valloire and the Col du Galibier and northward via the Col des Encombres, which in the past was used to reach local fairs and markets. Without vehicular access, it has lost its importance. The old town, in which some old streets and houses survive, is perched on a hillock. As it developed, the later town spread toward the modern communications routes, the cold-headed factory and the precision foundry, Métaltemple, the name indicating that this was once the site of a commandery of the Knights Templar. The associated communes of Thyl and Beaune are of interest, the first for its megaliths and the second for its 16th–17th-century church perched on a rocky promontory.

VALLOIRE. As the D902 climbs to the COL DU TÉLÉGRAPHE (5140 feet) on its way to Valloire, it passes a road on the left leading to VALMEINIER. The resort's beautiful skiing area is also the site of an annex for the vocational training college of Saint-Michel, which prepares students for the mountain professions. France's fourth-largest commune occupies a beautiful hanging valley. The principal village, Place, centered around its parish church (1630–82), is the heart of the resort. According to local legend the church was built from materials brought by the inhabitants each time they attended mass. Between the Col du Télégraphe and the Col du Galibier the road passes the commune's seventeen chapels and hamlets and reveals some truly magnificent landscapes. Above Saint-Michel the Vallée de l'Arc becomes a narrows trench. Until Napoleonic times people traveled along the south-facing slopes of the valley, via the hamlets of Orelle. When the modern road was built, the houses spread into the valley. A cableway now links Orelle with the Plan Bouchet (7545 feet) and the skiing areas of VAL-THORENS and LES TROIS VALLÉES.

LA PRAZ. Testimony to its industrial past, the village boasts the first self-supporting pressure pipeline in the world. It was built across the Arc river by Paul Héroult in 1893. Less obvious is the ultramodern underground power station, fed by the waters of the reservoir created by the Barrage de Bissorte, 3755 feet higher up on the opposite side of the valley. Le Freney and Saint-André lead to the Refuge de l'Orgère, one of the gateways of the Parc National de la Vanoise ▲ *264*.

MODANE-FOURNEAUX. The twin communes of Modane and Fourneaux form a town based on industry (iron ore was smelted at Fourneaux) and communications. In Roman times Bardonnecchia was reached via the Vallon du Charmaix and the Col de la Roue, which was dedicated to Jupiter, protector of mountain passes. In the Middle Ages travelers commended themselves to the Black Madonna of Charmaix. Modane reached its apogee in the 19th century, when the construction of the Fréjus rail tunnel made it a border station. Standing on a major communications route, it had to be fortified; 19th-century forts such as the Fort du Replaton and the Fort du Sapey, parts of the Maginot Line, Saint-Gobain, Le Lavoir and Le Pas-du-Roc can still be seen today. Although the road tunnel that opened in 1980 increased the volume of traffic, the abolition of borders within Europe significantly reduced the town's importance. Today tourism has taken over and the resort of VALFRÉJUS has been created in the Vallon du Charmaix, where ski championships have been held since 1910. The Musée de la Traversée des Alpes highlights the town's architectural heritage with an exhibition at the entrance to the tunnel, and offers a visit to the fort of Saint-Gobain and the illumination of the Fort du Replaton.

From the Col du Télégraphe there is a sweeping panorama of the Maurienne, a an obvious vantage point for a visual telegraph line on this major route.

TUNNEL DE FRÉJUS
Work on the Fréjus rail tunnel began on September 1, 1857. With the use of the pneumatic drill, which was invented by Germain Sommeiller (1815–71), the project could be completed by 1870.

NOTRE-DAME-DU CHARMAIX
The church was built in the 15th century to house the Black Madonna. It was enlarged and embellished in the 16th and 17th centuries is still a popular place of pilgrimage today.

THE MONOLITH OF SARDIERES
This impressive needle, 305 feet high, was climbed for the first time in 1957 by Michel Paquier.

THE HAUTE MAURIENNE

There are two possible itineraries: one via the N6 and Bramans; the other, along the south side of the valley, via Avrieux, Aussois and Sollières-Sardières.

AVRIEUX. The commune occupies a rocky cirque dominated to the east by the fortifications of L'Esseillon and scored to the north by the Cascade Saint-Benoît. The ÉGLISE D'AVRIEUX ● *82*, dedicated to Saint Thomas à Becket and in a flamboyant Baroque style, and, about 50 yards further on, the CHAPELLE NOTRE-DAME-DES-NEIGES, decorated in the early 17th century by Jean Clappier, are part of the commune's rich religious heritage. In striking contrast is the resolutely modern wind tunnel of the nearby national aerospace research center.

AUSSOIS. The plateau above the Esseillon fortifications has a history going back to prehistory. Cup-shaped hollows can be seen in the rocks and a late Bronze Age sickle and Iron Age rock carvings have been found there. The ÉGLISE NOTRE-DAME-DE-L'ASSOMPTION has some fine Baroque retables, carved benches and one of the most beautiful rood beams in Savoie. The Fort Marie-Christine, the nearest fort to the village, has been converted into a reception center and is also a gateway to the Parc de la Vanoise.

SOLLIERES-SARDIERES. Today the shoulders of Sollières-Sardières, at the foot of the monolith (*above*), are ideal for cross-country skiing. According to local tradition this was the scene of a battle in about 1000 between the semilegendary hero Bérold of Saxony and the Marquis of Susa reputedly recorded in the battle scenes carved on the door handle of the church of Sardières. (It is in fact a 16th-century sword guard.)

PONT DU DIABLE. Beyond Modane the N6 passes below the resort of La Norma and at the Pont du Nant skirts the Marie-Christine redoubt. From here a track leads down to the gorge carved through the limestone barrier by the Arc river. A footbridge over the river leads to the forts on the far bank.

BRAMANS AND THE VALLON D'AMBIN. From Bramans the Vallon d'Ambin and the Col Clapier lead to the Italian border. This is the route said to have been taken by Hannibal in 218 BC ● *43*. Those who want to retrace that historic itinerary will pass the ÉGLISE SAINT-PIERRE-D'EXTRAVACHE, the oldest church in the Maurienne, whose belfry seems to attempt to rival the lofty peak of the Dent Parrachée (12,130 feet).

THE ESSEILLON FORTIFICATIONS ● *85*
Built between 1817 and 1834 to protect Piedmont from invasion by the French, the Esseillon fortifications are a fine example of the Montalembert system of defense, which consisted of the fortifications lying at right angles to the line of attack and an artillery tower. The redoubt on the left side of the valley was linked to the forts on the right-hand side by the Pont du Diable

Medallions from the dome of the chancel in the Église Saint-Thomas-Becket in Avrieux

Termignon. Termignon is the third-largest commune in France, covering a quarter of the area of the Parc de la Vanoise ▲ *264*. Over 125 miles of footpaths enable visitors to follow in the footsteps of the commune's early inhabitants. The vast mountain pastures have always been a virtual cheese mine and the renowned and extremely rare Bleu de Termignon is a favorite with gourmets. In the 17th and 18th centuries local wealth financed the commissioning of the sumptuous retables that make the church of Termignon one of the most remarkable in the Maurienne.

Lanslebourg-Mont-Cenis. In the 18th century Lanslebourg, with a population of 1500, was an important staging post at the foot of Mont Cenis. Carriages had to be dismantled and carried over the pass by men and mules under the direction of local guides known as *marrons*. In winter the descent was made by sled. The road built in Napoleonic times was followed by a cog railway. In 1871, the opening of the Fréjus rail tunnel robbed the Lanslebourg of its importance, although village was revitalized by the creation of the Val-Cenis resort. The present church (1828-30), which has its original furniture, houses the Espace Baroque, one of the starting points of the Chemins du Baroque tour.

Mont-Cenis. The importance of the route over the Col du Mont-Cenis soon called for a hospice. Louis I, the Debonair, son of Charlemagne, pledged to construct one and the Frankish emperor Lothair I had it built in 825. Between 1803 and 1812, on the orders of Napoleon, 2000 to 3000 workmen were employed to build a complex of hospices and barracks on the edge of a trout lake. A series of dams enlarged the lake from 125 acres to 370 acres in 1912, and to 665 acres in 1924. It was further increased to 1650 acres after work carried out by the EDF (Électricité de France) between 1963 and 1968. The Napoleonic complex was submerged but is commemorated by a pyramid-shaped priory. The history of the pass is documented in a room beneath the chapel, surrounded by an Alpine garden. When Savoie became part of France ● *44* Napoleon III gave the Col Mont-Cenis to Italy. The Italians built four forts (Ronce, Variselle, Pattacreuse and Malamot) and France only two (La Turra and Le Mont-Froid). Even so France successfully held out against Italy in 1940.

Église d'Avrieux
The church has one of the most exuberant and richly decorated Baroque interiors in the Maurienne: notable features include the 17th-century door and the diptych (1626), from the former retable of the high altar, by local artist Jean-Pierre Bassand, and retables by Laurent Portaz and Augustin and Pierre Bertrand.

Saint-Pierre d'Extravache
According to tradition the oldest church in the Maurienne was founded by two of Saint Paul's disciples, Elias and Milet[us]. The ruins of this 11th-century building, destroyed by a fire in 1803, stand in a grandiose natural setting against the backdrop of the Dent Parrachée. The apse still has traces of wall paintings: the three groups of figures are those of Saint Andrew and Saint Philip on the left, Saint Thomas, Saint Bartholomew and Saint Matthew in the center, and Saint James and Saint Simon on the right.

Bonneval-sur-Arc.

The devil's own country
On a winter's evening in a byre in Bessans, behind an ass and a cow, the devil was born – a devil who was sculpted in wood and who carried a priest under his arm. This is a true story: in 1857 Étienne Vincendet, the parish sexton and a sculptor of religious statuettes, made the statue as a vengeful reply to the parish priest who had just dismissed him. Bessans, renowned from the 16th century onward for its school of Baroque sculptors, took Vincendet's statue as the emblem of their independent spirit. The art of *tsapoter* or *chapoter* (woodcarving) is today perpetuated by a few sculptors, among whom is Georges Personnaz.

The chapelle Saint-Sébastien
Paintings depicting scenes from the life of Saint Sébastian in 17 panels and scenes from the life of Christ in 36 panels decorate the chapel walls.

Lanslevillard.
Lanslevillard is the twin *commune* of Lanslebourg, with which it forms the resort of Val-Cenis. It has a rich archeological heritage: stones with cup-shaped hollows such as the Roche-aux-Pieds (on the right bank) and the Roche de Chantelouve (on the left bank), and tombs from the Iron Age to the Gallo-Roman period that have yielded a rich collection of fibulae. Of the many chapels the most beautiful is that of Saint-Sébastien (late 16th century) and the parish church has fine 17th-century furniture.

Bessans. Today this very open site, situated at an altitude of over 5580 feet, is a paradise for cross-country skiers. The mountain pastures of the Ribon and Avérole valleys are well suited to an agricultural and pastoral economy, which supports a population strongly attached to local culture and tradition, among which there are many artists. While the principal village was badly damaged during the war, the hamlets of Villaron and Avérole escaped more lightly. Religious and popular are combined to good effect. The Chapelle Saint-Antoine, next to the church, displays the virtues and vices, and portraits of Saint Anthony and Saint Voult de Lucques on its exterior walls. Within, the life of Christ is depicted in 42 panels. The paintings date from the late 15th or early 16th century and are similar to those in the chapel of Saint Sebastian in Lanslevillard. Bessans has produced several dynasties of artists, including the famous Clappier dynasty. Among more humble artists are those who sculpted the Passion crosses, an example of which stands at the end of the path leading to the church.

Bonneval-sur-Arc. The highest commune in the Maurienne has been attracting tourists for a long time. In 1895 the Club Alpin Français built a chalet that could hold 50 people. The site was preserved due to the policies of an exceptional mayor, Gilbert André. The old village, the hamlet of L'Écot, the Col de l'Iseran and Les Évettes are all sites of historic interest. It is a pleasure to walk in their narrow pedestrianized streets, especially at L'Écot. From L'Écot a path leads to the Refuge du Carro, offering a striking view of the Glacier des Sources de l'Arc and its moraine. Les Évettes, with its lake and refuge, is also popular.

Col de l'Iseran. As the road follows the Vallon de la Lenta to the Col de l'Iseran (9090 feet) it passes several chalets and the little Chapelle Saint-Barthélemy. On the col the Chapelle Notre-Dame-de-Toute-Prudence, built in 1939 by the architect Maurice Novarina, is decorated with a statue of the Virgin by Edgar Delvaux.

Alpine resorts, sports and leisure

▲ SKIING AREAS
The Bauges, Chartreuse, Les Aravis...

Manigod, huddled around its church.

Avoriaz, an innovative resort.

Nature reserves

The region's nature reserves keenly promote ecotourism.

Savoie-Grand-Revard
MONT REVARD, an ideal family resort for Alpine skiing (13 ski lifts), is also superb for cross-country skiing. It is linked to LA FÉCLAZ (snow-shoes and dog sleds) and SAINT-FRANÇOIS-DE-SALES by 95 miles of marked ski routes. LES AILLONS, in the heart of the Bauges, welcomes families and groups (25 lifts).

Vallée des Entremonts
The farmers who still live in the valley contribute to the atmosphere of this resort deep in the Parc Naturel Régional de Chartreuse. The idyllic Nordic ski center of the DÉSERT-D'ENTREMONT lies at the heart of 25 miles of cross-country routes and over 18 miles of snowshoe circuits. The small resort of GRANIER (4 ski tows) welcomes families and groups.

Massif des Aravis

La Clusaz
76 ski runs, a snow-park (snowboarding), two Nordic skiing plateaus with 45 miles of marked routes, a skating rink, swimming pool and snowshoe excursions with a meal en route.

Le Grand-Bornand
Farms, a Reblochon cheese market and a heritage center can be visited on skis. The resort has 42 ski runs, a snow-park, 35 miles of cross-country ski routes, 15 miles of snowshoe circuits, a skating rink and para-gliding.

Manigod
21 ski runs linked to La Clusaz and over 10 miles of cross-country ski routes.

Montmin
A 'snow stadium' ideal for beginners.

Plateau des Glières
One of the most beautiful Nordic ski plateaus, with 20 miles of cross-country ski routes and sled excursions.

Romme-sur-Cluses
A village ideal for cross-country skiers.

Saint-Jean-de-Sixt
Four ski slopes and a ski-bus for Le Grand-Bornand and La Clusaz.

Seythenex
A delightful skiing area (11 ski runs) with over 18 miles of cross-country routes.

Chablais and the Portes ...

The Portes du Soleil form one of the largest skiing areas in the world. Its 12 resorts have 375 miles of ski runs.

Avoriaz
The leading resort of the Portes du Soleil is an intensive skiing area with 95 miles of ski runs. More relaxed skiing in the 'children's village'.

Abondance
Farmhouse teas and visits to cheese dairies provide light relief for Alpine and cross-country skiers.

Bellevaux
The resort lies in two skiing areas (Hirmentaz-Habère-Poche and La Chèvrerie) and is linked to La Grande-Terche. 45 miles of cross-country ski routes, with beautiful woodland circuits.

Bernex
A family resort beneath the Dent d'Oche and above Lake Geneva: 30 miles of descents and over 8 miles of cross-country ski routes marked by the Nordic skiing center.

Les Brasses
A family resort with 15 descents and over 60 miles of cross-country ski routes on the magnificent plateau of Plaine-Joux (4100 feet).

La Chapelle-d'Abondance
The resort has a direct link with the Portes du Soleil, attractive ascents, a high-altitude restaurant (descent by torchlight) and 30 miles of cross-country ski routes.

Châtel
A large mountain village on the border of the Swiss canton of Valais and in the heart of the Portes du Soleil, popular for the quality of its snow and the variety of its descents. 13 miles of marked cross-country ski routes and 3 snowshoe circuits.

Drouzin-le-Mont
8 ski lifts and a cross-country ski circuit.

Les Gets
Apartments and hotels near the ski slopes. 11 miles of cross-country ski routes, tobogganing, snowshoes, skating and swimming.

La Grande-Terche
Family skiing along 15 wooded ski runs and a link with the Bellevaux-Val d'Enfer skiing area.

Reindeer from Lapland on Mont Revard in the early 20th century.

Portes du Soleil

Snowboarding.

From Flaine to Sixt on snowshoes.

... du Soleil

Les Habères
18 ski runs linked to the resort of Bellevaux-Hirmentaz, and 14 miles of cross-country ski routes designed by the Nordic skiing center in Les Moises.

Montriond
Linked to the Portes du Soleil, a favorite rendezvous for skaters, cross-country skiers, dog-sled enthusiasts and divers (under ice).

Morzine
A very large skiing area ▲ *198* (over 80 ski runs) linked to Avoriaz. Also five cross-country skiing areas with 60 miles of ski routes, as well as snowshoe and dog-sled excursions and curling.

Saxel
Two ski lifts and a small circuit for cross-country skiing.

Thollon
Fifteen ski runs offering a magnificent view of Lake Geneva. Cross-country skiing, para-jumping and late-night snowshoe excursions.

Vallée du Giffre and Faucigny

Morillon
A village resort on the Giffre river, linked to the Grand Massif. Cross-country skiers can follow the Giffre to the Cirque du Fer-à-Cheval ▲ *216.*

Samoëns
This listed village, has been turned into a resort. 45 miles of cross-country ski routes follow the Giffre river. Also 'archery on snowshoes', ice skating, sledding, ice climbing, horse riding and guided tours.

Sixt-Fer-à-Cheval
At the foot of its mountainous cirque, the resort has 20 miles of Alpine ski runs and 26 miles of cross-country ski routes. Also ice climbing on frozen waterfalls and snowshoe excursions in the nature reserve.

Praz-les-Lys-Sommand
A solarium and viewpoint with 47 descents for all levels of ability. Ideal for cross-country skiers, with 50 miles of sweeping circuits.

Le Grand Massif
Morrilon, Samoëns, Sixt, Flaine and Les Carroz offer a choice of 133 interconnecting ski runs, which are accessible with a single ski-pass, and 90 miles of cross-country routes.

Brizon
Three Alpine ski runs and a wild, sunny plateau for snowshoe excursions and cross-country skiing (15 miles).

Les Carroz
The south-facing resort is popular for its traditional villages, floodlit ski slope and balloon trips. The link with the skiing area of the Plateau d'Agy offers skiers 45 miles of cross-country routes. Children over the age of three can enjoy the 'snow garden'.

Flaine
One of the few integrated resorts in Haute-Savoie. It became famous when American architect Marcel Breuer ● *94* constructed the huge concrete buildings that echo the mineral world of the Désert de Platé. They are set around a central square that has works by Dubuffet, Picasso and Vasarely. The site, discovered by Émile Allias, has a superb skiing area with a magnificent view of Mont Blanc and the Grandes Platières and a wide variety of ski runs (snowpark). There is also an outdoor skating rink, indoor swimming pool, fitness center and indoor climbing wall, as well as late-night snowshoe excursions with a meal in an Alpine chalet.

Mont Saxonnex
Thirteen Alpine ski runs and a small cross-country ski circuit over 3 miles at the foot of Le Bargy. Snowshoe and dog-sled excursions.

Orange
A family resort with 2 ski lifts, a snow trail, summer tobogganing and 8 miles of cross-country ski routes.

Le Reposoir
A small village with 5 ski lifts, dominated by Le Bargy and La Pointe d'Areu.

Climbing waterfalls

The upper reaches of the Giffre river are spectacular in winter, when its waterfalls freeze in the sub-zero temperatures. Some thirty waterfalls – which are never the same from year to year because of varying climatic conditions – offer an irresistible challenge to ice climbers. The ascent is made with the aid of two special ice axes, a pair of rigid crampons, ice pitons and a helmet (for protection against falling ice). The sport is open to beginners, who can make the easier ascents with the help of guides.

Hikers in the solitude of the high mountains.

The Pays du Mont-Blanc offers 230 ski runs for all levels of ability linked to a number of other skiing areas. Holders of a special ski-pass may used all the ski lifts on the massif.

Vallée de Chamonix

In 1825 the writer Victor Hugo described the valley as a 'natural cabinet of curiosities, a sort of divine laboratory'.

Chamonix
Chamonix, which lies at the foot of Mont Blanc, in an area that is a World Heritage Site, attracts the more contemplative tourists as well as the powder-snow addicts. With 16 green, 18 blue, 27 red and 8 black ski runs, skiers are spoilt for choice. The favorite skiing areas are Le Brévent and Les Grands-Montets, whose high-altitude location – with a drop of 6560 feet – means that they can be used up until May. Chamonix has also produced several snow-boarding champions (snowpark). There are 30 miles of cross-country ski routes between Chamonix and Argentières, and over 10 miles of routes for hikers. Facilites include a water-sports center, skating rink, indoor tennis courts, a casino, the bridge club of the Majestic, eight bowling alleys and four nightclubs.

La Vallée Blanche

This is the descent that all skiers dream of making at least once in their life. Between the Aiguille du Midi (12,600 feet) and Chamonix, the route covers a distance of over 12 miles, with a drop in altitude of almost 9200 feet. It also demands the utmost caution since it crosses a glacier, whose movement and the dangers it presents in the form of seracs and crevasses leave no margin for error. This descent should be made only if the weather forecast is favorable (the best time is March-April) and only in the company of a guide.

Excursions

The proximity of the nature reserves and the vigilance of the environmental agencies have made possible the preservation of large expanses of unspoiled mountain landscape near the ski resorts. The massif therefore offers a number of possible ski excursions, some lasting for one day, others for several. There is, for example, the renowned Chamonix-Zermatt route. Off-piste skiing is not recommended and you would be well advised to seek the assistance of professional guides. This is particularly important on a massif where the most beautiful routes lie across glaciers. The guides' centers offer courses for beginners (Col de la Cicle and Croisse-Baulet) and for more advanced skiers (Col du Passon, Col du Chardonnet, Fenêtre du Tour, Glacier d'Argentère, and Buet). Spring is the best time for 'skins' excursions as then the snowpack should be stable.

Les Houches
The world's most experienced skiers are familiar with the famous black piste of Les Houches. However, for the less expert, the resort's 21 other ski runs offer more leisurely skiing, with a spectacular view of the Massif du Mont-Blanc and nearby Chamonix. Les Houches is also an ideal center for snowboarding, telemark, cross-country skiing, skijumping, dog sledding or simply enjoying the unspoilt rural surroundings.

Vallorcine
The village, with its impressive mantle of snow, occupies a postcard setting that is quite isolated. It is reached from Chamonix via a col (4795 feet) and will suit anyone looking for an unspoiled natural environment. Over 10 miles of cross-country ski routes wind between spruce and larches and there are Alpine skiing facilities (4 runs) both in the resort itself and at Les Grands-Montets, 5 miles away.

Passy-Plaine-Joux

A small family resort (Plaine-Joux) situated beneath the Chaîne des Fiz, on a sunny plateau with a fine view of Mont Blanc. Its has a famous church decorated by Léger, Chagall, Matisse and Braque and a 'sculptured route'.

Les Houches at dusk.

LE TÉLÉFÉRIQUE S^T GERVAIS-M^T D'ARBOIS

TOUS LES SPORTS D'HIVER FUNICULAIRE TÉLÉFÉRIQUES PATINOIRES_TREMPLINS

S^T GERVAIS-les-Bains

Val Montjoie

Les Contamines-Montjoie
The resort lies on the edge of a vast nature reserve, and so as not to spoil the landscape there is not a ski-lift in sight. This is an idyllic center for 'skins' enthusiasts and snowshoe excursions.
The resort's skiing area, linked to Hauteluce (Savoie), has a total of 44 ski runs, offering a range for all levels of ability. Experience the sensation of being in the frozen north by following 18 miles of cross-country routes around Notre-Dame-de-la-Gorge or learn how to drive a dog-sled team in the Val Montjoie. Alternatively you may prefer to learn about local traditions on a guided tour of a farm. Children will love to play at being Eskimos; there are snowshoe excursions designed especially for children and igloo-making sessions are laid on.

Saint-Gervais
Saint-Gervais preserves all the charm of a pre-1940s spa town. It also has an established reputation as an Alpine resort, with 88 ski runs linked to Les Houches and Megève. There is something for everyone, including slalom enthusiasts, who can try their skill in a special 'slalom stadium'. There are over 18 miles of cross-country ski routes, while snowshoe enthusiasts can dine in a mountain chalet before returning to the resort by moonlight. An Olympic skating rink hosts hockey matches, skating events and curling. Another challenging and very popular sport is 'ice climbing' up frozen waterfalls. It is suitable for all levels of ability, and ascents of varying difficulty are made under the supervision of a mountain guide. From the Plateau de Belleville (5900 feet) the Mont-Blanc tramway offers a panoramic view of the Chamonix valley.

Megève and the Val d'Arly

Megève
Megève was launched in the early 20th century by Baroness Noémie de Rothschild ● *65*. After World War Two it was the favorite resort of such people as Jean Cocteau, Roger Vadim, Jeanne Moreau and Juliette Greco. Its discreet luxury blends with the local agricultural environment: well-appointed chalets and four-star hotels subtly harmonize with well-weathered traditional wooden farm buildings where several dozen families make a living from their animals and ski-related occupations. It has 131 ski runs (including links with Saint-Gervais, Saint-Nicolas and Combloux) to suit skiers of all abilities, and 45 miles of cross-country ski routes on three skiing areas. Over 30 miles of marked footpaths enable hikers and snowshoe enthusiasts to enjoy walks and excursions in a natural setting, go 'hamlet hopping' or climb to high-altitude restaurants. Megève cultivates its image of a well-to-do resort where visitors can stroll along the pedestrianized streets, relax in the indoor swimming pool (saunas and steam baths are also available), enjoy gastronomic cuisine, the casino, skating rinks, the jazz club or a visit to the Musée du Haut Val d'Arly, which traces the pastoral development of the commune.

Combloux
By virtue of its balcony situation, Combloux offers a panoramic view of Mont Blanc, while attractive farm-chalets nestle around what is the region's finest onion-shaped belfry. The resort has a skiing area linked to Megève, Saint-Gervais and Saint-Nicolas-de-Véroce and one of the region's 35 floodlit ski runs. There are over 9 miles of cross-country ski routes and a special area for snowboarding. If you want a more restful holiday you can enjoy snowshoe or dog-sled excursions and farmhouse teas.

Cordon
An unspoilt traditional family resort nestling around a listed church. It has a small skiing area (8 ski runs) and its style is friendly and relaxed. Viisitors can enjoy snowshoe excursions (by lantern light after dark), sled rides and farmhouse teas.

The rooftops of Arêches.

Les Arcs, a well-integrated ski resort.

In the Tyrolean-style resorts between the Beaufortain and Val d'Arly traditional agriculture thrives alongside winter sports.

Val d'Arly

Praz-sur-Arly
One of the five village-resorts in the Val d'Arly ▲ *242*. Its skiing area (29 runs) is linked to Flumet and Notre-Dame-de-Bellecombe. There are cross-country ski routes to Megève and Flumet. Snowshoe enthusiasts can enjoy the varied relief and panoramic views of Mont Blanc and the Chaîne des Aravis, while balloon trips offer a bird's-eye view of the Alps.

Crest-Voland-Cohennoz
This traditional village-resort is linked to the skiing area of Les Saisies. Its snowshoe circuits run through fir forests and past high-mountain chalets.

La Giettaz
This traditional village at the foot of Les Aravis has a small skiing area (8 ski lifts), between 3610 and 8695 feet, set amid spruce forests.

Flumet-Saint-Nicolas-la-Chapelle
Flumet's chalets, typical of the Val d'Arly,give this resort a rustic atmosphere. Its skiing area lies between 3280 and 6790 feet.

Beaufortain

Arêches-Beaufort
In summer the famous Tarine cattle ● *57* graze in the most beautiful mountain pastures in Savoie. In winter these are transformed into vast snowfields on which the resort was created some fifty years ago. Here skiing is almost a religion and each year, in March, everyone helps to organize the 'Pierra Menta', the hardest Alpine ski event in Europe. Tourists who prefer to go at a more leisurely pace can use the resort's 13 ski lifts and enjoy 30 miles of cross-country routes, dominated by the Grand Mont (8815 ft).

Hauteluce
A delightful, well-situated village and a major resort whose skiing area is linked to Les Saisies and Les Contamines-Montjoie.

Le Saisies
The cross-country ski routes (60 miles) of this resort came to fame during the 1992 Winter Olympics: the Olympic champion Franck Piccard was born in the village. It has an excellent Alpine skiing area linked to the Espace Cristal (43 ski lifts with Crest-Voland and Cohennoz). It is also popular for para-jumping and balloon flights,which start from a plateau with a 180° view.

Tarentaise

Thanks to the impetus given by the development of the world's largest skiing area, built for the 1992 Winter Olympics, these mountains have been transformed.

Les Arcs
Arc-1600, Arc-1800 and Arc-2000 are three balcony-resorts located at different altitudes above Bourg-Saint-Maurice ● *92*. This vast skiing area comprises three levels: the first for budget and family tourism, the second for a wealthier clientele and the third for young people. A funicular transports skiers from the railroad station to the foot of the slopes (78 ski lifts).

Bozel
Peace and quiet in a genuine village setting, with free access to over 12 miles of ski slopes.

Brides-les-Bains
A spa that became a resort when it was linked to Les Trois Vallées by means of a cableway.

Champagny
An unspoilt village which, while opening up to the skiing area of La Plagne, has not become entirely dependent on winter tourism. Special routes allow visitors to tour the region's farms and take in its Baroque heritage ▲ *262*.
The village is located in a wooded setting near the Parc National de la Vanoise ▲ *264*.

Courchevel
The reputation of the 'queen' of the Trois Vallées is based on the beauty of its site, the ski runs devised by Émile Allais, its champions and its innovative winter sports facilities: skiing, skating, snowboarding, etc. It was designed as a 'snow front', the focal point for ski runs and lifts, and served as a model for many other resorts. In the center of the resort, where the streets are also laid out as ski runs, a

Meribel: stone and white wood.

Above La Plagne-Bellecôte.

balcony opens onto a stunning panoramic view. Courchevel was also the first 'experimental resort' in the *département*, which bought the land and built and managed the ski lifts, the buildings being left to the private sector. Courchevel is still at the cutting edge of winter sports facilities and it continues to attract a fashionable clientele.

Doucy-Combelouvière
This small family resort, which lies between 4430 and 7875 feet, has retained its rustic character. Skiers have access to the slopes of Valmorel.

Les Menuires
In the Vallée des Belleville, Les Menuires belongs to the generation of 'snow-front' resorts inspired by coastal resorts: open to the skiing area and traversed by shopping malls. Its ultramodern ski lifts are linked to the other resorts in the Trois Vallées.

La Plagne
La Plagne – ten resorts in one – offers a wide range of choice, including summer skiing on the Glacier de Bellecôte (10,660 feet), which dominates the vast skiing area. The site is so vast that a system of signposts is used to enable skiers to follow the ski routes from one massif to the next. Plagne-Centre is the epitome of the 1960s 'snow-front' resort, while visitors who like wood-cladding and pedestrianized streets tend to favor Belle-Plagne. The Olympic bobsled run is open to amateurs but is not for the fainthearted!

Méribel
Méribel nestles discreetly among forests of Arolla pines and enjoys an unrivaled view of the Glacier du Borgne. It is undoubtedly the most stylish of the resorts, and its luxury hotels and other buildings are well integrated with the the location. It is situated near the Parc National de la Vanosie: the route into the park is marked as far as the Lac du Tuéda.

Montchavin-les-Coches
This resort enjoys a magnificent view of Mont Blanc. In winter its mountain pastures form part of the vast skiing area of La Plagne.

Peisey-Vallandry
Winter visitors will appreciate the peace and quiet of the village, and its Baroque heritage. Access to the skiing area of Les Arcs.

Plagne-Montalbert
In a setting of larch and spruce, the resort offers access to the skiing area of La Plagne.

Pralognan-la-Vanoise
For over a century visitors have been coming to Pralognan to see the Glaciers de la Vanoise and to go mountaineering and skiing. In 1992 the village-resort became an Olympic site. It offers a range of activities, including cross-country skiing, snowshoe excursions and ice skating, and has 14 ski lifts.

La Rosière
The resort is set in a forest on the Italian border. Its skiing area is linked to La Thuile (33 ski lifts).

Saint-Martin-de-Belleville
A traditional village with narrow streets and direct access to the skiing area of the Trois Vallées.

La Tania
The most recently created resort in the Trois Vallées. Small apartment buildings and wooden chalets in a traffic-free zone: ideal for children. Sled and snowshoe excursions.

Valmorel
A neo-Savoyard village created in 1975, with stone-roofed houses clad in dark wood and with pedestrianized streets. It occupies a peaceful setting, with a skiing area linked to Saint-François-Longchamp ◆ *289*.

Val-Thorens
Part of the Trois Vallées system, Val-Thorens (7545 feet) is the highest resort in Europe. It appears to emerge from a white wilderness dominated by the Massif de Péclet-Polcet and the Cime de Caron (10,500 feet), which can be reached by cable car. Its high-altitude location ensures good-quality snow until spring. There are underground ski-lift stations, so that the ski slopes are free of pylons.

Major skiing areas, ski links and ski-passes

◆ The Trois Vallées, the world's largest skiing area (200 ski lifts and 375 miles of ski runs): Courchevel, Méribel, La Tania, Les Menuires, Val-Thorens, Saint-Martin-de-Belleville, Brides-les-Bains.

◆ The 'Espace Killy' linking Val-d'Isère and Tignes: 101 ski lifts, 185 miles of ski runs.

◆ La Grande Plagne: Champagny, Les Coches, Montalbert, Montchavin, and La Plagne: 112 ski lifts, 130 miles of ski runs.

◆ Les Arcs, linked to Peisey-Nancroix, Vallandry and Villaroger: 77 ski lifts and 125 miles of ski runs.

◆ Le Grand Domaine: Valmorel, Saint-François-Longchamp, Les Avanchers and Doucy-Combelouvière: 48 ski lifts and 100 miles of ski runs.

Haute Tarentaise

Sainte-Foy-Tarentaise
This relatively small skiing area (5 ski lifts) is a skier's and snowboarder's paradise. Excursions should only be undertaken with a guide.

Séez
Access to the skiing area of La Rosière (6070 feet) and almost 30 miles of cross-country ski routes (no charge).

Tignes
In the 1920s Alpine chasseurs and 'skins' enthusiasts ventured above the village, which was often cut off by avalanches. Since then a resort has been created above the reservoir that submerged the original village. Its excellent skiing area, open 365 days a year, is linked to Val-d'Isère. Tignes, which has a reputation as a winters sports and acrobatic ski center, also benefited from the boost given to the region by the 1992 Winter Olympics.

Val-d'Isère
For most French people, Val-d'Isère is the resort of Henri Oreiller, Jean-Claude Killy and the first skiing championship of the season. However skiing is only one of the attractions offered by this village, with its stone-walled and stone-roofed houses that can withstand the heaviest snow falls. The more contemplative visitors can enjoy the grandiose spectacle of the Aiguille de la Grande Sassière, the Pointe de Picheru, l'Iseran and the Rocher de Bellevarde renowned for the descent of the 1992 Winter Olympics. The Winter Olympics restored a real sense of identity to the village when the architect Jean-Louis Chanéac grafted a new, well-appointed complex onto the older buildings, with their stone columns, asymmetrical lines and exposed wooden framework.

Maurienne

The sunny plateaus and traditional villages of the Maurienne offer 'natural' skiing on a human scale, on slopes where you feel 'at home'.

Albiez-le-Jeune
A Nordic skiing area at an altitude of between 4430 and 4595 feet. Chamois and deer appear on its wooded plateau in the early morning.

Albiez-Montrond
A peaceful, sunny plateau dominated by the Aiguilles d'Arves, the Glacier de l'Étendard and the Chaîne de Belledonne. The skiing area lies between 4920 and 7220 feet and has 14 ski lifts. Cross-country skiing and dog sledding.

Aussois
One of the gateways to the Parc de la Vanoise. Eleven ski lifts on sunny slopes between 4920 and 9020 feet. The old village overlooks the Esseillon fortifications; the Marie-Christine fort has been converted into a *gîte* (lodge). A cross-country ski route leads to the Nordic plateau of Sollières-Sardières.

Bessans
This 'little Lapland' has exceptional snow cover due to its position and altitude (between 5740 and 7220 feet). Around 50 miles of marked cross-country ski routes and 4 ski lifts.

Bonneval-sur-Arc
A traditional village where climatic conditions are often extreme. The skiing area – 10 ski lifts between 5905 and 9840 feet – has an ideal snow cover, with ski runs open late in the season. Panoramic view of the glaciers dominating the upper valley of the Arc.

Les Bottières
A typical village in the Arvan valley. Its modest skiing area is linked to the Grand Large: 59 ski lifts with Le Corbier, La Toussuire, Saint-Jean-d'Arves and Saint-Sorlin-d'Arves.

Bramans
The best time to see Bramans ▲ *278* is on the day of the bobsled race held on the frozen road. The Nordic skiing area of Bramans-Val-d'Ambin offers 37 miles of ski runs. The oldest church in the Maurienne ▲ *279* can be visited on snowshoes.

Le Corbier
The resort has a dated urban development but a remarkable skiing area (Grand Large). It is also ideal for children, for whom there is a supervised snow garden.

Le Grand Coin
Four *communes* have created a Nordic skiing area with 25 miles of marked ski routes that pass well-preserved hamlets, picturesque chapels and forests.

Jarrier
A single ski lift but six chapels, twelve oratories, seventeen bread ovens, twenty-six hamlets and an unrivaled view of the Aiguilles d'Arves.

Bessans in the snow (early 19th century).

Mont Thabor.

Sculpture at Valloire.

La Norma
Created in 1971 in a forest dominated by the Aiguille de Scolette, the resort is still quite a modest size (3500 beds), favoring small, wood-clad buildings at the foot of the ski slopes with cars left outside the village. The skiing area lies between 4430 and 9020 feet and has 17 ski lifts. There are magnificent circuits for cross-country skiing and snowshoe excursions: Plateau de la Repose, Chemin du Petit Bonheur, Chemin des Forts de l'Esseillon.

Les Karellis
An integrated resort based on the idea of social tourism. Inclusive prices and activities are designed especially for young people. The skiing area – at 5250 to 8200 feet and with 17 ski lifts – suits all abilities.

Orelle
The longest cableway in Europe climbs from 2890 to 7710 feet and joins Val-Thorens and the Trois Vallées ◆ *287*. The resort's ten hamlets, with their narrow streets bordered by stone and wooden houses, and the church with its Baroque retables are in striking contrast to the largest skiing area in the world.

Saint-Jean-d'Arves
In the heart of the Arvan-Villards 25 scattered hamlets enjoy the view of the Aiguilles d'Arves and Chaîne des Grandes Rousses. A peaceful rural commune linked to the skiing area of the Grand Large.

Saint-Sorlin-d'Arves
A very sunny site, dominated by the Pic de l'Étendard (11,350 feet), and 55 miles of ski runs – between 4920 and 8530 feet – linked to the skiing area of the Grand Large. For those who want to spend a night at high altitude, the Refuge de l'Étendard (8200 feet) can be reached from the ski slopes.

La Toussuire
The extensive plateau, where ski races were held in the 1930s, is an ideal site for a resort. The area is well suited to various types of skiing. There are 19 ski lifts linked to the Grand Large.

Saint-Alban and Saint-Colomban-des-Villards
The modest size of the skiing area (4 ski lifts) is more than made up for by the charm of the unspoilt hamlets.

Sollières-Sardières
A paradise for cross-country skiers: 25 miles of ski routes wind across the sunny plateau at an altitude of 4920 feet) on the edge of the Parc National de la Vanoise.

Saint-François-Longchamp
The Grand Domaine complex lies at the foot of the Col de la Madeleine and is linked to Valmorel. It has 48 ski lifts and 100 miles of ski runs on north-facing and sunnier slopes at an altitude of 4690 to 8365 feet.

Termignon
Opposite the Glaciers de la Vanoise. Good snow cover for a small skiing area (6 ski lifts) and some fine cross-country circuits and itineraries for hikers.

Val-Cenis
Twenty-two ski lifts for 45 miles of ski runs between 4595 and 9200 feet. Visitors can take a break from skiing to visit the Espace Baroque (one of the starting points on the Baroque route) and the dairy cooperative.

Val-Fréjus
A forest resort whose streets are ski runs and which respects the style of the hamlet's traditional houses. Good snow cover and a skiing area with 12 ski lifts, lying between 5085 and 9020 feet.

Valloire
An attractive village huddled around its Baroque church. People have been skiing here for almost a century. Today it hosts international events. Linked to Valmeinier, it has ski runs for all abilities at 4690 to 8530 feet. An international ice sculpture competition is held in January.

Valmeinier
A village-resort that lies between 4920 feet and a more recent complex – where the streets are ski runs – at 5905 feet. The skiing area, dominated by Mont Thabor (10,425 feet), is linked to Valloire: (95 miles of ski runs).

A study in patience…

…and optimism.

Fishing

Rivers, mountain streams, pools, low-lying and mountain lakes offer anglers a wide variety of environments in which to try different fishing techniques. As well as the more common species (tench, perch, pike and whitefish), various species of the Salmonidae family (trout, grayling, dace and char) are found in the region's rivers and lakes. Do not miss the opportunity to fish in the mountain lakes, lying above 3935 feet. Reaching them may mean walking for one or two hours but as you cast your line you will find that the setting is well worth the effort.

Chablais-Genevois
The region has 300 miles of rivers that, in season, simply teem with brown trout: individuals weighing 12, 16 and as much as 22 pounds have been caught in the turbulent waters of the Dranse. You can also catch brown trout, rainbow trout and char in the ten lakes within the Chablais-Genevois region (220 acres).

Lac du Bourget
The lake is renowned for its perch, pike, lavaret (whitefish) and char.

The Alpine foreland
Although the Lac d'Aiguebelette and the Rhône and Guiers rivers are the best-known places for fishing in Savoie, anglers will find the many mountain streams and tributaries equallly rewarding.

◆ Do not ignore warnings on stretches of rivers lying below EDF (Électricité de France) reservoirs as the rate of flow can increase dramatically.

Swimming

In Savoie swimmers are spoilt for choice. There are the clear waters of the Lac d'Annecy – one of the purest lakes in the region, where temperatures in summer can exceed 70° F – and the pure, emerald-green waters of the Lac d'Aiguebelette, where temperatures can reach 75–80° F. There is no shortage of lakeshore beaches, which may be supervised, unofficial, free or private, some having organized areas with games and events. There are also 68 indoor and open-air public swimming pools.

Lakes

A wide range of watersports – from yatching, windsurfing, dinghy and catamaran sailing, to water-skiing, rowing and diving – can be practiced on the Rhône river and the Lac d'Annecy, Lake Geneva and Lac du Bourget. The lakes each have about ten marinas as well as clubs and leisure centers where equipment can be hired. Lessons and training courses are also available.

Aiguebelette

It was on the Lac d'Aiguebelette that the world rowing championships took place in September 1997. It is the most romantic of the French lakes. To preserve its peace and serenity only electrically powered boats are allowed on its waters.

INFORMATION
Rowing courses:
Base de Novalaise
Tel: 04 79 36 06 34

White water

With their lakes, mountains streams and rivers, the Alps of Savoie are ideal for canoeing, kayaking, rafting, canyoning, hydrospeed and other white-water sports. Many clubs offer courses for beginners as well as for more experienced enthusiasts. Some guides' associations organize multi-disciplinary adventure trails. Craft are allowed on the rivers only between the hours of 9am and 6pm.

◆ The upper reaches of the Isère river are ideal for kayaking and white-water rafting. The craft used for white-water rafting are inflatable dinghies that are paddled along under the direction of a professional helmsman. Experience the exhilaration of riding the rapids, although anyone wanting to go white-water rafting must be able to swim!

◆ Hydrospeed is a much more athletic sport. Swimmers wear a wet suit and flippers and swim down the river, steering themselves with a streamlined float that also acts as a fender.

Hiking
Miles of marked footpaths enable visitors to discover the changing colors of Savoie between May and November. The most beautiful excursions are described in brochures available from local tourist office and travel agents.

It doesn't matter what you're riding, provided you have a head for heights.

Climbing and caving

Climbing is becoming increasingly popular in a region that has produced some of the best climbers in the world. Indoor or outdoor artificial climbing walls are to be found in many communes.

Caving
◆ Haute-Savoie has ten officially recorded chasms and many more are yet to be discovered. In this region caving is a particularly strenuous sport since there is often a long walk to get to the site. The galleries are narrow, wet, cold and steep. The main chasms – the Gouffre Jean-Bernard, one of the deepest chasms in the world with a depth of 5255 feet, and the Mirolda (5050 feet) – are situated in the Samoëns region. The underground river of La Diau, in the Massif du Parmelan, is not to be missed. The descent – 2395 feet in 12 hours – is one of the most spectacular in France.
◆ In Savoie the main caving areas are in the Massif de Chartreuse and the Massif des Bauges.
◆ Comité Départemental de Spéléologie (Regional caving association)
172, rue du Paradis
74800 La Roche-sur-Foron
Tel: 04 50 98 84 86

On horseback and by bike

Cycle-touring
Themed routes, including a superb 300-mile route through Reblochon country, are on offer to cyclo-tourists, who must register at least two weeks in advance.
As well as roads and paths, there are a great many cycle tracks. One of the most picturesque follows the line of a disused railroad along the shores of the Lac d'Annecy as far as Sévrier.

Mountain bikes
The final of the mountain bike World Cup was held in Semnoz (Haute-Savoie) in 1997. Most resorts have marked routes and offer training courses for mountain bikers of all abilities, while sports shops rent out mountain bikes by the day or half-day.

On horseback
Marked bridle paths, over easy terrain in the Alpine foreland and more challenging in the mountains, allow horseback riders to explore the region on their own, at their own pace and according to their ability. Along the routes are over 100 lodges (*gîtes*), guest-houses (*chambres d'hôte*) and small rural hotels that will accommodate riders and their horses.
◆ Touring the Bauges on a donkey is an ideal way to explore these mountains. Donkey rides start from Bellecombe-en-Bauges
Tel: 04 79 63 36 97

Airborne sports

If you want to learn to paraglide, it is advisable to contact one of the fifteen or so schools belonging to the Fédération Française de Vol Libre (French free-flight federation), which offer beginners' courses and structured training courses. They have the very latest specialist equipment and teach pupils on sites suited to their ability. Instructors are also well acquainted with the aerological and meteorological conditions of mountain regions. A great many accidents are still caused by a poor understanding of landscape and wind conditions.

Dizzying heights

The *vie ferrate* ('iron ways') that have proved so successful in the Italian Dolomites are becoming ever more popular with climbers in Savoie. However, ecologists in some *communes* are less enthusiastic in view of the potential legal implications. If you like exhilarating experiences you will love these systems of rungs, gangplanks and metal cables that enable you to move up, down and along vertical – and vertiginous – rock faces midway between the sky and the ground. Those climbing a *via ferrata* for the first time will experience the sensation of hanging in a void and will see the mountains from a very different angle. But a word of warning: the specialist systems of the *vie ferrate* require special skills and equipment, and certain precautions. If you are doing this for the first time, make sure that you are accompanied by a mountain guide, who will explain how to use a harness, tethers and crabs, and who will ensure that you wear a protective helmet.

▲WINTER SPORTS:
something for everyone`

Winter sports are not a new idea. In the early 20th century people didn't 'go skiing', they 'did winter sports'. Today, as well as going to the mountains to ski, over 50 percent of people on holiday also want to enjoy the simple pleasure of walking or to discover new and exciting experiences: excursions in dog sleds or on snowshoes or climbing a frozen waterfall with ice axes and crampons.

Walking

Because you breathe in pure mountain air with every step, walking is an ideal way to refresh your mind and body as well as being excellent exercise. Many resorts have marked footpaths with a specially laid surface to make them more easily accessible for hikers. At La Clusaz an expert on survival techniques in the Canadian forests gives practical tips on how to survive in extreme conditions, for example how to light a fire without a lighter or matches in all weathers.
Tel: 04 50 32 65 00

Dog-sled teams

Amid the crunching of the sleds on the snow, the shouts of the drivers (*mushers*) and the panting of the Siberian huskies, with their blue eyes and wolf-like howls, dog-sled teams are a spectacularly disciplined operation. Sleds can be pulled by a team of up to twenty dogs, with a lead dog obeying the shouted commands of the *musher*.

Snowshoes

The concept of snowshoes dates from 10,000 BC, when the peoples of Central Asia migrated to the Canadian Far North. These early snowshoes consisted of a wooden frame covered with strips of animal hide.
Great advances were made in this field in the 1990s.
Today snowshoes, made of plastic or aluminum, are light and have special straps that allow the foot greater freedom of movement with each step. They can be used on the flat and on slopes, and even on hard snow, as small crampons are attached to the frame. Walking in snowshoes requires no particular skill and is something that people of any age can do. All you need is a pair of warm, waterproof boots. The Parc Naturel Régional de Chartreuse, for example, already has 30 miles of marked routes. But beware if you venture onto the Massif du Granier: this limestone massif is positively riddled with hundreds of treacherous potholes and fissures which are covered by snow in winter.
◆ Parc Naturel Régional de Chartreuse
38380 Saint-Pierre-de-Chartreuse
Tel: 04 76 88 65 07

High tension

Speed-record trial
You don't have to beat the world record (150 miles per hour) to experience the exhilaration of a speed-record trial. Try it, with a streamlined helmet and special skis, on the Olympic ski run of Les Arcs and receive an official certificate.
INFORMATION
Tel: 04 79 07 57

Bob-raft
For an exhilarating but safe experience try descending on La Plagne's Olympic bobsled run at over 50 miles per hour on a bob-raft with automatic steering and braking.
INFORMATION
Tel: 04 79 09 12 73

Icefalls

You do need to be fit and athletic to climb a frozen waterfall. Ascents are made with the aid of two special ice axes and crampons. However, the magical forms of the frozen water are not something that only experts are able to enjoy. In all the massifs in the region beginners' courses are available, with itineraries devised to suit prevailing temperatures and levels of freezing. At Les Gets an innovative evening course for beginners is offered in an underground gallery, where the quality of the ice is guaranteed.
Tel: 04 50 75 80 80

Practical information

Appendices:

Information: SNCF
All mainline (SNCF) stations are now linked to an information center, which provides a wide range of travel information and takes reservations and ticket orders
Tel. 08 36 35 35 35 (from within France),
Online: www.sncf.fr

BY TRAIN

Eurostar Ski Trains
Two Eurostar services per week from London Waterloo to Moûtiers, Aime-La Plagne and Bourg-Saint-Maurice. From here the resorts of Val d'Isère, Méribel, La Plagne and Tignes are easily accessible by local bus services.
◆ Roundtrip costs from £159 (overnight) or £179 (day) to £310 (first class)
◆ London Waterloo to Bourg-Saint-Maurice: 8 hrs 50mins
◆ Information:
Tel: 0990 186 186
www.eurostar.co.uk

Other connections
◆ Change at Paris Gare-de-Lyon for trains to Annecy, Chambéry, Megève, Aix-les-Bains, Modane, Saint-Michel-de-Maurienne, Saint-Jean-de-Maurienne.
◆ Change at Annecy or Lyons for Saint-Gervais (connections for Chamonix).
◆ Change at Chambéry for Albertville (bus link with Megève).
◆ Change at Bellegarde for Évian-les-Bains and Thonon-les-Bains

Reductions
The SNCF offers reductions (between 20 and 60 per cent).

Regional transport
◆ The region has a network of TER trains and buses. A regional transport guide is available from stations and tourist offices.
◆ There are SNCF bus services from all mainline stations.

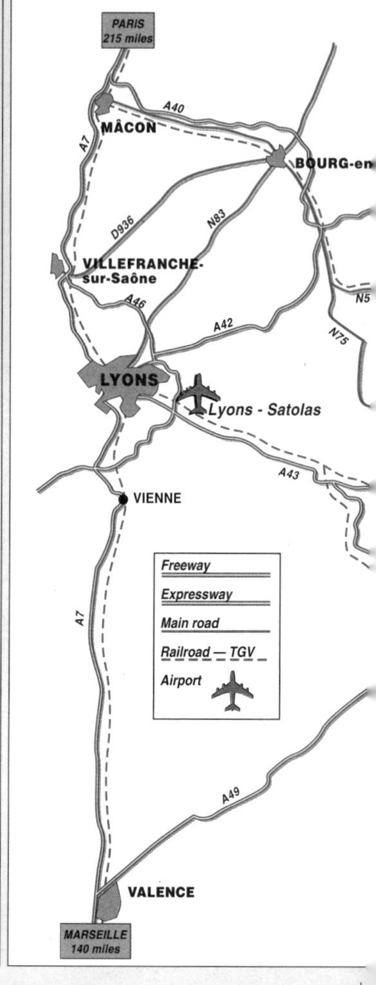

BY AIR

Formalities
Valid passport or identity papers needed for EC members.

International airports:
GENEVE-COINTRIN
Flights from the UK to Geneva by British Airways, Swiss Air and Easyjet.
Roundtrip flights from London to Geneva costs from £120 plus airport tax.
◆ Several buses a day from the bus station in Geneva to Annecy (1hr 15mins), Évian and Thonon-les-Bains.
◆ Between December and March, several buses a day from the airport to the resorts of Mont-Blanc, the Portes du Soleil, Grand Massif and Les Aravis. For the return journey (resort-airport), seats must be booked in advance at the tourist office or bus station.
◆ Airport Information
CP 100
1215 Geneva 15
Switzerland
Tel. (41) 22 717 71 11

LYON-SATOLAS
British Airways has direct flights from the UK to Lyons. Roundtrip flights from London to Lyons costs from £150 plus airport tax. There are also daily flights from Paris to Lyons.
◆ Shuttle service between the airport and the city center.
Tel. 04 78 67 09 10
◆ Daily bus services to Annecy.
Tel. 04 72 22 71 27 or 04 79 35 33 97
◆ Information
BP 113
69125 Lyon-Satolas
Tel. 04 72 22 72 21

ANNECY-MEYTHET
◆ Daily flights from Paris to Annecy.
◆ Bus services to the resorts.
◆ Information
Tel. 04 50 27 30 30 T

Telephone numbers

To telephone France from the UK: dial 00 33 followed by the regional code (omitting the initial 0), then the number you require.
To telephone the UK from France: dial 00 44 followed by the regional code (omitting the initial 0), then the number you require.

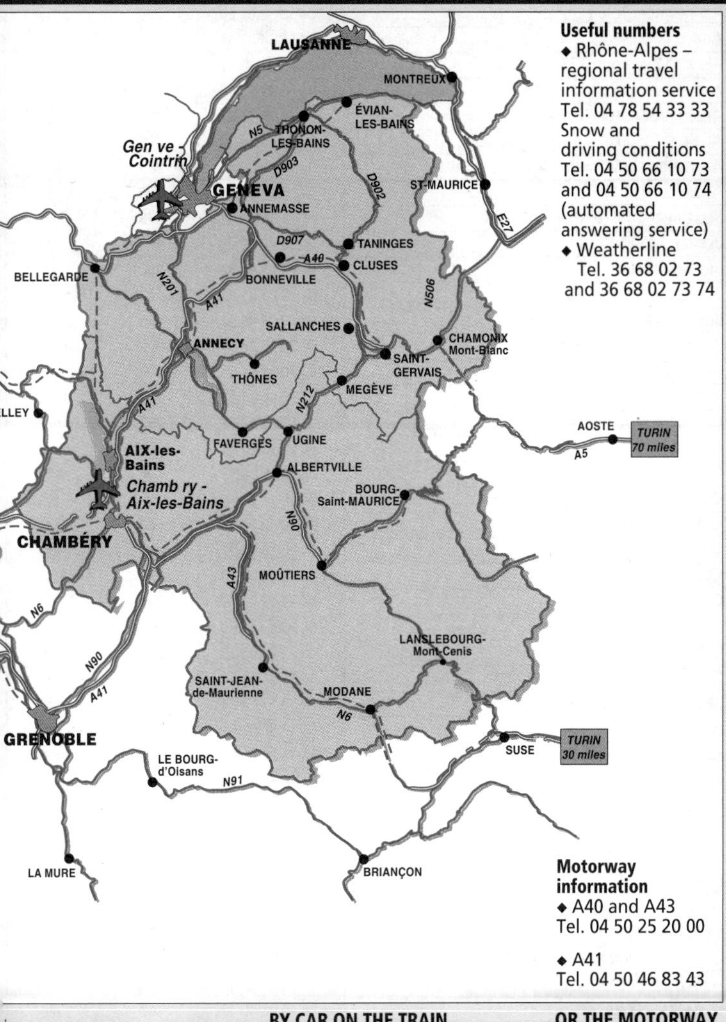

Useful numbers

◆ Rhône-Alpes – regional travel information service
Tel. 04 78 54 33 33
Snow and driving conditions
Tel. 04 50 66 10 73 and 04 50 66 10 74 (automated answering service)
◆ Weatherline
Tel. 36 68 02 73 and 36 68 02 73 74

Motorway information

◆ A40 and A43
Tel. 04 50 25 20 00

◆ A41
Tel. 04 50 46 83 43

AIRLINES

◆ Easyjet
Tel: 0990 29 29 29
www.easyjet.com
◆ British airways
Reservations:
Tel: 0345 222111
Information:
Tel. 0990 444000
www.britishairways.com
◆ Swiss air
Tel: 0845 601 0956
www.swissair.com
◆ Air France
Tel. 0845 0845 111
www.airfrance.com

BY CAR ON THE TRAIN ...

A practical, reliable and relaxing way of traveling to the Alps.
◆ Paris–Évian-les-Bains: daily from July 4 to August 31 and Friday evenings from December 19 to April 24.
◆ Paris-Saint-Gervais: daily
◆ Paris-Lyons: daily

Information
◆ Paris
Tel. 01 53 33 60 11
◆ Évian-les-Bains
Tel. 04 50 70 71 16
◆ Saint-Gervais
Tel. 04 50 78 45 64
◆ Lyons
Tel. 04 72 40 10 82

Le Shuttle
Eurotunnel's 'Le Shuttle' train transports motor vehicles through the Channel Tunnel between England (Folkestone) and France (Calais).

Information:
Tel. 0990 353535
www.eurotunnel.co.uk

OR THE MOTORWAY

The region is serviced by a number of motorways (autoroutes): A 40, A41, A43 and A430. All ski resorts are within 20 miles of a motorway exit.
◆ Autoroute FM 107.7 Mhz

Maps
◆ Michelin:
France n° 989, Rhône-Alpes n° 244
Departmental maps n° 70, 74, 77

◆ PRINCIPAL SKI RESORTS

	Telephone numbers	No of beds: hotels	No beds: holiday resorts
Abondance 74360	04 50 32 65 00	259	2 518
Agy	04 50 34 82 50		
Albiez-Montrond 73300	04 79 59 30 48	150	1950
Arbusigny	04 50 03 36 68		
Arèches-Beaufort 73270	04 79 38 37 57	367	1562
Aussois 73500	04 79 20 30 80	380	1000
Avant-Pays savoyard 73470 Novalaise	04 79 36 09 29	335	1140
Avoriaz 74110	04 50 74 02 11	180	9 771
Bellevaux 74 470	04 50 73 71 53	378	1 908
Bernex 74500	04 50 73 60 72	174	1 927
Bessans 73480	04 79 05 96 52	250	980
Bonneval-sur-Arc 73480	04 79 05 95 95	172	1346
Bourg-Saint-Maurice 73700 Les Arcs	04 79 07 04 92	420	1000
Brides-les-Bains 73570	04 79 55 20 64	1545	2224
Brizon / Solaison	04 50 96 91 61		
Canton de la Chambre 73130	04 79 56 33 58	670	4600
Carroz-d'Arâches 74300	04 50 90 00 04	232	5 018
Chamonix-Mont-Blanc 74400	04 50 53 00 24	4 012	25 450
Champagny-en-Vanoise 73350	04 79 55 06 55	490	2500
Châtel 74380	04 50 73 22 44	1 364	7 195
Combloux 74920	04 50 58 60 49	688	5 141
Cordon 74700	04 50 58 01 57	436	1 441
Courchevel 73120	04 79 08 04 10	4500	14000
Courchevel 73120	04 79 08 00 29	4500	14000
Courchevel 73120 Le Praz	04 79 08 41 60	4500	14000
Courchevel 73120 Moriond	04 79 08 03 29	4500	14000
Crest-Voland 73590 Cohennoz	04 79 31 62 57	350	6000
Drouzin-le-Mont 74430 Le Blot	04 50 72 12 28	36	1 642
Flaine 74300	04 50 90 80 01	544	8 058
Flumet 73590 St-Nicolas-la-Chapelle	04 79 31 61 08	250	4000
La Chapelle-d'Abondance 74360	04 50 73 56 04	492	4 699
La Chapelle-Rambaud	04 50 03 36 68		
La Clusaz 74220	04 50 32 65 00	1 436	10 184
La Féclaz 73230	04 79 25 80 49	380	500
La Giettaz 73590	04 79 32 91 90	310	2000
La Norma 73500	04 79 20 31 46	400	3000
La Plagne 73210	04 79 09 79 79	1200	37000
La Plagne-Montalbert 73210	04 79 09 77 33	155	1450
La Rosière-Montvalezan 73700	04 79 06 80 51	600	2500
La Tania 73120	04 79 08 40 40	162	2700
La Toussuire 73300	04 79 56 70 15	1168	4000
Le Corbier 73300	04 79 83 04 04	150	6500
Le Grand-Bornand 74450	04 50 02 78 00	782	8 913
Le Praz de Lys	04 50 43 02 72		
Le Reposoir 74950	04 50 98 18 01	0	693
Le Revard 73100 Aix-les-Bains	04 79 54 00 83	70	120
Le Salève	04 50 32 10 33		
Le Semnoz	04 50 33 02 10	2 912	4 446
Le Sulens	04 50 44 92 44		
Les Aillons 73340 Aillon-le-Jeune	04 79 54 63 65	112	3800
Les Arcs 73700 Bourg-Saint-Maurice	04 79 07 12 56	3808	21000
Les Bottières 73300 Saint-Pancrace	04 79 83 27 09		350
Les Brasses 74250 Viuz-en-Sallaz	04 50 36 86 24	202	3 484
Les Contamines-Montjoie 74 170	04 50 47 01 58	380	4 610
Les Gets 74280	04 50 79 76 90	1 116	9 690
Les Habères 74420 Habère-Poche	04 50 39 54 46	108	1 884

	Altitude of the resort	Marked cross-country ski routes (kilometers)	No. of ski tows/lifts
Abondance 74360	930		13
Agy	1250	56	
Albiez-Montrond 73300	1550	15	13
Arbusigny	900-950	28	
Arèches-Beaufort 73270	1050	43	13
Aussois 73500	1500	35	11
Avant-Pays savoyard 73470 Novalaise	230-2000	69	15
Avoriaz 74110	1 800		36
Bellevaux 74 470	900	58	23
Bernex 74500	1 000	14	18
Bessans 73480	1740	80	4
Bonneval-sur-Arc 73480	1800		10
Bourg-Saint-Maurice 73700 Les Arcs	810	30	77
Brides-les-Bains 73570	580	33	1
Brizon / Solaison	1 500	26,5	
Canton de la Chambre 73130	500	45	21
Carroz-d'Arâches 74300	955	56	17
Chamonix-Mont-Blanc 74400	1 035	43	59
Champagny-en-Vanoise 73350	1250	35	113
Châtel 74380	1 200		40
Combloux 74920	980	13	14
Cordon 74700	871		7
Courchevel 73120	1550	50	4
Courchevel 73120	1850	50	38
Courchevel 73120 Le Praz	1300	50	2
Courchevel 73120 Moriond	1650	50	23
Crest-Voland 73590 Cohennoz	1230	90	17
Drouzin-le-Mont 74430 Le Blot	1 200		7
Flaine 74300	1 600	56	32
Flumet 73590 St-Nicolas-la-Chapelle	1000	25	10
La Chapelle-d'Abondance 74360	1 000	27	14
La Chapelle-Rambaud	950	30,2	
La Clusaz 74220	1 040	69	39
La Féclaz 73230	1350	160	14
La Giettaz 73590	1100	6	8
La Norma 73500	1350	6	17
La Plagne 73210	1250-2000	90	113
La Plagne-Montalbert 73210	1350	25	10
La Rosière-Montvalezan 73700	1850	12	19
La Tania 73120	1350-3200	50	68
La Toussuire 73300	1800	25	19
Le Corbier 73300	1550	25	44
Le Grand-Bornand 74450	1 000	56	42
Le Praz de Lys	1450	60	
Le Reposoir 74950	900		6
Le Revard 73100 Aix-les-Bains	1550	160	14
Le Salève	1 180	29,5	
Le Semnoz	1 430	50	9
Le Sulens	800	14	
Les Aillons 73340 Aillon-le-Jeune	1000	50	24
Les Arcs 73700 Bourg-Saint-Maurice	1600-2000	15	77
Les Bottières 73300 Saint-Pancrace	1300	4	3
Les Brasses 74250 Viuz-en-Sallaz	900	50	16
Les Contamines-Montjoie 74 170	1 164	23	22
Les Gets 74280	1 172	39	35
Les Habères 74420 Habère-Poche	850	20	8

◆ PRINCIPAL SKI RESORTS

	TELEPHONE NUMBERS	NO OF BEDS: HOTELS	NO BEDS: HOLIDAY RESORTS
LES HOUCHES 74310	04 50 55 50 62	724	7 410
LES KARELLIS 73870	04 79 59 50 36		300
LES MENUIRES 73440	04 79 00 73 00	1700	18300
LES SAISIES 73620 HAUTELUCE	04 79 38 90 30	400	10000
LULLIN-COL DU FEU 74470	04 50 73 82 05	102	212
MANIGOD / LA CROIX-FRY / MERDASSIER 74230	04 50 44 92 44	90	1 850
MASSIF DES BAUGES 73630 LE CHÂTELARD	04 79 54 84 28	550	5000
MEGÈVE 74120	04 50 21 27 28	1 888	13 269
MÉGEVETTE	04 50 35 74 32		
MÉRIBEL 73550	04 79 08 60 01	2600	25000
MIEUSSY-SOMMAND 74440	04 50 43 02 72	72	2 163
MONT-SAXONNEX 74130	04 50 96 97 27	88	1 024
MONTCHAVIN-LES COCHES 73210	04 79 07 82 82	160	7200
MONTMIN 74210	04 50 44 60 24	68	252
MONTRIOND 74110	04 50 79 04 06	158	1 538
MORILLON 74440	04 50 90 15 76	112	7 052
MORZINE 74110	04 50 79 03 48	2 770	12 589
NANCY-SUR-CLUSES 74300	04 50 90 94 90	0	66
NOTRE-DAME-DE-BELLECOMBE 73590	04 79 31 61 40	400	4500
ORANGE 74800 LA ROCHE-SUR-FORON	04 50 03 36 68	144	566
PASSY / PLAINE JOUX 74480	04 50 58 80 52	414	2 398
PEISEY-VALLANDRY 73210	04 79 07 94 28	520	3500
PLATEAU DES GLIÈRES	04 50 22 40 31		
PRALOGNAN-LA-VANOISE 73710	04 79 08 79 08	1160	2500
PRAZ-SUR-ARLY 74120	04 50 21 90 57	268	3 447
SAINT-COLOMBAN-DES-VILLARDS 73130	04 79 56 24 53	54	500
SAINT-FRANÇOIS-LONGCHAMP 73130	04 79 59 10 56	560	3712
SAINT-GERVAIS-LES-BAINS 74170	04 50 47 76 08	970	13 823
SAINT-JEAN-D'ARVES 73530	04 79 59 72 97	30	1100
SAINT-JEAN-D'AULPS 74430	04 50 79 67 95	116	3 130
SAINT-JEAN-DE-SIXT 74450	04 50 02 70 14	118	1 558
SAINT-SORLIN-D'ARVES 73530	04 79 59 71 77	575	1500
SAINTE-FOY-TARENTAISE 73460	04 79 06 95 19	90	450
SAMOËNS 74340	04 50 34 40 28	646	11 963
SAXEL 74420	04 50 39 00 70	40	350
SERVOZ	04 50 47 21 68		
SEYSSEL / SUR LYAND	04 50 59 26 56		
SEYTHENEX 74210	04 50 44 60 24	66	387
SEYTROUX	04 50 79 65 09		
SIXT-FER-À-CHEVAL 74740	04 50 34 49 36	150	1 370
SOLLIÈRES-SARDIÈRES 73500	04 79 20 52 45	60	234
SOMMAND	04 50 34 25 05		
TANINGES-PRAZ-DE-LYS 74440	04 50 34 25 05	336	5 177
TERMIGNON-LA-VANOISE 73500	04 79 20 51 67	33	460
THOLLON-LES-MÉMISES 74500	04 50 70 90 01	198	3 270
TIGNES 73320	04 79 06 15 55	1158	28000
VAL-CENIS-LANSLEBOURG 73480	04 79 05 23 66	755	3934
VAL-D'ISÈRE 73150	04 79 06 06 60	2435	10845
VAL-THORENS 73440	04 79 00 08 08	1400	18400
VALFRÉJUS 73500 MODANE	04 79 05 33 83	400	3100
VALLÉE DES ENTREMONTS 73670	04 79 65 81 90	145	500
VALLOIRE 73450	04 79 59 03 96	900	8500
VALLORCINE 74660	04 50 54 60 71	154	1 285
VALMEINIER 73450	04 79 59 20 77	985	1815
VALMOREL 73260	04 79 09 85 55	350	8150

	Altitude of the resort	Marked cross-country ski routes (kilometers)	No. of ski tows/lifts
Les Houches 74310	1 045	35	12
Les Karellis 73870	1600	40	19
Les Menuires 73440	1850	28	48
Les Saisies 73620 Hauteluce	1650	100	24
Lullin-col du Feu 74470	850		3
Manigod / La Croix-Fry / Merdassier 74230	935		18
Massif des Bauges 73630 Le Châtelard	650-2200	230	24
Megève 74120	1 113	63	43
Mégevette	900	23	
Méribel 73550	1450	33	57
Mieussy-Sommand 74440	636		10
Mont-Saxonnex 74130	1 000		7
Montchavin-Les Coches 73210	1250-1450	12	113
Montmin 74210	1 045		2
Montriond 74110	950		10
Morillon 74440	700	63	10
Morzine 74110	1 000		36
Nancy-sur-Cluses 74300	1 100		4
Notre-Dame-de-Bellecombe 73590	1150	8	18
Orange 74800 La Roche-sur-Foron	1 100		3
Passy / Plaine Joux 74480	710	50	8
Peisey-Vallandry 73210	1650	40	77
Plateau des Glières	1 450	35	
Pralognan-la-Vanoise 73710	1410	25	14
Praz-sur-Arly 74120	1 036		14
Saint-Colomban-des-Villards 73130	1150	15	5
Saint-François-Longchamp 73130	1450-1650		16
Saint-Gervais-les-Bains 74170	800		26
Saint-Jean-d'Arves 73530	1550		26
Saint-Jean-d'Aulps 74430	810		9
Saint-Jean-de-Sixt 74450	960	16	2
Saint-Sorlin-d'Arves 73530	1550	20	14
Sainte-Foy-Tarentaise 73460	1550	15	5
Samoëns 74340	710	63	17
Saxel 74420	900		2
Servoz	820	12	
Seyssel / Sur Lyand	1240	38	
Seythenex 74210	721	27	5
Seytroux	850-950	10	
Sixt-Fer-à-Cheval 74740	760	63	8
Sollières-Sardières 73500	1600	45	
Sommand	1450	60	
Taninges-Praz-de-Lys 74440	600		12
Termignon-la-Vanoise 73500	1300	30	7
Thollon-les-Mémises 74500	920		17
Tignes 73320	2100	21	51
Val-Cenis-Lanslebourg 73480	1400	10	23
Val-d'Isère 73150	1850	24	51
Val-Thorens 73440	2300	3	27
Valfréjus 73500 Modane	1550	2	12
Vallée des Entremonts 73670	650-1550	54	13
Valloire 73450	1430	40	33
Vallorcine 74660	1 260	20	3
Valmeinier 73450	1500-1800	15	35
Valmorel 73260	1400	20	50

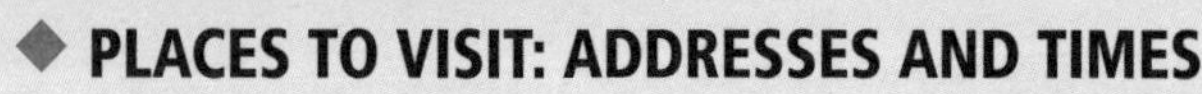

PLACES TO VISIT: ADDRESSES AND TIMES

Towns are listed in alphabetical order.
The letter and number (e.g. E6) relate to the *communes* on the departmental maps:
Savoie at the front of the guide,
Haute-Savoie at the end of the guide.

KEY TO PREFIXES
M : mairie (town hall)
OT : office de tourisme (tourist office)
SI : syndicat d'initiative (tourist bureau)
MT : maison du tourisme (tourist center)

CHAMBÉRY, COMBE DE SAVOIE, CHARTREUSE

Place	Details		Map	Page
CHAMBÉRY	**73000**	*OT 04 97 33 42 47*	**B4**	
Cathédrale Saint-François Place Métropole	*Open June–Sept.: 8–11.45am and 1.30–6pm; off season: 9–11.45am and 2–6pm. Closed Sun. Guided tour as part of the tour of the old town organized by the Tourist Office.*			▲ 124
Château des Ducs de Savoie and Sainte-Chapelle	*Guided tours by appt. at the Tourist Office: 2.30pm, 3.30pm and 4.30pm. Tour as part of the tour of the old town organized by the Tourist Office.*			▲ 121
Église Notre-Dame Rue Saint-Antoine	*Open July–Sept.: Tues.–Fri. 3–6pm, Sat. 9am–noon and 4–5.30pm; Oct.–June: Wed.–Thur. 2.30–5pm, Sat. 9am–noon and 4–5.30pm. Guided tours by appt. at the Tourist Office.*			
Church and crypt of Saint-Pierre-de-Lémenc	*Open Sat. 5–6pm, Sun. 9.30–10.30am. Guided tours (by appt.) by the guides of the Fil de l'Eau (☎ 04 79 35 05 92).*			
Grand Carillon du Château	*Guided tours by appt. at the Tourist Office. Concerts Sat. 10.30am and 6pm.*			
Les Charmettes ☎ 04 79 33 39 44	*Guided tours April–Sept. 10am–noon and 2–6pm, Oct.–March 10am–noon and 2–4.30pm. Closed Tues. and pub. hols.*			▲ 130 ▲ 129
Médiathèque Jean-Jacques Rousseau Carré Currial	*Open Tues., Thur. and Fri. 1.30–7pm, Wed. and Sat., 10am–6pm. From Oct. to March additional opening on the 3rd Sun. of the month 2–6pm.*			▲ 126
Musée des Beaux-Arts Place du Palais-de-Justice ☎ 04 79 33 75 03	*Open 10am–noon and 2–6pm. Closed Tues. and pub. hols.*			
Musée Savoisien Square de Lannoy-de-Bissy ☎ 04 79 33 44 48	*Open 10am–noon and 2–6pm. Closed Tues. and pub. hols.*			▲ 126
Patrimoine en Lumière 'Chambéry, Ville Lumière'	*Guided tours of the Palais de Justice, Musée Savoisien and Musée des Beaux-Arts, cathedral and Carré Curial by guides recognized by the French Ministry of Culture. Aug. 1–Sept. 15: Mon. and Thur. 9pm. Rest of year: group visits by appt. at the Tourist Office.*			
Quartier Curial	*Guided tours by appt. at the Tourist Office.*			▲ 129
MONTMÉLIAN	**73800**	*M 04 79 84 07 31*	**C5**	
Town, fort, museum	*Guided tours (by appt.) by the association Les Amis de Montmélian (☎ 04 79 84 25 73)*			▲ 133
MYANS	**73800**	*M 04 79 28 11 69*	**C5**	
Église Notre-Dame ☎ 04 79 28 11 65	*Open 6am–7pm.*			▲ 132
SAINT-PIERRE-D'ALBIGNY	**73250**	*OT 04 79 71 44 07*	**D5**	
Château de Miolans ☎ 04 79 28 57 04	*Open July–Aug.: daily 10am–7pm; May–June and Sept.: daily 10am–noon and 1.30–7pm; April: guided tours Sat., Sun. and pub. hols. 1.30–7pm. Group visits throughout the year by appt.*			▲ 133
SAINT-PIERRE-D'ENTREMONT	**73670**	*OT 04 79 65 81 90*	**B5**	
Château de Montbel	*Unrestricted access via the GR 9.*			▲ 134
YENNE	**73170**	*OT 04 79 36 71 54*	**A3**	
Church	*Open throughout the day. Guided tours by appt. at the Tourist Office.*			▲ 136

AIX-LES-BAINS–LAC DU BOURGET

Place	Details		Map	Page
AIX-LES-BAINS	**73100**	*SI 04 79 36 05 92*	**B3**	
Aquarium and Maison du lac Petit-Port ☎ 04 79 61 08 22	*Open July–Aug.: daily 10–11am and 2–7pm; May–June: daily 2–6pm; Sept.–Nov. and Feb.–April: Sat., Sun. and pub. hols:. 2–5pm, Wed. and school hols.: 2–4pm.*			
Casino Grand Cercle ☎ 04 79 35 16 16	*Open Mon.–Thur. and Sun.: noon–3am, Fri.–Sat. noon–4am. Guided tours (by appt.) by the guides of the Fil de l'Eau (☎ 04 79 35 05 92).*			▲ 142
Musée Faure 10, boulevard des Côtes ☎ 04 79 61 06 57	*Open 10am–noon and 1.30–6pm. Closed Tues., pub. hols. and Dec. 20–Jan. 4. Guided tours (by appt.) by the guides of the Fil de l'Eau (☎ 04 79 35 05 92).*			

Site	Information		Map	Page
Palace-Hotels of Aix	*Guided tours (by appt.) by the guides of the Fil de l'Eau (☎ 04 79 35 05 92), taking in the Splendide, Excelsior, Bernascon, Grand Hôtel, Astoria, and the Château de la Roche du Roi. The Chalet Charcot is not open to the public.*			▲ 142
Parc des Thermes	*Open to the public.*			▲ 142
Thermes Marlioz ☎ 04 79 61 79 61	*Open Mon.–Fri. 8am–noon and 2–4.30pm, Sat. 8am–noon and Sun. 9–11.30am. Guided tours (by appt.) by the guides of the Fil de l'Eau (☎ 04 79 35 05 92).*			▲ 140
Public baths, Roman baths and thermal springs ☎ 04 79 35 38 50	*Guided tours in season: Tues.–Sat. 3pm; low season once or twice a week at 3pm.*			▲ 141
Villa Chevalley	*Not open to the public.*			▲ 142
Villa de Solms	*Not open to the public.*			▲ 142
BOURDEAU	**73370**	*M 04 79 25 03 41*	**B3**	
Château de Bourdeau	*Privately owned: not open to the public.*			▲ 145
Grotte de Lamartine	*Unrestricted access.*			▲ 145
BRISON-SAINT-INNOCENT	**73310**	*M 04 79 54 33 60*	**C3**	
Maison Despine	*Open on Heritage Days (journées du patrimoine).*			▲ 150
CHANAZ	**73310**	*M 04 79 54 57 50*	**B2**	
Portout pottery works ☎ 04 79 54 26 01	*Open throughout the year. Spring: guided tours for groups by appt. Special events in summer.*			▲ 149
Maison de Boigne Town hall	*Open on Heritage Days (journées du patrimoine).*			▲ 150
CHAUTAGNE	**73310**	*OT 04 79 54 54 72*	**B2**	
Chemin du Terroir	*Signposted tourist route; meet local producers (wine growers, beekeepers, millers, farmers).*			
Peupleraie ☎ 04 79 54 27 10	*Tours by appointment.*			
CHINDRIEUX	**73310**	*M 04 79 54 20 36*	**B2**	
Château de Châtillon ☎ 04 79 54 28 15	*Gardens open Easter–Whitsun: Wed. 2–5pm.*			▲ 150
LE BOURGET-DU-LAC	**73370**	*OT 04 79 25 01 99*	**B3**	
Château de Thomas II	*Individual guided tours July–Aug.; group tours throughout the year by appt. Info. from Tourist Office.*			
Priory, Église Saint-Laurent, crypt, cloisters	*Church, cloisters and gardens: open daily. Full guided tour July–Aug.; throughout the year by appt. at the Tourist Office. Bird-watching observatory. Contact FRAPNA: (☎ 04 79 85 31 79)*			▲ 145
SAINT-PIERRE-DE-CURTILLE	**73310**	*OT 04 79 54 25 48*	**B3**	
Abbaye de Hautecombe ☎ 04 79 54 26 12	*Audio guided tour 10–11.00am and 2–6pm. Closed Tues.*			▲ 145
MASSIF DES BAUGES, THE ALBANAIS				
AILLON-LE-JEUNE	**73340**	*OT 04 79 54 63 65*	**C4**	
Chartreuse d'Aillon	*Tours in July–Aug., with a Heritage guide. Info. from Tourist Office.*			
ALBY-SUR-CHÉRAN	**74540**	*OT 04 50 68 11 99*	**C5**	
Église Notre-Dame-de-Plainpalais Opposite the maison de Pays	*Open throughout the day.*			▲ 158
Musée de la Cordonnerie Town hall	*For opening times and guided tours by Heritage guides contact the Tourist Office.*			
ALLÈVES	**74540**	*M 04 50 77 54 92*	**C9**	
Grotte de Banges Hameau de Martinod	*Dangerous access.*			▲ 153
BELLECOMBE-EN-BAUGES	**73346**	*OT 04 79 54 84 28*	**D3**	
Sawmill at grand cadre	*Group tours by appt.; contact the Association Oxalis (☎ 04 79 63 36 97).*			▲ 154

◆ MASSIF DES BAUGES, THE ALBANAIS, ANNECY, THE SHORES OF THE LAC D'ANNECY

KEY TO PREFIXES
M : mairie (town hall)
OT : office de tourisme (tourist office)
SI : syndicat d'initiative (tourist bureau)
MT : maison du tourisme (tourist center)

CLÉRY	**73460** *M 04 79 38 59 69* **E4**	
ÉGLISE SAINT-JEAN-BAPTISTE	*Key at the town hall.*	▲ 156
LE CHÂTELARD	**73630** *OT 04 79 54 84 28* **D3**	
COVERED MARKET (GRENETTE)	*Open 10am–noon and 3–7pm.* *Closed Sept.–June: Mon.–Fri.*	▲ 156
MAISON DES BAUGES Place de la Grenette ☎ 04 79 54 84 28	*Open Mon.–Sat.: 9am–noon and 2–6pm.*	
ÉGLISE SAINT-JEAN-BAPTISTE	*Evening tour in July–Aug., included in the tour of the village. Info. from the Maison des Bauges.*	▲ 156
LE SEMNOZ	**74** **C8**	
MAISON DU SEMNOZ ☎ 04 50 01 19 41	*Open July–Aug.: daily noon–6.30pm.* *Group tours by appt. in June and Sept.* *Situated on the car park, below the summit.*	▲ 157
LOVAGNY	**74330** *M 04 50 46 23 37* **C7**	
CHÂTEAU DE MONTROTTIER ☎ 04 50 46 23 02	*Open June–Aug.: daily 9.30am–noon and 2–6pm; March 15–May and Sept.–Oct. 15: Mon., Wed.–Sun. 9.30am–noon and 2–6pm.*	▲ 158
GORGES DU FIER ☎ 04 50 46 23 07	*Open July–Sept. 15: daily 9am–7pm; March 15–May and Sept. 16–Oct. 15: daily 9am–noon and 2–6pm.*	▲ 158
MERCURY	**73200** *M 04 79 32 30 17* **E3**	
CHURCH	*Tours July–Aug.: Wed. 6pm, meet in front of the church. Info. from town hall.*	▲ 156
CASTLE	*Privately owned: not open to the public.*	▲ 156
PLANCHERINE	**73200** *M 04 79 32 46 02* **E3**	
ABBAYE DE TAMIÉ ☎ 04 79 31 15 50	*Church: open daily throughout the year.* *Reception center with slide shows: open in summer: 10am–noon and 2.30–6pm; Oct.–April: 10am–noon and 2.30–5pm. Closed Sun. am and Mon. am.*	▲ 156
RUMILLY	**74150** *OT 04 50 64 58 32* **B7**	
ÉGLISE SAINTE-AGATHE	*Open 8am–7.30pm.*	▲ 158
MUSÉE DE L'ALBANAIS Avenue Gantin ☎ 04 50 01 19 53	*Open July–Aug.: 10am–noon and 3–7pm.* *June and Sept. 1–15: 9–11am and 2–6pm.* *Closed Tues.*	▲ 158

ANNECY, THE SHORES OF THE LAC D'ANNECY

ANNECY	**74000** *OT 04 50 45 00 33* **C7**	
TOURIST OFFICE Centre Bonlieu 1, rue Jean-Jaurès ☎ 04 50 45 00 33	*Guided tour of Old Annecy and theme tours.*	
BASILIQUE DE LA VISITATION 11, avenue de la Visitation	*Open 7am–noon and 2–8.30pm (summer), 6pm (winter). Tours of the carillon: mid-June–mid-Sept.: Sat. 4pm. Group tours by appt. (☎ 04 50 66 17 37).*	▲ 171
CATHÉDRALE SAINT-PIERRE 13, rue J.–J.–Rousseau	*Open throughout the day.*	▲ 170
CONSERVATOIRE D'ART ET D'HISTOIRE 1, avenue du Trésum ☎ 04 50 51 02 33	*Open Mon.–Fri. 9am–noon and 2–6pm, Sat. 10am–noon and 2–6pm. Closed Sat. (except during exhibitions) and Sun.*	▲ 171
ÉGLISE SAINT-FRANÇOIS 4, place Saint-Maurice	*Open throughout the day.* *Mass in Italian: Sun. 10.30am.*	▲ 169
ÉGLISE SAINT-MAURICE Place de l'Hôtel-de-Ville	*Open throughout the day.*	▲ 168
SAINT-FRANÇOIS-DE-SALES MEMORIAL Quai du Semnoz	*Not open to the public.*	▲ 171
MUSÉE-CHÂTEAU Place du Château ☎ 04 50 33 87 30	*Open June–Sept.: daily 10am–6pm; Oct.–May: Mon., Wed.–Sun. 10am–noon and 2–6pm.* *Guided tours by appt. throughout the year.*	▲ 164
PALAIS DE L'ÎLE MUSÉE D'HISTOIRE D'ANNECY Passage de l'Île ☎ 04 50 33 87 30	*Open June–Sept.: daily 10am–6pm; Oct.–May: Mon., Wed.–Sun. 10am–noon and 2–6pm. Guided tours by appt. throughout the year.*	▲ 168
ANNECY-LE-VIEUX	**74940** *M 04 50 23 86 00* **C7**	
ÉGLISE SAINT-LAURENT Rue Jean-Mermoz	*Open 8.30am–6.30pm.* *Key to the belfry at the town hall.*	▲ 173

Site	Information	Page
VILLA DE LA TOUR Lieu-dit Petit-Port	*Privately owned: not open to the public.*	▲ 173
VILLA DUNAND Rue Jean-Mermoz	*Town hall administrative offices: not open to the public.*	▲ 173
DOUSSARD	**74210** M 04 50 44 30 45	**D8**
RÉSERVE DU BOUT DU LAC Access via the hamlet of Verthier	*Unrestricted access with a signposted route.*	▲ 173
DUINGT	**74410** OT 04 50 68 67 07	**D8**
CASTLE RN 508	*Privately owned: not open to the public.*	▲ 172
FAVERGES	**74210** OT 04 50 44 60 24	**F9**
LES AMIS DE FAVERGES M. Michel Duret ☎ 04 50 32 45 99	*Group tour of the Gallo-Roman villa, the Église Saint-Jean-Baptiste and the Musée de Viuz-Faverges.*	
CASTLE	*Privately owned: holiday center.*	▲ 173
ÉGLISE SAINT-JEAN-BAPTISTE Viuz	*Tours organized by Les Amis de Faverges.*	
MUSÉE DE VIUZ-FAVERGES Route de Viuz	*Open July–Aug.: Mon.–Sun. 2.30–6.30pm; Sept.–June: Mon.–Fri. 2.30–6.30pm.*	▲ 173
GALLO-ROMAN VILLA	*Tours organized by Les Amis de Faverges.*	▲ 173
SÉVRIER	**74320** OT 04 50 52 40 56	**C7**
ÉCOMUSÉE DU COSTUME SAVOYARD Place de l'Église ☎ 04 50 52 41 05	*Open June–Sept.: Tues.–Sat. 10am–noon and 2.30–6.30pm, Sun. 2.30–6.30pm. Group tours throughout the year by appt.*	▲ 172
MUSÉE DE LA CLOCHE RN 508 ☎ 04 50 52 47 11	*Museum: Tues.–Sat. 10am–noon and 2.30–5.30pm, Sun. 2.30–5.30pm. Closed Dec. 1–15. Foundry: April–Oct.: Fri. and Sun. 2.30–5.30pm, Sat. 10am–noon and 2.30–5.30pm.*	▲ 172
SEYTHENEX	**74210** M 04 50 44 51 51	**E9**
CAVE AND WATERFALL ☎ 04 50 44 55 97	*Open end May–mid-Sept.: daily. Guided tour of the cave.*	▲ 173
TALLOIRES	**74290** OT 04 50 60 70 64	**D8**
BENEDICTINE ABBEY	*Now a hotel-restaurant.*	▲ 176
CHAPELLE SAINT-GERMAIN Plateau de Saint-Germain	*Open throughout the day.*	▲ 176
PRIORY Route de la Colombière	*Privately owned: not open to the public.*	▲ 176
RÉSERVE ROC DE CHÈRE	*Unrestricted access.*	

LES ARAVIS

Site	Information	Page
ALEX	**74290** M 04 50 02 87 05	**D7**
ÉGLISE NOTRE-DAME	*Key at the town hall.*	▲ 185
DINGY-SAINT-CLAIR	**74230** M 04 50 02 06 27	**D7**
ÉGLISE SAINT-ÉTIENNE	*If closed, key at the farm, opposite the church.*	▲ 185
ENTREMONT	**74130** M 04 50 03 51 90	**F6**
CHURCH 200 yards from the baker's	*Open May–Oct.: 9am–6pm or by appt. with M. Albert Pessay (☎ 04 50 03 52 18).*	▲ 182
LA BALME-DE-THUY	**74230** M 04 50 02 16 89	**D7**
EXCAVATION About 400 yards from the village toward Thônes	*Guided tour July–Aug.: Thur. afternoon. Info. from Tourist Office in Thônes (☎ 04 50 02 00 26).*	▲ 185
LA CLUSAZ	**74220** OT 04 50 32 65 00	**F7**
CHAPELLE SAINTE-ANNE Col des Aravis	*Open in summer.*	▲ 179
ÉGLISE SAINTE-FOY	*Open throughout the day. Concerts in summer.*	▲ 181
LE GRAND-BORNAND	**74450** OT 04 50 02 78 00	**F6**
CHAPELLE NOTRE-DAME-DES-NEIGES Village of Chinaillon	*Tour included in the tour of old Chinaillon, by appt. at the Maison du Patrimoine.*	▲ 181
MAISON DU PATRIMOINE Next to the ice rink ☎ 04 50 02 79 18	*Open July–Aug.: Tues.–Sat. 10am–noon and 3–5.30pm, Sun. 4–7pm; Dec.–April: school holidays. Mon.–Fri. 5–7pm; term time Tues. and Fri. 5–7pm.Themed exhibitions.*	▲ 181
MAISON DU REBLOCHON	*Opening planned for 2000; info. from town hall (☎ 04 50 02 78 20).*	

◆ LES ARAVIS, THE GENEVOIS, LAKE GENEVA

KEY TO PREFIXES
M: mairie (town hall)
OT: office de tourisme (tourist office)
SI: syndicat d'initiative (tourist bureau)
MT: maison du tourisme (tourist center)

LES VILLARDS-SUR-THÔNES	**74230** M 04 50 02 07 88	**E7**	
ÉGLISE SAINT-LAURENT	*Irregular opening times.*		
MANIGOD	**74230** OT 04 50 44 92 44	**E7**	
ÉGLISE SAINT-PIERRE	*If closed, enquire at the town hall (☎ 04 50 44 90 20).*		▲ 185
STANDING STONE OF LA CROIX-FRY RD 16	*Unrestricted access.* *In front of the Maison de la Ruche.*		▲ 184
THÔNES	**74230** OT 04 50 02 00 26	**E7**	
ÉCOMUSÉE DU BOIS ET DE LA FORÊT Sawmill at Les Étouvières Toward Montremont	*Tours July–Aug.: Mon., Tues., Thur., Fri. and Sun. (if raining) 11am and 3pm, Wed. 2pm (book at the Tourist Office); April–June and Sept.–Oct.: Tues. and Thur. 4pm; off season group tours by appt. at the Tourist Office.*		▲ 183
ÉGLISE SAINT-MAURICE	*Open throughout the day.*		▲ 183
MANOIR DE LA TOUR Martinet	*Privately owned: not open to the public.*		
MUSÉE DÉPARTEMENTAL DE LA RÉSISTANCE Morette ☎ 04 50 02 08 14	*Open June 15–Sept. 15: daily 10am–noon and 2–7pm.*		▲ 185
MUSÉE DU PAYS DE THÔNES 2, rue Blanche ☎ 04 50 02 97 76	*Open July–Aug.: Mon.–Sat. 10am–noon and 3–7pm; off season: Thur. and Fri. 9am–noon, Mon., Wed. and Sat. 9am–noon and 1.30–5.30pm.*		▲ 183
THORENS-GLIÈRES	**74570** OT 04 50 71 55 55	**D6**	
CASTLE Dir. plateau des Glières ☎ 04 50 22 42 02	*Open May–June and Sept.: Sat., Sun. and pub. hols. 2–6pm; July–Aug.: daily 10am–noon and 2–6pm.*		▲ 186
GILIOLI MONUMENT Plateau des Glières	*About 15 mins. from the village.*		▲ 186

THE GENEVOIS

ANDILLY	**74350** M 04 50 44 21 43	**C5**	
CHAPEL Village of Charly	*Key at the house next to the chapel.*		
CHAUMONT	**74270** M 04 50 44 73 01	**B6**	
CASTLE	*Tours July–Aug.: Fri. 5pm; off season by appt., taken by Heritage guides:* *Mme Marie-Christine Baudet (☎ 04 50 44 71 18) or Mme Denise Revillon (☎ 04 50 44 72 04).*		▲ 190
CHEVRIER	**74520** M 04 50 04 37 45	**B5**	
CHAPEL Near the War Museum	*Open on Heritage Days (journées du patrimoine).*		▲ 189
CLERMONT	**74270** OT 04 50 32 26 40	**B6**	
CASTLE ☎ 04 50 69 63 15	*Open June–Sept.: daily 10.30am–noon and 1.30–6.30pm; May and Sept. 1–15: Sat., Sun. and pub. hols.*		▲ 190
FRANGY	**74270** OT 04 50 69 63 69	**B6**	
CHURCH	*Open throughout the day.*		▲ 190
MARLIOZ	**74270** M 04 50 77 84 22	**C6**	
CHÂTEAU DE SALLENÔVES	*Open on Heritage Days (journées du patrimoine).*		▲ 190

LAKE GENEVA

ALLINGES	**74200** M 04 50 71 21 18	**F3**	
CHÂTEAUX DES ALLIGNES ☎ 04 50 71 22 12	*Open daily 8.30am–7pm.*		▲ 193
AMPHION-LES-BAINS	**74500** M 04 50 70 82 14	**F2**	
VILLA BASSARABA RN 5 1½ miles from Amphion	*Privately owned: not open to the public.*		▲ 196
ÉVIAN-LES-BAINS	**74500** OT 04 50 75 04 26	**G2**	
BUVETTE DE LA SOURCE CACHAT 19, rue Nationale	*First floor: exhibition on mineral water. Open beginning May–mid-June and Sept. 15–30: 2.30–6.30pm; mid-June–mid-Sept.: 10.30am–12.30pm and 3–7pm. Tours of the bottling factory.*		▲ 196
CASINO Quai Baron-de-Blonay	*Open daily 10am–2am.*		▲ 197

Site	Information	Page
Église Notre-Dame-de-l'Assomption Rue du lac	*Open 9am–6pm.*	▲ 196
Établissement Thermal The Évian spring Place de la Libération ☎ 04 50 75 02 30	*Open mid-Feb.–mid-Nov.: Mon.–Sat. 9am–noon and 2.30–7pm.* *Visits May–Sept.: Mon.–Sat. 4pm.*	
Villa Lumière Rue de Clermont	*Historical part of the villa open: Mon.–Fri. 9–11.30am and 1.30–5pm. Open to visitors on Heritage Days (journées du patrimoine).*	▲ 197
THONON-LES-BAINS	**74200** OT 04 50 71 55 55 **F2**	
Tourist Office Place du Marché ☎ 04 50 71 55 55	*Scenic tour of the Chablais, taking in frescos, local history and exploration of the Réserve Naturelle de la Dranse.*	
Couvent des Minimes Rue Hôtel-Dieu	*Former convent due to become the court building.*	▲ 194
Château de Ripaille Quai de Ripaille – Rives ☎ 04 50 26 64 44	*Castle: open Feb.–March and Oct.–Nov.: 3pm; April–June, Sept.: 11am, 2.30pm, 4pm; July–Aug.: 11am, 2.30pm, 3pm, 3.30pm, 4pm, 4.30pm and 5pm.*	▲ 195
Fondation Ripaille	*Tours of the Réserve Naturelle du Delta de la Dranse organized by FRAPNA (☎ 04 79 85 31 79).*	▲ 195
Arboretum Chemin de la Forêt – Rives ☎ 04 50 26 28 22	*Open May–Sept.: Tues.–Sun. 10am–7pm; Oct.–April: Tues.–Sun. 10am–4.30pm. Closed Dec.*	
Musée du Chablais Château de Sonnaz Place de l'Hôtel-de-Ville ☎ 04 50 70 26 96	*Open July–Aug.: daily 10am–noon and 2.30–6.30pm; Sept.: Tues.–Sun. 2.30–6.30pm.* *Group tours by appt. throughout the year.*	▲ 195
Église Saint-Hippolyte Grande-Rue	*Open June 15–30 and Sept. 1–15: 3–7pm; July–Aug.: 10am–noon and 3–7pm.*	▲ 195
Établissement Thermal Boulevard de la Corniche ☎ 04 50 26 17 22	*Guided tours for groups throughout the year by appt.*	
Monastère de la Visitation Place du Marché	*Temporary exhibitions, library, Tourist Office.*	▲ 194
YVOIRE	**74140** M 04 50 72 80 21 **E2**	
Jardin des Cinq Sens Rue du Lac ☎ 04 50 72 88 80	*Open mid-April–mid-May: 11am–6pm; mid-May–end Sept.: 10am–7pm; end Sept.–mid-Oct.: 1–5pm.*	▲ 193

THE CHABLAIS

Site	Information	Page
ABONDANCE	**74360** OT 04 50 73 02 90 **H3**	
Tourist Office ☎ 04 50 73 02 90	*Themed excursions: visits to the mountain pastures and farms where cheese is made; cheese tastings.*	
Abbaye Notre-Dame-de-l'Assomption ☎ 04 50 81 60 54	*Church: closed during services.* *Cloisters: open May–Oct. 15: daily 10am–noon and 2–6pm; Dec. 15–April: daily 10am–noon, 2–5pm.*	▲ 202
BOËGE	**74420** M 04 50 39 10 01 **E4**	
Church	*Open throughout the day.*	▲ 210
BURDIGNIN	**74420** M 04 50 39 11 86 **F4**	
Church	*If closed, key from Mme Dupraz, opposite the town hall.*	▲ 210
LA CHAPELLE-D'ABONDANCE	**74360** OT 04 50 73 51 41 **H3**	
Tourist Office ☎ 04 50 73 51 41	*Info. for visits to a farm making Abondance cheese.*	
Church	*Open Mon.–Thur. and Sat.–Sun. until 6pm.*	▲ 203
LA FORCLAZ	**74200** M 04 50 71 76 44 **G3**	
Church	*Open throughout the day.*	▲ 209
LA VERNAZ	**74200** M 04 50 72 10 40 **G3**	
Gorges du Pont du Diable **Gorges de la Dranse** RD 902 ☎ 04 50 72 10 39	*Open July–Aug.: 9am–7pm; May–June and Sept.: 9am–6.30pm.*	▲ 209
LES GETS	**74260** OT 04 50 75 80 80 **G4**	
Church	*Open throughout the day. In season, guided tours of the organ organized by the museum.*	▲ 207

◆ THE CHABLAIS, VALLÉE DU GIFFRE AND THE FAUCIGNY

KEY TO PREFIXES
M : mairie (town hall)
OT : office de tourisme (tourist office)
SI : syndicat d'initiative (tourist bureau)
MT : maison du tourisme (tourist center)

MUSÉE DE LA MUSIQUE MÉCANIQUE ☎ 04 50 79 85 75	*Open July–Aug.: 10am–noon and 2.30–7pm; off season: 2.30–7pm. Closed Nov.–Dec. 20.*		▲ *207*
MONTRIOND	**74110**	*OT 04 50 79 12 81*	**G4**
CASCADE D'ARDENT	*Unrestricted access, difficult in winter. Dir. of the lake, about 1½ miles (2 km) from the village, turn along a small path on the right, 100 yds after an avalanche barrier.*		▲ *206*
CHURCH	*Open throughout the day. If the main door is closed, use the side door.*		▲ *206*
MORZINE	**74110**	*OT 04 50 74 72 72*	**H4**
CHAPEL Village of Avoriaz	*Service: in summer: Sun. 6pm.*		▲ *207*
ÉGLISE SAINTE-MARIE-MADELEINE	*Open throughout the day.*		
SAINT-JEAN-D'AULPS	**74430**	*OT 04 50 79 65 09*	**G3**
ABBAYE D'AULPS	*Church: open throughout the day. Abbey: guided tours May, June and Sept.: Sat., Sun. and pub. hols. 4pm; July–Aug.: Info on 04 50 72 16 16 or from Tourist Office.*		▲ *208*
VACHERESSE	**74360**	*M 04 50 73 10 18*	**G3**
CHAPELLE DU VILLARD Village of Villard	*Open on request by Mme Germaine Tupin-Bron, house opposite the chapel.*		
VILLARD	**74420**	*M 04 50 39 12 40*	**F4**
CHURCH	*If closed, key from Mme Madeleine Delavoet.*		▲ *210*

VALLÉE DU GIFFRE AND THE FAUCIGNY

BONNEVILLE	**74130**	*OT 04 50 97 38 37*	**E5**
CHÂTEAU DE BÉATRICE Avenue du Coteau	*Under restoration; not open to the public.*		
ÉGLISE SAINTE-CATHERINE	*Open throughout the day.*		▲ *221*
MUSÉE DÉPARTEMENTAL DE LA RÉSISTANCE Rue Sainte-Catherine ☎ 04 50 97 07 48	*Open Wed. and Sat. 2–6pm. Group visits by appt.*		▲ *221*
CLUSES	**74300**	*OT 04 50 98 31 79*	**G5**
ÉGLISE SAINT-NICOLAS 4, rue de l'Hôtel-de-Ville	*Open 9am–7pm.*		▲ *222*
MUSÉE DE L'HORLOGERIE ET DU DÉCOLLETAGE Espace Carpano-et-Pons 100, place du 11-Novembre	*Open 10am–noon and 2–6pm. Closed July–Aug.: Sun. am; off season: Sun. Group visits Sun. by appt.*		▲ *222*
CONTAMINE-SUR-ARVE	**74130**	*M 04 50 03 60 17*	**E5**
CHURCH Road opposite the post office	*Guided tour July–Aug.: Tues. pm; off season by appt. with M. Michel Pessey (☎ 04 50 03 70 11).*		▲ *220*
PRIORY	*Now a college.*		▲ *220*
CORNIER	**74800**	*M 04 50 25 55 49*	**E5**
COMMANDERIE DE MOUSSY	*Private property; not open to the public.*		▲ *219*
ÉVIRES	**74570**	*M 04 50 62 01 72*	**D6**
GLAZED POTTERY Famille Hermann Follow the signpost ☎ 04 50 62 01 90	*Workshop: visits by appt. Shop: open 8–11am and 1.30–7pm. Museum: open Easter–Whitsun: visits by appt.*		▲ *220*
LA ROCHE-SUR-FORON	**74800**	*OT 04 50 03 36 68*	**E5**
TOURIST OFFICE Place André-Vétan ☎ 04 50 03 36 68	*Guided tour of the medieval town and visit to the tower of the counts of Geneva. Tower: open June 15–Sept. 15: daily 10am–noon and 2–6.30pm.*		
CASTLE Quartier du Plain-Château	*Open during shows and exhibitions. Info. from Tourist Office.*		▲ *219*
CHÂTEAU DE L'ÉCHELLE Quartier du Plain-Château	*Open on certain Heritage Days; Info. from Tourist Office.*		▲ *219*
CHÂTEAU DU SAIX Rue du Plain-Château	*Open throughout the day.*		▲ *219*
ÉGLISE SAINT-JEAN-BAPTISTE Place Saint-Jean	*Open throughout the day.*		▲ *219*

VALLÉE DU GIFFRE & THE FAUCIGNY, PAYS DU MONT-BLANC, VAL D'ARLY, THE BEAUFORTAIN

Site	Information	Page
LE REPOSOIR	**74950** — *SI 04 50 98 18 01* — **F6**	
CHARTREUSE DU REPOSOIR ☎ 04 50 98 29 31	*Open summer: 8.30am–noon and 2.30–6.30pm, 5.30pm in winter. Guided tours – by appt. at the Syndicat d'Initiative – by Heritage guides.*	▲ 221
MARNAZ	**74460** — *M 04 50 98 35 05* — **F5**	
GLAZED POTTERY Maison Guyot Rue de la Poterie ☎ 04 50 98 35 49	*Shop and workshop: open July–Aug.: Mon.–Sat. 7am–noon and 1.30–6.30pm, Sun. 9am–noon and 2–6.30pm; off season: Mon.–Sat. 7am–noon and 1.30–6.30pm. Closed 2 wks. between end Sept. and beginning Oct.*	▲ 220
MIEUSSY	**74440** — *OT 04 50 43 02 72* — **F4**	
CHURCH	*Open throughout the day.*	▲ 219
CONSERVATION ORCHARD Hameau de Saint-Denis ☎ 04 50 43 05 64	*Apple and pear orchard. Tours by appt.*	▲ 213
MORILLON	**74440** — *OT 04 50 90 15 76* — **G5**	
ÉGLISE SAINT-CHRISTOPHE Village	*If closed, enquire at the Tourist Office. Tours by Heritage guides.*	▲ 214
SAINT-JEOIRE-EN-FAUCIGNY	**74490** — *OT 04 50 35 91 83* — **F5**	
CHÂTEAU DE BEAUREGARD	*Privately owned: not open to the public.*	▲ 220
ÉGLISE SAINT-GEORGES	*Open throughout the day.*	
SALLANCHES	**74700** — *OT 04 5058 04 25* — **G7**	
ÉGLISE SAINT-JACQUES	*Open throughout the day, entrance through side door.*	▲ 222
SAMOËNS	**74340** — *OT 04 50 34 40 28* — **H5**	
TOURIST OFFICE ☎ 04 50 34 40 28	*Tour of the historic town and of the surrounding hamlets.*	
CHÂTEAU DE LA TOUR Next to the church	*Conference rooms of the town hall: not open to the public.*	▲ 214
ÉGLISE NOTRE-DAME-DE-L'ASSOMPTION	*Open throughout the day.*	▲ 214
GOUFFRE JEAN-BERNARD	*Open only to speleologists.*	▲ 215
ALPINE GARDEN 'LA JAŸSINIA' Place du Jardin-Botanique ☎ 04 50 34 49 86	*Open May–Sept.: daily 8am–noon and 1.30–7pm; Oct.–April: daily 8am–noon and 1.30–5.30pm. Closed during snowfalls and when icy.*	▲ 215
SIXT-FER-À-CHEVAL	**74740** — *OT 04 50 34 49 36* — **H5**	
ABBAYE AND ÉGLISE SAINTE-MADELEINE	*Tours organized by Heritage guides: school hols: Tues. and for groups throughout the year by appt. at the Tourist Office.*	▲ 215
MAISON ALLAMANS Near the presbytery	*Privately owned: not open to the public.*	▲ 215
RÉSERVE DE SIXT	*Maison de la Réserve (in the village): open July–Aug. and school hols.: daily 9am–12.30pm and 2.30–7pm; off season: daily 9am–noon and 2–6pm. Chalet de la Réserve (Cirque du Fer-à-Cheval): open July–Sept.: 2–6pm.*	▲ 216
TANINGES	**74440** — *OT 04 50 34 25 05* — **G5**	
CHARTREUSE DE MÉLAN Village of Mélan	*Open during exhibitions: daily 3–7pm. Off season: group tours by appt. at the Tourist Office.*	▲ 214
ÉGLISE SAINT-JEAN-BAPTISTE	*Open throughout the day: entrance by the post office.*	▲ 213
VIUZ-EN-SALLAZ	**74250** — *M 04 50 36 80 39* — **E4**	
MUSÉE PAYSAN ☎ 04 50 36 89 18	*Open throughout the year: Mon.–Sat. 9am–noon and 1.30–6.30pm; extra opening in season: Sun. 2–7pm.*	▲ 220

PAYS DU MONT-BLANC, VAL D'ARLY, THE BEAUFORTAIN

Site	Information	Page
ALBERTVILLE-CONFLANS	**73200** — *OT 04 79 32 04 22* — **E3**	
CHÂTEAU MANUEL DE LOCATEL	*Tours: July–Aug.: daily for individuals; group tours throughout the year by appt. with the Guides de Conflans (☎ 04 79 32 29 93).*	
ÉGLISE SAINT-GRAT	*Open daily 9am–7pm.*	▲ 248
MAISON ROUGE (MUSEUM) ☎ 04 79 32 57 42	*Open April–May: Mon., Wed.–Fri. 2–7pm, Sat.–Sun. 10am–noon and 2–7pm; June–Sept.: daily 10am–noon and 2–7pm; Oct. and school hols. (November): Mon., Wed.–Sun. 2–5pm; school hols. (Christmas, Feb. and Easter): daily 2–5pm. Guided tours throughout the year by appt.*	▲ 248

◆ PAYS DU MONT-BLANC, VAL D'ARLY, THE BEAUFORTAIN

KEY TO PREFIXES
M : mairie (town hall)
OT : office de tourisme (tourist office)
SI : syndicat d'initiative (tourist bureau)
MT : maison du tourisme (tourist center)

MAISON DES 16èmes JEUX OLYMPIQUES D'HIVER ☎ 04 79 37 75 71	*Open July–Aug.: Mon.–Sat. 9am–7pm, Sun. and pub. hols. 2–7pm; off season: Mon.–Sat. 9am–noon and 2–6pm.*	▲ *248*
ARÊCHES	**73270** *OT 04 79 38 15 33*	**G3**
ÉGLISE SAINT-JEAN-BAPTISTE ☎ 04 79 38 37 57	*Open throughout the day. Guided tour as part of the village tour during school hols.*	▲ *246*
ARGENTIÈRE	**74400** *M 04 50 54 02 14*	**I6**
CHURCH	*Open throughout the day.*	▲ *239*
CHAPEL Village of Le Tour	*Open throughout the day in summer.*	▲ *239*
BEAUFORT-SUR-DORON	**73270** *OT 04 79 38 37 57*	**G3**
DAIRY COOPERATIVE ☎ 04 79 38 33 62	*Open Mon.–Sat. 8am–noon and 2–6pm.*	▲ *245*
ÉGLISE SAINT-MAXIME	*Open throughout the day. Tours organized by FACIM.*	▲ *245*
CHAMONIX	**74400** *OT 04 50 53 02 25*	**I7**
TOURIST OFFICE 85, place du Triangle-de-l'Amitié ☎ 04 50 53 02 25	*Guided tours of Chamonix and tailor-made tours on request.*	
ANGLICAN CHAPEL Chemin du Temple	*Tours organized by Heritage guides (Claudie Apertet ☎ 04 50 53 03 38).*	▲ *237*
ÉGLISE SAINT-MICHEL	*Open throughout the day.*	▲ *237*
ENSA 35, route du Bouchet ☎ 04 50 55 30 30		▲ *236*
MAISON DE LA MONTAGNE 190, place de l'Église ☎ 04 50 53 00 88	*Office de la Haute Montagne, École de Ski Français. Compagnie des Guides: themed excursions: geology of the valley, glaciology, dinosaurs in the region (book the day before).*	▲ *237*
MER DE GLACE	*Musée de la Faune Alpine: 9.30am–4pm, Grotte du Glacier: 10am–4pm, Galerie des Cristaux: 9.30am–4pm. Opening times correspond to the Montenvers train. Inclusive tickets available.*	▲ *238*
MUSÉE ALPIN 89, avenue Michel-Croz ☎ 04 50 53 25 93	*Open June–Oct. 15: 2–7pm; Dec. 20–May 1: 3–7pm.*	▲ *237*
AIGUILLE DU MIDI CABLEWAY ☎ 04 50 53 30 80	*Open throughout the year.*	▲ *238*
MONTENVERS RAILROAD ☎ 04 50 53 12 54	*Open mid-Dec.–Nov. 15.*	▲ *238*
COMBLOUX	**74920** *OT 04 50 58 60 49*	**G7**
TOURIST OFFICE ☎ 04 50 58 60 49	*Exploring Combloux on foot: nature, history, heritage and cheese tasting.*	
ÉGLISE SAINT-NICOLAS-DE-COMBLOUX	*Open throughout the day.*	▲ *241*
SENTIER BAROQUE	*Marked footpath (about 12 miles) for hikers and mountain bikes. Starts from the church in Combloux.*	▲ *241*
FLUMET	**73590** *OT 04 79 31 61 08*	**F2**
ÉGLISE DE CHAUCISSE	*Open throughout the day. Tours organized by FACIM.*	▲ *243*
ÉGLISE SAINT-NICOLAS-LA-CHAPELLE	*Open throughout the day. Tours organized by FACIM.*	▲ *243*
FORTIFIED RESIDENCE OF THE COUNTS OF BIEUX	*Privately owned: not open to the public.*	▲ *243*
HAUTELUCE	**73620** *M 04 79 38 80 31*	**G3**
ÉCOMUSÉE ☎ 04 79 38 80 31	*Open July–Aug.: daily. Off season: admission by appt.*	▲ *245*
ÉGLISE SAINT-JACQUES-D'ASSYRIE	*Open throughout the day. Tours organized by FACIM.*	▲ *245*
LES CONTAMINES-MONTJOIE	**74170** *OT 04 50 47 01 58*	**H8**
CHAPELLE NOTRE-DAME-DE-LA-GORGE Notre-Dame-de-la-Gorge	*Open throughout the day.*	▲ *241*
RÉSERVE NATURELLE DES CONTAMINES	*Permanent exhibition, next to the post office: July–Aug.: Mon.–Sat. 10am–noon and 3–7pm, Sun. 3–7pm; off season: Mon.–Fri. 3–7pm. Info. ☎ 04 50 91 51 36.*	▲ *241*

Brochures giving details and times of tours and permanent exhibitions organized by FACIM (☎ 04 79 96 74 19) are available from Tourist Offices.

Site	Information	Map / Page
LES HOUCHES	**74310** *OT 04 50 55 50 62*	**H7**
ÉGLISE SAINT-JEAN-BAPTISTE	*Open throughout the day.* *Guided tours July–Aug.: Wed. 10am.*	▲ 224
MUSÉE MONTAGNARD 2, place de l'Église ☎ 04 50 54 54 74	*Open school hols.: Mon., Wed., Fri. 3–6.30pm;* *term time: Mon., Thur. 3–6pm.*	
ORATOIRE NOTRE-DAME-DES-VOYAGEURS Village of Les Chavants	*Unrestricted access.*	▲ 225
MERLET NATURE RESERVE Le Coupeau ☎ 04 50 55 52 19	*Open July–Aug.: 9.30am–8pm;* *May–June and Sept.: 10am–6pm.*	▲ 225
MEGÈVE	**74120** *OT 04 50 21 27 28*	**G7**
CALVARY	*Tours organized by Heritage guides.* *Info. from Tourist Office.*	
ÉGLISE SAINT-JEAN-BAPTISTE	*Open 9am–6.30pm.*	▲ 242
MUSÉE DU HAUT-VAL-D'ARLY 88, rue du Vieux-Marché ☎ 04 50 91 81 00	*Open June 20–Sept. and Dec. 20–April: Mon., Wed.–Sun. 2.30–6.30pm.*	
PASSY	**74480** *OT 04 50 58 80 52*	**H7**
ÉGLISE NOTRE-DAME-DE-TOUTE-GRÂCE Village of Le Plateau d'Assy	*Open throughout the day.*	▲ 240
QUEIGE	**73780** *M 04 79 38 00 91*	**F3**
ÉGLISE SAINTE-AGATHE	*Open in summer, with tours organized by FACIM.*	▲ 244
SAINT-GERVAIS-LES-BAINS	**74170** *OT 04 50 47 76 08*	**H7**
ÉGLISE DE SAINT-GERVAIS Opposite the town hall	*Open throughout the day.*	▲ 241
ÉGLISE SAINT-NICOLAS Viillage of Saint-Nicolas-de-Véroce	*Open throughout the day.*	▲ 241
THERMAL SPRINGS Village of Le Fayet ☎ 04 50 47 54 54	*Open daily 8am–12.30pm and 2–8pm.*	▲ 240
SERVOZ	**74310** *OT 04 50 47 21 68*	**H7**
CHURCH	*Open throughout the day.*	
GORGES DE LA DIOSAZ Allée des Gorges	*Open July–Aug.: daily 9am–6.30pm;* *May–June and Sept.–Oct.: daily 10am–5pm.* *Info.: Mme Albertine Mugnier (☎ 04 50 47 21 13).*	▲ 224
UGINE	**73400** *OT 04 79 37 56 33*	**F3**
CHÂTEAU DE CREST-CHEREL (MUSÉE D'ARTS ET DE TRADITIONS POPULAIRES DU VAL D'ARLY)	*Open June 15–Sept..15: daily 2–6pm;* *off season: guided tour by appt. at the Tourist Office.*	▲ 243
ÉGLISE SAINT-LAURENT	*Irregular opening times.*	▲ 243
VALLORCINE	**74660** *OT 04 50 54 60 71*	**I6**
MUSÉE VALLORCIN	*Open July 20–Aug. 20: 2–6pm;* *off season: visits by appt. at the Tourist Office.*	▲ 239
VILLARD-SUR-DORON	**73270** *M 04 79 38 38 96*	**G3**
ÉGLISE SAINT-PIERRE	*Open in summer; info. from town hall.* *Tours organized by FACIM.*	▲ 244

THE TARENTAISE

Site	Information	Map / Page
AIME	**73210** *SI 04 79 55 67 00*	**G4**
BASILIQUE SAINT-MARTIN	*Open throughout the day. Tours organized by FACIM.*	▲ 258
CHAPELLE SAINT-SIGISMOND	*Open July–Aug.: throughout the day. Tours organized by FACIM.*	▲ 258
PARISH CHURCH	*Open throughout the day. Tours organized by FACIM.*	▲ 258
BOURG-SAINT-MAURICE	**73700** *OT 04 79 07 04 92*	**H4**
CHAPELLE SAINT-GRAT (VULMIX)	*Guided tours (by appt.) organized by Heritage guides (☎ 04 79 07 04 92).*	▲ 260
PARISH CHURCH	*Open daily 9am–6pm.*	▲ 260
BOZEL	**73350** *OT 04 79 22 10 41*	**G5**
SAINT-FRANÇOIS-DE-SALES CHURCH	*Tours organized by FACIM.*	▲ 255
TOUR 'SARRASINE' ☎ 04 79 55 03 77	*Open to the public.*	▲ 255

◆ THE TARENTAISE, PARC NATIONAL DE LA VANOISE, THE MAURIENNE

KEY TO PREFIXES
M : mairie (town hall)
OT : office de tourisme (tourist office)
SI : syndicat d'initiative (tourist bureau)
MT : maison du tourisme (tourist center)

BRIDES-LES-BAINS	**73570** *OT 04 79 55 20 64*	**F5**	
THERMAL WATERS ☎ 04 79 55 23 44	*Open Jan.–March: 8am–noon and 2–6pm and April–Oct. 7am–8pm. Closed Sun.*		▲ 255
CHAMPAGNY-EN-VANOISE	**73350** *OT 04 79 55 06 55*	**G5**	
ÉGLISE SAINT-SIGISMOND	*Tours organized by FACIM and by the Tourist Office.*		▲ 256
COURCHEVEL	**73120** *OT 04 79 08 41 60*	**G6**	
ÉGLISE DE SAINT-BON	*Open throughout the day. Tours organized by FACIM.*		▲ 255
HAUTEVILLE-GONDON	**73700** *OT 04 79 07 04 92*	**H4**	
ÉGLISE SAINT-MARTIN	*Tours organized by FACIM and by the Tourist Office.*		▲ 259
MUSÉE DE LA HAUTE-TARENTAISE	*Open July–Aug.: 2–6pm (closed Tues. and pub. hols.); off season: by appt. at the Tourist Office.*		▲ 259
MOÛTIERS	**73600** *OT 04 79 24 04 23*	**F5**	
CATHÉDRALE SAINT-PIERRE	*Open daily 9am–noon and 2–6.30pm. Tours organized by FACIM and by the Tourist Office.*		▲ 253
MUSÉE DE L'ACADÉMIE DE LA VAL D'ISÈRE	*Guided tours by appt. at the Tourist Office.*		▲ 253
PEISEY-NANCROIX	**73210** *OT 04 79 07 94 28*	**H4**	
ÉGLISE DE LA TRINITÉ	*Irregular opening times; info. from Tourist Office. Tours organized by FACIM.*		▲ 259
SANCTUAIRE NOTRE-DAME-DES-VERNETTES	*Irregular opening times; info. from Tourist Office. Tours organized by FACIM.*		▲ 259
SAINT-JEAN-DE-BELLEVILLE	**73440** *OT 04 79 08 93 09*	**F5**	
CHAPELLE NOTRE-DAME-DES-GRÂCES	*Open throughout the day. Tours taken by FACIM.*		▲ 254
SAINT-MARTIN-DE-BELLEVILLE	**73440** *OT 04 79 08 93 09*	**F6**	
CHAPELLE NOTRE-DAME-DE-LA-VIE	*Open throughout the day. Tours organized by FACIM.*		▲ 254
ÉGLISE DE SAINT-MARTIN-DE-BELLEVILLE	*Open throughout the day. Tours organized by FACIM.*		▲ 254
SÉEZ	**73700** *OT 04 79 41 00 15*	**H4**	
ÉGLISE DE SAINT-PIERRE	*July–Aug.: irregular opening times; info. from the Tourist Office. Tours organized by FACIM and by the Tourist Office.*		▲ 261
ARPIN TEXTILE MILL ☎ 04 79 07 28 79	*Visits Mon.–Fri. at 9am, 9.45am, 10.30am, 11.15am, 2.30pm, 3.15pm, 4pm, 4.45 pm; extra tours during school hols. at 1.45pm. Also open Fri. am and Sat., although the machinery is not in operation.*		▲ 261
VAL-D'ISÈRE	**73150** *OT 04 79 06 06 60*	**I5**	
PARISH CHURCH	*Open throughout the day. Tours organized by FACIM.*		▲ 262
PARC NATIONAL DE LA VANOISE			
GENERAL INFORMATION			
COMPAGNIE DES GUIDES DE LA VANOISE 73700 Bourg-Saint-Maurice ☎ 04 79 07 62 11			▲ 264
PARC NATIONAL DE LA VANOISE 135, rue du Dr-Julliand 73000 Chambéry ☎ 04 79 62 30 54	*Open Mon.–Fri.: 8am–noon and 2–6pm.*		▲ 264
MAISON DU PARC ET DU TOURISME 73170 Pralognan-la-Vanoise ☎ 04 79 08 71 49	*Refuge reservations from May 15. Open summer 8.30am–12.30pm and 2–6.45pm; June and Sept.: 9am–noon and 2–6pm.*		
SYNDICAT NATIONAL DES ACCOMPAGNATEURS EN MONTAGNE 73530 Saint-Jean-d'Arves ☎ 04 79 59 70 06	*Guides for the Massifs de Savoie (mid-altitude mountains).*		▲ 264
THE MAURIENNE			
AUSSOIS	**73500** *OT 04 79 20 30 80*	**H7**	
ÉGLISE NOTRE-DAME-DE-L'ASSOMPTION	*Open throughout the day. Tours organized by FACIM.*		▲ 278
L'ESSEILLON FORTIFICATIONS	*Guided tour: info. from the Tourist Office. Unrestricted access to some forts.*		▲ 278

Brochures giving details and times of visits and permanent exhibitions organized by FACIM (☎ 04 79 96 74 19) are available from Tourist Offices.

Site	Postcode / Details	Tel.	Map	Page
AVRIEUX	**73500**	*M 04 79 20 33 16*	**H7**	
Chapelle Notre-Dame-des-Neiges	*Open Mon.–Fri. on request at the town hall; guided tour by appt.*			▲ 278
Église Saint-Thomas de Canterbury	*Open Mon.–Fri. on request at the town hall; guided tour by appt.*			
BESSANS	**73480**	*MT 04 79 05 96 42*	**I6**	
Chapelle Saint-Antoine	*Tours organized by FACIM and by the Maison du Tourisme for groups.*			▲ 280
BRAMANS	**73500**	*M 04 79 05 10 71*	**H7**	
Église de Saint-Pierre-d'Extravache	*Open throughout the day. Tours organized by FACIM.*			▲ 278
FONTCOUVERTE-LA-TOUSSUIRE	**73300**	*OT 04 79 83 06 06*	**E7**	
Pôterie de la Lune ☎ 04 79 56 75 78	*Open July–Aug. 9am–8pm; off season: by appt.*			▲ 275
JARRIER	**73300**	*SI 04 79 64 16 79*	**E7**	
Église Saint-Pierre	*Tours organized by FACIM and by the Syndicat d'Initiative in July–Aug. by appt.*			▲ 275
LANSLEVILLARD	**73480**	*OT 04 79 05 99 10*	**I7**	
Chapelle Saint-Sébastien	*Tours organized by FACIM.*			▲ 280
Église Saint-Michel	*Tours organized by FACIM.*			
MODANE	**73500**	*M 04 79 05 04 01*	**G8**	
Fort de Saint-Gobain ☎ 04 79 05 01 50	*Open Fri., Sat., Sun., Mon. and school hols. 10am–noon and 2–7pm; off season: group tours by appt.*			▲ 277
Notre-Dame-du-Charmaix	*Open July–Aug.: Sun. to 10.30am.*			▲ 277
MONTAIMONT	**73130**	*M 04 79 56 35 45*	**E6**	
Chapelle Notre-Dame-de-Beaurevers	*Tours organized by FACIM.*			▲ 273
MONTROND	**73300**	*OT 04 79 59 30 48*	**E7**	
Parish church	*Tours by appt. with Louis Bellet (☎ 04 79 59 30 18).*			▲ 274
SAINTE-MARIE-DE CUINES	**73130**	*OT 04 79 56 33 58*	**E6**	
Church	*Tours by appt. at the Tourist Office.*			▲ 273
SAINT-JEAN-D'ARVES	**73530**	*OT 04 79 59 72 97*	**E7**	
Parish church	*Opening and tours organized by FACIM.*			▲ 275
SAINT-JEAN-DE-MAURIENNE	**73300**	*OT 04 79 83 51 51*	**E7**	
Cathedral	*Cathedral and cloisters: open throughout the day. Crypt: guided tour by the Tourist Office in July–Aug. Guided tours throughout the year (by appt.) by the GPPS. Info. from Tourist Office.*			▲ 272
Musée Opinel ☎ 04 79 64 04 78	*Open Mon.–Sat.: 9am–noon and 2–7pm. Closed Sun. and pub. hols.*			▲ 272
SAINT-RÉMY-DE-MAURIENNE	**73660**	*OT 04 79 83 13 70*	**E6**	
Parish church	*Open end June–beginning Sept. Info. Mme Fligeat (☎ 04 79 83 11 13).*			▲ 273
SAINT-SORLIN D'ARVES	**73530**	*OT 04 79 59 71 77*	**E7**	
Église Saint-Saturnin	*Open July–Aug.: Tues.–Sun. 3–6pm. Tours organized by FACIM.*			▲ 275
Cheese cooperative of Les Arves ☎ 04 79 59 70 16	*Tours by appt. (mornings only).*			▲ 275
TERMIGNON	**73500**	*OT 04 79 20 51 67*	**H7**	
Église Notre-Dame-de-l'Assomption	*Open in season; info. from Tourist Office. Tours organized by FACIM.*			
VALLOIRE	**73450**	*M 04 79 59 03 11*	**F8**	
Église Notre-Dame-de-l'Assomption	*Tours organized by FACIM and GPPS; contact M. Martin (☎ 04 79 59 01 36).*			

AIGUEBELETTE-LE-LAC

Post code 73610

HOTEL-RESTAURANT

LA COMBE-CHEZ MICHELON
La Combe (2½ miles d'Aiguebelette-le-Lac par la D 41)
Tel. 04 79 36 05 02
Fax 04 79 44 11 93
Closed Mon. eve to Tues.; start of Nov. until start of Dec.
9 rooms: 210–330 F
Menus: 130–240 F
À la carte: 280 F
Traditional cuisine
A country inn in an idyllic setting with a view of the lake and forest worthy of Jean-Jacques Rousseau. In addition to the attractive park, terrace and garden and access to the beach, Jean Dufour offers a traditional and extremely popular cuisine: terrine of salmon with crawfish sauce, lavaret in cream sauce or small plump quail from the Drôme.

AILLON-LE-JEUNE

Post code 73340

TABLE & CHAMBRES D'HÔTES

ROBERT BAULAT
Hameau des Curiaz
Tel. 04 79 54 61 47
3 rooms, 260 F
Half-board: 200 F per person.
Guests only can dine here.
An inexpensive and pleasant way to discover the forest roads and marked footpaths of the Bauges mountains. Proprietor Robert Baulat has renovated a house above the village with self-contained, spacious and comfortable rooms. Baulat, a former restaurant owner, is a dedicated host, providing information on the local fauna and flora, and ideas for walks and excursions in the region. His guests return to enjoy farm-reared rabbit with polenta, fondue or tartiflette, washed down with wine from the sunny slopes of the Combe de Savoie.

AIME

Post code 73210

HOTEL-RESTAURANT

LA TOURMALINE
175, rue de la Fortune
Tel. 04 79 55 62 93
Fax 04 79 55 52 48
29 rooms, 290–370 F
Menus: 68–115 F
A comfortable hotel
On the road to the resorts of the Haute Tarentaise, a delightful little hotel and an ideal starting point for some beautiful excursions. Aime is renowned for the 'goose cooked in milk with ocher-colored flour and juniper berries' extolled by the Roman consul Actius. It is also famous for Savoyard fondues and lavaret cooked with sorrel.

AIX-LES-BAINS

Post code 73100

HOTELS-RESTAURANTS

L'ARIANA
Le Grand Café Adélaïde
111, av. de Marlioz
Tel. 04 79 61 79 79
Fax 04 79 61 79 00
60 rooms, 465–720 F
Menus: 125–185 F
À la carte: 185 F
Traditional cuisine
Situated in the balneotherapy center of Aix-Marlioz. Spacious rooms with thick-pile carpets, large bay windows and quiet corners provide a setting for the simple yet delicious bistro cuisine of Bruno Lechène: rillettes of lake trout with spices, tartiflette, freshwater pike-perch and dumpling gratin with Beaufort. This is regional cuisine at its very best.

LE MANOIR
37, rue Georges-Ier
Tel. 04 79 61 44 00
Fax 04 79 35 67 67
73 rooms, 375–895 F
Menus: 145–265 F
À la carte: 250 F
Traditional and regional cuisine
Le Manoir combines the buildings of two manor-hotels in a shady, flower-filled park with a view of the lake. An oasis of peace and quiet in the town center, with rooms that are more like the guest room in a local family home. A restrained and sophisticated cuisine that reflects the lake and the region: fillet of Le Bourget perch and other freshwater fish. Although the numbers of fishermen on the lake are declining, fish is still very much on the menu, each ensuring the other's survival!

PARK HOTEL
Avenue Charles-de-Gaulle
Tel. 04 79 34 19 19
Fax 04 79 88 11 49
Restaurant closed Sun. eve. in winter
92 rooms, 650–930 F
10 suites, 1200–2900 F
Menus 80–160 F
À la carte 160 F
Traditional cuisine
Part of the prestigious hotel-casino complex. A comfortable, four-star hotel with a pleasantly modern restaurant.

ALBERTVILLE

Post code: 73200

HOTEL-RESTAURANT

★ MILLION
8, place de la Liberté
Tel. 04 79 32 25 15
Fax 04 79 32 25 36
Restaurant closed Sun. eve.–Mon. lunchtime
26 rooms, 350–650 F
Menus: 150–550 F
À la carte: 350 F
Gastronomic cuisine
This former coaching inn, now a Relais & Châteaux, *stands in a magnificent garden with a vast, shady terrace in summer. It is an extremely traditional establishment that has been in the family for generations. The distinction of its cosy rooms (some with fireplaces) is complemented by the careful continuity of Philippe Million's cuisine. But continuity is not a routine matter, as evinced by the fillet of féra (Lake Geneva trout) grilled in fine wheat flour or the grilled calf's sweetbreads served with leek vinaigrette. Also on the menu are more traditional and regional dishes: prawn dumplings served with a creamy, spider-crab sauce or prawns with a truffle vinaigrette. Bar, terrace and garden. Carefully prepared and moderately priced cuisine.*

ANNECY

Post code: 74000

RESTAURANTS

L'ATELIER GOURMAND
2, rue Saint-Maurice
Tel. 04 50 51 19 71
Closed end August to start of Sept. and end Feb. to start of March; Feb.–May and Sept.–Oct.: Sun.–Mon.; June–August and Nov.–Jan.: Sun. eve.–Mon.
Menus: 195–450 F
À la carte: 400 F
Traditional cuisine
A delightful new setting adds to the attraction of the consistently good cuisine based on local ingredients – fish from the lake, mushrooms – and regional traditions. Other dishes and ingredients include pigeon and truffle parfait, warm pâté and seasonal vegetables; spiced frog and prawn consommé; fillet of venison with cranberries. The restaurant has two beautiful, large and pleasantly decorated dining rooms, and extremely polite service.

LA CIBOULETTE
10, rue Vaugelas
Impasse du Pré-Carré
Tel. 04 50 45 74 57
Closed end June to end July; Sun.–Mon.
Menus 140–215 F
À la carte 300 F
Traditional cuisine
An almost dazzling technique and excellent ingredients. Georges Paccard provides all the ingredients for an excellent meal while his wife supervises the well-stocked cellar. Chestnut salad served with hot pheasant sausage; smoked féra (Lake Geneva trout) with creamy horseradish sauce; free-range chicken with Tricastin truffles.

LE CLOS DES SENS
13, rue Jean-Mermoz
Annecy-le-Vieux
Tel. 04 50 23 07 90
Closed Sat. lunch, Sun. eve. and Mon. except in July–August; two weeks in Sept. and one week from Jan. 1.
Menus: 135–380 F
À la carte: 320 F
Traditional cuisine
One of the town's best restaurants, Le Clos de Sens has a light and airy decor and a magnificent view from the terrace. Chef Laurent Petit effortlessly produces complex combinations of textures and flavors, without neglecting the aromatic aspect of the ingredients. An amazing selection of cheeses. Specialties include pan-fried scallops with truffles; féra (Lake Geneva trout) in sesame pastry; spit-roasted Challans duckling.

HOTEL

LES MARQUISATS
6–8, ch. de Colmyr
Tel. 04 50 51 52 34
Fax 04 50 51 89 42
22 rooms, 350–500 F
This delightful hotel stands on the edge of the town, on the shores of the lake. It occupies a hillside site overlooking the bay of Annecy. Rooms with a personal touch and a delightfully daring breakfast room. Peaceful setting with morning mists on the lake.

HOTEL-RESTAURANT

L'IMPÉRIAL PALACE
32, av. d'Albigny
Tel. 04 50 09 30 00
Fax 04 50 09 33 33
98 rooms, 1200–4000 F (suite)
7 apartments, 2200 F
Restaurant La Voile:
Menus: 150–190 F
À la carte: 160 F
High-quality hotel
A prestigious hotel set in carefully maintained gardens, on the shores of the lake. The spacious rooms, which are furnished in a contemporary style – steely tones and white wood – enjoy an exceptional view of the lake.

ANNEMASSE

Post code: 74100

HOTEL

HÔTEL DU PARC
19, rue de Genève
Tel. 04 50 38 44 60
Fax 04 50 92 75 71
Closed Christmas to start of Jan.
30 rooms, 240–380 F
A centrally located hotel popular for

LES ARCS

Post code 73700

RESTAURANT

★ BELLIOU-LA-FUMÉE
Pré-Saint-Esprit
Les Arcs 2000
Tel. 04 79 07 29 13
Open for lunches; winter and summer.
Menus 105–150 F
À la carte: 120 F
Regional cuisine
This high-altitude restaurant, whose name was inspired by Jack London, is a typical Tarentaise stone chalet. At lunchtime groups of skiers occupy the tables on the terrace where, with the help of the sun and the famous Mondeuse wine, the atmosphere is extremely pleasant. On the table, sausages and pâtés worthy of the rugged but subtle Allobrogi include pâté de foie with juniper, uncooked ham and diots (small rustic sausages), as well as dumplings made with buckwheat flour (crozets) and excellent Beaufort, the vital ingredient of a fondue washed down with dry white wine from Apremont. A warm welcome and family atmosphere. Access on skis or by road.

the quality of its service and its lush setting. Comfortable rooms.

LES ARCS

Post code 73700

HOTEL-RESTAURANT

HÔTEL-RESTAURANT DU GOLF LATITUDES
Village du Charvet
Tel. 04 79 41 43 43
Fax 04 79 07 49 87
250 rooms, 615–880 F per person half-board (compulsory)
Menus: 195 F
À la carte: 175 F
White or green, on the 'snow front' or below the golf course, the architecture of Bernard Taillefer and the Atelier d'Architecture en Montagne is modern in its use of space and its interior design. But it is also well integrated into the site and traditional in its use of materials (larch façades). The restaurant (Le Green) offers sophisticated and innovative cuisine. Open-air swimming pool.

ARGENTIÈRE

Post code 74400

HOTEL-RESTAURANT

LES BECS ROUGES
Montroc (¾ mile north on the N506)
Tel. 04 50 54 01 00
Fax 04 50 54 0051
Closed Nov. 5–Dec. 20
24 rooms, 510–655 F
Menus: 115–298 F
À la carte: 175 F
A delightful hotel
At the foot of the Aiguille Verte, this Relais du Silence *enjoys a spectacular view of Mont Blanc and the Chamonix valley from the loggias of its rooms. Terrace and flower-filled garden. The hotel's owner is Danish – which explains the presence of a wide range of smoked fish dishes on the menu.*

AUSSOIS

Post code 73500

RESTAURANT

FORT MARIE-CHRISTINE
Tel. 04 79 20 36 44
Closed off season: Sun. eve.; end April–end May and Nov. to mid-Dec.
Menus: 88–165 F
À la carte: 120 F
Regional cuisine
Magnificent view from this tastefully renovated restaurant in one of the five forts built by the Piedmontese and Austrians between 1817 and 1834. Lunch in the interior courtyard in summer. Regional cuisine at reasonable prices. Efficient, friendly service and a well-stocked cellar.

BEAUFORT-SUR-DORON

Post code 73270

HOTEL-RESTAURANT

LE GRAND MONT
Place de l'Église
Tel. 04 79 38 33 36
Fax 04 79 38 39 07
Closed end April to start of May and first week in Nov.
13 rooms, 285–295 F
Menus: 98–160 F
À la carte: 120 F
Regional cuisine
The restaurant gives pride of place to Beaufort, the soft, uncooked mountain cheese, whose rind is salted, washed and rubbed as it matures over a six month period. It is prepared in all kinds of ways: in tarts, salads, omelettes and even with the dumplings (crozets) that accompany the diots (sausages) cooked in white wine. Friendly welcome and very reasonable prices.

BERNEX

Post code 74500

HOTEL-RESTAURANT

CHEZ TANTE MARIE
Langin
Tel. 04 50 73 60 35
Fax 04 50 73 61 73
Closed Oct. 15–Dec. 15
27 rooms, 370–410 F
Menus: 98–240 F
À la carte: 170 F
Comfortable hotel
There's no need to climb the Dent d'Ocheto to enjoy your stay in this hotel with its magnificent view. In summer meals are served in a flower-filled garden. Carefully prepared cuisine.

BOËGE

Post code 74420

RESTAURANT

AUBERGE DU CHALET
Chez Novelly
Tel. 04 50 39 12 35
Restaurant closed spring to Sept.; Wed. and Sun. eve.
3 rooms, 190–280 F
Menus: 90–120 F
À la carte: 90 F
Savoyard cuisine
The inn – a stone building with a

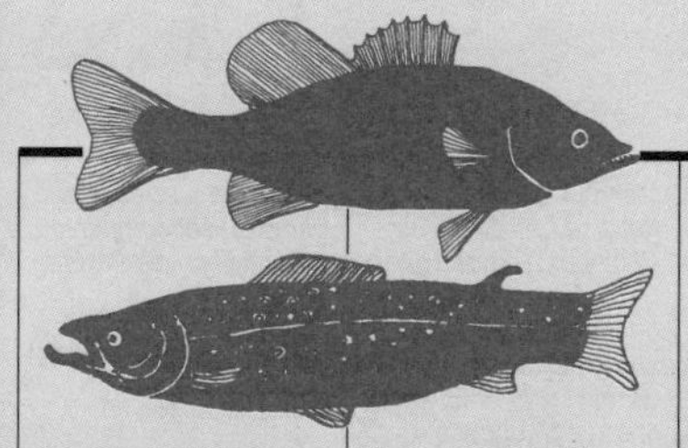

Savoyard balcony – is situated high on the slopes, about 2 miles from the village, and enjoys a magnificent view of the Vallée Verte. Guests can visit a farm, which sells Tomme de Savoie and Abondance cheeses, and sample regional cuisine: Savoyard fondue made with Abondance cheese and mushrooms; forcemeat from the Pays du Mont-Blanc; diots (small sausages) cooked in white wine, and salad with white Tomme de Savoie.

BONNEVAL-SUR-ARC

Post code 73480

RESTAURANT

LE PRÉ CATIN
Tel. 04 79 05 95 07
Closed Mon.;
May 3–June 18
and Sept. 25–Dec. 19
Menus: 115–160 F
À la carte: 140 F
Regional cuisine
Charming traditional chalet – lauzes (roofing stones), a romantic fireplace and softly lit dining room – and superb cuisine: raclette (fondue), Bresse poultry with crozets (dumplings) and diots (sausages) cooked in white wine. In summer, guests can sip the 'wines of Allobrogia' on the shady terrace.

BONNEVILLE

Code postal 74130

HOTEL-RESTAURANT

SAPEUR HÔTEL L'EAU SAUVAGE
Place de l'Hôtel-de-Ville
Tel. 04 50 97 20 68
Fax 04 50 25 73 48
Restaurant: closed
Sun. eve.–Mon.
15 rooms, 280–400 F
Menus: 100–440 F
À la carte: 350–450 F
Gastronomic cuisine
When the restaurant was established 100 years ago, forcemeat and farçon (crusted mashed potato with eggs and herbs) were dishes served on special occasions. Its trout and salmon were caught in the Arve or the Risse, and its terrines and pâtés were made from local game. The regional cuisine of Patrick Guénon is inspired by long-standing traditional recipes: crêpet made with char and summer truffles, trout grilled in wild celery butter and 'biscoin' of lamb with 'pimpiolet'. A quiet and peaceful setting and an extensive wine list.

LE BOURGET-DU-LAC

Post code 73370

RESTAURANTS

LA GRANGE-À-SEL
Près de la plage
Tel. 04 79 25 02 66
Closed Wed.;
Nov.–May 5
Menus: 180–310 F
À la carte: 300 F
Traditional cuisine
A former salt warehouse, dating from the 16th century, whose terrace offers a magnificent view of the lake in its lush setting. Gilles Bloway takes pride in his simple, rustic and extremely aromatic cuisine: marbré of ox cheeks, fillets of perch with salad or fresh cod puréed with garlic and coriander oil. A few olive trees flourish in the shelter of the rocks on the shores of the lake.

AUBERGE LAMARTINE
Bourdeau, route du Tunnel-du-Chat
Tel. 04 79 25 01 03
Closed throughout the year: Sun. eve.–Mon.; off season: Tues. lunch; mid-Dec.–end Jan.
Menus: 150–390 F
À la carte: 300 F
Regional cuisine
From the terrace, an idyllic view of the mountains and lake extolled by the French poet Lamartine, whose grande passion

LE BOURGET-DU-LAC

Post code 73370

HOTEL-RESTAURANT

★ OMBREMONT LE BATEAU IVRE
Route du Tunnel-du-Chat (1½ miles from Le Bourget-du-Lac, on the N 504)
Tel. 04 79 25 00 23
Fax 04 79 25 25 77
Open May–Nov.
Restaurant closed Tues. lunch and Wed. lunchtime except in July–Aug.
17 rooms, 880–1400 F
Menus: 260–590 F
À la carte: 500 F
Gastronomic cuisine
The hotel terrace offers a romantic view of the surrounding mountains and the Lac du Bourget. Set in an impressive park with trees several hundred years old and a lakeside swimming pool. The dazzling cuisine of Jean-Pierre Jacob pays homage to the lake's fish with such inspired dishes as his adaptation of lavaret browned in sesame oil and served crisp with a soft-boiled egg. Eating here gives credit to the assertion of the French gastronome, Brillat-Savarin (1755–1826), that great cuisine is the sign of a great civilization. The delicacy of pan-fried fillets of perch served with potato salad, and a few prawns browned in spices, accompanied by the best wines from nearby Chautagne, complements the magnificent landscape.

does not appear to have spoiled his appetite. Fish from the lake are still the basis of a wide range of delicately flavored dishes: char in a truffle sauce and lavaret with a crawfish coulis. In season there are also delicious game

dishes and roasted Bresse pigeon stuffed with garlic.

BOURG-SAINT-MAURICE

Post code 73700

HOTEL-RESTAURANT

HOSTELLERIE DU PETIT-SAINT-BERNARD
74, avenue du Stade
Tel. 04 79 07 04 32
Fax 04 79 07 32 80
20 rooms, 290–370 F
Menus: 97–138 F
À la carte: 150 F
Regional cuisine
A good, centrally located restaurant, which promotes traditional cuisine: diots (sausages) cooked in white wine, tartiflette, fondue and fillet of perch. Once a week a special Savoyard menu is prepared for the guests staying in this comfortable hotel.

BRIDES-LES-BAINS

Post code 73570

HOTELS-RESTAURANTS

GRAND HÔTEL DES THERMES
Parc Thermal – BP 36
Tel. 04 79 55 29 77
Fax 04 79 55 28 29
Closed Nov.–Dec. 26
102 rooms, 660–800 F
4 apartments, 1000 F
Menus: 140–250 F
À la carte: 200 F
A good, traditional hotel
A vast establishment, with well-appointed rooms, offering dietetic cures. Brides-les-Bains is a spa town and a popular fishing center (Lac du Praz and Doron). If this is not reason enough to take a relaxing break, there are the added attractions of a beautiful location, excursions in the Parc de la Vanoise, and the high-altitude ski resorts.

LES CARROZ D'ARÂCHES

Post code 74300

RESTAURANT

ALPAGE DE L'AIRON
Route de Flaine
(1½ miles along a track suitable for vehicles or 15 mins on foot from the car park)
Tel. 04 50 90 33 84
Closed Sept. 15–June 1
À la carte: 45–90 F
Savoyard cuisine
A mountain chalet situated above the cluse (gorge) of the River Arve and opposite the summits of the Croix de Fer and Les Grandes Platières. You can see farmhouse cheese being made and sample some delicious regional wines. Diots (sausages) made with cheese and white wine, polenta with Beaufort; sirac with shallots and raspberry vinegar, a mountain cheese board; sabayon (zabaglione) and gâteau de Savoie.

CHALLES-LES-EAUX

Post code 73190

HOTEL-RESTAURANT

HOSTELLERIE DES COMTES DE CHALLES
247, montée du Château
Tel. 04 79 72 86 71
Fax 04 79 72 83 83
46 rooms, 425–750 F
Menus: 160–350 F
À la carte: 250 F
An historic hotel
A former 15th-century fortified residence set in a park. A good restaurant offering regional dishes. Superb rooms with a view of the Dent du Chat or the Combe de Savoie. A vineyard region where fondue made with Beaufort reigns supreme, served in a casserole rubbed with garlic and accompanied by white 'vin de Savoie'.

CHAMBÉRY

Post code 73000

HOTEL

HÔTEL MERCURE
183, place de la Gare
Tel. 04 79 62 10 11
Fax 04 79 62 10 23
81 rooms, 620 F
A centrally located, comfortable hotel, near the station. No restaurant.

HOTEL-RESTAURANT

CHÂTEAU DE CANDIE
38, rue Bobby-Sands
Tel. 04 79 96 63 00
Fax 04 79 96 63 10
17 rooms, 500–1200 F
3 split-level apartments
Restaurant
closed Sun. eve.
Menus: 150–380 F
À la carte: 300 F
Traditional cuisine
The entire history of Savoie is encapsulated in this impressive 14th-century building, set in a park, with beautiful individually designed rooms. The chef, who trained with Alain Ducasse, takes the setting into account when preparing a sophisticated cuisine

CHAMBÉRY

Post code 73000

RESTAURANT

★ L'ESSENTIEL
183, place de la Gare
Tel. 04 79 96 97 27
Closed Sat. lunch and Sun. eve.
Menus: 130–200 F
À la carte: 300 F
Traditional cuisine
The atmosphere of this restaurant is largely due to Jean-Michel Bouvier's excellent 'harmonie gourmande' menu. His is a carefully prepared cuisine, based on seasonal produce. The restaurant's modern setting, beneath a glass pyramid, the elegant and sophisticated table decor, and the efficient but unobtrusive service, add to its gastronomic pleasures: browned-vegetable tart with basil, rabbit and rosemary stew served with a root-vegetable gratin, blue-veined cheese made with buttermilk, strawberries in lemon-balm syrup. The lavaret with baby vegetables and herb sauce ('land and sea' menu) or the duckling cooked with spices highlight the skill and ability of the chef, and his taste for an inventive but carefully controlled cuisine. Excellent choice of wines.

CHAMONIX

Post code 74400

HOTELS-RESTAURANTS

★ LE HAMEAU ALBERT-Ier
119, impasse du Montenvers
Tel. 04 50 53 05 09
Fax 04 50 55 95 48
Closed one week in May; Nov. Restaurant closed off season: Wed. lunch
32 rooms, 690–3200 F, 7 apartments, 3 chalets
Menus: 195–500 F
À la carte: 350 F
Gastronomic cuisine
The memories of the Pension du Montenvers evoked by Pierre and Martine Carrier highlight the progress made since the beginning of the 20th century by four generations of restaurant owners. The rooms in the little chalets dotted about the flower-filled park form what must be one of the most delightful hamlets ever. A discreet and efficient service, and a cuisine based on local traditional fare but with the emphasis firmly on lightness and accuracy, maintain the restaurant's well-established reputation. The extensive wine cellar gives pride of place to 'vins de Savoie'. Char in vegetable butter; knuckle of veal braised with truffles.

pervaded by a sense of occasion: fish from the lake, including roast perch on a bed of fennel. Delicious poultry dishes, sophisticated cheeses, a prestigious wine cellar, an idyllic setting and reasonable prices.

RESTAURANT

LE TONNEAU
2, rue Saint-Antoine
Tel. 04 79 33 78 26
Closed Sun. eve.–Mon.
Menus: 120–250 F
À la carte: 120 F
Regional cuisine
An attractive, centrally located restaurant with a beautiful shady terrace in summer. Simple, traditional dishes, such as fillet of lavaret with black pepper, embody the pleasures of Savoyard cuisine. No Savoyard feast would be complete without Tomme de Savoie, an ideal cheese to end a meal and accompany the wines from the Combe de Savoie. Very attentive service.

CHAMONIX

Post code 74400

RESTAURANT

LA MAISON CARRIER
Rte du Bouchet
Tel. 04 50 53 00 03
Closed Mon. and mid-Nov. to mid-Dec.
Menus: 145–240 F
À la carte: 200 F
Savoyard cuisine
For ten years, Pierre Carrier salvaged old barns and abandoned chalets to create this truly amazing restaurant in the grounds of the

Hôtel Albert-Ier. The warmth of an old wood decor, the huge chimney used for smoking sausages and hams, and portraits of famous mountaineers recreate the atmosphere of a traditional mountain chalet. Traditional Savoyard cuisine completes the delightful effect.

HOTELS-RESTAURANTS

AUBERGE DU BOIS PRIN
69, chemin de l'Hermine
Aux Moussoux
Tel. 04 50 53 33 51
Fax 04 50 53 48 75
Closed end April–beg. May and Nov. Restaurant closed Wed. lunch
11 rooms, 840–1380 F
Menus: 180–430 F
À la carte: 180 F
Relais & Châteaux
An elegant Savoyard chalet with a terrace and flower-filled balconies, opposite the Massif du Mont-Blanc. Materials and spaces adapted from the lifestyle of yesteryear and rooms equipped with the latest in modern comfort. The traditional, light cuisine of Denis Carrier is complemented by an excellent choice of Savoyard cheeses and wines.

HÔTEL MONT-BLANC RESTAURANT LE MATAFAN
62, allée du Majestic
Tel. 04 50 53 05 64
Fax 04 50 55 89 44
Closed Oct. 7–Dec. 18
34 rooms and 8 apartments, 574–974 F
Menus: 150–320 F
À la carte: 250 F
Traditional cuisine
The hotel, with its luxuriously furnished rooms and suites, is one of the brilliant legacies of 19th-century Chamonix, already regarded as the capital of mountaineering. Alain Corvi is an experienced chef who combines regional ingredients with inspired cuisine. Sole and scallop pancakes; veal cutlets simmered with morel mushrooms; roast breast of pigeon with cocoa beans.

BEAUSOLEIL
Au Lavancher
(3½ miles north of Chamonix on the N 506)
Tel. 04 50 54 00 78
Fax 04 50 54 17 34
15 rooms, 380–580 F
Closed Sept. 20–Dec. 20. Restaurant closed for lunch in the off season.
Menu: 90–150 F
À la carte: 180 F
Chalet-hotel
This smart inn near the cross-country ski routes at the foot of the Aiguille du Midi and Mont Blanc offers a simple, family welcome. Comfortable, cosy rooms in traditional mountain style. Flower-

filled garden in summer and tennis court. Carefully prepared cuisine.

LA CHAPELLE-D'ABONDANCE

Post code 74360

HOTEL-RESTAURANT

LES CORNETTES
Tel. 04 50 73 50 24
Fax 04 50 73 54 16
Closed Oct.20–Dec. 20
43 rooms, 320–440 F
Menus: 110–320 F
À la carte: 250 F

Chalet-hotel
This huge chalet owned by Bernard and Philippe Trincaz has retained all the charm of yesteryear while keeping up with modern trends, especially with regard to cuisine. Rooms with 'kitchenettes'. Heated indoor swimming pool.

CHÂTEL

Post code 74390

HOTEL-RESTAURANT

HÔTEL FLEUR DE NEIGE – LA GRIVE GOURMANDE
Route de Morgins
Tel. 04 50 73 20 10
Fax 04 50 73 24 55
Open start June to mid-Sept. and mid-Dec. to start April
37 rooms, 490–680 F
Menu: 190–400 F
À la carte: 300 F
Traditional cuisine
This large chalet enjoys a magnificent panoramic view of mountain pastures, only a stone's throw from a cableway, in winter, and from the swimming pool in Châtel, in summer. Ideal for serious gourmets: escalope of foie gras served on a bed of lettuce flavored with ginger; quail 'en besace' with wild woodland mushrooms; traditional pot-au-feu.

CHINDRIEUX

Post code 73310

HOTEL-RESTAURANT

RELAIS DE CHAUTAGNE
7, route d'Aix
Tel. 04 79 54 20 27
Fax 04 79 54 51 63
Closed Dec. 28–Feb. 12; Sun. eve. and Mon. except July–August
32 rooms, 240–260 F
Menu: 90–180 F
À la carte: 155 F
Regional cuisine
The Chautagne vineyards, to the north of the Lac du Bourget, produce one of the best Roussettes, a clear, pale gold wine. Here white wine accompanies carefully prepared fish dishes: matelote (fish stew) made with fish from the lake – lavaret, mountain trout, féra (Lake Geneva trout), char and perch. In the hunting season, dishes prepared with local game attract gourmets to this delightful rural restaurant, founded in 1921.

LA CLUSAZ

Post code 74220

RESTAURANT

LE BERCAIL
Crêt du Merle
Tel. 04 50 02 43 75
Open Sept.–Dec.: weekends; throughout the year: Mon.–Sun. Closed mid-April to start July
Menus: 32–98 F
À la carte: 150 F
Traditional cuisine
A 265-year-old chalet situated in mountain pastures at an altitude of 4920 feet. It still has an old wooden chimney (bourne) used for smoking hams and sausages. Only the very best ingredients are served in this ski-slope restaurant where customers arrive on skis or by free shuttle service in winter, and on foot or by shuttle in summer. White Tomme de Savoie (made at the restaurant) and potato fritters; pormonniers (pig's offal and green vegetable sausages) cooked in the ashes; tartiflette des Aravis.

COISE-SAINT-JEAN-PIED-GAUTHIER

Post code 73800

HOTEL-RESTAURANT

CHÂTEAU DE LA TOUR DU PUITS
Route du Puits
Tel. 04 79 28 88 00
Fax 04 79 28 88 01
Closed Jan.; Sun. eve. and Mon.
8 rooms, 750–950 F
Menus: 120–530 F
A charming hotel and restaurant
An 18th-century castle nestling in 17 acres of forest and orchards. Rooms of character in which old parquet floors and traditional Savoyard furniture are combined with the latest in modern comfort. The 'Table du Baron' serves delicious regional dishes prepared with local fish and game. Terrace shaded by plane trees in summer and a swimming pool discreetly concealed amongst the trees. Helipad.

COMBLOUX

Post code 74920

HOTELS-RESTAURANTS

AU CŒUR DES PRÉS
152, chemin du Champet
Tel. 04 50 93 36 55
Fax 04 50 58 69 14
Open mid-Dec. to mid-April and June to end Sept.
33 rooms, 420–560 F
Menus: 125–200 F
À la carte: 180 F
Comfortable hotel
This spacious Savoyard chalet, with its attractive rustic decor and comfortable rooms, enjoys a view of the Chaîne des Aravis and Mont Blanc. A warm, friendly atmosphere and courteous welcome. Sauna, jacuzzi, terrace, garden and swimming pool. Carefully prepared cuisine.

LE ROND-POINT DES PISTES
Au Haut-Combloux
Rte de la Cry-Cuchet
(2 miles west of Combloux)
Tel. 04 50 58 68 55
Fax 04 50 93 30 54
29 rooms 550–650 F
Open June 15–Sept. 15 and Dec. 20–April 15
Menus: 140–180 F
À la carte: 200 F
Charming hotel
This typical Savoyard chalet stands on a steep slope, near the ski runs. View of Mont Blanc from the terrace and comfortable, well-appointed rooms for skiers and hikers. Sauna. Sophisticated cuisine.

CORDON

Code postal 74700

HOTEL-RESTAURANT

LES ROCHES FLEURIES
La Scie
Tel. 04 50 58 06 71
Fax 04 50 47 82 30
Hotel closed mid-April to mid-May and end Sept. to mid-Dec.
19 rooms and 6 suites,

COURCHEVEL

Post code 73120

RESTAURANT

LE BATEAU IVRE
Courchevel 1850–
Les Chenuts
Tel. 04 79 08 36 88
Fax 04 79 08 38 72
Open Dec. 15–April 15
Menus: 250–590 F
À la carte: 700 F
Gastronomic cuisine
A magnificent panoramic view of La Vanoise, in a comfortably modern setting. The modern cuisine is complemented by Jean-Pierre Jacob's careful selection of good cheese-makers, attentive fruit and vegetable pickers and successful fishermen, while his creativity has root in tradition. Oysters à la meunière with potato salad, roasted scallops and crunchy pig's trotters with gentian sauce reflect a way of life: cuisine, customs, respect for ingredients, where everything is linked to the pleasures of the palate. 'Vins de Savoie' are also very much in evidence: Crépy, Mondeuse and the clear, pale gold of Roussette de Seyssel. Warm welcome from Josy Jacob.

600–1200 F
Menus: 148–320 F
À la carte: 260 F
Traditional cuisine
An attractive chalet opposite Mont Blanc. Cosy, well-appointed rooms with terraces to enjoy the view. Dominique Weber's cooking makes skillful use of regional ingredients – filet of rabbit with pesto sauce and Beaufort – lingers over subtle blends of flavors– honey and roast prawns – and pays homage to tradition with a tourtière (flaky-pastry tart) of calf's sweetbreads and morel mushrooms.

COURCHEVEL

Post code 73120

HOTELS-RESTAURANTS

LES AIRELLES
Le Jardin Alpin
Tel. 04 79 09 38 38
Fax 04 79 08 38 69
Open mid-Dec.–end April
7 suites and 52 rooms, 3700–6800 F
Menus: 380–520 F
À la carte: 750 F
Luxury hotel and restaurant
An exceptional hotel-restaurant in an extremely comfortable, luxury chalet with painted façades. A little corner of Savoie in its own setting, with staff dressed in traditional costume. Fine traditional cuisine in the 'Table du Jardin Alpin' or top-of-the-range regional cuisine in the 'Coin Savoyard' (evenings only). Carefully selected Savoie cheeses and regional wines. A choice of vintage Bordeaux wines.

L'ANNAPURNA
Courchevel 1850 Route de l'Altiport
Tel. 04 79 06 04 60
Fax 04 79 08 15 31
Open mid-Dec. to mid-April
4 apartments, 64 rooms, 2460–3820 F
Menus: 295–350 F
À la carte: 300 F
Luxury hotel
One of the best hotels in a resort where competition is fierce. Wood decor and comfortable, spacious rooms with views of the ski slopes and the mountains of the Tarentaise. Remarkable cuisine and the latest modern facilities: bar, terrace, fitness center with a swimming pool, jacuzzi and steam bath.

HÔTEL DU GOLF
Courchevel 1650
Moriond
Tel. 04 79 00 92 92
Fax 04 79 08 19 93
Open mid-Dec. to mid-April
41 rooms, 880–940 F
6 split-level apartments
À la carte: 235 F
Luxury hotel
An impeccable establishment efficiently run by Françoise Beff. Attached to the hotel is a fitness center near a beautiful dining room decorated in modern Alpine style.

LES PEUPLIERS
Courchevel 1300
Le Praz-de-Saint-Bon.
Tel. 04 79 08 41 47
Fax 04 79 08 45 05
Closed April;
mid-Oct. to mid-Dec.
33 rooms, 700–800 F
Menus: 105–250 F
À la carte: 105 F
Extremely comfortable
Norbert Gacon extends a warm welcome in this modern Savoyard chalet, with fitness facilities and an unrivaled view of the Olympic ski-jumps. In the restaurant, as everywhere else in Savoie, the chef combines tradition and modernity. Try the truly amazing crème caramel. Spacious well-appointed rooms.

LA SIVOLIÈRE
Courchevel 1850
Tel. 04 79 08 08 33
Fax 04 79 08 15 73
Closed start May to start Dec.
32 rooms, 890–2900 F (suite)
Menu: 120–360 F
À la carte: 250 F
Extremely comfortable
Madeleine Cattelin and Nadine Vercellino felt that children were happier on their own rather than fidgeting on a chair next to their parents. So they created a separate children's area with specially adapted meals, and an elegant dining room with a wood decor, huge flower arrangements, and modern Savoyard cuisine for the adults. 'Les Grisons' salad with Beaufort provides a touch of local color, while veal cutlets with morel mushrooms and pumpkin gratin are also on the menu. All this in the friendly atmosphere of a spacious chalet with its view of snow-covered fir trees.

★ LE CHABICHOU
Courchevel 1850
Les Chenuts
Tel. 04 79 08 00 55
Fax 04 79 08 33 58
Open end June to start Sept. and mid-Dec. to end April
44 rooms, 900–2090 F per person (half-board only)
Menus: 340–650 F
À la carte: 400 F
Gastronomic cuisine
Michel Rochedy is the host and chef of this beautiful and

impeccably run chalet. He is a talented professional whose cuisine is as precise and efficient as the welcome extended by his excellent staff on a vast terrace with a panoramic view of the valley and dominated by La Saulire. Specialties include croûton savoyard and cream of prawn soup with cottage cheese, terrine of chamois with

hazelnuts, chicken liver mold with truffles and crawfish. Regional dishes, enhanced and skillfully recreated, are very much a part of this innovative cuisine: for example the lightly spiced duck suprême accompanied by a gratin savoyard with mushrooms. The magnificent and luxurious wine list is equal to the setting.

CRUSEILLES

Post code 74350

HOTEL-RESTAURANT

L'ANCOLIE
Route des Dronières
Tel. 04 50 44 28 98
Fax 04 50 44 09 73
Closed Sun. eve. and public holidays in Nov. and Feb.
10 rooms, 365–520 F
Menus: 125–365 F
À la carte: 220 F
Traditional cuisine
The setting – broad bay windows overlook the shores of a small lake and the surrounding park – adds to the sophisticated pleasures of the chalet's traditional cuisine. Excellent filet of beef with marrowbone garnish.

DUINGT

Post code 74410

HOTEL-RESTAURANT

HÔTEL DU LAC
Tel. 04 50 68 90 90
Fax 04 50 68 50 18
Hotel: closed Nov.–Jan.
Restaurant: closed end Sept.–end April
23 rooms, 310–410 F
Menus: 98–225 F
À la carte: 250 F
Traditional cuisine
This established hotel enjoys an unrivaled location on the shores of the Lac d'Annecy, opposite Talloires, which marks the division between the Grand Lac and the Petit Lac. The rooms have been modernized, but retain their individual character. The delights of a menu that changes each day are enhanced by the very reasonable prices.

ÉVIAN-LES-BAINS

Post code 74500

RESTAURANTS

LE CHALET DU GOLF
Domaine du Royal Club Évian
Tel. 04 50 75 56 34
Open for lunch only, except in July–August.
Closed Nov. 30–Feb. 7
Menu: 190 F
À la carte: 200 F
Regional cuisine
This mountain chalet, with its stone fireplace, exposed beams and wooden balconies, stands on the edge of the golf course. Its

lunch and dinner (in season) menus offer simply prepared regional specialities: péla with farmhouse Reblochon; filets of perch à la meunière; portions of spit-roasted beef with a preserved shallot sauce.

LE LIBERTÉ
On the right of the casino
Tel. 04 50 26 87 50
Menus: 64–110 F
À la carte: 150 F
International cuisine
The bar-restaurant-terrace, opened in July 1997, provides a modern and relaxed atmosphere: videos on a giant screen, bands in summer and 'surfing' on the Web. An eclectic cuisine offers prawns sautéed in saké and black mushrooms (Asia), guacamole casa fiesta (South America) and grilled ostrich in a sweet-and-sour guava sauce (Australia).

HOTELS-RESTAURANTS

HÔTEL ERMITAGE LE GOURMANDIN
Domaine du Royal Club Évian
Tel. 04 50 26 85 54
Fax 04 50 75 29 37
Closed Nov. 11–Feb. 6 except week of Jan. 1
87 rooms 610–1090 F per person
4 suites 1300 F per person
Menus: 200–380 F
À la carte: 340 F
Regional cuisine
This huge Anglo-Norman-Savoyard chalet is discreetly comfortable and luxurious. The restaurant, with its warm tones, traditional decor and furniture, provides an ideal setting for the traditional Savoyard cuisine: filet of féra (Lake Geneva trout) roasted with bacon and wild mushrooms; suprême of roast duck in pastry flavored with spices.

LES PRÉS FLEURIS SUR ÉVIAN
Route de Thollon (on the D 24)
Tel. 04 50 75 29 14
Fax 04 50 74 68 75
Open May 15–Oct. 1
12 rooms, 900–1600 F
Menus: 300–440 F
À la carte: 450 F
Traditional cuisine
roasted filet of beef; soufflé with Morello cherries and kirsch.

ÉVIAN-LES-BAINS

Post code 74500

HOTEL-RESTAURANT

★ LA VERNIAZ AT SES CHALETS
Avenue d'Abondance
Neuvecelle-Église
Tel. 04 50 75 04 90
Fax 04 50 70 78 92
Closed mid-Nov. to mid-Feb.
34 rooms, 750–1500 F; 5 chalets, 2300–2800 F
Menus: 210–380 F
À la carte: 250 F
Traditional cuisine
Relais & Châteaux
The idyllic landscape has been much admired since Jean-Jacques Rousseau came here in the 18th century. The magnificent view of the lake and mountains is one of the major assets of this beautiful hotel whose 'Relais & Châteaux' listing is a guarantee of comfort and good service. The superb park dotted with chalets is worth a visit in its own right, but the classic cuisine of Christian Métreau, who uses quality ingredients, is another major attraction. A warm welcome is extended by the Verdier family. Specialties include fish from Lake Geneva; spit-

LE GRAND-BORNAND

Post code 74450

RESTAURANT

★ LA FERME DE LORMAY
Lormay
Tel. 04 50 02 24 29
Closed May–June 20, Sept. 10–Dec. 15; winter: lunch during the week; summer: Tues. lunch
À la carte: 170
Savoyard cuisine
Situated 4½ miles from Le Grand-Bornand and the magnificent farms below the Massif des Aravis, which make farmhouse Reblochon. Meals are served in the old living accommodation of a farm, built in 1786, which still has the old wooden chimney typical of the valley. The delightfully traditional cuisine of Albert Bonamy adds to the charm of the setting. Fricassée de caïon (pork stew); attriaux (pork-offal and herb sausage); chicken with crawfish (in summer).

MANIGOD

Post code 74230

HOTEL-RESTAURANT

★ CHALET HÔTEL DE LA CROIX-FRY
Chez Marie-Ange Guelpa-Veyrat
Route de la Croix-Fry
Tel. 04 50 44 90 16
Fax 04 50 44 94 87
Closed 15 Oct.–15 Dec. and April 15–June 15
9 rooms and 3 suites, 550–1500 F
Menus: 150–400 F
À la carte: 200 F
Regional cuisine
An old family farm, converted into a comfortable Savoyard residence: spacious well-appointed rooms (old Savoyard furniture), some split-level, with a balcony and 'balneo' bath. Heated swimming pool and tennis court. Marie-Ange, the sister of Marc Veyrat, runs this delightful chalet-hotel and applies the same exacting standards to her selection of quality ingredients: traditional tartiflette; wild mushroom omelette; foie gras maison; wild fruit desserts.

Relais & Châteaux.
This former mid-19th-century farmhouse stands at an altitude of 2790 feet (850 m) in a panoramic and grandiose setting. Its cuisine, prepared by owner Roger Frossard is in perfect harmony with the setting and only includes seasonal ingredients fresh from the market. Ideal for those in search of peace and quiet. Fricassée of wild woodland mushrooms; fish from the lake; veal cutlets en cocotte.

FLUMET

Post code 73590

HOTEL-RESTAURANT

LE PARC DES CÈDRES
Promenade des Aravis
Tel. 04 79 31 72 37
Fax 04 79 31 61 66
Open Dec. 20–March and June 15–Sept. 15
18 rooms, 250–350 F
Menus: 85–225 F
À la carte: 150 F
A charming hotel-restaurant
Beyond the Gorges de l'Arly, at the foot of the Chaîne des Aravis, Flumet has for a long time been a busy winter and summer resort. The 100-year-old hotel, which stands in a

traditional terraced park, offers guests the comfort of yesteryear, without the nostalgia! Carefully prepared cuisine.

LANSLEVILLARD -LANSLEBOURG

Post code 73480

HOTEL-RESTAURANT

ALPAZUR
Lanslebourg
Tel. 04 79 05 93 69
Fax 04 79 05 86 55
Open Dec. 20–April 20 and June–Sept. 20
24 rooms, 290–450 F
Menus: 100–360 F
À la carte: 220 F

This family hotel, run by Jean-Pierre Jorcin, stands on the edge of the Parc de la Vanoise and at the foot of the ski slopes. Classic comfort in a traditional village that places the emphasis on good food. Pleasant and carefully prepared cuisine.

LA LÉCHÈRE

Post code 73260

HOTEL-RESTAURANT

LE RADIANA
Parc Thermal
Tel. 04 79 22 61 61
Fax 04 79 22 65 25
Hotel open start Feb. to start March and end

March to end Oct.
Restaurant open end March to end Oct.
87 rooms, 340–770 F
Menus: 105–155 F
Spa hotel
Hotel and residential hotel dependant on the baths. Excellent cuisine. A terrace and garden enhance a pleasurable experience.

MEGÈVE

Post code 74120

RESTAURANTS

L'ALPETTE
220, route du Téléphérique
Tel. 04 50 21 03 69
Closed Sept. 10–Dec. 15 and April 20–June 30
Menu: 138–165 F
À la carte: 200 F
Regional cuisine
This charming restaurant is perched high in the mountains, at the top of the cableway, in a grandiose setting. Owned by a former pork butcher, its extremely friendly atmosphere is reflected in the generosity of the dishes: Savoyard meat and vegetable stew; country sausage with two kinds of potato; Reblochon pie.

FLOCONS DE SEL
75, rue Saint-François
Tel. 04 50 21 49 99
Closed Tues.–Wed. lunch off season and 3 weeks in May
Menus: 110–310 F
À la carte: 280 F
Regional cuisine
An amazing little restaurant, in a slightly out-of-the-way location in the old part of Megève. The chef, who trained with Marc Veyrat, offers an original and innovative cuisine.

HOTELS-RESTAURANTS

CHALET-HÔTEL L'IGLOO
3120, route des Crêtes
Tel. 04 50 93 05 84
Fax 04 50 21 02 74
Closed April 20–June 20 and Sept. 20–Dec. 15
12 rooms, 650 F–1050 F per person (half-board only)
Menus: 140–200 F
À la carte: 180 F
Regional cuisine
An elegant mountain chalet recently built (with sauna, jaccuzi, pool, solarium) opposite the summit of Mont d'Arbois, at an altitude of 2705 feet (825 m). Reached by cableway or four-by-four. Very friendly welcome. Regional and traditional cuisine: mountain ham; Savoyard péla with Abondance cheese; mountain salad.

LE TRIOLET
Route du Bouchet
Tel. 04 50 21 08 96
Fax 04 50 74 68 75
Open Christmas–Easter
10 rooms, 3 chalets
850–1800 F
Menus: 300–440 F
À la carte: 450–500 F
Traditional cuisine
A chalet with huge, south-facing bay windows, situated near the Teléphérique de Rochebrune. Good-quality, seasonal ingredients fresh from the market. Fricassée of scallops and prawns; fish from Lake Geneva (char, trout); Bresse poultry in a creamy tarragon sauce.

LES MENUIRES

Post code 73440

HOTEL-RESTAURANT

L'OURS BLANC
Reberty 2000

MEGÈVE

Post code 74120

HOTEL-RESTAURANT

★ LES FERMES DE MARIE
Chemin de Riante-Colline
Tel. 04 50 93 03 10
Fax 04 50 93 09 84
Hotel closed April 15–June 15 and Sept. 15–Dec. 15
Restaurant open end June–beg. Sept. and Dec. 20–April 10
69 rooms including 11 suites, 1220–3880 F
Menus: 230–350 F
À la carte: 400 F
Traditional cuisine
A new chalet with 13 rooms has been added to this delightful little hamlet of Savoyard farms, renovated and furnished in traditional style. The complex is 5 minutes from the center of the resort, in a pleasant park with a swimming pool, sauna, jaccuzi and health farm. Delicate cuisine supervised by Nicolas Le Bec and impeccable service. Foie gras and leek salad; roasted farm-reared pigeon with slow-cooked peas; baked peaches and creamed rice with caramel custard.

LES MENUIRES

Post code 73440

HOTEL-RESTAURANT

★ LE GRAND CŒUR
Route du Grand Cœur
Tel. 04 79 08 60 03
Fax 04 79 08 58 38
Open Dec. 15–April 15
41 rooms, 1050–3000 F
Menus: 175–360 F
À la carte: 300 F
Gastronomic cuisine
Together with historian Monique Lansart, Michel Dach, the Alsace-born chef of the Grand Coeur, has become passionately interested in the 15th-century recipes of Maître Chiquart, the chef of Duke Amadeus VIII. Each year, in January, 'forgotten recipe' enthusiasts can enjoy skillfully recreated dishes washed down with regional wines: lively whites and reds with the subtle aroma of autumn flowers. The everyday cuisine is deeply rooted in the present, in the lake and mountain environment, with mountain ham and nuts accompanied by Beaufort flan, char and féra (Lake Geneva trout) à la meunière, carrots flavored with thyme, cabbage pie à la vigneronne with a sauce thickened with wine and bitter cherries. Comfortable bar, inglenook and a sunny terrace overlooking the ski slopes and footpaths.

N.-D.- DE BELLECOMBE

Post code 73850

RESTAURANT

★ LA FERME DE VICTORINE
Route du Planay
Tel. 04 79 31 63 46
Closed Nov. 15–Dec. 15; off season: Sun. eve.–Mon.
Menus: 119–210 F
À la carte: 210 F
Regional cuisine
A grandiose rural landscape, at the foot of Mont Joly, dominated by the distant Massif du Mont-Blanc. Villages, the houses clustered round a church, and hamlets of a few chalets, barns and haylofts punctuate the green pastures. Traditionally, cattle live in the stone base of a chalet, while in the wooden upper story are the living quarters and hayloft. In the restaurant's dining room, which has a traditional wooden chimney, guests can gaze through a bay window at the byre. The rustic cuisine promotes the culinary heritage of the Beaufortain: mushroom fondue, tartiflette made with Tamié (a type of Reblochon produced in the nearby abbey), poulard with morel mushrooms, forcemeat and reblochonnade. These tasty dishes are washed down with Abymes, Apremont and Mondeuse, described by Columella as the 'wine of Allobrogia'.

Tel. 04 79 00 61 66
Fax 04 79 00 63 67
Open Dec. 3–April 24
47 rooms, 600–670 F
Menus: 95–250 F
À la carte: 250 F
Comfortable hotel
Les Menuires, a resort whose very streets are ski runs, is situated in the Vallée des Belleville, in the heart of Les Trois Vallées. The Ours Blanc, a comfortable hotel with carefully prepared cuisine, offers a pleasant winter break in a friendly winter-sports setting.

MÉRIBEL-LES ALLUES

Post code 73550

HOTELS-RESTAURANTS

ALTIPORT HÔTEL
Tel. 04 79 00 52 32
Fax 04 79 08 57 54
Closed April 20–June and Sept. 15–Dec. 15
41 rooms, 975–1620 F
Menus: 125–300 F
À la carte: 150 F
High-altitude hotel
This white-wood chalet, typical of Méribel, stands at the top of the resort, near the ski runs and golf course. Magnificent view from the terrace, and swimming pool in summer. Gilles Gourvat's traditional cuisine places the emphasis on flavor, color and lightness, even when it comes to preparing duck parmentier (duck and potatoes) with truffle sauce or crawfish risotto.

HÔTEL ANTARÈS
Route du Belvédère
Tel. 04 79 23 28 23
Fax 04 79 23 28 18
63 rooms, 1890–2200 F
13 apartments
Restaurants:
Le Cassiopée: open July 13–Aug. and Dec. 20–April 20
Menus: 190–460 F
À la carte: 350–500 F
Altaïr (dinner only): open Dec. 20–April 20
À la carte: 220–330 F
Luxury hotel
In the magnificent setting of the hotel's beautiful modern dining rooms, chef Christian Farenasso, from the département *of the Var, presents a subtle blend of aromas and flavors in his traditional and regional cuisine. He uses noble ingredients with great skill and inventiveness: freshwater pike-perch in a light curry sauce, ravioli made with preserved onions, Bresse poultry with traditional stuffing, and 'chicken's oyster' and green vegetable sausage. A meticulous and consistently good cuisine that carefully avoids the over-use of spices and herbs. Excellent sommelier.*

MORZINE

Post code 74110

RESTAURANT

LA CHAMADE
La Crusaz
Route de Thonon
Tel. 04 50 79 13 91
Open daily in season
Menu: 250 F
À la carte: 200 F
Regional cuisine
The intelligence and humor of Thierry Thorens has made him the favorite chef of a local – seasonal and permanent – clientele. The restaurant's three dining rooms serve simple pizzas, regional specialties or a more elaborate pork dish washed down with a choice bottle of wine (more than 1000 to choose from). Hot filet of féra (Lake Geneva trout) and smoked salmon, beetroot and nut salad, grilled suckling pig and potato fritters; Mont Chablais sausage (attriaux).

HOTEL-RESTAURANT

LE DAHU
Chemin du Mas-Métout (télécabine de Super-Morzine)
Tel. 04 50 75 92 92
Fax 04 50 75 92 50
Closed Sept. 15–Dec. 15 and April 15–June 15
Restaurant: closed Tues. in winter
40 rooms, 325–880 F
Menus: 155–280 F
This large chalet-hotel, in a superb location outside the resort, has something for everyone: swimming pool, gym and body-building equipment for health; sauna, jacuzzi and

PEISEY-NANCROIX

Post code 73210

RESTAURANT

★ L'ANCOLIE
Tel. 04 79 07 93 20
Closed Oct.–Nov., May; winter: Mon.
Menus: 149–210 F
À la carte: 200 F
Regional cuisine
L'Ancolie, perched high above the Gorges du Ponturin on the slopes of the Montagne de Bellecôte, was founded as an inn in 1760. It enjoys a magnificent view of the Pointe des Pichères. A special 'day in the mountains' menu offers customers a taste of regional cuisine: potato salad with pormonniers (pig's offal and herb sausages), fricassée de caïon (pork), blanquette de cabri (kid) with sage or the famous diots (sausages cooked in white wine) and crozets (dumplings), followed by little Reblochon 'cakes' with nuts. The old farm implements on show and dried flowers decorating the tables evokes the Savoie of yesteryear. Regional cuisine based on old recipes in a traditional decor and an unspoiled landscape.

steam bath for pleasure;
bar, terrace and gardens for relaxation.

LA PLAGNE

Post code 73210

HOTEL-RESTAURANT

GRACIOSA
Tel. 04 79 09 00 18
Fax 04 79 09 04 08
Hotel open: July–August and Dec.–April
Restaurant open: Dec.–April
14 rooms, 480–520 F
Menus: 175–235 F
Traditional cuisine
A hotel with spacious, renovated rooms, offering half-board at very reasonable prices during the winter season.

PLANCHERINE

Post code 73200

RESTAURANT

CHALET DES TRAPPEURS
Col de Tamié
(7 miles from Albertville)
Tel. 04 79 32 21 44
Closed Mon.
Menus: 85–150 F
À la carte: 130 F
Regional cuisine
This attractive wood chalet stands in an impressive forest setting on the Col de Tamié, where the monks of the abbey still produce a type of Reblochon cheese.
Its terrace and high-altitude garden are delightful in summer.
A delicious rustic menu includes dishes popular with hikers: Reblochon melted over a wood fire, tartiflette, fondue, gratins and cheese omelettes. Charming decor, very reasonable prices and a fine list of regional wines.

PRALOGNAN-LA-VANOISE

Post code 73710

HOTEL-RESTAURANT

LE GRAND BEC
Tel. 04 79 08 71 10
Fax 04 79 08 72 22
Open June to mid-Sept. and mid-Dec. to mid-April
39 rooms, 480 F
Menus: 125–205 F
À la carte: 150 F
Traditional cuisine
Guests can admire the vast expanses of the Massif de la Vanoise, even if they can't climb the often extremely steep slopes which bear out the old Savoyard proverb: 'water always runs to the river'. A cosy, well-run hotel in a pleasant and peaceful mountain setting. Comfortable rooms with a view of La Vanoise. Traditional cuisine.

LA ROCHE-SUR-FORON

Post code 74800

RESTAURANT

LE MARIE-JEAN
Route de Bonneville
Amancy
Tel. 04 50 03 33 30
Closed Sun. eve. to Mon.; August 3–25
Menus: 160–280 F
À la carte: 350 F
Traditional cuisine
Jean-Pierre Signoud holds a very traditional view of Savoyard cuisine that is particularly exemplified by his calf's sweetbread pie with seasonal mushrooms. Although trout from the Arve and game pâtés are becoming increasingly rare in the region, Ayse still produces an excellent wine. Renowned for its carefully prepared cuisine and efficient service. Scallop and wild mushroom chartreuse; crisp, crunchy mullet with potatoes and basil.

LA ROSIÈRE

Post code 73700

HOTEL-RESTAURANT

LE PETIT-SAINT-BERNARD
Tel. 04 79 06 80 48
Fax 04 79 06 83 40
Open June 22–Sept. 10 and Dec. 20–April 20
20 rooms, 240–340 F
Menus: 70–115 F
À la carte: 140 F
Comfortable hotel
A typical small Alpine hotel, whose guests appreciate its comfort and the friendly welcome of Germain Arpin. Simple but carefully prepared cuisine.

SAINT-FRANCOIS-LONGCHAMP

Post code 73130

HOTEL-RESTAURANT

LE CHEVAL NOIR
Tel. 04 79 59 10 88
Fax 04 79 59 10 00
Closed start of Sept. to mid-Dec. and end April to end June
30 rooms, 280–380 F
Menus: 98–175 F
À la carte: 90 F
Regional cuisine
Regional cuisine at affordable prices in this beautiful hotel at the foot of the ski slopes. Claude Daumas knows how to treat his guests: reviving soups, fondue gratin, talmouse (puff-pastry triangles) filled with Beaufort, longeoles (pork sausages) with fennel and farçon (crusted mashed potatoes with eggs and mixed herbs) are washed down with lively wines.

SAINT-GENIX-SUR-GUIERS

Post code 73240

HOTEL-RESTAURANT

GOURJUX-LES BERGERONNETTES
Champagneux
Tel. 04 76 31 81 01

Fax 04 76 31 61 29
18 rooms, 240–310 F
Menus: 70–200 F
À la carte: 125 F
Regional cuisine
A pleasant family establishment on the slopes of the village, with a terraced garden offering a view of the surrounding landscape.

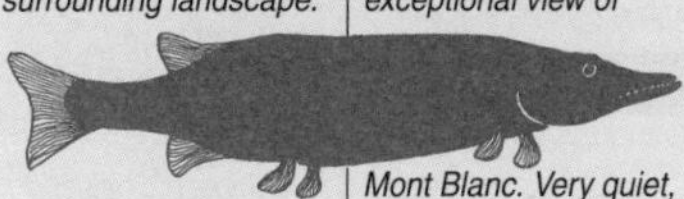

Serge Gourjux likes frogs and serves them in some delicious dishes. He is also an expert on cheeses, an indissociable part of Savoie, and serves wine produced on the stony ground of the region's glacial scree slopes. Simple, uncomplicated cuisine: veal mignon in a cream sauce and tarte tatin. A regular paradise!

SAINT-GERVAIS-LES-BAINS

Post code 74170

HOTELS-RESTAURANTS

'CHEZ LA TANTE'
Route des Crêtes,
Le Mont d'Arbois
Tel. 04 50 21 31 30
Fax 04 50 21 31 33
Closed May–June and Oct.–Dec. 15
26 rooms, 280–380 F per person (half-board only)
2 dormitories, 250 F per person (half-board only)
Menus: 75–140 F
À la carte: 140 F
Regional cuisine
Situated at an altitude of 6070 feet, on the major ski slopes of Megève, Saint-Gervais and Saint-Nicolas-de-Véroce, with a south-facing terrace and an exceptional view of Mont Blanc. Very quiet, with a number of walks. Reached by cableway. Braserade; fondue savoyarde.

SAINT-JEAN-DE-MAURIENNE

Post code 73300

HOTEL-RESTAURANT

HÔTEL DU NORD
Place du Champ-de-Foire
Tel. 04 79 64 02 08
Fax 04 79 59 91 31
19 rooms, 265 F
Menus: 78–210 F
À la carte: 170 F
Regional cuisine
An old coaching inn on the road to Italy. Charming historic decor (vaulted rooms) and a warm welcome. Simple but delicious cuisine of yesteryear: the inevitable fondue but also a superb wild-woodland-mushroom omelette, the restaurant's own smoked salmon and medallions of burbot with bilberries.

SAINT-JULIEN-EN-GENEVOIS

Post code 74160

RESTAURANT

LA FERME DE L'HOSPITAL
Rue du Molard,
Bossey (3 miles east of Saint-Julien on the N206)
Tel. 04 50 43 61 43
Closed Sun. eve. to Tues. lunch; end Feb. to start March and 3 weeks in August
Menus: 190–340 F
À la carte: 300 F
Traditional cuisine
Traditional dishes and innovative cuisine. The cooking of Jean-Jacques Noguier encapsulates the difference between simply repeating recipes – even to perfection – and the real work of a chef, including the occasional mistakes. Roasted saddle of young rabbit served on the bone with a mild garlic sauce; lobster and snail parmentier (with potatoes), cooked in natural juices.

SAINT-MARTIN-DE-BELLEVILLE

Post code 73440

RESTAURANT

LA BOUITTE
Saint-Marcel
Tel. 04 79 08 96 77
Open: July–Aug. and Dec. 15–May 1
Menus: 135–290 F
À la carte: 300 F
Gastronomic cuisine
When it comes to cuisine, La Bouite doesn't settle for anything short of the very best. In the cosy dining room of this mountain chalet, good-quality ingredients and perfect preparation produce a truly successful meal. Fresh codfish with shredded leeks cooked in Mondeuse, pan-fried prawns and oysters wrapped in spinach leaves, snail flan with a creamy nettle sauce and sophisticated desserts are living proof that René Meilleur lives up to his name.

LES SAISIES

Post code 73620

HOTEL-RESTAURANT

LE CALGARY
Tel. 04 79 38 98 38
Fax 04 79 38 98 00
Closed May to mid-June and mid-Sept. to mid-Dec.
41 rooms, 320–750 F
Menus: 145–210 F
À la carte: 200 F
Attractive rooms with a balcony, from where guests can watch the skiers and hikers on the slopes of Mont Bisane, a modest summit and magnificent observatory opposite the Chaine des Aravis and Mont Blanc. Truly amazing cuisine:

LES SAISIES

Post code 73620

RESTAURANT

★ LE CHAUDRON
Col des Saisies
Tel. 04 79 38 92 76
Open Dec.–April 25 and July–Aug.
Menus: 72–170 F
Regional cuisine
A delightful road climbs through the spruce forests and clearings of Mont Lachat, where wild mushrooms are found in season. This is the most picturesque route to the Val d'Arly, via Crest-Volant, and Les Saisies, originally the site of an isolated cheese dairy. The split-level restaurant, with its traditional wooden chimney, has a pleasant rustic decor and the warm and friendly atmosphere associated with après-ski and excursions. The terrace looks toward Mont Blanc and the menu offers Savoyard specialties – fried fish, soup, Savoyard salad, diots, trout, tartiflette – or something for special occasions – filet of féra (Lake Geneva trout),

frogs' legs, snails or Savoyard steak with cheese, which calls for one of the restaurant's wide selection of major vintages. A warm welcome and dedicated and friendly service.

terrine of wild mushrooms, free-range poultry with crawfish, excellent Beaufort and a good selection of 'vins de Savoie'.

SALLANCHES

Post code 74700

HOTEL-RESTAURANT

LES PRÉS DU ROSAY
285, route du Rosay
Tel. 04 50 58 06 15
Fax 04 50 58 48 70
Closed May 1–10 and Jan. 1–10.
Restaurant: closed Sun. eve. to Mon. lunch (except July 10–Aug. 20 and Dec.–March)
15 rooms, 2 suites 500–1000 F
Menus: 150–320 F
À la carte: 250 F
Gastronomic cuisine
At the crossroads of some of the leading Alpine resorts. A cosy hotel whose spacious rooms have a loggia offering a view of mountain pastures and Mont Blanc. A beautiful shady terrace in summer and a dining room with a wood decor. Michel Perrin offers sophisticated and inventive cuisine at reasonable prices: char, a 'trilogy' of foie gras, bayadère of duck and saddle of lamb. A cellar stocked with some top-ranked growths.

SAMOËNS

Post code 74340

HOTEL-RESTAURANT

NEIGE ET ROC
Tel. 04 50 34 40 72
Fax 04 50 34 14 48
32 rooms, 550 F
18 studios, 2400–3700 F per week
Open June–Sept. and Dec. 20–April 15
Menus: 120–200 F
À la carte: 200 F
With its various options – spacious rooms or well-appointed studios with 'kitchenette' – this is an ideal place for mountain enthusiasts. Excellent service. Leisure and fitness facilities. Extremely popular cuisine.

SÉVRIER

Post code 74320

HOTEL-RESTAURANT

L'AUBERGE DE LETRAZ
921, route d'Albertville
Létraz
Tel. 04 50 52 40 36
Fax 04 50 52 63 36

25 rooms, 360–820 F
Closed Oct. to end May: Sun. eve. to Mon.
Menus: 198–420 F
À la carte: 250 F
Situated in a garden, overlooking the lake, the inn is a charming place to stay on 'the far' shore of the lake. Everything about it is comfortable and tasteful. Bernard Collon's delightful cuisine, inspired by traditional recipes and regional ingredients, gives pride of place to fish: steaks of roast féra (Lake Geneva trout), cheese flan with leek purée.

TALLOIRES

Post code 74290

HOTEL-RESTAURANT

L'ABBAYE
Route du Port
Chemin des Moines

SCIEZ

Post code 74140

HOTEL-RESTAURANT

★ CHÂTEAU DE COUDRÉE
Tel. 04 50 72 62 33
Fax 04 50 72 57 28
19 rooms, 720–1580 F
Closed Nov.
Menus: 160–390 F
À la carte: 500 F
Bistrot François Ier:
Meal: 180–246 F
Relais & Châteaux
This former 12th-century castle of the counts of Savoie – once a formidable fortress flanked by a massive keep – stands in a garden setting on the shores of Lake Geneva. The renovations carried out by successive generations have preserved the original coffered ceilings, tapestries, stained-glass windows, monumental fireplaces and wood paneling, an ideal setting for the restaurant's candlelight dinners. Chef Gilles Doré places great emphasis on the freshness of the ingredients and a blend of very modern flavors: stuffed courgette flowers and fricassée of wild mushrooms; mullet tartlets with Swiss chard; pan-fried filet of lamb and potato purée with olive oil. An exceptional wine cellar.

Tel. 04 50 60 77 33
Fax 04 50 60 78 81
Closed Jan.–Feb.
Restaurant closed Oct.–March: Sun. eve. to Mon.
32 rooms, 730–1350 F
Menus: 195–540 F

À la carte: 450 F
Relais & Châteaux
This 17th-century Benedictine abbey has a terrace and shady garden. The French painter Paul Cézanne, who stayed at the abbey in 1896, described it as a 'superb legacy of bygone days'. The monks' cells have been converted into comfortable and luxuriously furnished rooms. Reverence is certainly not the order of the day at the table when guests sample traditional dishes and regional wines.

TANINGES

Post code 74440

RESTAURANT

LA CRÉMAILLÈRE
Route d'Annemasse
Lac Flérier
Tel. 04 50 34 21 98
Closed Sun. eve. and Wed. except in July-August; Jan. 3–Feb. 1
Menus: 155–225 F
À la carte: 200 F
Regional cuisine
On the shores of Lac Flérier, Jean-Pierre Bonjean excels in his adaptations of traditional Savoyard cuisine to meet the demand for lightness and moderation. Forcemeat; frogs' legs in chopped parsley and garlic; fricassée of lobster in Sauterne.

TALLOIRES

Post code 74290

HOTEL-RESTAURANT

★ L'AUBERGE DU PÈRE BISE
Route du Port
Tel. 04 50 60 72 01
Fax 04 50 60 73 05
Open mid-Feb. to start Nov.
Restaurant closed Mon.–Tues. from mid-Feb. to mid-April and in Oct.
21 rooms, 1200–3000 F
5 apartments
Menus: 490–820 F
À la carte: 700 F
Gastronomic cuisine
Relais & Châteaux
According to the present owners, this 100 year-old inn perpetuates the gastronomic tradition established by its first cooks. Curnonsky praised the talents of François Bise: 'His cuisine was perfection', he said of the man whose menu invariably included char, grilled chicken and gratin savoyard. The cuisine is still extremely traditional. L'Auberge, which stands on the shores of the lake, in the bay of Talloires, enjoys a charming and peaceful setting with a view of the water and mountains and a shady terrace in summer. Extremely comfortable rooms. Gratin of crawfish tails 'Marguerite Bise'; tatin of potatoes with truffles and foie gras; braised chicken with a creamy tarragon sauce.

THONON-LES-BAINS

Post code 74200

RESTAURANT

LE PRIEURÉ
68, Grande-Rue
Tel. 04 50 71 31 89
Closed Sun. eve.–Mon.
Menus: 200–380 F
À la carte: 300 F
Regional cuisine
Charles Plumex is a past master at using spices in moderation and adapting regional recipes to produce interesting variations for his accompaniments for freshwater fish. Filet of perch with mixed herbs roasted au savagnin; féra (Lake Geneva trout) stuffed with grilled bacon and served with cumin-flavored veal juices; char cooked in slightly salted butter with a sauce made with wine from the Jura. Smooth, efficient service.

HOTEL-RESTAURANT

AUBERGE D'ANTHY
Anthy (3 miles west of Thonon on the N 5 and the D 3)
Tel. 04 50 70 35 00
Fax 04 50 70 40 90
Closed hols. in Nov. and Feb. and Mon. eve.–Tues. except in July and Aug.
7 rooms, 252–309 F
Menus: 78–240 F
À la carte: 200 F
A charming and moderately priced hotel-restaurant, with very acceptable rooms and varied cuisine which gives pride of place to

fish – féra (Lake Geneva trout), char, perch – without neglecting Savoyard caïon (pork). A fine choice of regional and, generally undervalued, Swiss wines.

THÔNES

Post code 74230

HOTEL-RESTAURANT

NOUVEL HÔTEL DU COMMERCE
5, rue des Clefs
Tel. 04 50 02 13 66
25 rooms, 230–410 F
A comfortable, smart hotel offering gastronomic and regional cuisine which gives pride of place to traditional forcemeat from Haute-Savoie.

TIGNES

Post code 73320

HOTELS-RESTAURANTS

LES CAMPANULES
Tel. 04 79 06 34 36
Fax 04 79 06 35 78
Open July–Aug. and Nov.–May 1
32 rooms, 480–950 F per person (half-board only)
12 apartments
Menus: 140–195 F
À la carte: 220 F
Extremely comfortable hotel
The hotel, which has a superb location opposite the ski slopes in the center of the resort, offers good value for money. Extremely comfortable rooms with a large balcony. A warm welcome, excellent service and carefully prepared cuisine.

LE SKI D'OR
Val Claret
Tel. 04 79 06 51 60
Fax 04 79 06 45 49
Open Dec.–April
22 rooms, 900–1050 F per person (half-board only)
Menus: 135–245 F
À la carte: 300 F
Traditional cuisine
A comfortable, picturesque hotel in a modern chalet with a truly exceptional panoramic view. Light, sophisticated cuisine: seafood and delicious Savoyard recipes. Large seafood buffet, fillet of féra (Lake Geneva trout) with sorrel and pumkin gratin. Delightful welcome.

VILLAGE MONTANA
Le Lac
Tel. 04 79 40 01 44
Fax 04 79 40 04 03
Open Dec. to start May and mid-June to mid-Sept.
78 rooms, 4 suites, 48 apartments
350–745 F per person per day.
Menus: 95–180 F
À la carte: 150 F
The Village Montana stands on the edge of the resort with a view of the Lac de Tignes and the Glacier de la Grande Motte to the west. This large hotel – freestone façade, double-pitched roof and warm wood – is owned by a collector of traditional Savoyard objects, who has given it a distinctive montagnard style combined with modern comfort and facilities: swimming pool, saunas, gymnasium. One of the restaurants, whose narrow benches and creaking floor are in the syle of the old byres, offers typical Savoyard cuisine.

VAL-D'ISÈRE

Post code 73150

HOTELS-RESTAURANTS

LE KANDAHAR LA TAVERNE D'ALSACE
Tel. 04 79 06 02 39
Fax 04 79 41 15 54
Open July 4–Sept. 1 and Nov. 28–May 5
29 rooms, 320–730 F per person per day
À la carte: 130 F
Cuisine from Alsace
Within the space of ten years, Savoie was annexed by France and

Alsace by Germany. At the time a number of families from Alsace were living in the Savoie region. Traditions were maintained and theTaverne d'Alsace perpetuates the memory of good cooked meats, sausages and pâtés, crunchy sauerkraut and the savory tarts known as Flammenküche. An extremely comfortable hotel.

LE BLIZZARD
Avenue Olympique
Tel. 04 79 06 02 07
Fax 04 79 06 04 94
Open July–Aug. and Dec.–May 2
67 rooms, 820–2840 F
Menus: 150–250 F
À la carte: 300 F
Luxury hotel
This luxury hotel is always extremely lively: you can work out in the fitness center and swimming pool during the day and in the discothèque at night. The rooms are ultra-cosy and the welcome and service first class.

CHRISTIANIA
Tel. 04 79 06 08 25
Fax 04 79 41 11 10
Open beg. Dec. to beg. May
69 rooms, 1700–2900 F
Menu: 280 F
À la carte: 360 F
Luxury hotel
This large mountain chalet is located at the foot of the ski slopes. An impressive building whose framework, furniture, fittings and decor (communal rooms, bedrooms and bathrooms) are all in wood: a special homage to the forests of Savoie. Extremely comfortable; very carefully prepared cuisine.

LA SAVOYARDE
Tel. 04 79 06 01 55
Fax 04 79 41 11 29
Open Dec.–May 5 and Aug. 5–22
46 rooms, 600–1100 F per person (half-board only)
Menus: 125–280 F
À la carte: 200 F
Extremely comfortable hotel
This huge, centrally located chalet has a fully-equipped fitness center, complete with sauna, jacuzzi and steam bath. Spacious rooms and beautiful bathrooms. Sophisticated cuisine.

VALLOIRE

Post code 73450

HOTELS-RESTAURANTS

GRAND HÔTEL VALLOIRE ET GALIBIER
Tel. 04 79 59 00 95
Fax 04 79 59 09 41
Open Dec. 15–April 15 and June 15–Sept. 15
46 rooms, 300–420 F
Menus: 90–250 F
À la carte: 150 F
A beautiful, traditional mountain hotel in this lively resort where skiers are replaced by cyclists in summer. All services, the

comfortable rooms, the quality of the welcome are highly recommended. Carefully prepared cuisine.

VEYRIER-DU-LAC

Post code 74290

HOTEL-RESTAURANT

★ AUBERGE DE L'ÉRIDAN
13, vieille route des Pensières
Tel. 04 50 60 24 00
Fax 04 50 60 23 63
Closed end Oct. to end March
Restaurant closed Mon.
9 rooms, 1250–4650 F (suite)
Menus: 395–995 F
À la carte: 650 F
Gastronomic cuisine
Relais & Châteaux
Yarrow with pan-fried mullet and anchovy sauce; scallops decorated with cow parsnip; carvi (mountain cumin) with duckling sauvageonne; juniper to heighten the flavor of pigs trotters en aumônière; the delicious combination of beef and wormwood sauce... The extremely original flavors imparted by the wild herbs are perfectly matched to the ingredients, cooking times and juices, sauces, light, aromatic stocks, decoctions and infusions. The art of Marc Veyrat, an inspired montagnard, lies in his ability to use the regional setting as the medium for his very individual culinary creations. Taking into account the garden on the shores of the lake, the dozen or so luxury rooms, the successfully renovated decor and a cellar well-stocked with excellent regional wines at affordable prices, one cannot but admire the great merit of this restaurant – the most prestigious in the département – which is limited only by the financial means of its clientele. Vegetable ravioli redolent of woodland and meadow; grilled féra (Lake Geneva trout) in a herb-bennet sauce; calf's sweetbreads and lake crawfish flavored with oregano.

LE GASTILLEUR LA SÉTAZ
Rue de la Vallé-d'Or
Tel. 04 79 59 01 03
Fax 04 79 59 00 63
Closed April 20–June 1 and Sept. 21–Dec. 10
22 rooms, 360–490 F
Menus: 125–190 F
À la carte: 250 F
Regional and traditional cuisine
Jacques Villard does the cooking while his wife Monique ensures that guests receive the perfect welcome. This comfortable hotel (which also has a swimming pool) is particularly inviting in winter. All the charm of mountain pastures and recreated traditional cuisine, with an extremely varied gourmet menu: pâté in a pastrycrust, fondue, scrambled eggs with wild mushrooms, snails in Mondeuse wine, preserved pig's trotters with leeks à la savoyarde and cardoon gratin.

VAL-THORENS

Post code 73440

HOTEL-RESTAURANT

FITZ-ROY HOTEL
Tel. 04 79 00 04 78
Fax 04 76 00 06 11
Open Dec.–May 1
36 rooms, 1050–1500 F per person (half-board only)
Menus: 180–500 F
À la carte: 350 F
Extremely comfortable hotel
An elegant stone and wood building situated near the ski slopes. Deep armchairs around a central fireplace in an atmosphere of elegance and comfort. The cuisine of Francis Prudent places great emphasis on ingredients and is not without a few surprises:

fondue savoyarde with truffles or gilthead bream in vanilla-flavored chestnut bread.

VEYRIER-DU-LAC

Post code 74290

HOTEL

LA DEMEURE DE CHAVOIRE
71, route d'Annecy
Tel. 04 50 60 04 38
Fax 04 50 60 05 36
Closed Nov. 11–20
10 rooms, 800–1100 F
suites 1350–1650 F
A delightful hotel
Situated on the shores of the Lac d'Annecy. The spacious, well-furnished rooms have every modern comfort and a view of the lake. An ideal place to prove – or disprove with a few walks on steep mountain paths – the feeling of calm and fulfillment known as the 'lethargy of the lake'. Limited restaurant service for residents.

YVOIRE

Post code 74140

RESTAURANT

LES JARDINS DU LÉMAN
Grande-Rue
Tel. 04 50 72 80 32
Closed Wed. and Dec. 15–Feb. 8
Menus: 165–310 F
À la carte: 250 F
Regional cuisine
This delightful, flower-filled medieval village, perched on a promontory above Lake Geneva, has experienced an understandable increase in tourism that does not always attract gourmets. The restaurant's Italian chef has for a long time been using seasonal ingredients to present a very individual menu which includes tureen of crawfish with truffles and breast of free-range guinea-fowl with wild mushrooms.

Blanc in the background © F. Isler.
261 Logo of the Arpin mill © Arpin, Séez.
262 Chalet, La Gurraz © F. Isler. Le Monal in the snow © J. Sierpinski. Poster for Bernard Favre's film 'La Trace', 1983 © Ciné Plus
263 Guardian angel, Église de Val-d'Isère; great retable of the Église Saint-Martin d'Hauteville-Gondon; tabernacle of the Église Saint-Pierre de Séez © Facim/R. Vidalie for the series of the photos.
264 Logo of the Parc National de la Vanoise © P.N.V.
265 Bonneval-sur-Arc above the Gorges de la Reculaz © idem.
266-267 Illus. F. Desbordes and J. Chevallier.
267 Ibex on the Grand Infernet, view toward Lac Blanc © P.N.V./J. Perrier.
268 Glacier de Gébroulaz © P.N.V./J. Perrier. Thick-billed nut-cracker, illus. J. Chevallier. Lac Blanc and the Dent Parrachée © P.N.V./F. Grosset. Marmots © Médialp/ A. and E. Lapied.
269 Gorges de Malpasset © P.N.V./ Ph. Benoit. Male ibex jousting © P.N.V./ J.-P. Ferbayre. Forêt de l'Orgère © P.N.V./ Ph. Benoit. Illus. F. Desbordes. Villarodin-Barget © PNV./ M. Mollard
270 View of Saint Alban-des-Hurtières, p.c. © M.C.
271 Les Aiguilles d'Arves © Médialp/ S. Coupé. Portrait of General Ferrié © Harlinque/Viollet, Paris.
272 Knife from the Opinel collection © coll. Opinel, Cognin.
272-273 Illus. Ph. Candé.
273 Relic of Saint John the Baptist © Médialp/ D. Ngo Dinh Phu.
274 Col de la Croix-de-Fer © Diaf/Biollay. Col du Glandon © Médialp/S. Coupé.
275 Montrond and Les Aiguilles d'Arves © Médialp/S. Coupé. House in Jarrier, illus. M. Pommier. Saint-Sorlin-d'Arves © Médialp/R. Hémon.
276 Statue of Saint Peter, great retable in the church of Valloire © Facim/R. Vidalie. Col du Galibier © J. Sierpinski.
276-277 Vallée de l'Arc from the Col du Télégraphe © P. Huchette
277 Notre-Dame-de-Charmaix © P. Dompnier.
278 The monolith of Sardières © J. Sierpinski. Marie-Thérèse redoubt at Aussois © Médialp/ Macherel.
278-279 Église Saint-Pierre-d'Extravache, illus. F. Bony.
279 Details from the dome of the chancel of Saint-Thomas-Beckett in Avrieux © Médialp/ F. da Costa. Snow-covered sign on the Col du Mont-Cenis © Diaf/Pratt-Pries.
280 View of Bonneval © Médialp/S. Coupé. Saint Bernard shackling the devil with his stole, carved wood by B. Clappier, 18th cent. © G. Personnaz, Bessans. The Last Judgement, fresco, Chapelle Saint-Sébastien, Lanslevillard © J. Sierpinski.
281 View of Courchevel © M.J.O.A/L. Maccaro.
282 Manigod © Médialp/ G. Hertzol. Avoriaz © D. Vidalie. Reindeer on Mont Revard, p.c. © J. Routin, Chambéry.
283 Snowboarding at Avoriaz © T.O. d'Avoriaz/agence Nuts. From Flaine to Sixt on snowshoes © L. Collinet. Climbing waterfalls at Sixt © C. Gardien.
284 On the Mer de Glace © Scope/ M. Colonel. La Vallée Blanche © M. Colonel.
285 Les Houches © Médialp/E. Moy. Poster for Saint-Gervais by R. Broders, 1935 © Artéphot/Perrin/ADAGP, Paris 1997/Wagons-Lits Diffusion, 1997.
286 View of Arêches © A.T.D.S. Les Arcs © J. Sierpinski. Snow shoes in Savoie © Médialp/Ph. Royer.
287 Méribel © J. Sierpinski. La Plagne-Bellecôte © idem.
288 Le Corbier, Les Aiguilles d'Arves © J. Sierpinski. Jean-Claude. Killy presenting 'Dynamic' skis © Roger-Viollet.
289 Bessans in the snow, p.c. © M.C. Refuge du Mont-Thabor © Diaf. Ice sculpture, Valloire, 1992 © Médialp/S. Coupé. Alpine sled, fresco by Bastian in Lanslebourg © Diaf/G. Biollay.
290 Fishing in the River Fier © Médialp/Hertzog. Sailing on the Lac d'Annecy © Médialp/ S. Coupé. White-water rafting © Médialp/Arnal. Illus. de M. Pommier.
291 The Alps on horseback © Médialp/Simon. Mountain bikes at Plampraz © Médialp/ B. Magnien. Para-gliding at Chambéry © T.O. Chambéry. *Via ferrate* at La Daille © A.T.D.S./D. Givois.
292 Snow shoes at Les Arcs © Médialp/Arnal Climbing an icefall © Médialp/Ph. Royer.
293 Illus. de M. Pommier
304 Illus. de M. Pommier

We would like to thank the following people and institutions for their valuable assistance:

G. Billet, H. Marcadal, D. Debiolles and A. Guignaud (A.T.D. de Haute-Savoie)
Agence Médialp
L. Collinet
M. Colonel
P. Gallay
B. Gillet
F. Isler
R. Robert
G. Sommer
J.-F. Tanghe
D. Vidalie
M. Andréoni (Archives Départementales de la Haute-Savoie)
M. Dubosson (Conservatoire d'Art et d'Histoire)
W. Saadé (Curator, Musée-Château d'Annecy)
S. Robillard (Researcher, Musée-Château d'Annecy)
C. Blaser (Curator, Musée de l'Élysée de Lausanne)
Mme Chevallier (Librarian, Musée d'Ethnographie de Genève)
P. Vinit (PNR du Massif des Bauges)
P. Monnerot (S.A. des Eaux Minérales d'Évian)
Soeur Marie-Patricia Burns
Michel Germain (collector)
Agence Médialp.
C. Blanc et O. Manéra (A.T.D. de Savoie)
Cl. Grangé, director, and M. Gibert (Maison des XVIes Jeux Olympiques d'Hiver)
D. Richard, curator, and F. Parrot (Facim, Chambéry)
F. Isler (photographer)
F. Pion (Arpin mill)
I. Brunel (T.O. Aix-les-Bains)
I. Legrand (T.O. Courchevel)
J. Luquet (Curator, Archives Dép. de Savoie)
J.-P. Bergerie (T.O. Moûtiers)
J. Routin, Chambéry
J. Sierpinski (photographer)
J.-L. Sevez et M. Dissez (J.-L. Sevez Organisation, Chambéry)
J.-M. Jeudy (photographer)
Librairie des Alpes, Paris
L. Rey (Ugine-Savoie)
L. Sadoux, Mme Déjammet,
J.-P. Girou (Musée Savoisien, Chambéry),
The director of the T.O. Albertville
The researcher of the CAUE de Chambéry
Le Vieux Campeur, Paris
M. Opinel and his assistant (Société Opinel, Cognin)
M. Taupiac and M. Charpin (T.O. Chambéry)
M. Vedrine (Curator of the Bibliothèque de Chambéry)
M. et Mme Davat, Aix-les-Bains
M. Girard-Reydet (photographer)
M. Liatard (Curator, Musée Faure, Aix-les-Bains)
P. et C. Louvel, Aix-les-Bains.
P. Folliet (photog. dept. of the Parc National de la Vanoise)
P. Vinit (PNR du Massif des Bauges).

People

General index

◆ A ◆

◆ D ◆

◆ E ◆

◆ F ◆

◆ G ◆

◆ H ◆

◆ I - J - K ◆

◆ L ◆

◆ M ◆